INSIDERS' GUIDE® TO
COLORADO SPRINGS

HELP US KEEP THIS GUIDE UP TO DATE

We would love to hear from you concerning your experiences with this guide and how you feel it could be improved and kept up to date. Please send your comments and suggestions to:

editorial@GlobePequot.com

Thanks for your input, and happy travels!

INSIDERS' GUIDE® TO

COLORADO SPRINGS

FIRST EDITION

LINDA DuVAL & MARTY BANKS

INSIDERS' GUIDE

GUILFORD, CONNECTICUT
AN IMPRINT OF GLOBE PEQUOT PRESS

All the information in this guidebook is subject to change. We recommend that you call ahead to obtain current information before traveling.

INSIDERS' GUIDE ®

Editor: Kevin Sirois
Project Editor: Lynn Zelem
Layout: Joanna Beyer
Text Design: Sheryl Kober
Maps: Sue Murray © Morris Book Publishing, LLC

ISBN 978-0-7627-6469-3

Printed in the United States of America

CONTENTS

CONTENTS

Directory of Maps

ABOUT THE AUTHORS

Linda DuVal grew up in the Midwest but has lived in Colorado Springs for more than 40 years. She attended St. Cloud State University in Minnesota for three years, finishing her degree at the University of Southern Colorado. She was a reporter, staff writer, and section editor for *The Gazette* in Colorado Springs for 32 years. She has been freelancing since 2004, focusing on travel journalism but also writing about food, wine, architecture, and general features. She has been a member of the Society of American Travel Writers since 1999 and is a Lowell Thomas award-winner. She specializes in Colorado and the Rocky Mountain West. She also has a local website, Pikes Peak on the Cheap (www.pikespeakonthecheap.com), which tells both residents and visitors about freebies, bargains, and deals for dining, lodging, shopping, and events. Linda is a regular contributor to regional magazines and newspapers, and her work has appeared in *The Writer*, a national publication, and online for HGTV, AOL Travel, and other websites. After all this time, she still is fascinated by Colorado and the Pikes Peak region and takes every opportunity to tell others about it.

Marty Banks has a long and deep history with Colorado. While growing up in Southern California, she spent a few summers in Fort Collins with her college-age brothers. Simply to be different, she chose to attend the University of Colorado-Boulder. After earning a degree in journalism, Marty moved to Colorado Springs where she's been ever since—minus a few journeys along the way. She has been an associate editor at *Western Horseman* magazine, a technical editor at Digital Equipment Corporation, a marketing writer and account executive for clients such as the United States Olympic Committee, and now is a freelance writer. Marty also writes fiction. She's attended the University of Iowa Writer's Workshop, has published adult short stories and creative nonfiction, and is a member of the Society of Children's Book Writers and Illustrators. Her children's picture book, *The Splatters Learn Some Manners,* was honored as a finalist in children's literature at the 2010 Colorado Book Awards. Learn more from her website: www.martymoklerbanks.com.

ACKNOWLEDGMENTS

Writing this book was a real learning experience! Between us, we have lived in the Pikes Peak region and written about it for more than 65 years. Still, we learned something new every day as we pursued information to fill the various chapters. Needless to say, this book wasn't written in a vacuum.

First, we need to thank Rick DuVal for his enduring and sometimes frustrating work on the maps that accompany and illustrate the text in this book. Without the maps, you might be disoriented, indeed.

We also need to thank some local sources of assistance and information: Matt Mayberry of the Colorado Springs Pioneers Museum for vetting the history chapter; and, for quick answers to endless questions, Chelsy Murphy of Experience Colorado Springs, Floyd O'Neil of the Manitou Springs Chamber of Commerce, Leslie Weddell at Colorado College, and Kurt Schroeder at the city of Colorado Springs Parks, Recreation & Cultural Services.

Also thanks to Sean Anglum at the Kennedy Center Imagination Celebration; and Jackie McGee, Stephanie Kasanicky, and Lynette Wheaton at ERA Shields Real Estate. And, for their expert guidance, we are grateful to Lisa Heaston, Jeff Cooper, and Rob McGee.

Also, thanks to the countless others who answered questions, returned phone calls, filled out questionnaires, and responded to e-mails. They each, in their own way, helped write this book.

Finally, we want to thank Globe Pequot Press for the opportunity to really explore our region, and a special thanks goes to Kevin Sirois, the most laid-back, reasonable, and cooperative editor ever!

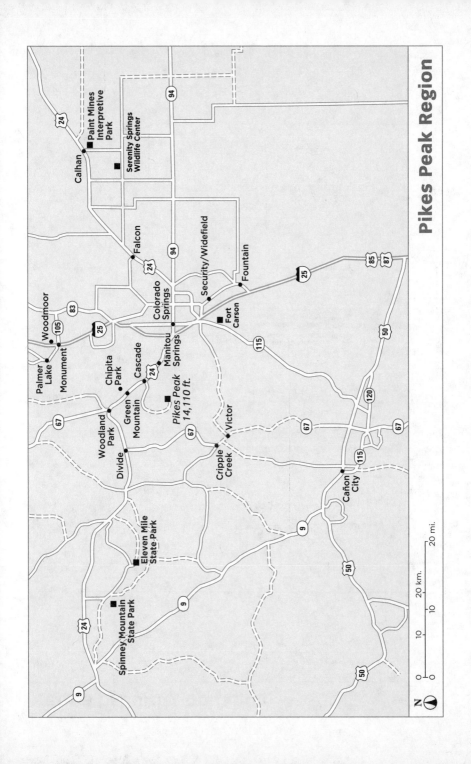

Pikes Peak Region

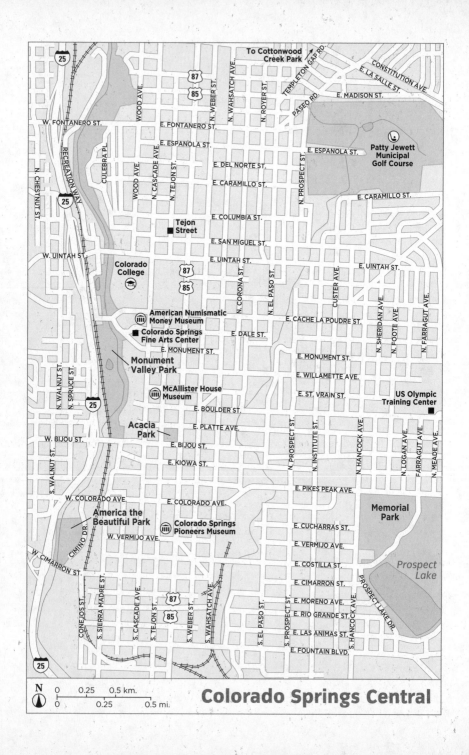

Colorado Springs Central

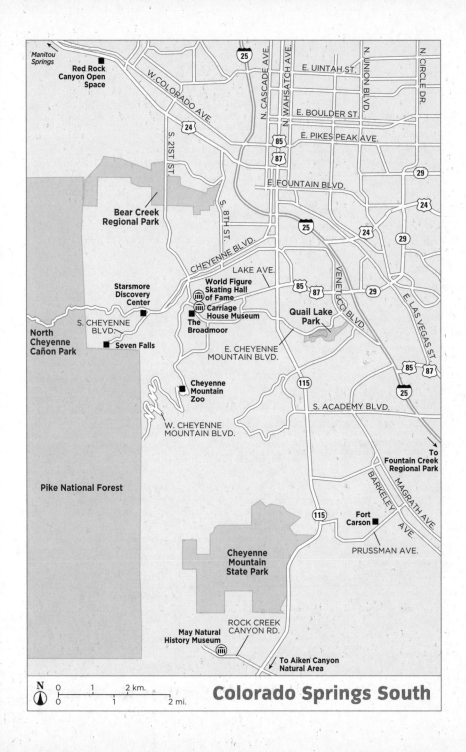

Colorado Springs South

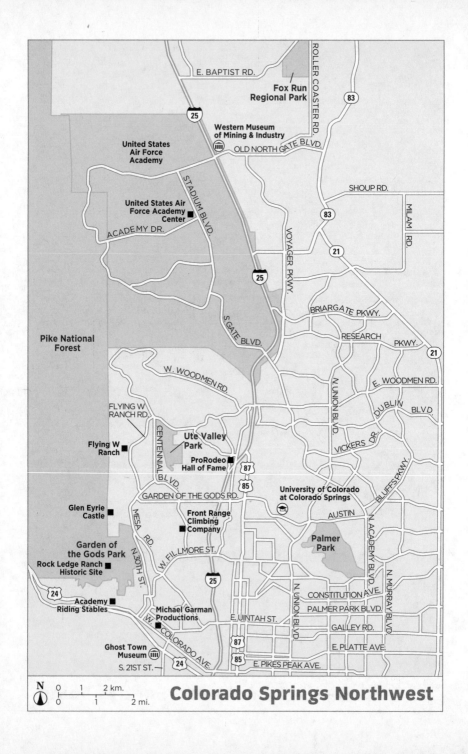

Colorado Springs Northwest

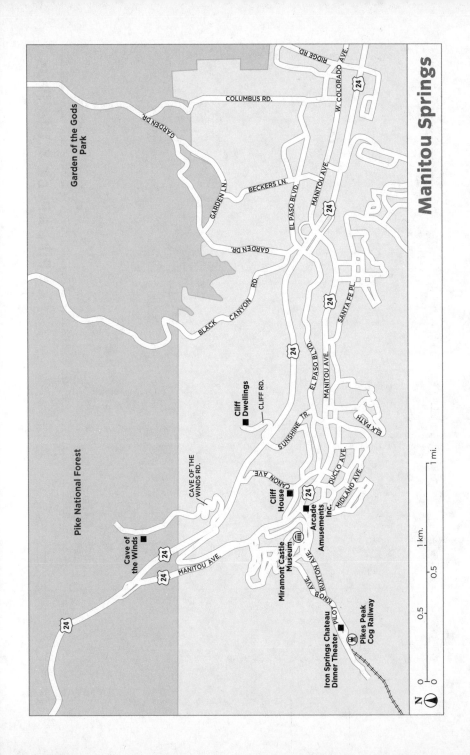
Manitou Springs

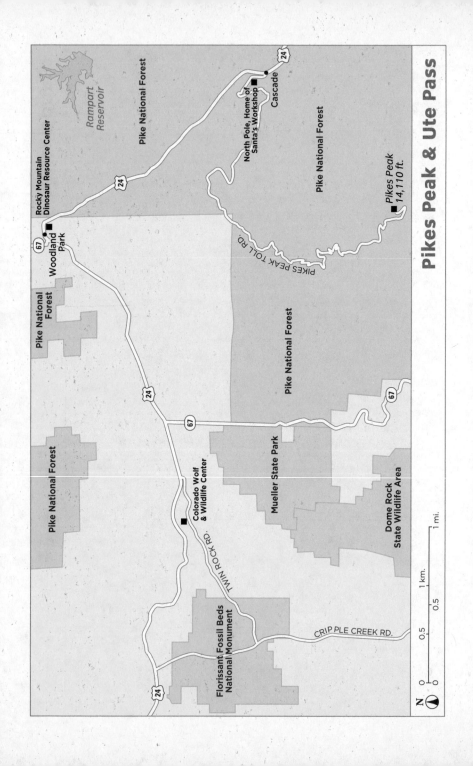

Pikes Peak & Ute Pass

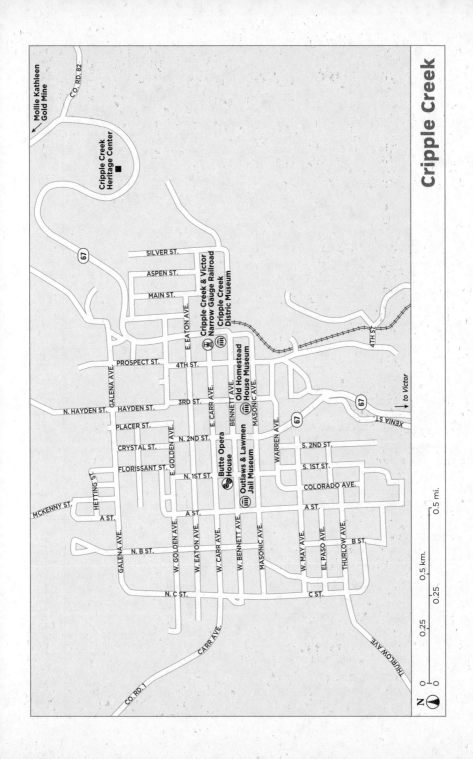

Cripple Creek

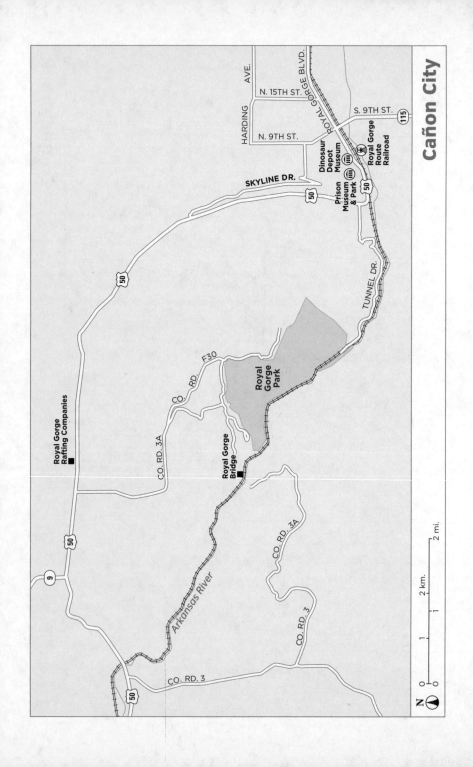

Cañon City

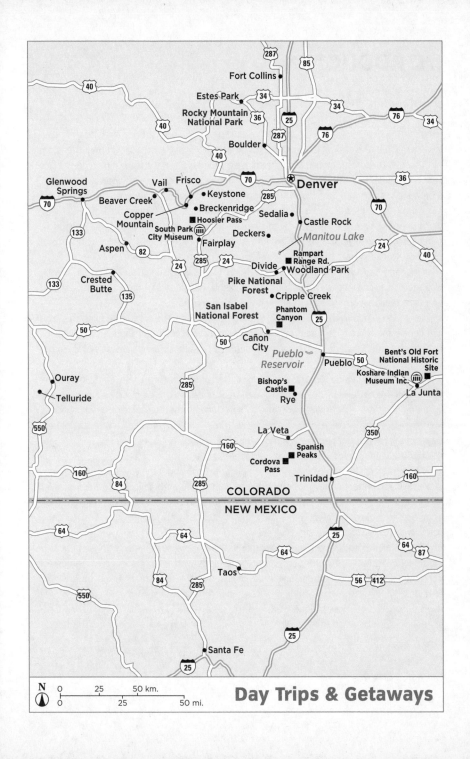

Day Trips & Getaways

INTRODUCTION

What a marvelous place this is! Colorado Springs and the Pikes Peak region not only offer stunning scenery, a fantastic climate, an abundance of things to see and do, but it's a great place to live as well as visit. For a city of its size, it has remarkable resources for outdoor recreation, a broad range of great dining, plenty of lodging in all price ranges, abundant nightlife, a real love of the arts, an eclectic mix of shopping opportunities, and enough attractions to keep visitors coming back year after year. Sure, there are a few tourist traps—but they're mostly fun. What you'll find really appealing here is its authenticity—rare geological features and a great outdoors you can't beat. Its history is short (compared to many cities) but well preserved.

Colorado Springs was named one of the 2011 Dozen Distinctive Destinations by the National Trust for Historic Preservation. Its walkable historic areas, natural attractions and ample recreational opportunities helped it win this distinction.

It's a family-friendly city, with tons of stuff to do with kids. There are more parks than you can count, and more hiking trails than you could master in years of wandering. Open space has been planned into the rapidly growing metropolitan area, so there's always a place to run with your dog or take off on your bike.

Maybe you are visiting for the first time, or the 10th time. Maybe you're moving here—being stationed at one of the local military installations or coming to school here. Maybe you're retiring here—and boy, are you in luck there! It has endless resources for senior citizens. But no matter why you're reading this guide, we hope it will help you enjoy your stay or new home in a way you might not have without this information. We hope it gives you insight into this region's culture, idiosyncrasies, and uniqueness.

The beauty of this book is that we were able to tell you about the little secrets that might make your visit better or more interesting: a great little restaurant, a unique B&B, a fun store for shopping, or an unusual haunt for night owls. We warn you about the vagaries of high-altitude living and possible encounters with wildlife, and we tell you about some of the colorful characters who helped shape our city.

Best of all, we got to be honest. Restaurants, hotels, and such were all chosen for their worthiness. We looked for businesses or organizations with good track records—most of which we have experienced personally. We've dined at the restaurants, hiked the trails, or attended events at the local venues. Or we know someone trustworthy who did! OK, we have personal preferences, but those are borne of experience. Now go have your own experiences and don't be afraid to jot down the information in the margins, if need be. This is your book—use it well.

HOW TO USE THIS BOOK

Welcome to Colorado Springs and the Pikes Peak region. This book will help you navigate your way around, decide where to go, what to do, where to stay, and where to dine. Whether you're a first-time visitor or a frequent one, whether you are on vacation or looking at relocation, this book should help you understand the communities and the region better. That's because, as insiders, we are allowed to have opinions. We can direct you to the places we'd send our own family and friends who visit. We don't owe allegiance to anyone but our readers. You'll notice there's no advertising in this book. The authors drew from their cumulative years of experience in the community to come up with suggestions we feel comfortable recommending. We made every effort to include fun shops, great attractions, and interesting diversions of all kinds (sports, recreation, hiking, scenic drives). If nothing else, this book will get you started.

A good place to start, when planning your trip, is the Getting Here, Getting Around chapter. Then, if you have time during your journey here, read the History chapter for background on this colorful, fascinating city. You might want to consult the Accommodations chapter to pick a place to stay. Then, once you're here, figure out what dining establishments are near your lodgings or activities from the Restaurants chapter. We've included price ranges, so you know about how much you'll pay for lodging and dining. In the Restaurants chapter, we've also focused on locally owned restaurants—you can eat at the chains in any town. That's not quite as easy with lodgings, but we have included a number of local hotels, motels, and bed-and-breakfast inns. And we've categorized them geographically, to help you plan your stay.

Then, of course, you need to decide how to best spend your time here. The Attractions chapter is a good place to start. The Pikes Peak region has so many, you'll never do them all in one (or two, or three . . .) trips. So we've broken it into manageable pieces—where to find more history, where to get some thrills, how to explore the local geography, and so on. We've even included some scenic drives you can do in a day from here. Need to shop? We'll tell you where to find unique, local stores in the Shopping chapter. In the Parks and Sports & Recreation chapters, we outline the extensive choices you have among local and regional parks and the almost unlimited options for exploring recreational opportunities from mountain biking to rock climbing. After a day of hiking, gallery-gazing, whitewater rafting, or museum-hopping, you might be looking for some evening entertainment. That's where the Nightlife and The Arts chapters might come in handy.

Traveling with children? Check out the Kidstuff chapter for fun, mostly affordable, and often unique explorations and adventures for the younger crowd. Want to explore more of Colorado using this as your base camp? It's a good idea, and you'll find lots of options in the Day Trips & Getaways chapter. Maybe you want to plan your visit around a special event (a writer's conference, film festival, or holiday activities), so go to the Annual Events & Festivals chapter for that.

Along the journey through this guide, you'll find some insider's tips (dealing with the high, dry climate, for example) and we've profiled some fascinating local people and institutions. We'll tell you everything from how to get a local driver's license to where to find a good, locally brewed beer or cup of coffee.

You'll also find listings accompanied by the ✳ symbol—these are our top picks for attractions, restaurants, accommodations, and everything in between that you shouldn't miss while you're in the area. You want the best this region has to offer? Go with our **Insiders' Choice.**

Moving to the Colorado Springs area or already live here? Be sure to check out the blue-tabbed pages at the back of the book, where you will find the **Living Here** appendix that offers sections on relocation, child care, education, health care, retirement, and media.

Understand that this book is just a start. There are so many more places to stay and eat, so many more things to see and do—the list is too long to include them all in one guidebook. We encourage you to expand on our suggestions, because that's just what they are: suggestions. We tried to make them good suggestions, though! Also understand that due to the vagaries of the economy, and life in general, restaurants and stores and such do come and go. We tried to choose those with good reputations and an established track record, but even a business that has been around for 25 years can close overnight.

In all, we hope this book offers a well-rounded roundup of what Colorado Springs and the Pikes Peak region have to offer. We've included a few maps to get you oriented, but take time to just drive the city and explore on your own. Colorado Springs is a city that is constantly changing and growing. Who knows? You might discover something we missed!

AREA OVERVIEW

"O beautiful, for spacious skies,
For amber waves of grain,
For purple mountain majesties
Above the fruited plain . . ."

Welcome to Colorado Springs, the second-largest city in Colorado and the inspiration for one of the most beloved songs in America. Katharine Lee Bates, a visiting professor at Colorado College in 1893, wrote these words that later became the song "America the Beautiful." Though the poem (and song) address the beauty and spirit of the nation as a whole, it was written after she took in the vast views of Colorado, as seen from the summit of Pikes Peak.

In its inception, the city was situated on a barren prairie at the base of Pikes Peak, bisected by a creek that flowed from the north to the south and another that came in from the west and joined it. But the city's founder, Gen. William J. Palmer, soon saw to it that trees were planted and neat plats laid out for homes, with broad streets bearing regional names like Wahsatch or Cache la Poudre. Trees grew, houses were built, and a downtown began to emerge with hotels, theaters, and public buildings. A city was born.

What drew many people to Colorado Springs initially was not only the natural beauty, but the climate—it was healthful and it felt good. Those things still draw new residents, as well as visitors, every year. It wasn't a gold camp or a Wild West town, despite the fact that it was ringed by ranches, farms, and mining towns, but instead it was an oasis of refinement and culture in a sea of roughness.

Many military men and women have been stationed here over the years, and many decided to make this their home when they retired. The city also has had a long history of clean industry, particularly micro-technology, bringing workers from other states here. A number of sports organizations and Christian ministries have their corporate headquarters here, too. It's an outdoorsy kind of town, with lots of natural diversions. It has good schools and a clean environment and a low crime rate, which makes it a great place to raise a family. So it has many ways to appeal to many groups of people, and they merge here, at the base of America's mountain, to pursue the quality of life we all want.

ENVIRONMENT

It's high. It's dry. And it takes a bit of getting used to. But folks once came here to cure tuberculosis, so the climate must be good for you!

Colorado Springs lies at the foot of 14,110-foot Pikes Peak. The city's average altitude is just over 6,000 feet. That's almost 1,000 feet higher than the "Mile High City" of Denver. And at this elevation, you only have about three-fourths of the oxygen you get at sea level. Don't be embarrassed if you get winded climbing just a few steps.

So take some time to acclimate. Don't go running a marathon your first day in town. Don't go up Pikes Peak (which has only half the oxygen you get at sea level). Take it easy. Hit some museums or, if you must, take a gentle walk in Garden of the Gods. After your body adjusts to the altitude, in a couple of days, then head up the peak or get on a bike. It's also extremely dry here—pack some lip protection and drink way more water than you think you need!

i The TV weather guy or gal talks about virga. What's virga? Well, if you're looking off in the distance and see rain clouds, and rain coming out of the clouds, then disappearing before it hits the ground, that's virga. The climate is so dry, a light shower may evaporate on its way to the ground.

As Ms. Bates mentioned in her "America, the Beautiful," the region goes from high plains on the east to high peaks on the west. The city of Colorado Springs lies in a shallow valley that runs north and south along the Front Range. Elevations can vary widely from one part of town to another, as can the terrain. And there are many micro climates, as well. You can live a mile from someone who gets a foot of snow during a storm and not have any significant precipitation at your house. Some neighborhoods are flat as a pancake; others are so hilly, people need four-wheel-drive to get home during a snowstorm. Snow really isn't a deterrent for those who have lived here a while, but newcomers (especially from places that don't get it) may be spooked a bit. Don't worry. Usually, the sun comes out after a snowstorm and melts everything off in a day or two. Yes, really.

In summer, we may experience afternoon showers on many days—just enough to cool things off for the evening. Do be aware that the Pikes Peak region gets an extraordinary number of lightning strikes, so if a storm does blow up, get to shelter. More than one golfer has rued the day he didn't pay attention to the storm clouds.

JUST THE FACTS

Time Zone

Colorado Springs—and all of Colorado, actually—is in the **Mountain Time Zone.** That's an hour ahead of the West Coast and two hours behind the East Coast. We observe Daylight Savings Time, turning the clocks back one hour in the fall and one hour ahead in the spring, in accordance with most of the rest of the country.

The Economy

Like the rest of the nation, Colorado Springs and the Pikes Peak region have suffered during the recent recession. Jobless rates were high and foreclosures abundant, but we fared better than many other places.

Keep in Mind . . .

Here are some things to be aware of when visiting the Pikes Peak region:

- **Altitude sickness:** Most people adjust just fine, but keep an eye on any-one with breathing or heart problems, young children, elderly people, and women who are pregnant or menstruating. Be aware of the signs of altitude sickness (more likely when you go higher than the city). Alti-tude sickness affects about 25 percent of visitors to Colorado to some degree. About 500 cases a year are treated on the top of Pikes Peak.

   Many cases are mild; some are serious. Symptoms include deep fatigue, headache, nausea, dizziness, and shortness of breath. If symp-toms are severe, or the person loses consciousness, get emergency medi-cal aid right away. The cure? Getting them back down to a lower altitude as quickly as possible usually does the trick. More serious cases may need medical attention.

- **Dehydration:** Drink lots of water to avoid dehydration in this semi-arid climate. Avoid alcoholic beverages the first few days here; they'll only dehydrate you further. So does caffeine, so take it easy on the coffee and colas. Drink extra water, especially before you hike or otherwise exercise, and carry water with you. Signs of dehydration include thirst (naturally), dry mouth, sunken eyes (or sunken soft spot on a baby's head), very yel-low urine, and skin that doesn't bounce back quickly when pinched.

- **Sunburn:** Let's face it. At 6,000 feet and higher elevation, you're just that much closer to the sun. And we get lots of sunshine—as many as 300 days a year. Each 1,000 foot gain in elevation above sea level increases ultra-violet exposure by 4 to 5 percent. Which means exposure here is about 25 to 30 percent higher than the flatlands. Serious sunburn can occur in just 30 minutes. Protect your skin at all times with SPF 30 or higher sunblock, applying 15 minutes before exposure and reapplying as needed. Also limit exposure between 10 a.m. and 3 p.m. on very hot, clear days or when ski-ing or on water—adding reflection to the mix. And don't forget a hat and sunglasses. They're an essential part of any resident's, or visitor's, ward-robe. Eyes can be damaged by intense sunlight, too.

The cost of living is moderate here, and you can still buy a really nice house for less than $300,000. One reason the economy is more stable here is due to the military influ-ence—its presence is a fairly constant one and seems to be always growing.

Safety

In general, Colorado Springs is a safe place to visit. Tourists are seldom involved in crimes. If a problem does occur, there are local resources to help you deal with it. If your car is stolen, for example, you can call the **Colorado Springs Police Department** (719-444-7000); only use 911 in case of a real emergency. Because of budget cuts in recent years, however, a police officer might not respond to a minor theft and you will be asked to report the crime online or in person at a police station. Car break-ins are sometimes a problem in parking areas of popular tourist attractions, so keep valuables out of sight if you must leave them in your car. But that's good advice anytime, anywhere.

A few local laws that might be good to know: The speed limit in neighborhoods is 25 miles per hour unless otherwise posted; traffic cameras monitor major intersections, and you will be fined if photographed running a red light; and it is illegal to leave your car running while you are not in it.

If you want to see a local crime report, complete with the latest statistics, go online to **www.springspolice.com** and click on Documents and Records.

> **i** During the night, especially late fall through spring, you might hear wind howling outside your bedroom window. The next morning, the air is practically balmy, with temperatures much warmer than the night before, and snow (if there is any) disappearing before your eyes. It's a chinook wind. Locals call it "the promise of spring."

CITY HIGHLIGHTS

Remember that Colorado Springs is neatly divided by **I-25** (north and south) and **US 24** (east and west). That gives you four distinct quadrangles—northwest, northeast, southwest, and southeast. But it's not that simple. Major roads and streets meander and loop around, and there are a couple of creeks to

contend with, but they mostly run parallel to major highways.

Most of the highlights for visitors lie to the west—**Pikes Peak, Garden of the Gods,** and the bulk of the tourist attractions. On the north end is the **U.S. Air Force Academy,** balanced by **Fort Carson** on the south, with several more military installations east of the city. **Downtown** also is important in the scheme of things, with fine museums, arts complexes, restaurants, and nightlife. The city airport is on the southeast side of town, and many of the major hotel chains are situated on the city periphery in all directions (except west).

This chapter, and hopefully this book, will help you set out to explore the fascinating, endlessly entertaining Pikes Peak region.

COLORADO SPRINGS NEIGHBORHOODS

If you're one of those people who like exploring the neighborhoods in a new city, or if you're thinking of moving here, these are some of the more interesting and desirable neighborhoods you might want to check out.

Downtown

Downtown houses are mixed with businesses, in some cases, and are fairly modest one- and two-story homes dating back as far as the late 1800s. Many are rentals and in need of repair; others are well-preserved family homes. Some have been converted into offices or other businesses. If you love history, the **Old North End,** just north and west of downtown, reflects the city's heritage. Large, stately homes that date back to the late 1800s mingle with smaller ones (built later). Many of these homes are on the National Register of Historic Places. Doctors, lawyers, college professors, and other professionals tend to live in this area, as well as third and fourth generations of moneyed families. It's a liberal pocket in the otherwise conservative-leaning city. Just east of the Old North End, on the other side of Nevada Avenue, is the **Audubon** neighborhood, where houses are somewhat newer (built in the 1940s and 1950s) and more modest. It's a stucco-and-brick neighborhood of retirees, teachers, and professionals who don't want to shuck out the bucks for a more prestigious address. Young families are starting to move in and remodel.

East

Because the mountains efficiently block westward development, the city tends to flow eastward. There are dozens of different neighborhoods, few with any distinctive construction other than a lot of it! **Academy Boulevard** was once (in the 1970s) the eastern edge of the city—now, it's almost city center, geographically speaking. A boom in the 1990s sent houses spilling out over the plains where once cattle grazed and winter wheat grew. **Powers Boulevard** soon became the new frontier, and now even that has been passed by the ever-reaching tentacles of development. Homes and stores have usurped antelope, prairie dogs, and coyotes. The eastern part of the city also is home to the Skysox baseball team's home stadium and a number of huge shopping complexes. It's an affordable place to live, with great views of the mountains to the west, and convenient for workers at the air force bases and city airport.

Northeast

Though not an architecturally distinctive neighborhood, **Briargate,** in the northeast quadrant of the city, does encompass a huge chunk of real estate with affordable, roomy homes. Though it once looked like a cookie-cutter neighborhood, maturing landscapes and personal touches have set the homes apart from one another. Situated on a slight hill, it has good mountain views. Families are attracted to it for its affordability, and because of its inclusion in the excellent **Academy School District.** Many families have two working parents and many are also in the military or work for local Christian organizations. Though still young in some respects, there's a strong sense of community (such as an annual all-neighborhood garage sale).

North of Briargate is the **Pine Creek** neighborhood. The lessons developers learned from Briargate led them to create the more upscale and personable adjacent neighborhood, which is where Briargate residents tend to want to move when they have the income to do so.

Beyond these lies **Black Forest,** probably named because it reminded someone of that region of southern Germany, thickly covered in places with dense evergreens. Here, large lots (some with substantial acreage) make for a rural-feeling community. A major crossroads is the closest thing they have to a "town center" and most folks there like it that way. Houses range from little log cabins to multimillion-dollar mansions. All with a lot of privacy.

Northwest

In the northwest quadrant of the city, **Rockrimmon** was developed in the 1970s in the foothills, which means there isn't a straight street in the whole place. Odd-shaped lots sit on hillsides covered with scrub oak and it's not unusual to see a herd of deer or bighorn sheep stopping traffic. The Brady Bunch houses have lots of windows and conform to the lots. Expect to see the neighbors going to work in uniform. A lot of higher-ranking military officers live here because of its proximity to the US Air Force Academy. You'll also find white-collar professionals, teachers, and business owners. Some choose this area because of its inclusion in the excellent Academy School District.

Peregrine, developed later than Rockrimmon, is nonetheless the rich uncle here. Its homes are even larger and more distinctive, on oversized and irregularly shaped lots, with great city views and lots of wildlife. It's an area for people who value privacy.

South

In the **Broadmoor** neighborhood, old money mixes with new money in what is arguably the region's most prestigious neighborhood. Built in the 1920s to 1940s, its stately mansions have been joined by pricey remodels and a few new mansions, most within walking distance of the historic, grand, world-famous Broadmoor hotel and resort. People who live here don't necessarily work for a living, but those who do tend to be doctors, lawyers, generals, and real estate developers. Don't be surprised to see a golf cart parked in the garage. And most folks here know their neighbors and rub elbows with them at the hotel's fine restaurants and world-class golf courses.

Built in the 1980s, to the south of the Broadmoor area, is **Broadmoor Bluffs,** which features large homes on large lots covered with scrub oak and frequented by

wildlife. It's more affordable than old Broadmoor, but draws many of the same type of residents. They also enjoy the same great school district—**Cheyenne Mountain**—and often have great nighttime views of the city lights.

West Side

One of the city's oldest and most eclectic neighborhoods, the **West Side,** and **Old Colorado City** within it, are just minutes from downtown. The homes, still affordable for retirees and growing families on a budget, vary from stately Victorians to cute cottages and everything in between. This mixed neighborhood even includes some new houses built on lots that have been vacant for years (or where an old house was torn down). The Old Colorado City section of the West Side draws lots of tourists, with shops aplenty. Colorado Springs has its blue-collar roots in the West Side and Old Colorado City. The mine owners lived in the Old North End, but the mine workers lived on the West Side. Colorado Springs was dry, and Colorado City had saloons. Today, the neighbors have as much character as the houses.

Farther west, **Pleasant Valley** was once the poshest neighborhood outside of the Broadmoor and the Old North End. Today, Pleasant Valley is an enclave of small ranch-style homes inhabited by retirees who raised their families here. New families are moving in, however, and enjoy the nearby Garden of the Gods and the feeling of being tucked away from it all.

THE PIKES PEAK REGION

The Pikes Peak region encompasses a number of small communities outside of Colorado Springs, mostly in El Paso County (but

Visitor Information

Experience Colorado Springs Convention & Visitors Bureau
515 S. Cascade Ave., Colorado Springs
(719) 635-7506 or (800) 368-4748
www.visitCOS.com
Go online to request a free visitors' guide be sent to you prior to your visit. Or stop by when you get into town and visit their office in person to get the visitor guide, free brochures on specific attractions, and lots of great information from the front-desk staff.

Manitou Springs Chamber of Commerce & Visitors Bureau
354 Manitou Ave., Manitou Springs
(719) 685-5089 or (800) 642-2567
www.manitousprings.org
If you are especially interested in visiting Manitou Springs, you can get great information at the office, right on the main drag. You also can get brochures on local attractions outside the city's limits.

Cañon City Chamber of Commerce
403 Royal Gorge Blvd., Cañon City
(719) 275-2331 or (800) 876-7922
www.canoncity.com/visitors.php
Cañon City lies about an hour southwest of Colorado Springs and is worth a side trip on its own, with enough diversions to fill a long day, or even a weekend.

Cripple Creek Heritage Center
9283 S. Highway 67, Cripple Creek
(719) 689-3289 or (877) 858-4653
www.visitcripplecreek.com
The historic gold camp, about an hour west of Colorado Springs and deep in the mountains, offers a wide array of attractions and entertainment, from museums to casinos.

also in Teller and Fremont Counties), all within view of Pikes Peak. They vary wildly in character and demographics. A few, like Manitou Springs, are self-contained communities that have everything their residents might need. Others are really bedroom communities where folks who work on a military base or in "the city" find their nightly refuge. Here is a bit about each one:

Cañon City

An hour southwest of Colorado Springs, Cañon City is the county seat and the most populous city of Fremont County. The small city of 16,000 people lies in the "banana belt" of central Colorado, and is home to nine state and four federal prisons and penitentiaries, which provide many jobs to support the local economy. Cañon City straddles the Arkansas River and is a popular tourist destination for whitewater rafting and rock climbing.

Established in 1858 during the Pikes Peak or Bust gold rush, it then lay idle until 1860, when the first building was erected. Intended as a commercial center for mining to serve South Park and the upper Arkansas River area, it became a site of many metal ore smelters in the 1890s.

Situated as it is on US 50, it always has had heavy through-traffic, supporting local hotels and restaurants. Its proximity to the Royal Gorge, where a world-famous bridge and park draw countless tourists every year, it continues to thrive. It's also home to the resurrected Royal Gorge Route railroad, which now is a tourist attraction; a dinosaur museum; and much more (see the Attractions and Day Trips & Getaways chapters).

Manitou Springs

Before Colorado Springs was a gleam in General Palmer's eye, Manitou Springs already existed as a gathering place. Its many mineral springs drew the Ute Indians and several Plains Indian tribes to visit its healing waters. It was considered a sacred place and all could visit without fear of conflict.

Zebulon Pike didn't notice the springs in his thwarted effort to climb Pikes Peak. That honor was left to Dr. Edwin James, team botanist for the Long Expedition, in 1820. James, also the first European to conquer the peak, spread the word about the "boiling springs." Early visitors included Daniel Boone's grandson, who visited in 1833 to "take the cure," as it was then called.

First called La Font, the town was laid out in 1871 and then renamed Manitou Springs (after the Native American word for "spirit"). A railroad spur from Colorado Springs incited rapid growth in this forested box canyon tucked between Garden of the Gods and the base of Pikes Peak. Hotels, bathhouses, dance pavilions, restaurants, and a mineral water bottling plant sprang up. Visitors to this "Saratoga of the West," as it was dubbed, included P. T. Barnum, Thomas Edison, and several presidents.

The town stagnated a bit in the 1960s and 1970s, becoming a low-cost haven for aging hippies. But locals became involved in saving the mineral springs and boosting the arts. In the early 21st century, a complete revitalization of the downtown was undertaken and now you can't find a parking spot on a summer's day!

Enclosed by natural boundaries, this home-rule city of about 5,000 residents really can't grow much. But what is growing is its economy—stores that were doing poorly elsewhere in the region have moved here and are now thriving.

A designated National Historic District, today's downtown doesn't have a single chain restaurant or lodging. It bustles with life, fun events (like a fruitcake toss after the holidays), a farmers' market, and a plethora of attractions, from Cave of the Winds to the historic Miramont Castle (see the Attractions chapter). Manitou today is a happening place, and you're likely to spend some time there on any visit to the Pikes Peak region.

Eastern Plains

Falcon

About 14 miles northeast of Colorado Springs, along US 24, lies Falcon, an unincorporated exurb in El Paso County. A railroad hub in the early 20th century, the town was for many decades simply a quiet ranching community. The Falcon Land and Town Company was established in 1896 and the enclave included two hotels, a newspaper office, six saloons, a pool hall, two general stores, a blacksmith, a school, and extensive stockyards. When a flood washed out one set of railroad tracks in 1935, they weren't rebuilt and the town declined. By 1975, only the school and a few homes remained.

Then, in the 1990s, the city of Colorado Springs reached its borders and suddenly Falcon experienced a boom in residential development. A town of a few hundred country folks exploded into a burg of more than 10,000 residents. Now, major grocery and discount stores, restaurants, and dozens of other retail entities can be found here. In 2010, a new branch of the Pikes Peak Library District was opened to serve the growing community, and locals love playing on the Antler Creek Golf Course, known as the longest in the state and second-longest in the nation.

Calhan

Home to the annual El Paso County Fair, Calhan is one of the few communities in the region that has actually declined in population. Fewer than 1,000 residents make up this farm/ranch community. What draws visitors here are the Calhan Paint Mines Interpretive Park (see the Parks chapter), the aforesaid county fair, and the big cats of Serenity Springs Wildlife Center (see the Attractions chapter) rescue operation.

There aren't many restaurants or stores for visitors, but the folks there are friendly and welcome anyone who takes the time to stop by.

Fountain Valley

Security/Widefield

The combination of Security, an incorporated town, and the exurb of Widefield totals a population of about 30,000 people, many of whom are stationed at Fort Carson, just west of the area. In fact, it was built in the 1950s and 1960s (and beyond) primarily to serve the mountain post. Affordable family homes were its hallmark. It has its own school district and a smattering of stores and restaurants, but Colorado Springs is so close, many residents seek their entertainment and employment in the city. New housing developments continue to expand the parameters of the two. This area is just north of the city of Fountain and just southeast of Colorado Springs.

It's Miller Time!

Colorado Springs and the Pikes Peak region experience an annual influx of a pesky insect, the **miller moth,** which doesn't do any harm but can be a nuisance, anyway. The moth migrates from the plains to the mountains—right through Colorado Springs—starting in late May or early June and hangs around for a few weeks, less if it's really dry. No one is quite sure why they do this migration. They get their name because they are covered with fine "dusty" scales (sort of like flour on a miller's apron) that come off on everything they touch. They don't eat clothes, they don't lay eggs, and they don't bite. They do congregate in outdoor light fixtures and other odd places—don't drive off the road when one flies out of your air vent in your dashboard! As quickly as they come, they're gone. Leaving just a dusty memory.

Fountain

About 10 miles south of Colorado Springs is the city of Fountain, another popular residence for military families from nearby Fort Carson. Founded in 1859 as a ranching community, it wasn't incorporated until 1903. It's the kind of town where lots of folks know your name but it's still big enough to have most of the amenities you need for everyday living. Being farther out on the prairie, it also has great mountain views. About 20,000 people call it home, and they're proud of its designation, in 2002, as an All-American City by the National Civic League. Fountain has its own school district.

It's usually a quiet place, but early in the morning on May 14, 1888, it was the site of an enormous train wreck, referred to locally as "the blast," when a freight train carrying 18 tons of explosives collided with a passenger train right in town. Only three people were killed, amazingly enough, but the crash destroyed a nearby grocery store and church, and reportedly created a crater 40 feet in diameter and 15 feet deep. People still talk about it.

The Gold Camps

Cripple Creek

The famous gold camp of Cripple Creek sits at 9,000 feet on the southwest slope of Pikes Peak on the opposite side from Colorado Springs and Manitou Springs. Its riches, the result of volcanic activity eons ago, served to draw miners and others during the last Gold Rush of the 1890s. You can explore its history at the Cripple Creek Heritage Center or at the Mollie Kathleen Mine, both just outside of town. Although mountain men and Native Americans explored the area prior to that, it was pretty much a cow pasture until Robert "Bob" Womack discovered gold there in

1890. Within three years, 10,000 people lived there. More than $500 million in gold was taken out of the area, and it's widely believed that the "mother lode" still hasn't been found. It was a wild 'n' woolly town, with bars, red-light districts, gunfights, and the stuff of Western legends. All that came crashing down in the early 1900s, as the gold mines played out and the price of gold dropped. By the 1970s, it was practically a ghost town, with just a couple hundred residents. But it was still a popular tourist attraction, with its quaint old buildings, a few rustic restaurants, and a melodrama at the old Imperial Hotel.

But in 1991, the state legalized gaming in three of the old gold-mining towns, including Cripple Creek, and the economy rebounded. More than a thousand residents live there today and are supported by the gambling industry and tourism. (See also the Attractions and Day Trips & Getaways chapters.) Mining has returned to the area, too, with new methods for extracting gold and new jobs for locals. Its annual events include the fun and funky Donkey Derby Days each summer. (See the Annual Festivals chapter.)

Victor

Just 5 miles from Cripple Creek, Victor also was a booming gold camp in the 1890s, especially after Winfield Scott Stratton, a Colorado Springs carpenter, discovered a major gold strike in 1891. His Independence Mine remains one of the world's largest producers of gold ever. The reintroduction of gold mining in the area has revitalized the town a bit, but it still is sparsely populated (with fewer than 500 residents at last count). Many of its historic buildings date back to 1899 (rebuilt after a major fire), but many are in poor repair. The town declined, along with its sister city of Cripple Creek, in the

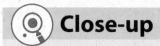

Close-up

Lowell Thomas and the News

Author, world traveler, and newsman **Lowell Jackson Thomas** was born in 1892 in Ohio and moved to Victor, Colorado, with his family when he was a child. His father, a doctor, and his mother, a teacher, were welcome additions to the rough mining camp. He attended school there, later working as a gold miner, a cook, and as a reporter on the local newspaper. After graduating from Victor High School in 1910, he attended college, getting his master's degree from the University of Denver and a job with the *Chicago Journal*. He also was a professor (teaching oratory at a law school) and later got a second master's degree at Princeton, where he also taught.

On a trip to Alaska, he hit upon the idea of creating a travelogue, an account of his travels, which so impressed President Woodrow Wilson, Thomas was asked to write a history of the conflict of World War I. Thomas thought the piece would lend itself to a new medium: film. His reporting brought him to T. E. Lawrence, a captain in the British Army, who was inciting the Palestinians to revolt against the invading Turks. His story and the film footage were so compelling, *Lawrence of Arabia* became the stuff of legends. And Lowell Thomas became a household name. Thomas later wrote a book, *With Lawrence in Arabia,* in 1924 and it was his first of 56 books in total.

In 1930, he became a broadcaster with CBS radio network, switching to NBC two years later. He hosted the first-ever television news broadcast in 1930 and the first regularly scheduled TV newscast in 1940. But he favored radio over television and continued reporting on the world until he retired in 1976. A book about his career, *Lowell Thomas: The Stranger Everyone Knows,* was published in 1968. He narrated several films and had a hit TV series, *High Adventure,* in the 1950s and another, *Lowell Thomas Remembers,* in the 1970s.

Lowell Thomas died in 1981 at his home in New York. His many books are a testament to his travels and fascination with the world. They include topics ranging from Eskimos to shipwrecks and several autobiographical works, including *Good Evening Everybody,* and *So Long Until Tomorrow.* The nationally prestigious Explorers Club presents their Lowell Thomas award annually to men and women who have distinguished themselves in the world of travel, and the Society of American Travel Writers has bestowed awards in his name (in many categories) every year since 1985.

1900s and does not have legalized gaming to boost its economy. (See Close-up: Lowell Thomas and the News.)

The Palmer Divide

Monument

North of Colorado Springs at exit 161 on I-25, the town of Monument is the nexus of the Tri-Lakes area (that includes Palmer Lake to the west and unincorporated Woodmoor to the east). The first settlers here, at the foot of the Rampart Range of the Rockies, are thought to be Iowans headed for California. However, they got to this spot, saw the high meadow grass and virgin soil, and decided to homestead here instead of taking their chances at crossing the Rockies to get to the gold fields. There were some minor skirmishes with the Plains Indians, but eventually a town was established and incorporated in 1879.

It became a supplier of potatoes, dairy products, and grains (wheat, rye, and oats) in the region, aided by the Denver & Rio Grande Railroad passing through town. Monument didn't really grow rapidly, however, till 1954 when it was announced that the US Air Force Academy would be built just south of it. Suddenly, grazing and farm land became housing developments to accommodate the military personnel who would move here.

Today, it's also a bedroom community for people who work in Colorado Springs and Denver. The wooded township of Woodmoor, to the east, borders the Black Forest. The current population of Monument is about 3,000 people. But take in the nearby enclaves and it's enough to support a variety of major stores, smaller shops and businesses, and a scattering of decent local restaurants. It also has an active arts community.

Palmer Lake

In the 1860s it was an area of homesteads and ranches, but Palmer Lake today is more of a cozy small town with a population of a few thousand folks who commute elsewhere for work. Tucked back into the foothills of the Rampart Range, with a small lake, it's Colorado's version of Mayberry. A nice little library, a few good restaurants, quaint shops, and a mix of historic and attractive contemporary homes lend to its charm.

Established in 1871 (and incorporated in 1889) by Colorado Springs' founder, William J. Palmer, the town served as a water stop for his Denver & Rio Grande trains after they struggled up the incline now known as the Palmer Divide (over Monument Hill).

Because it was higher than either Denver or Colorado Springs, it was a popular summer retreat and cooling-off spot for city residents back then, too. Many of its original buildings were summer cottages. Visitors indulged in picnicking, fishing, and boating. One stately home, the Queen Anne–style Estemere mansion (www.estemere.com) still stands as an architectural centerpiece—a private home that is occasionally open for tours for special occasions and fundraisers.

Of all the towns in the Pikes Peak region, this one came closest, perhaps, to the image of the Wild West. There were some Indian raids, a few scalpings and saloon shootings, and a couple of forts built for refuge during troubled times. Today, though, it's a quiet refuge from the bustle of nearby cities.

Ute Pass

Cascade

Just minutes west of Colorado Springs, up Ute Pass, is the scenic mountain community of Cascade. About 3,000 folks live here, in the shadow of Pikes Peak. The town is named for the nearby waterfalls and has long been a mountain retreat for city folks escaping the summer heat. Today, it's more of a bedroom community for Colorado Springs. One of its historic homes, Eastholme Inn, was built in 1885. It's said that Dwight and Mamie Eisenhower once stayed there. Cascade, on US 24, is a spot in the road to passersby, but the front door to Pikes Peak for those seeking the Pikes Peak Highway. It's also home to the North Pole/Santa's Workshop and a fun creek-side eatery, Wines of Colorado, where you can sample some of the state's award-winning vintages.

Recommended Reading: A Legacy in Letters

For a look at Colorado Springs in more contemporary times, pick up a copy of *Gifts from the Heart,* by Lucille Gonzales Oller. Growing up in Colorado Springs in the 1950s and '60s, Lou Gonzales (as she was known under her byline for the daily newspaper, *The Gazette*) offered a different perspective on the city. She wrote about her Hispanic roots, about remarkable people, and about the city's growth and changes, in an insightful way. She died in 2003 of Lou Gehrig's disease, or ALS, and those who loved, admired, and respected her work compiled this collection of stories, essays, columns, and memories into the book, published in 2010. The profits from the book go to a scholarship in her name, benefiting other nontraditional women students who attend the University of Colorado at Colorado Springs, like she did. The book is available at the UCCS bookstore (719-255-3247), Friends of the Pikes Peak Library District bookstore (www.friendsppld.org), Hooked on Books (719-596-1621), and from the CU Foundation office at UCCS, (719) 255-5105 or (719) 255-5104.

Chipita Park

Situated between Cascade and Green Mountain Falls is Chipita Park, another of the collection of towns along the Ute Trail, which later was paved and became US 24. With a population nearing 2,000, it is still mostly a bedroom community and vacation getaway site (cooler than the cities below because of its 7,500-foot elevation). It was long a popular summer destination for Kansans and Texans seeking cooler climes, but today most of the houses there are permanent residences.

Green Mountain Falls

This tiny, picturesque town in Ute Pass, with fewer than 1,000 residents, played an important role in local history. Long before the town existed, a trail ran by the site of present-day Green Mountain Falls. This pathway, the Ute Pass Trail, was first used by the Ute Indians, then Spanish explorers and finally by white settlers moving west. Green Mountain Falls was one of three towns set up as vacation spots first for dust-weary Kansans, then upper-class Easterners. Today, the trail has been paved over and is still used as US 24. It boasts a gourmet restaurant, the Black Bear; a trading post; and a small lake where locals love to go ice skating in the winter. If it sounds like a Victorian painting, in many ways it is.

Woodland Park

Once a way station and stopover for miners and others on their journey from Colorado Springs to the mining camps of Cripple Creek and Victor, Woodland Park has finally come into its own. Today with more than 7,600 residents, Woodland Park is a flourishing community of people seeking some solace and a high quality of life. Tourism fuels the economy, but it also is a bedroom community for folks who work in Colorado Springs. About 18 miles west of the Springs, it is the largest city in Teller County (and just over the line from El Paso County).

Woodland Park is surrounded by spectacular views of Pikes Peak and the Rampart

Vital Statistics

Founded: July 31, 1871

Area code: 719 for the entire Pikes Peak region

Population: 416,000 (city limits), and 622,000 (metro area), as of 2009

County: El Paso County

State capital: Denver

Time zone: Mountain Standard Time, Mountain Daylight Time

Area cities: Manitou Springs, Woodland Park, Cripple Creek, Monument, Palmer Lake, Fountain, Falcon, and Cañon City

Area: 186 square miles

Elevation: (average for city) 6,035 feet

Nickname: The Springs

Average temperatures: January, 42 degrees (high) and 15 degrees (low); July, 84 degrees (high) and 54 degrees (low)

Annual precipitation: About 16 inches

Average days of sunshine: 300

Colleges and universities: Colorado College; the University of Colorado at Colorado Springs; Pikes Peak Community College; and a number of smaller, private, for-profit universities

Military installations: Fort Carson, the US Air Force Academy, Peterson Air Force Base, Shriever Air Force Base, NORAD, and Cheyenne Mountain Air Station

Major area employers: Fort Carson, Peterson Air Force Base, US Air Force Academy, Schriever Air Force Base, Memorial Health System, Colorado Springs School District 11, Academy School District 20, City of Colorado Springs, El Paso County, and Colorado Springs Utilities

Famous natives: Western literary writer Frank Waters; silent film star Lon Chaney; pro baseball pitcher Richard "Goose" Gossage; character actor Cassandra Peterson (aka Elvira, Mistress of the Dark); Broadway and TV actor Michael Boatman; and TV actor Kelly Bishop

Famous temporary residents: Author Helen Hunt Jackson; science fiction writer Robert Heinlein; author Truman Capote (stationed at Fort Carson); *Peanuts* creator Charles M. Schulz;

figure skaters Peggy Fleming, Dick Jenkins, and others; and a number of other Olympic athletes, including Apollo Ohno

Major airports: Colorado Springs Municipal Airport

Public Transportation: Mountain Metro city bus system

Driving laws: Persons 15 to 21 years old must go through the graduated license process, which can be started any time after reaching age 15. You can get a Minor License at age 16 after taking a written and driving test. If you move here from out of state, you have 90 days to establish residency and another 30 days to obtain a Colorado driver's license. Active military and their families are exempt. All drivers and passengers must wear seat belts. Children from 1 to 4 weighing 20 to 40 pounds must be in front-facing safety seats. Children younger than 1 year or less than 20 pounds must be in a rear-facing safety seat; children 4 to 7 years old (or under 4 feet, 9 inches or less than 80 pounds) must be in a booster seat. Text messaging while driving is prohibited. Drivers younger than 18 years old are prohibited from using cell phones while driving. For more information, go online to www.colorado.gov/revenue and click on Driver's License.

Drinking laws: Colorado law says that persons 21 years of age and older may purchase and consume alcoholic beverages. Bars must close at 2 a.m. Liquor stores may be open on Sun.

Tobacco laws: The minimum age to purchase tobacco products in Colorado is 18. Smoking ordinances prohibit smoking indoors in public places and places of business, except cigar bars. Hotels may set aside rooms for smokers.

Daily newspapers: *The Gazette*, established in 1872

City sales tax: 2.5 percent

County sales tax: 1 percent

Emergency phone numbers: The universal number of 911 is used for medical emergencies, including child abuse. Poison center: (800) 332-3073. Suicide Prevention Hotline: (800) 273-8255. Runaway Hotline: (800) 786-2929

City website: www.springsgov.com; or for visitors, www.visitCOS.com

Chambers of Commerce: The Greater Colorado Springs Chamber of Commerce, 6 S. Tejon St., Suite 700, Colorado Springs, CO 80903; (719) 635-1551; www.coloradospringschamber .org. Manitou Springs Chamber of Commerce & Visitors Bureau, 354 Manitou Ave., Manitou Springs, CO 80829; 719-685-5089; www.manitousprings.org

Range. Thick stands of spruce, pine, and aspen mark its perimeter. It offers bed-and-breakfasts, motels, campgrounds, RV parks, hiking and biking trails, shopping, restaurants, and full services. Use it as your base camp to explore the world-famous mining towns of Victor and Cripple Creek, the historic Florissant Fossil Beds National Monument, and Mueller State Park & Wildlife Area and to fish in Rampart Reservoir or Manitou Lake. Go hiking or horseback riding (or, in winter, cross-country skiing or snowshoeing) in the adjacent Pike National Forest. Or visit the dinosaur center, a local history museum, or have a fine meal at one of their good local restaurants. (See also the Attractions and Restaurants chapters.)

GETTING HERE, GETTING AROUND

Colorado Springs was founded by Gen. William Jackson Palmer, a railroad man who wanted to make his home at the foot of Pikes Peak. Palmer brought his Denver & Rio Grande Railroad to town in the 1870s and that's how most early visitors arrived—by train. Well, except for those who came in covered wagons or on horseback.

Passenger trains no longer serve the city, and for most airlines it's the end of the road (or, rather, tarmac). For the most part, flights initiate and terminate here but don't stop over and then go on to other cities.

Six major airlines service the Colorado Springs Municipal Airport, and there are direct flights to nearly a dozen major cities, but many destinations require passengers to go through Denver. The airport is located on the far southeast corner of the city, has ample parking, and is easy to navigate. There is a separate airport, Peterson Air Force Base, also on the east edge of town, which serves the multitude of military flights in and out of the city. It's where military officers and national dignitaries, such as the sitting President or Vice President of the United States, fly in and out. There also are several small private airports.

Driving the city is fairly manageable, but it will take a while to learn your way around. There are several reasons: because each neighborhood has its own "grid," because of the hilly terrain, and because so many streets end after a while and give way to a whole new set of streets. Many streets have similar names (Columbine Street, Boulevard, Avenue, Drive, Place, and Road). The only streets that seem to have a reliable square-grid pattern are downtown, which was laid out by the city's founder. With great foresight, he made the downtown streets broad, mostly to accommodate the street cars of the era, but now they also handle fairly heavy traffic well.

OVERVIEW

There are only a few one-way streets. But "avenues" can be north-south or east-west (e.g., Nevada Avenue is north-south and Platte Avenue is east-west). Many streets curve (Circle Drive, Academy Boulevard) and some stop in one place and pick up in another.

Our advice? Get a good city map, a seasoned local guide, directions from someone who has lived here a while, or invest in a GPS unit!

The city's medians (dividing major streets) used to be showpieces of flower beds and plantings, but that's no longer so. The economic downturn of recent years has either left them neglected or they have been adopted by neighbors or volunteers. A few are still maintained by the parks department as funds allow.

The drive to Denver on I-25 is always busy, and you'll hit volume slowdowns in certain areas almost any time of the day. Midday is the best time to make that drive. Or you can ride the Front Range Express (FREX) bus, while funding lasts. It's no faster, but you can read a book instead of pounding the steering wheel.

If you don't drive, be aware that the city bus system is minimal, with limited routes and hours. Also, local folks rarely take taxis for regular transportation, and this isn't New York, so call well ahead if you need one.

DRIVING

The city is at the confluence of two major roadways: **I-25,** which runs north and south, and **US 24,** which runs east and west, up Ute Pass, and into the Rampart Range of the Rocky Mountains. If you drive here, chances are you'll arrive by one of those two highways.

It's a driving kind of town, and sometimes the drive can make you crazy! The infrastructure has not kept up with the population growth, so morning and evening rush hours are sometimes brutal on the interstate and other major thoroughfares, especially when there's road construction or an accident.

Within the city, there is no good east-west thoroughfare. Even US 24 has jogs and quirks and lots of traffic lights, especially downtown. And if you're on the interstate in town and see a sign for the Fontanero Street exit, don't take it. It doesn't really go anywhere.

North-south thoroughfares are a little better. They tend to curve around the perimeter of the city, but will get you from point A to point B, providing those two points aren't in a straight line. **Powers Boulevard,** the most recent north-south throughway, probably is the fastest of these. Be aware that intersections are far apart on Powers, and drivers tend to treat it like a freeway with stoplights!

i **Parking can be tough in Manitou Springs in summer. If you have trouble, head to the very west end of town, where there's a parking lot many don't know about—and it's just a few blocks walk back to the historic district.**

Because Colorado Springs has so many tourists and newcomers who move here from elsewhere, the drivers are (to put it nicely) eclectic in their habits. Some won't turn right on red; some think speed limits are just casual suggestions. Drive defensively and obey the traffic laws—the city strongly enforces them and needs the money. Be especially careful in school zones.

BY AIR

COLORADO SPRINGS MUNICIPAL AIRPORT
7770 Milton E. Proby Pkwy.
(719) 550-1900
www.ifly.com/city-of-colorado-springs-municipal-airport
The Colorado Springs Municipal Airport is so easy to get in and out of, folks from south Denver sometimes drive down to use it. Especially if they're flying somewhere that local flights go directly.

The airport, about 11 miles southeast of downtown, serves 2 million passengers a year and sets the stage nicely for visitors, with its panoramic view of Pikes Peak and the Front Range. It sits on 7,135 acres at 6,200 feet in elevation. Don't be surprised to see a coyote, prairie dogs, or antelope hanging around the perimeter.

There are more than 100 arrivals and departures each day. It's served by six airlines and has nonstop direct flights to about a dozen major cities. Other cities can be reached via connections through Denver (most common) or any of its other direct-connection cities.

Carriers include Allegiant, American, Continental, Delta/Northwest, Frontier, and United Airlines.

There are nonstop flights to Atlanta, Chicago, Dallas/Fort Worth, Denver, Houston, Las Vegas, Los Angeles, Long Beach (CA), Minneapolis, Phoenix-Mesa, Salt Lake City, San Francisco, and Washington DC–Dulles.

The recently remodeled airport has new works of art, comfortable seating, lots of electrical outlets, free wireless Internet access, several food vendors, gift shops, and 16 gates included in its spacious 280,000 square feet. Lines tend to move pretty quickly.

Because of the uncongested surrounding air and ground space, flight delays are among the lowest in the country. Passengers seldom wait more than 10 minutes to get baggage. The farthest gate is less than 1,000 feet from the ticket counters and baggage claim.

Parking is convenient. There are more than 9,000 uncovered parking spaces, and parking fees are modest by today's standards: Short-term parking is $1 for each half hour, $8 per day maximum; long-term parking is $1 per hour with a daily maximum of $6. Valet parking is $14 per day (or $2 for the first hour and $4 for each additional hour up to the maximum).

Commercial Airlines

Allegiant Airways
(702) 505-8888
www.allegiantair.com

American Airlines
(800) 433-7300
www.aa.com

Continental Airlines
(800) 523-3273
www.continental.com

Delta
(800) 221-1212
www.delta.com

Frontier Airlines
(800) 432-1359
www.frontierairlines.com

United Airlines
(800) 864-8331
www.united.com

Parking lots are safe, clean, and well-lighted, with frequent car-to-terminal shuttle service and assistance for the disabled traveler.

Private Airports

COLORADO JET CENTER
1575 Aviation Way
(719) 591-2288
www.coloradojetcenter.com
UNICOM: 122.95
Arinc Number: 130.575
The largest fixed-base operation (FBO) in the Pikes Peak region is located on the west side of the Colorado Springs Municipal Airport. The center handles both small private planes and larger jets (private, commercial charters, and military) and has three large hangars and about 20 smaller ones. About 45 aircraft are based there. The number of operations

per day varies wildly, but it has probably 25 a day on average. There is a helicopter flight school on-site. The center provides fuel for general aviation, military, and commercial customers.

CUTTER AVIATION
1360 Aviation Way
(719) 591-2065
www.cutteraviation.com
UNICOM: 125.3

This private airport also is located in the Colorado Springs Municipal Airport complex and has been operating since 2006. It handles private planes and jets, has 58 hangars (9 of them accommodate the larger jets) and has approximately 60 aircraft based there. They also have an on-site flight school.

MEADOW LAKE AIRPORT
13625 Judge Orr Rd., Peyton
(719) 683-3062
www.meadowlakeairport.org
UNICOM: 122.95

Meadow Lake is a pilot-owned and -controlled airport that handles small planes—an average of 162 daily, according to the FAA. On a busy day, there may be as many as 300 operations out of this airport, located near Falcon on the prairie east of Colorado Springs. About 400 small planes are based here. Private businesses offer flying lessons, ultralight instruction, and more. It has been in operation since 1965.

GROUND TRANSPORTATION
Airport Shuttles & Rental Cars

Many local hotels offer shuttle service to their site from the airport, so ask if that service is available when you book your room.

However, it's likely you will need a rental car, anyway.

Most major car rental companies serve the Colorado Springs Municipal Airport. Cars are on-site or have shuttles to nearby lots. And if you fly in, you *will* want a rental car, because driving is the best (and sometimes only) way to see the local attractions. Car rental desks are near the baggage carousels. They include:

ADVANTAGE
(719) 574-8756 or (800) 777-5500
www.advantage.com

ALAMO/NATIONAL
(719) 574-8579 or (800) 327-9633
www.alamo.com

AVIS
(719) 596-2751 or (800) 331-1212
www.avis.com

BUDGET
(719) 597-1271 or (800) 527-0700
www.budget.com

ENTERPRISE
(719) 591-6644 or (800) 736-8222
www.enterprise.com

HERTZ
(719) 596-1863 or (800) 654-3131
www.hertz.com

PUBLIC TRANSPORTATION
Taxis & Limos

Yellow Cab dominates the taxi scene, but there are several town car services and more than a dozen limousine services that have a wide range of prices and availability. They seem to come and go, but current ones are listed in the Colorado Springs Yellow Pages. Most also are listed online at www.limos .com/airports/united-states/COS.

YELLOW CAB
4625 Town Center Dr.
(719) 634-5000 or (719) 777-7777
www.yellowbot.com/yellow-cab-
colorado-springs-co.html
The Yellow Cab Company serves the Colorado Springs airport and city at large. There's always a line of them waiting at the airport. A typical taxi fare from the airport to a downtown hotel is about $26 plus tip.

Buses

The city's bus service is . . . well, serviceable. It gets riders to work or appointments and back, but not necessarily in an easy or timely fashion. There is a bus to Denver and one to the casinos in Cripple Creek. There also is some effort to bring back tourist trolleys in Colorado Springs and Manitou Springs, but so far they serve a very limited area and funding is somewhat unpredictable.

FRONT RANGE EXPRESS
1015 Transit Dr.
(719) 636-FREX (3739)
www.frontrangeexpress.com
There's also the city-run Front Range Express (FREX) bus that runs from Colorado Springs to Denver several times a day. The one-way cash fare is $11. The cash fare for senior citizens (60 and older), children (ages 6 to 11), students (12 to 18), and Medicare/disabled passengers during non-peak hours (9 a.m. to 3:15 p.m.) is 50 percent off the posted one-way cash fare. Proper ID or proof of

eligibility required. Children 5 and younger ride free with an adult. Drivers can only take exact change or a prepaid bus pass. Note: It's worth the money just to avoid driving on heavily congested I-25 between the two cities.

GREYHOUND BUS LINES
120 S. Weber St.
(719) 635-1505 or (800) 231-2222
www.greyhound.com
The local bus station does some passenger business, with nearly a dozen buses a day heading north and south along I-25. Much of their business is package transportation. Few visitors arrive or depart this way and you should be aware that the bus stop area is a little intimidating, especially at night. It is somewhat deserted, on the edge of a warehouse district, and not as well lighted as it could be.

MOUNTAIN METRO BUS
1015 Transit Dr.
(719) 385-RIDE (7433)
www.springsgov.com
The only real public transportation in town is the Mountain Metro Bus System, operated by the city of Colorado Springs. Routes have been curtailed due to the economy, but many local residents depend on it to get around. They're not likely to be convenient for vacationers, however. Buses run from about 5:30 a.m. to about 7 p.m. weekdays, except major holidays. The main terminal is downtown at the intersection of Nevada Avenue and Kiowa Street. The basic adult fare is $1.75, but kids and seniors ride for 85 cents. The city bus system routes do not include the airport.

RAMBLIN EXPRESS
3465 Astrozon Place
(719) 590-8687
www.ramblinexpress.com

The Ramblin Express takes residents and visitors from several locations in Colorado Springs to Cripple Creek. It also runs daily from the Colorado Springs Airport to The Broadmoor hotel complex. Round-trip fares from Colorado Springs to Cripple Creek are $25 ($20 if you purchase in advance online) and a one-way trip to The Broadmoor is $23. But check their website for group rates, plus numerous deals and packages.

WALKING & BICYCLING

Except for dedicated enclaves of shopping and dining, such as downtown Colorado Springs, Old Colorado City, and Manitou Springs, walking really is not an option for exploring most of the city, which is quite spread out. That said, there are lots of recreational hiking and walking trails throughout the city's park system (see the Parks and Sports & Recreation chapters).

HISTORY

There are no springs in Colorado Springs. No hot springs. No mineral springs. It was called Colorado Springs even though no springs exist within the city limits—they're all over in Manitou Springs, to the west. But this was the train stop to get there, so the name made sense to someone!

And though it's a distinctly Western city, Colorado Springs never was a "Wild West" kind of town. From its earliest days, it was more refined—or tried to be. There were no famous outlaws living here, no shoot'em-up showdowns downtown outside some saloon. In fact, there were no saloons.

When Gen. William Jackson Palmer established the city in 1871, the founding father established it as a "dry" town. No saloons. (No brothels, either.) Instead, there were opera houses, tea shops, and fine hotels. Easterners getting off the railroad to visit the place discovered a city that reminded them of home—with mountains. In fact, its early nickname was "Little London."

Ladies could stroll the boardwalk with their parasols, shopping. Business was the order of the day for men, with banks and, somewhat later, mining exchange buildings growing up in the downtown to support the mining industry in the nearby goldfields of Cripple Creek and Victor.

There were parades of flower-bedecked wagons in an annual celebration called Shan Kive, a historical pageant meant to entice tourists, but that mostly entertained locals. The event culminated in an amateur rodeo at Garden of the Gods. All this was the precursor to today's Pikes Peak or Bust Rodeo and annual pre-rodeo parade.

The resort city has always drawn tourists because of its spectacular setting and many attractions, some crafted by nature and much older than the city itself. Tourism still is one of its economic mainstays.

OVERVIEW

The arrival of the military in the 1940s changed the face of the city, encouraged a sprawling expansion, and altered its cultural nature. And it brought an economic boom that remains the strongest factor in its financial picture today.

Health and wellness also have had a major impact on the city's formation. In the early days, patients from all over the world came here for "the cure" for tuberculosis. The high altitude and clean, dry mountain air were thought to be beneficial. It must have been, because many of them stayed on, became productive members of the community, and lived to a ripe old age. Little sleeping porches were added to many homes in the core city, and TB patients became boarders. The first hospitals specialized in the care of the disease. Strong health service providers remain a mainstay of the city, and some of the best doctors in the country live and practice here.

In recent years, the city has successfully recruited a number of "clean" industries—mostly electronics and high-tech companies—and has become a corporate headquarters for a variety of religious organizations.

Always re-creating itself, Colorado Springs has seen tough times like every other city, but always has managed to come up with a new way to make it flourish.

In Colorado Springs and the Pikes Peak region, history and modern amenities stand side by side, comfortably rubbing elbows across time. Its history is short (compared to Eastern cities) but rich, tied to the Gold Rush, the military, high-tech industry, and tourism.

Pikes Peak probably is America's most famous mountain. Everyone knows about NORAD (made famous in films) and the US Air Force Academy (especially if he or she follows sports). The US Olympic Training Center is here. The city often makes the national news.

But how it was shaped into the city it has become is a complex story we will try to tell you in this chapter. Learn about some of the movers and shakers who made the city what it is today—a beautiful, healthful place to live with lots of industries that keep it thriving.

PREHISTORY

At the Paint Mines in Calhan, there is evidence that prehistoric man visited the site as far back as 9,000 years ago. The abundant colorful clays here were used by American Indians for making pottery and ceremonial paints. The site's geologic features, including spires and hoodoos, also may have made it a ceremonial place.

As far as anyone knows, the Ute Indians were the first regular inhabitants of the Pikes Peak region. Primarily a mountain tribe, they spent time in what is now Colorado Springs, seeking the healing waters that eventually named Manitou Springs, and visiting the ceremonial site of the Garden of the Gods for gatherings. You might say they were the first tourists.

By definition, we know little of the city's pre-history because it wasn't recorded! But archeology, oral history, and reports by early mountain men confirm much of this. At some point, probably in the late 1700s or early 1800s, the Arapaho and Cheyenne Indians—plains tribes, and avid hunters—visited the area in search of game. Later, there were clashes between the Indians and the invading Europeans in various parts of the state, but it is generally not thought that any significant battles were fought here.

DISCOVERY

In 1806, young Zebulon Pike, then a captain in the US Army, was sent west, leaving from St. Louis and ending up more than a year later in what is now Natchitoches, LA (a "guest" of the army of New Spain, which thought he was a spy—but that's another story). Battling hardships, including harsh winter weather, he and his ill-equipped party managed to explore a good portion of the West not touched by Lewis and Clark.

Now, more than 200 years after Pike's trek through the uncharted wilds of the Louisiana Purchase, his efforts are being

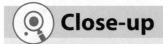 **Close-up**

General Palmer & His Queen

William Jackson Palmer was enamored of the Pikes Peak region the first time he laid eyes on it. This was where he wanted to make his home.

Palmer was born and raised a Quaker, but fought in the Civil War because he so abhorred slavery. By all accounts, his military service was exemplary—he won a Congressional Medal of Honor for his actions. But as soon as the war was over, he headed west and saw the future: railroads. He built several, and traveled extensively, before settling on Colorado Springs as his home.

He met and married the daughter of one of his business associates, the petite, pretty **Mary Lincoln Mellen,** nicknamed "Queen" by her grandmother and called that by her husband her whole life.

Palmer promised his Queen (who, according to some accounts, disliked the rustic West) that he would build the grandest home he could afford, and bought the valley and adjacent canyon north of the Garden of the Gods in 1870. First, they built what is today the carriage house, where they lived on the 2,000-acre estate until the 22-room frame house was built.

Palmer engaged a Scottish landscape architect to sculpt the barren grounds into a veritable park, complete with fruit trees and a rose garden. The architect dubbed the valley Glen Eyrie (valley of the eagles), a name the Palmers liked and adopted. Eagles still live there, along with deer, bighorn sheep, mountain lions, coyotes, ringtails, wild turkeys, and a variety of small mammals and birds.

When this grand estate was built, it had all the modern conveniences. Electric gates. A milk pasteurization plant. Greenhouses for growing vegetables and flowers. Its own laundry. An indoor bowling alley. Telephones in the house. Stables for the fine horses Palmer raised and loved (he hated cars).

All this, and his beloved bride was gone.

Young Queen had a mild heart attack in 1880 and was advised by her doctor to move to a lower altitude. She moved back to the East Coast, and later to England, where she died in 1894 at the age of 44, leaving Palmer and their three daughters.

There are lots of stories about what transpired during this time. All that's known for sure is that Palmer's business interests were in the West, and that Queen moved east. Some say she found life in the West too lacking in culture. Others claim theirs was a real love story to which fate dictated an unhappy ending. In any case, Palmer did visit her as often as possible, and their letters to each other bear this out.

In the early 1900s, Palmer decided to transform the frame house into a stone castle. Work began in 1904 and was finished in less than two years. Then, in 1906, the accomplished horseman was thrown while riding an unfamiliar mount and broke his neck. He was paralyzed from his rib cage down.

Still, he managed his family and business for several more years until his death at age 72 in 1909.

reexamined and evaluated. Much has been made of his failure to climb the mountain named for him, but by the time he reached the peak, it was November. Winter weather was upon him and he and his men were inadequately dressed in summer gear.

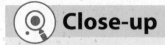

Close-up

The Penrose Legacy

If ever there were a power couple in Colorado Springs's early history, it was Spencer and Julie Penrose.

Born in 1865 in Philadelphia, **Spencer Penrose** (nicknamed "Spec" or "Speck," depending on which source you read) was an Eastern blue blood from a well-established prominent family.

He came to Colorado Springs in 1891 and, with his friend, Charles Tutt, invested in real estate, plus gold and copper mines in Utah, and became a wealthy man. An avowed bachelor, his life was devoted to the business of making money.

Enter Julie Villiers Lewis McMillan, the daughter of the mayor of Detroit and widow of Jim McMillan, whom she had married in 1888. The McMillans moved to Colorado Springs to help him recover from tuberculosis. He died in 1901, leaving Julie, a daughter and a son. Their son, Jimmie, died the same year of appendicitis. That left Julie and her daughter, Gladys.

Some say she decided she didn't want to spend the rest of her young life as a widow and set her sights on the eligible and handsome copper millionaire, Spencer Penrose. Details of their courtship are varied and contradictory, but Julie and Spec ended up marrying—at ages 35 and 41, respectively—in April 1906 in London.

After returning to Colorado Springs, she pursued the arts and he pursued the money. Then, a decade after their marriage, they decided to build a grand resort hotel like those they had visited in Europe. **The Broadmoor** opened in 1918 and the Penroses moved to a nearby estate, which they named **El Pomar,** for its apple orchards. Julie then donated her beautiful former home on Dale Street to **The Broadmoor Art Academy,** which laid ground for the later **Colorado Springs Fine Arts Center.**

Together, they also started or built the Pikes Peak Highway, the Pikes Peak Hill Climb car race, the Cheyenne Mountain Zoo, the Fountain Valley School, the Pikes Peak or Bust Rodeo, The Broadmoor World Arena, and the Will Rogers Shrine.

Her philanthropy inspired him and, in 1937, they started the **El Pomar Foundation,** just two years before Spec died.

From his death until her own in 1956, Julie Penrose was president and CEO of El Pomar, directing disposition of its funds. After Spencer's death, Julie wore black almost exclusively for the next two decades.

She also moved out of El Pomar, donating it to the Sisters of Charity, and moved into a penthouse at the hotel. El Pomar later became the headquarters of the foundation.

Today, the El Pomar Foundation is one of the largest philanthropies in the state and its mark is everywhere in Colorado Springs—from performing arts centers, sports complexes, health facilities, and local colleges—and beyond. That's the Penrose legacy.

Pike, who had been promoted to general, died young and heroically—at age 34, in the War of 1812. He never got the glory and recognition that Lewis and Clark received, but today there are hundreds of landmarks, attractions, and businesses named for him in the—what else—Pikes Peak region.

THE GOLD RUSH

In 1859, Pikes Peak became a beacon for miners and prospectors headed for the Rockies in the West's second big Gold Rush (after California). The first finds were actually in the Denver area, but for travelers the mountain became a landmark in an unmarked land. Gold was not really found in this area till 1891, when prospector Robert Womack discovered gold in Cripple Creek, creating one of the great gold mining towns of the century.

In 1861, when Congress established the Colorado Territory, President Abraham Lincoln appointed William Gilpin as the first Territorial governor. Congressional delegates were chosen and, in September, the state's first assembly selected Colorado City—situated between what later will be Colorado Springs and Manitou Springs—as the Territorial capital. A log cabin that marks the place stands in Bancroft Park in Old Colorado City, now a western suburb of Colorado Springs.

In 1862, however, the Second Territorial Legislature met for a few days at Colorado City, adjourned to Denver, and selected Golden as the new capital.

BIRTH OF A CITY

In the early 1870s, Civil War veteran and railroad magnate Gen. William Jackson Palmer arrived on the scene. Taken with the natural beauty of this high plain at the foot of an enormous mountain, he decided it was here he would bring his railroad, build a city, and make his own life. Fresh from his honeymoon, Palmer decided to bring his Denver & Rio Grande Railroad to Colorado Springs and parts south.

He and his business partners set about developing a city that was both beautiful and practical. Wide streets accommodated coaches and carriages as well as a streetcar system. Lots were spacious enough to accommodate mansions. Trees by the hundreds were planted, turning the prairie into a woodland. Water was siphoned from Fountain Creek and Monument Creek to feed them, along with lawns, flowers, and other plantings.

A downtown emerged: the Antlers Hotel, among others; several opera houses; a plethora of churches; plus schools, banks, businesses, and offices. It was a genteel city fit for his bride, the blue-blooded Queen Mellen (and daughter of one of his business partners).

Colorado College was founded in 1874, just a few years after the city, on land and with funds donated by General Palmer. It remains one of the most prestigious (and expensive) private liberal arts colleges in the country.

In the same year, The Colorado Institute for the Education of Mutes was founded by Jonathan R. Kennedy. Kennedy had previously served as the steward of the Kansas School for the Deaf in Olathe. With an appropriation of $5,000 from the Territorial Legislature, Kennedy opened the school on April 8, 1874. It later became known as the Colorado School for the Deaf and the Blind, which continues to educate and train students who are either deaf or blind (or both) today.

Another early influential resident was Winfield Scott Stratton, a carpenter who in 1891 discovered one of the richest gold mines on earth, the famous Independence Mine, in the Cripple Creek and Victor goldfields.

A generous man, he became an early mover and shaker in the development of the city. He lived in a relatively modest house,

History Timeline

1500s: Ute Indians inhabit mountain areas of southern Rocky Mountains making these Native Americans the oldest continuous residents of Colorado Springs and the Pikes Peak region.

1682: Explorer La Salle appropriates for France all of the area now known as Colorado east of the Rocky Mountains.

1803: Through the Louisiana Purchase, signed by President Thomas Jefferson, the US acquires a vast area that includes what is now most of eastern Colorado.

1806–1807: Lt. Zebulon M. Pike and small party of US soldiers sent to explore southwestern boundary of Louisiana Purchase; discovers a peak that later bears his name, but fails in effort to climb it.

1858: Green Russell's discovery of small placer gold deposits near confluence of South Platte River and Cherry Creek precipitates gold rush from the East and "Pikes Peak or Bust" slogan.

1859: Colorado City is established as the first permanent settlement in the Pikes Peak Region. Located at the foot of Ute Pass, the town becomes a supply center for miners heading to the goldfields of the central Rockies.

1861: Congress establishes Colorado Territory with boundaries of present state; President Lincoln appoints William Gilpin as first Territorial governor; Colorado City chosen as Territorial capital.

1862: Second Territorial Legislature meets for a few days at Colorado City, adjourns to Denver, and selects Golden as the new capital.

1871: Colorado Springs is founded by Gen. William J. Palmer, who builds the Denver & Rio Grande Railroad southward from Denver.

1872: *Out West,* later the *Colorado Springs Gazette,* is established.

1874: Colorado College is founded. Also established is the Colorado School for the Deaf and the Blind.

1876: Colorado is admitted to Union as the 38th or "Centennial" State.

1880: Denver & Rio Grande lays tracks through Royal Gorge and on to Leadville.

1881: Ute tribes are removed onto reservations.

1887: St. Francis Hospital is established.

1888: The first TB sanatorium opens in Colorado Springs ("The Bellevue"). More than a dozen other major sanatoriums will open subsequently.

1890: Glockner Tuberculosis Sanitarium is privately founded. Later becomes Penrose Hospital, operated by the Sisters of Charity.

1891: Robert Womack's discoveries open great goldfield of Cripple Creek. Pikes Peak cog railroad begins operation.

1893: National panic brings great distress to Colorado. Repeal of Sherman Act strikes silver mining a paralyzing blow and adds to already acute unemployment problems.

1900: Gold production reaches peak of more than $20 million annually at Cripple Creek, the second richest gold camp in the world.

1902: Myron Stratton Home for the needy is established.

1903: Mine, mill, and smelter workers strike in many camps for higher wages and better working conditions; at Cripple Creek, strike results in much property damage and loss of life; all strike objectives in gold field are lost.

1915: Toll road for auto travel to top of Pikes Peak built by Spencer Penrose. Construction of The Broadmoor resort hotel at Colorado Springs starts (opens in **1918**).

1928: Alexander Film Company becomes a major industry in Colorado Springs.

1936: Colorado Springs Fine Arts Center established.

1938: Broadmoor World Arena opens at the hotel, hosting figure skating and hockey matches.

1942: Camp Carson (later Fort Carson) is established.

1958: Air Force Academy is built near Colorado Springs and first class graduates in June 1959.

1963: NORAD's main facility built inside Cheyenne Mountain.

1965: The University of Colorado at Colorado Springs is established on the site of a former Cragmor Sanitarium.

1973: The community saves the 1903 El Paso County Courthouse for use as the Colorado Springs Pioneers Museum (city's first historic preservation victory).

1978: The US Olympic Training Center opens on the site of the former Ent Air Force Base.

1982: The Pikes Peak Center performing arts facility is built.

1998: Colorado Springs World Arena opens, replacing old Broadmoor World Arena, which was razed to build Broadmoor West, an addition to The Broadmoor hotel complex.

2001: The September 11 terrorist attack on the World Trade Center in New York and on the Pentagon puts all local military bases on high alert. Visitors are not allowed, or very cautiously allowed, for several years. In all, it has a negative impact on local tourism for several years.

2009: Voters turn down a tax increase needed to keep police and fire departments at full staff, and reduce park maintenance and the number of streetlights.

not a mansion (as many of the other new millionaires did), and he donated the land for the first city hall, the first post office, and the 1902 county courthouse and built the Mining Exchange Building. Before he died in 1902, he also founded the Myron Stratton Home on the south end of the city. The home was designed to aid the itinerant children and elderly who were struggling in the community. Today, the organization still provides housing, support services, and grants to improve the quality of life for the needy in the community.

A NEW CENTURY

Colorado Springs had become a destination for tuberculosis patients seeking its dry climate. The healing waters of Manitou Springs also drew patients of various kinds. Sanitariums and hospitals were built. St. Francis Hospital was founded by the Sisters of St. Francis in 1887. And in 1890, the Glockner Tuberculosis Sanitarium was started by Marie Glockner in memory of her husband, who died from the disease. She later transferred its operation to the Sisters of Charity and, after a large donation, it was renamed after Spencer Penrose. The city became famous for its level of health care.

Word of the healthful climate and natural attractions spread, and tourism blossomed, too. Zeb Pike never climbed Pikes Peak, but plenty of others were determined to do it. And in 1858, Julia Archibald Holmes became the first woman on record to climb it. Many others—men and women—followed. For those not hearty enough to do it on foot, there were wagon rides to the top.

Others discovered the grandeur of the Garden of the Gods city park and explored it on foot, by horse and donkey. Many early tourist photos show vacationers on burro-back posing at the various famous formations, such as the Balanced Rock.

The growth of Colorado Springs and its reputation as a city of note inspired new ventures.

Enter Spencer Penrose, a copper tycoon who, with his wife, Julie, decided to build a resort hotel that would rival the grand hotels they had seen on their travels in Europe. The hotel was completed in 1918, and included luxury rooms, restaurants, bars, ballrooms, terraces, and even its own lake.

The mining operations in Cripple Creek and Victor lost steam as World War I took every bit of mechanical know-how the country possessed. Things stagnated here, as they did elsewhere, during the Great Depression.

One bright spot was in 1928, when the Alexander Film Company relocated its operation here. By the early 1950s Alexander was producing 2,000 to 3,000 advertisement films a year, shown in theaters all over the country. In its heyday, it provided more than 600 jobs. The advent of television dealt a hefty blow to the company and today it is a much smaller video production enterprise.

THE POST-WAR YEARS

In the 1940s, new economic hope arrived in the guise of a military base. Camp Carson was established on land the city had bought and set aside for such a use. It eventually became Fort Carson and remains one of the strongest Army bases in the country.

And that was just a start. In the 1950s, Colorado Springs was among the cities chosen to consider for the site of the newest American military academy—the US Air Force Academy. It graduated its first class of eager cadets in 1959.

Recommended Reading

Frank Waters
Nowhere has the story of early Colorado Springs been captured so vividly as in Frank Waters's trilogy about Pikes Peak.

Waters was born on July 25, 1902, in Colorado Springs, the son of May Ione Dozier Waters and Frank Jonathon Waters. His father, who was part Cheyenne, had a profound influence in Waters's perception of and interest in the American Indian experience. The elder Waters took his son to the Navajo Reservation in New Mexico in 1911. Frank Sr. died in 1914, when young Frank was 12. Waters studied engineering at Colorado College, and worked a number of different jobs, mostly in various Western states, but wrote in his spare time. In 1944, he moved to Taos, NM, where he became a newspaper editor.

He started publishing novels in 1941, including the acclaimed *Man Who Killed the Deer,* and, in 1971, the Pikes Peak trilogy. He was both lauded and criticized for his novels about Indians, and nominated several times for the Pulitzer Prize for Literature. Frank Waters died at his home in Arroyo Seco, NM, in 1995. There is a small park in downtown Colorado Springs named for him.

Helen Hunt Jackson
Though she hailed from Amherst, MA, Helen Jackson took Colorado Springs to heart when she moved here with her second husband and railroad executive, William Jackson, in 1875—when the city was newborn. She had been here as a tuberculosis patient, for "the cure," when she met her husband a few years earlier. Moved by the plight of the Native Americans, she wrote *A Century of Dishonor,* published in 1882, about the government's treatment of native tribes. Two years later, she published *Ramona,* the fictional story of a beautiful Scots-Indian orphan girl who is raised as gentry but falls in love with Allesandro, a handsome and courageous Indian. Their love story turns tragic and illustrates the power of prejudice. It caused quite a stir. Jackson died the following year, 1885, of stomach cancer.

Other Reading
- **Marshall Sprague,** who wrote about Colorado Springs's early history and people in *Newport in the Rockies* and *Money Mountain.*
- **Nancy Loe,** a historian who wrote *Life in the Altitudes: An Illustrated History of Colorado Springs*—hard to find except online or from rare book dealers.
- **Elena Bertozzi-Villa,** for many years the Broadmoor hotel's historian, who wrote *Broadmoor Memories: The History of the Broadmoor,* still available at the Broadmoor West Gift Shop.

Note: Some of these books are out of print, but can be found at the local library or online bookstores.

The influx of military personnel who had traveled the world brought a new racial and ethnic mix to the city, expanding its awareness of its place in the world.

Also raising its national profile was the construction of the Broadmoor World Arena, an ice rink across the lake from the original hotel, a place where figure skaters could practice and hockey matches could be played. It was razed in 1994 to build an addition to the hotel complex, Broadmoor West.

The Broadmoor Skating Club, established in 1939 as the Pikes Peak Skating Club, is one of the most famous and prestigious figure skating clubs in the US. Many of the Broadmoor Skating Club's members have won medals at national, Olympic, and world figure skating events. They practiced and performed at the Broadmoor World Arena, which was started by Thayer Tutt, then executive director of The Broadmoor hotel. World-class skaters who called it home included Olympic champions Peggy Fleming, Hayes Allen Jenkins, and David Jenkins, among others.

POPULATION EXPLOSION

The population boom started in the 1950s, and in the 1970s the city exploded. The military presence had expanded to include more air bases and NORAD (North American Aerospace Defense Command). Many military folks who were stationed here at one time or another returned to retire in the temperate climate and clean environment.

It became a mecca for retirees of all kinds, giving rise to senior services such as Silver Key, and beautiful retirement complexes.

The city began to court any kind of clean industry it could, especially the new companies that specialized in technology. Defense contractors proliferated. The University of Colorado opened a Colorado Springs campus, which was small and without dorms, but today is one of the fastest-growing campuses in the nation.

Because of its natural attractions and clean air, and because it was such a family-oriented city, it also became attractive to the US Olympic Committee as a place to house and train athletes at high altitude, thereby giving them a slight edge at lower-altitude competition venues.

It also attracted large religious organizations wanting to relocate their corporate offices. Dozens are now based here.

THE 21ST CENTURY

The economic downturn of the first decade of the 21st century has affected business and industry. Some of the major electronics manufacturers—Digital Equipment, Litton Industries, and Intel, for example—have closed their doors. Hewlett Packard, a longtime player in the local economy, is now Agilent Industries but continues to be a significant employer. Real estate sales and construction have, for the time being, stagnated.

Local citizens have voted down tax measures that would keep police and fire departments at full staff, parks and public flower beds watered, museums open, and streetlights fully functional, and the city has gotten some negative national press for those actions.

However, the city still is an affordable, desirable place to live and visit. It's a safe, healthful place to raise families. Tourism has rebounded. The beauty doesn't change. The climate remains enticingly temperate. And so the city continues attract new residents in large numbers every year.

ACCOMMODATIONS

ecause it gets 6 million visitors a year, the Pikes Peak region has got rooms galore! Not only is there no shortage of accommodations, but there also is a wide array of lodgings from which to choose.

You can stay in a historic hotel at the foot of Pikes Peak, a world-class resort nestled near Cheyenne Mountain, or a funky little motel that has been around since the 1920s. There are a number of locally owned accommodations along with well-known national chain hotels, and dozens of chain motels with familiar surroundings. All the major players are here, from Motel 6 to La Quinta to the Hyatt and Marriott.

Where you stay depends on two things: how much you want to spend and your reason for being here. If you're looking at budget lodgings, you can find them. If you're looking for a luxury vacation, that's here, too. And there's everything in between, including some retro motels along Manitou Avenue, complete with neon signs that date back to the '50s. You also can stay at the home of the city's founder (Glen Eyrie) or at one of the world's classiest resorts (The Broadmoor).

Let's face it. Manitou Springs probably has more bed-and-breakfast inns per capita than anywhere else in the state. And Colorado Springs has its share, too. A number of historic B&Bs offer lodging with personality and a personal touch. To find them all, go online (www.bedandbreakfast.com/colorado-springs-colorado.html). Big hotels offer more anonymity and amenities, including spas and golf courses. For a price. Most hotels have ample parking of their own. The only major downtown hotel (Antlers Hilton) has its own parking garage. The Broadmoor properties (Main, South, and West) all use valet parking or an on-site parking garage. Use the valet parking—it's free! (Though it's rare that folks don't tip.)

OVERVIEW

If you're here strictly as a tourist, chances are you'll want to stay on the west side or in Manitou Springs. If you're here on business, downtown or south are probably your best bets. South-end lodgings also will serve you well if your business is at Fort Carson, but you'll want to head to the north end if you are visiting the US Air Force Academy. East-side lodgings will suit visitors to the local air force bases or those who need to be near the airport.

Lodging in Colorado Springs and the Pikes Peak region, with a few notable exceptions, is generally more reasonably priced than in many cities of its size. Prices are higher in summer, of course, during the peak tourist season. They're also likely to be higher during special events, such as the Air Force Academy graduation in May.

Because the Pikes Peak region has a glut of hotels ranging from cheapie chains to grand hotels, you can pick your price: Spend $59 a night or $590 a night—it's your call.

We have arranged this chapter by type of accommodations, then by geographic region.

Most places are wheelchair accessible and kid-friendly but if they aren't (like some B&Bs), we'll tell you. We'll also note if they are pet-friendly (or not) and what their smoking policies are. Colorado law prohibits smoking in public areas, and many accommodations are smoke-free in their entirety, but lodgings may set aside "smoking" rooms—and some do. All addresses are Colorado Springs unless we note otherwise. Because this is such a popular tourist destination, we've also included a few nearby RV parks and campgrounds.

Price Code

This price code guide helps you decide where to stay based on cost. The prices are average room rates, per night, for up to two people, in peak visiting season. Most lodgings offer lower prices in shoulder- and off-season. Most charge a nominal fee (like $5 to $10) for an extra person in the room. Many accommodations also offer special deals and packages at certain times of the year, so check their websites for those (for example, a "sweetheart" package at Valentine's Day). Unless otherwise noted, all take major credit cards and request reservations.

$	less than $70
$$	$70 to $100
$$$	$100 to $200
$$$$	$200 to $300
$$$$$	more than $300

HOTELS & MOTELS

Downtown

ANTLERS HILTON HOTEL   **$$$**
4 S. Cascade Ave.
(719) 955-5600 or (866) 299-4602
www.antlers.com
The original Antlers Hotel was built as a centerpiece of downtown Colorado Springs in 1883 by the city's founder, Gen. William J. Palmer. Two years later, it burned down and an even more elegant hotel was built on the spot. Unfortunately, that grand edifice was torn down and replaced with an architecturally uninspiring modern building in 1967. (Its saving grace is that it has as its backdrop the stunning outline of Pikes Peak.) But inside, you'll figure out why it's a four-diamond property. Elegantly appointed guest rooms are particularly suitable for business travelers, with every amenity one could want. And don't miss the lobby-level Judge Baldwin's microbrewery. With its pub food and dark wood, it's just the place to relax (locals love it). Also, be sure to swim in the hotel pool with floor-to-ceiling windows and a panoramic view of the Front Range.

East

HILTON GARDEN INN—AIRPORT   **$$$**
2035 Aerotech Dr.
(719) 622-0300
www.coloradospringsairport.hgi.com
After a long flight, relax at the Hilton Garden Inn near the airport. Just grab the free airport shuttle and within minutes you can be in your room, sinking into a Garden Sleep System king bed with a European-style duvet to keep you cozy. All 119 guest rooms come with a refrigerator, coffeemaker, and microwave. You can press your own wrinkled shirts (an iron is provided) or send your duds to the on-site laundry. For those who need to be connected, there's free wireless and wired high-speed Internet access (with secure, remote printing to the business center, if needed). There's a large desk area and ergonomic desk chair for those who have to do some serious work while here. After all that work, relax in the heated pool or de-stress at the workout facility. Room service is available in the evenings, or you can dine in their Great American Grill any time of the day. Nonsmoking and wheelchair accessible rooms are available, and if you rent a car there is plenty of free parking on property. Pets are not allowed.

RADISSON HOTEL—
   COLORADO SPRINGS AIRPORT   **$$$**
1645 Newport Rd.
(719) 597-7000
www.radisson.com/
coloradospringsco_airport
Conveniently located near the Colorado Springs Airport, the Radisson Hotel has a complimentary 24-hour airport shuttle available. This 100-percent smoking-free facility is

equipped to handle business travelers with its full-service business center and high-speed Internet access in rooms. Spacious suites and guest rooms also feature Sleep Number beds (kings or doubles), micro-waves, refrigerators, in-room coffee service, and bottled water. Take advantage of the free full breakfast buffet each morning, and the 20 percent discount they'll give you on meals in their restaurant, Bistro Colorado, or on room service. There's a fitness center and heated swimming pool with a sun deck and hot tub for those who need to unwind after a hectic day of work or travel. There's a game room for fun and some rooms are pet-friendly (with a refundable deposit). Forgot to bring a book? There's a library, too. They must be doing something right: This Radis-son ranks No. 1 in their nationwide chain for guest satisfaction.

North

**BEST WESTERN
  THE ACADEMY HOTEL** $$
8110 N. Academy Blvd.
(719) 598-5770 or (800) 766-8524
www.theacademyhotel.com
This 200-room full-service hotel is conve-niently located for visitors who have cadets enrolled at the nearby US Air Force Academy. It has a cool, Colorado-style lobby with lots of wood and stone. Your stay includes a full breakfast, with an omelet bar, waffles, and a buffet, not one of those skimpy stale-muffin-and-bad-coffee things! There's a full bar and restaurant on-site and a 24-hour pool. Rooms come with free local calls and HBO movies. Pets can be accommodated in one wing of the hotel. Kids will love the arcade and adults will like the well-equipped business center. For the amenities, it's a great value.

COLORADO SPRINGS MARRIOTT $$$
5580 Tech Center Dr.
(719) 260-1800
http://marriott.com/cosmc
The Colorado Springs Marriott is a luxury hotel with 309 rooms, Southwestern din-ing, and elegantly appointed event space. It opened in 1986 but was recently renovated. Visitors are greeted first by a warm great room, featuring a brick fireplace and rich wood decor. Guest rooms, with either a king bed or 2 doubles, feature plush bed-ding packages and dual screen plasma HD televisions. Other amenities include a coffee maker, iron and board, and hair dryer. This hotel is plugged in, with an in-room laptop safe, two-line telephone with voicemail and message light, high-speed Internet access, and dataport. For exercise, there are indoor and outdoor pools, a fitness center with individual cardio theaters, sauna and whirl-pool, plus nearby jogging and hiking trails and three 18-hole golf courses. Later, sample a flavored tequila cocktail from the Lobby Lounge before dining in Zebulon's Grill and Tequileria. The entire hotel is nonsmoking and only service pets are allowed. You can request a rate with breakfast included, if you like. This Marriott is proud to be rated among the top five in the chain for service.

GLEN EYRIE CASTLE $$$
3820 N. 30th St.
(719) 634-0808 or (800) 944-4536
www.gleneyrie.org
Colorado Springs's city founder, Gen. William J. Palmer, built his stone castle in a small valley just north of Garden of the Gods. He named it Glen Eyrie for the eagles that nested there. Over the years, it has changed ownership several times but is now owned by The Navigators, an international Christian

organization. For some years, it was used as a Christian retreat and was not open to the public. Over the past 30 years, the group has reopened the castle and its grounds to the public with high tea and tours and overnight stays. If you want to stay in a real castle, this is it! The castle and adjacent buildings have 97 guest rooms with double, queen, and king beds. Prices are commensurate with the lodgings, and there's a fee of $14 to $16 for an extra person in the room. Most rooms have phones, hair dryers, coffee machines, and bath amenities. There is a large bookstore on the property and breakfast is available daily, but other meals may not be (check when you make your reservation). Set on 800 acres of glen and canyon property, there are 17 hiking trails for guests to explore, including one up to a waterfall. There is a tennis court, a basketball court, sand volleyball court and large lawns for Frisbee or touch football games. Daily tours are scheduled of the castle. The entire property is nonsmoking and pets are not allowed in any of the buildings. Children 16 and younger are not permitted in the historic castle rooms, but they are allowed in the lodges. There are no televisions in the rooms because the property is designed as a retreat, for rest and renewal. Don't forget to book a high tea for yourself during your stay. It's a treat.

HYATT SUMMERFIELD SUITES
COLORADO SPRINGS $$$
5805 Delmonico Dr.
(719) 268-9990
http://coloradosprings.summerfield
suites.hyatt.com/hyatt/hotels/
summerfield

This smoke-free property, with 125 rooms, is conveniently located just off I-25, which makes it minutes from just about anything you might want to visit, from the Air Force Academy to Pikes Peak. Their spacious, apartment-style suites include just about any size beds or accommodations arrangements you can imagine: 44 studio king suites with a queen pull-out couch, 63 one-bedroom king suites (the bedroom is separate from the living room and the living area in this room has a queen pull-out couch), 12 studio double rooms (with 2 double beds and a queen pull-out sofa), 4 wheelchair accessible suites with full beds, and 2 two-bedroom suites with king beds in each bedroom. All rooms come with fully equipped kitchens. The hotel even throws in complimentary grocery shopping service and a 24-hour gourmet convenience market! A full complimentary hot breakfast buffet is available every day and a complimentary evening social is held from 5:30 to 7 p.m. Monday through Thursday (includes light appetizers, salads, breads, beer, wine, and soft drinks). The business center has everything a traveler could want, from free high-speed Internet access to a printing center. They have a fully equipped 24-hour fitness center and laundry facilities that never close. In other words, if you stay here, you don't even have to leave the property to get everything you need, except entertainment. Oh, and pets are allowed, but there's a $20 per night charge.

INN AT PALMER DIVIDE $$$
443 S. Highway 105, Palmer Lake
(719) 481-1800 or (877) 684-3466
www.innatpalmerdivide.com

This small, intimate hotel, situated on wooded acreage between Monument and Palmer Lake, offers a retreat from the city. With just 24 rooms (2 queens or 1 king bed), there's never a mob scene when trying to check in or out. It opened in 2006, and rooms come with such amenities as flat-screen TVs with a satellite feed, a work desk, iron and ironing board, and coffeemaker. They don't allow smoking or pets, and there's a small extra charge for an additional adult or child in a room. But they do offer a fine dining restaurant, MoZaic, with a good local reputation. Weekdays, they include continental breakfast; Saturday, there's a hot breakfast; and Sunday, you get a half-price coupon for their Sunday brunch.

THE LODGE AT GARDEN OF THE GODS CLUB　$$$$
3320 Mesa Rd.
(719) 632-5541 or (800) 923-8838
www.gardenofthegodsclub.com

For many decades, only members could stay at the club, but in recent years The Lodge has opened to the public. The views of the Garden of the Gods and Pikes Peak just to the west will take your breath away. This prestigious property is perched on a ridge overlooking the scene. With this kind of view, who can play attention to golf? But do! It's a 27-hole championship course. They have 87 rooms with either 2 doubles or king beds and every amenity you can imagine. Most rooms (all nonsmoking and pet-free) have a fireplace, in front of which you can snuggle on chilly Colorado evenings, and patios where you can indulge in an outdoor breakfast while reading the daily paper. The rooms are spacious, but if you want even more privacy, book a golf cottage of your own. Business travelers will love the dual-line phones, dataports, and high-speed Internet. Take a swim in one of their 2 outdoor pools (and a splash park for children), spend a little time playing games in the rec center (kids especially love it), or

connect with one of the walking trails that lead to the Garden of the Gods. Also be sure to enjoy their upscale cuisine in 2 fine restaurants—one formal, one casual—the elegant spa, and well-kept tennis courts (both indoor and out). It's an indulgence, but a memorable place to stay.

South

＊THE BROADMOOR　$$$$$
1 Lake Ave.
(719) 577-5775 or (866) 837-9520
www.broadmoor.com

If you're looking for a luxury vacation, it just doesn't get any better than The Broadmoor, a 744-room world-class resort hotel complex, and Colorado's only five-diamond, five-star property. With a backdrop of Cheyenne Mountain and a lake of its own, the ornate 1918 main hotel looks like a postcard of an imaginary wonderland. But it's very real—and very expensive. But you get the best service, the best food, endless amusements, and diversions, from a world-class spa to 54 holes on some of the best golf courses in the West. Guest rooms and suites (with kings or 2 doubles) are located in Broadmoor Main, the Broadmoor West, or the South Tower. The Broadmoor Cottages are separate from the main hotel, situated along the 18th fairway of the east golf course. There are 6 cottage buildings with anywhere from 2 to 8 bedrooms, with the choice of either a king bed or 2 queen beds.

Some rooms are pet-friendly, too. Well, more than friendly. For your pet's comfort, the staff will place special bedding and food bowls in the room for use during your stay. A complimentary pet treat also will be provided. You also can join the Pitty Pat Pet Club for additional perks. Note that there is a pet fee of $35 per day and a maximum of two pets per room. A dozen restaurants cater to your every culinary whim—from a confection and coffee shop to the state's only five-diamond restaurant, the Penrose Room. Plush beds, sumptuous linens, elaborately appointed bathrooms with high-end amenities, thick carpets, and robes make every guest feel like royalty. Don't be surprised to be addressed by name—it's a mystery how they do that, but it makes a guest feel pretty special! (See also the Restaurants chapter.)

CHEYENNE MOUNTAIN RESORT $$$
3225 Broadmoor Valley Rd.
(719) 538-4000 or (800) 428-8886
www.cheyennemountain.com
Overlooking Broadmoor Valley, with unobstructed views of an 18-hole golf course and Cheyenne Mountain beyond, the Cheyenne Mountain Resort will remind visitors of mountain properties they've visited in Vail and Aspen. Having undergone a $20 million renovation, the resort's 316 rooms and suites, as well as its public areas, got a fresh, new look early in 2011. For even more privacy, consider renting one of its 8 residential lodges. There are 3 dining rooms that vary from casual to upscale Colorado fusion cuisine. It is particularly famous—and popular locally—for its elaborate Sunday brunch. And local golfers say it's more affordable than The Broadmoor but just as much fun to play. It's also a popular conference hotel, with plenty of meeting space for groups of all sizes. Check out their various room and activity packages online. Pets are allowed—a maximum of two dogs per room, each weighing less than 50 pounds, and there's a $35 per pet nightly fee.

DOUBLETREE HOTEL COLORADO SPRINGS WORLD ARENA $$$
1775 E. Cheyenne Mountain Blvd.
(719) 576-8900
www.coloradospringsworldarena
.doubletree.com
How often do you check into a hotel and get a fresh chocolate chip cookie before you even pocket your room key? Well, you do here! The Doubletree Hotel at the Colorado Springs World Arena is a beautifully remodeled hotel in a majestic mountain setting. With 299 oversized (all nonsmoking) guest rooms, many with balconies and spectacular mountain views, it's also conveniently located near a multiplex theater, shopping, and restaurants—not to mention the World Arena, host to many major concerts and sporting events in the city. Choose from among single queen-, double queen- or king-bed rooms. All come with a coffee maker, hair dryer, iron and board, daily paper, and Hilton's "Sweet Dreams" bedding package. Some rooms have refrigerators and microwaves. Room service is available. Or check out their 2 full-service restaurants (Atrium and Maxi's Bar and Grille) and a coffee bar that offers Starbucks brews. Maxi's Bar and Grille is a family-friendly sports lounge with a 12-foot projection television and 5 other flat-screen TVs so you can follow your favorite sporting events. Two pool tables and an air hockey table are also available. DJ and live music are scheduled each month with two separate dance floors. The Atrium is located in the main lobby and hosts a full hot breakfast buffet. Work off all those calories in the hotel's large fitness center, or walk in the courtyard and admire the fountain. The hotel has complimentary shuttle service to the Colorado Springs airport and easy access to many of the region's top attractions.

ACCOMMODATIONS

West

*CLIFF HOUSE AT PIKES PEAK $$$
306 Canon Ave., Manitou Springs
(719) 685-3000 or (888) 212-7000
www.thecliffhouse.com

This lovely landmark in Manitou Springs was the *haute*-est thing going when it was built in 1873. Over the years, it deteriorated and when a fire nearly gutted the place in 1982, it was boarded up. An investor stepped in and saved the historic property, bringing it back to its original glory in the late '90s. Packed with charm and antiques, no two rooms (of the 54) are alike. (The turret rooms are fun.) It's all part of the pleasure of staying in a place where the history is richer than the people who once stayed there—Henry Ford, various presidents, movie stars, and J. Paul Getty, among others. Guests love the heated toilet seats, the 400-count bed linens, and complimentary bountiful breakfast buffet. A four-diamond restaurant, a well-stocked wine cellar, a fun bar (The Red Mountain Bar and Grill), and a fitness room round out the hotel's amenities. The hotel is nonsmoking in its entirety and pets are not allowed. The lushly landscaped grounds (oh, the flowers in summer!) add to its ambience. In the evenings, grab a rocker and sit out on the front porch to enjoy the fresh mountain air.

EL COLORADO LODGE $$$
23 Manitou Ave., Manitou Springs
(719) 685-5485 or (800) 782-2246
www.elcolorado.net

One of the oldest businesses in Manitou Springs (since 1926), El Colorado Lodge is a trip back in time . . . or maybe to old-style Santa Fe. The 17 adobe cottages with 26 units total feature wood-burning kiva fireplaces and lodgepole pine ceiling beams that just scream "Southwest." And the decor was here long before it was popular! Each cabin is a little different and bed options include doubles, queens, and kings. They offer nonsmoking rooms only, but pets are welcome. Only one cabin is wheelchair accessible. Outside, the grounds are scattered with picnic tables, barbecue grills, and a children's playground. Not to mention horseshoes, shuffleboard, basketball hoop, and a volleyball court. And they have the largest outdoor heated swimming pool of any lodging in Manitou. Families love this place and it's a popular site for family reunions. They don't serve breakfast, but Uncle Sam's Pancake House is right across the street.

BED-AND-BREAKFAST INNS

Downtown

ST. MARY'S INN $$$
530 N. Nevada Ave.
(719) 540-2222
www.thestmarysinn.com

The St. Mary's Inn, Bed and Breakfast, opened in 2006, and quickly became one of the most award-winning B&Bs in the area. It was a winner of one of the industry's most prestigious awards, Best of the Rockies, for 4 years in a row. With 10 spacious and beautifully decorated rooms and a 2-bedroom extended-stay apartment (with a full kitchen), it is small enough to feel homey, large enough so there are a variety of other guests with which to mingle, if you like. Rooms come with queen or king beds, and daybeds for extra guests (a $25 charge), plus every amenity: ceiling fans, individual heating and air conditioning, a daily newspaper, all private baths (some with Jacuzzi tubs), complimentary robes, and more. Check out the upscale Aveda amenities and the 600-thread-count sheets! For business travelers, there's high-speed

Internet access and desks. This all comes with a full hot gourmet breakfast, of course. There's plenty of free on-site, off-street parking. There's no smoking on the premises and they are not wheelchair accessible. Children younger than 16 are not permitted, and neither are pets.

West

1892 VICTORIA'S KEEP $$$
202 Ruxton Ave., Manitou Springs
(719) 685-5354 or (800) 905-5337
www.victoriaskeep.com

One more elegant choice among Manitou's bed-and-breakfast selections is Victoria's Keep, a restored 1892 Queen Anne Victorian home that just oozes charm. Surrounded by trees, it feels secluded. There are spacious, beautifully furnished rooms. All in all, that spells romantic. The award-winning establishment has been voted the "best place to celebrate honeymoons and anniversaries" in *Arrington's Inn Traveler's Magazine* (2004, 2005, and 2006, before they ceased publication). It also was voted by BedandBreakfast .com as being among the "Best Undiscovered Inns for Romance." Recently renovated, all 6 rooms (and 2 cottages) have a private bath and either queen or king feather beds. Most have fireplaces and Jacuzzi tubs for two. They'll also supply comfy robes, coffee makers, hair dryers, iron and board, wireless Internet services, assorted beverages, and a bottomless cookie jar. And for breakfast? Prepare yourself for an extra-fancy eggs Benedict or Grand Marnier stuffed French toast. They don't allow smoking, or pets, or children. Ask about their en suite massage packages. And note they are a "green" operation. If you're looking for an adult retreat, this is the place.

HOLDEN HOUSE 1902 BED &
BREAKFAST INN $$$
1102 W. Pikes Peak Ave.
(719) 471-3980 or (888) 565-3980
www.holdenhouse.com

This lovely 5-room historic property in Old Colorado City opened in 1986 by Sallie and Welling Clark set the standard for others to follow. Each suite has a queen bed, sitting area, fireplace, oversized tub for two, and plump robes for apres-bath. Despite the charming Victorian decor, it also has all the electronic amenities, too (TV, DVD, and CD players). In case you haven't guessed, they specialize in romantic getaways. Guests can get a fresh cup of coffee 24 hours a day and there's a bottomless cookie jar. Afternoon wine with snacks will whet your appetite for dinner and one of the area's fine restaurants. Turn-down service includes a poem and a handmade chocolate peanut truffle. You'll be eager to rise and shine when a full gourmet breakfast awaits you downstairs. Think ruffled crepes, German puffed pancakes with spiced apples, or maybe a sticky-bun casserole? Guests may sit on the front porch swing or rocking chair with a view of the gardens. The suites are scattered among three homes. One suite is wheelchair accessible. There are two resident cats who won't mind if you pet them, and you can arrange to bring a pet if you like—but not children. It's supposed to be romantic, remember?

OLD TOWN GUESTHOUSE $$$
115 S. 26th St.
(719) 632-9194 or (888) 375-4210
www.oldtown-guesthouse.com

The Old Town GuestHouse was newly built in 1997 as a bed-and-breakfast with 8 luxury rooms (1 king, the rest queen beds). The three-story brick building is in perfect harmony with the 1859 period construction of the historic Old Colorado City, which surrounds it. The inn is located on the site of the 1892 city hall, fire station, and jail, which was flanked by saloons, gambling parlors, and brothels. Today, its neighbors are candy shops and great little restaurants—a little more tame. Though it looks old, the amenities all scream 21st century: Rooms come with a hot tub or steam shower, coffeemaker, iron, refrigerator, hairdryer, TV, DVD, VCR, CD/MP3 players, and phone with messaging. Guests also get Internet access (Wi-Fi and wired). On the cozy size, they also have fireplaces and private balconies. Need some diversion? Check out the pool tables, pinball machine, darts, or the exercise equipment. Unlike some B&Bs, this one is wheelchair accessible. They don't take pets, but children are allowed under certain conditions (ask) . . . and smoking is permitted only on the balconies. Don't leave without breakfast! It's a full three-course meal with a hot entree, warm muffins or bread, fresh fruit, and cereal. Tea and juice are available, and the coffee pot is on all the time. If all this isn't enough to convince you, the GuestHouse has had a AAA four-diamond rating for 12 years running and it's often voted the best B&B in local surveys. It's also a member of the Select Registry.

ONALEDGE $$$
336 El Paso Blvd., Manitou Springs
(719) 685-4515 or (888) 685-4515
www.onaledge.net
Historic Onaledge in Manitou Springs is listed in the National Register of Historic Places and offers lodging with the warmth and charm that Manitou Springs has become known for. The Arts & Crafts style inns Red Crags, Onaledge, and Rockledge line El

Paso Boulevard above the town of Manitou Springs, and collectively make up Red Crags Estates. The inn's gourmet breakfast is served at Rockledge Country Inn for all guests of Red Crags Estates. Onaledge's 6 guest rooms all have king-size beds, fireplaces, and private baths. Architect, builder, and coppersmith Roland Boutwell, an Englishman, built the Onaledge estate in 1912 in the style of the Arts & Crafts movement, which emphasized simplicity and craftsmanship with high design standards in all architectural details. The inn is not wheelchair accessible, and pets are not allowed. Children are welcome.

i Most bed-and-breakfasts pride themselves on meeting your personal needs. If you have special dietary concerns, let your hosts know well in advance so they can plan an appropriately delicious meal for you.

RED CRAGS BED & BREAKFAST INN $$$
302 El Paso Blvd., Manitou Springs
(719) 685-4515 or (888) 685-4515
www.redcrags.com
Red Crags Bed and Breakfast Country Inn of Manitou Springs is a magnificent four-story Victorian mansion that has been a landmark in the Pikes Peak region for more than 130 years. It became a bed-and-breakfast in 1989. The 7,000-square-foot main house of this 8-room country inn dominates the 2-acre estate, prominently situated as it is on a bluff overlooking Manitou Valley. Views from the inn include Pikes Peak, Garden of the Gods, and the City of Colorado Springs. High ceilings, hardwood floors, and beautiful antiques decorate the common areas of the main floor. A lovely parlor with a large bar, antique piano, and fireplace is a great place for conversation and the solarium is

wonderful for relaxing on a sunny day. Or sit on one of the covered decks or stroll around the grounds, which include a stream, and visit the herb garden. The formal dining room features a rare cherrywood Eastlake fireplace—the perfect backdrop for a gourmet breakfast, served at Rockledge Country Inn next door. They can accommodate special dietary needs with advance notice. Guest rooms all have king-size beds, fireplaces, and private baths. Pets are not allowed; neither is smoking. Children 10 and older are welcome.

ROCKLEDGE COUNTRY INN $$$
328 El Paso Blvd., Manitou Springs
(888) 685-4515 or (719) 685-4515
www.rockledgeinn.com
Rockledge Country Inn in the National Historic District of Manitou Springs provides a private, peaceful destination for the discriminating traveler. It's also just minutes from downtown Colorado Springs and many attractions, including the nearby Garden of the Gods, ancient mineral springs, the Pikes Peak Cog Railway, and a number of interesting shops and excellent restaurants. With just 6 rooms, there's lots of privacy. Upon entry, guests will immediately notice the two-story copper-hooded stone fireplace, the cherry furnishings in the dining room, and, in the living room, an 1875 Steinway grand piano and an Italian marble fireplace. Here, guests can relax and enjoy the audio, video, and print libraries and parlor games. The solarium and patio are perfect for enjoying the outdoors. Explore the stone terraces and walk the gardens of the 4-acre historic Arts & Crafts estate. In summer, play croquet on the lawn, soak in the outdoor heated spa, or just relax with a world-class view of Pikes Peak. If it's booked, try one of its sister properties,

Red Crags or Onaledge (both in this chapter). Children are not allowed here; nor are pets. The entire property is nonsmoking.

TWO SISTERS INN $$$
10 Otoe Place, Manitou Springs
(719) 685-9684 or (800) 2-SIS-INN
(274-7466)
www.twosisinn.com
The list of awards is long: Colorado's Best Bed and Breakfast–2010, *Frommer's;* Colorado's Best and Breakfasts–2010, *The Huffington Post;* Colorado's Best in the State–Golden Muffin Award 2009-2010 and the 2008 Longevity Award, Bed & Breakfast Innkeepers of Colorado; Best Kept Secret in North America, *Arrington's B&B Journal;* and Colorado's Best B&B Innkeepers, Colorado Hotel & Lodging Association. Oh, we could go on! The point is, you'll like this place—as long as you don't mind double beds. They don't allow pets, smoking, or children younger than 10. But they will accommodate special dietary needs. They're known for their award-winning mandarin orange streusel muffins and other delectable breakfast treats. The inn is located in the center of a historic district, within a block of many old, renovated mineral springs, exceptional restaurants, and distinctive shops and galleries that mark Manitou Springs.

GUEST RANCHES

Guest ranches are an option with their own special character. The original "all-inclusive" vacation, they usually include lodging, meals, and entertainment in the package. Horseback riding is inevitably involved, but there are also other pursuits at many ranches, including fly fishing in summer and cross-country skiing in winter. They're a good choice for families, where kids can roam and interact with the ranch animals and mom and dad can relax and know they're in a safe, contained environment. Meals are homey, as a rule, and if a kid doesn't like beef stew for dinner, the cook is usually happy to whip up a grilled cheese sandwich. In other words, it's a laid-back vacation far from the maddening crowds of high-end resorts and city life.

EMERALD VALLEY GUEST RANCH $$$
7855 Old Stage Rd.
(719) 635-2468
www.emeraldvalleyranch.com

For a couples retreat, family reunion, or group getaway, it doesn't get any better than this secluded guest ranch southwest of Colorado Springs. There are 9 cabins with queen beds and bunk beds (kids will love them!) scattered over the lush acreage of this place, which opened in 1982. Cabins sleep from two to eight people in various configurations. There's no restaurant on the property, but many are a short drive away. And, besides, each cabin has a full kitchen, so you can bring your own grub and fix it there. Because the cabins are older, they are not wheelchair accessible, but the owner does have a ramp that can be moved from one cabin to another if it is needed. There's no swimming pool, but there are ponds for fishing, not to mention plenty of trails for hiking. Horseback riding is available nearby, for a fee. Cabins are decorated in Western chic—not too rustic, but not too elegant. It's a comfy kind of place.

GREY WOLF RANCH $$$$
2631 County Rd. 86, Victor
(719) 302-5906
www.greywolfranchcolorado.com

Located about an hour or so southwest of Colorado Springs, near the historic gold mining town of Victor, Grey Wolf Ranch lies in the heart of Pikes Peak country. You'll get stunning views of Pikes Peak, the Sangre de Cristo Mountain range, aspen groves, spectacular rock outcroppings, and acres and acres of rolling, wooded terrain, pasture, and prairie. It's all about horses here. Their equine programs deliver a unique horse experience, from basic horseback riding lessons to an equine management workshop. After you master your horseback riding skills, take a trail ride adventure with an hour, a half-day, or all-day ride. The ranch, which opened to guests in 2007, offers all-inclusive family vacations, romantic retreats, and corporate meeting spaces. They describe the decor of their lodging as "rustic elegance" in the private cabins, each complete with a queen bed, loft, kitchen, dining area, wood-burning stove, and full bathroom with a "grotto" shower. Larger groups can stay in the Horse Barn Lodge, a 1,900-square-foot cabin with 2 bedrooms on the lower level and a private suite on the upper level. The elegant upper level suite offers a full kitchen, living room, master bedroom, master bathroom with a Jacuzzi tub. Two private decks offer great views. There's no pool, and it's entirely nonsmoking, but they are wheelchair accessible and welcome kids and pets. There's also no restaurant on property, so stock up on groceries before you arrive. They do serve a continental breakfast of pastries and fruit each morning. If you get tired of riding horses, head into nearby Cripple Creek for a little gambling, a few attractions, and some affordable restaurants.

RUSTY SPUR BUNK & BARN $$$
583 South Forty Rd., Woodland Park
(719) 687-4260
www.rustyspurbunkandbarn.com

In this case, B&B stands for bunk and barn! Yes, this ranch outside Woodland Park accommodates not only humans, but horses (and dogs, too). So saddle up and head up Ute Pass for a different kind of stay. They have 4 rooms (sleeping 10 total), with names like the Buffalo Bill Room (which has a king bed), the Annie Oakley (with a queen bed and a double), and 2 more with queen beds. Rooms share 2 baths. Additional adults in a room are $20 per night; horses range from $10 to $25 a night; and dogs are charged $10 a night and allowed in rooms with their owners. Open since 2007, the inn is open year-round (many guest ranches aren't). There's a communal hot tub on the 1,000-square-foot patio, a gas grill, and firepit for guests' use. The TV room features a 36-inch wall-mounted screen. For horses, there are four 10-by-28-foot corrals with loafing sheds and a communal pasture. Hiking, biking, and horseback riding trails surround the property. The indoor areas are all nonsmoking, and because the rooms are on the second floor, the inn is not wheelchair accessible. Kids are always welcome. The owner grows her own garden and uses her fresh herbs and vegetables in her creative egg dishes each morning.

RV PARKS & CAMPGROUNDS

Did you BYOB? Bring your own bed? Many RV-ers find the Pikes Peak region irresistible and some folks just prefer to camp. There are numerous campgrounds in the mountains, but finding one in town is a little tougher. Still, there are some nice spots to park your RV or tent for a night or two. If you camp, note that nights here are quite a bit chillier than daytime temperatures, so bring a sleeping bag even in the summer. Keep fires in fire pits or other designated areas—it can be dry here at any time of year and the current fire danger is usually listed on a sign somewhere. Do not drink out of streams or other "natural" water sources—you can get an intestinal parasite (giardia) that will plague you for months.

CHEYENNE MOUNTAIN STATE PARK $
410 JL Ranch Heights
(719) 576-2016 or (800) 678-2267
www.parks.state.co.us

Just south of Colorado Springs off CO 115 lies one of the crown jewels of the Colorado State Park system—Cheyenne Mountain State Park. This 1,680-acre park, one of the newest in the state (since 2006), lies beneath the eastern face of Cheyenne Mountain and borders the plains of Colorado for a startling transition from plains to peaks. Cheyenne Mountain offers superior facilities and recreational opportunities, including a 20-mile trail system good for both hiking and mountain biking. Along with great trails, the park offers top-notch facilities for overnight guests, including 61 spectacular campsites, most with a paved parking area, grill ring/fire pit, 10-foot-by-10-foot tent pad, picnic table, and panoramic views of Colorado Springs and Cheyenne Mountain. Most campsites (51 total) are full-service, with water, electrical, and sewer hookups for RV campers. Tent campers may use these RV sites, but there are also 10 unique walk-in sites among the scrub oak, reserved for tents only. A nearby camper-services building is where you get permits and park information, and find flush toilets, coin-operated showers, and a coin-operated laundry room. There's also an activity room and a camp store that sells everything from books and souvenirs to snacks and camping necessities. Playgrounds, additional restrooms, a beautiful amphitheater, and easy trail access are also available from the campgrounds. Reservations are strongly recommended (use the 800-number above). Group camping also is available through the local office. (See also Camping in the Sports & Recreation chapter.)

COLORADO SPRINGS KOA $
8100 Bandley Dr., Fountain
(719) 382-7575
www.coloradospringskoa.com
This KOA member site offers a number of different accommodations: RV sites, pull-throughs and back-ups, with different combinations of services available from water and electric to full service. Creek-front deluxe sites come with a patio table and chairs and barbecue grill. Tent sites also are available with tent pads and covers—or rent a cabin, available in 1 or 2 rooms. Cabins are not pet-friendly and you supply your own linens. Amenities are pretty much what you would expect from a KOA campground, such as a clean shower and laundry, and you'll also find a full-line convenience store, kennels, and corrals. Services include free Wi-Fi and assistance in planning your activities once you arrive.

i | When camping or RV-ing, it's pleasant to stay by a stream. But if there's heavy rainfall, check on flash flood warnings, which can affect even small creeks and streams and do a lot of damage. You may want to move away from the water.

GARDEN OF THE GODS
CAMPGROUND $
3704 W. Colorado Ave.
(719) 475-9450 or (800) 248-9451
www.coloradocampground.com
Situated near the gorgeous Garden of the Gods city park, the Garden of the Gods Campground may just be the best place to go camping in the Colorado Springs/ Manitou Springs area. With more than four decades of service, they offer it all. There are large pull-through sites, huge back-in sites, new mountain suites, and the treetop suites along with bunkhouse rooms and camper cabins. Centrally located, there's easy access from I-25 and US 24. Amenities include 2 pools, an indoor whirlpool, TV lounge, pavilion, game room, free Wi-Fi hot spot access and free Internet service, clean restrooms and showers, laundry facilities, barbecues, picnic tables, and even a playground. Add to all this spectacular views of Pikes Peak and a gorgeous, wooded setting and your camping vacation will become a memorable one.

GOLDEN EAGLE RANCH RV PARK &
CAMPGROUNDS $
710 Rock Creek Canyon Rd.
(719) 576-0450
www.maymuseum-camp-rvpark.com
Located south of Colorado Springs next to the May Natural History Museum (see the Attractions chapter), this huge, family-operated RV park has 300 sites, including long pull-through sites for big rigs. They have sites with no hookups, partial hookups, and full hookups—all affordable. This campground and park opened in the 1960s and still is a favorite of large groups. Pets must be leashed, and there's no restaurant or pool or other fancy accoutrements, just a scenic spot to park your RV or tent. There is,

however, Wi-Fi access, plus laundry facilities and picnic tables and, best of all, campfire rings. Campers get a $1 off admission to the May Museum on-site.

PIKES PEAK RV PARK
& CAMPGROUND $
320 Manitou Ave., Manitou Springs
(719) 685-9459
http://pprvpk.com/default.aspx
For the price of a nice hotel room for one night, you can stay for a whole week at this quiet creek-side campsite in Manitou Springs. You can walk along Fountain Creek to downtown Manitou and to some local attractions. There are 55 back-in sites with water-sewer-electric hookups. You can fish in the creek. There's free Wi-Fi, access to laundry facilities, and, they say, "extra-clean bathrooms." There's a limit of six people and two pets per site. Tents are not allowed on the RV sites.

RESTAURANTS

The dining scene in Colorado Springs and the Pikes Peak region is surprisingly eclectic and quite sophisticated at times. You might think of it as a steak-and-potatoes kind of town, but the city has always been culturally aware and a diverse influx of ethnic groups has provided it with equally diverse cuisines.

There are more than 1,200 restaurants in the region, serving roughly half a million people. That means when you go out, any night of the week, you can expect other diners to have the same idea. Some restaurants, especially along heavily traveled corridors, are busier than others. Better restaurants take reservations and it's always a good idea to make them!

Local restaurants will make steak-eaters happy, to be sure. Beef is a big industry in the West and many locals want nothing more than a good hunk of beef when they go out to dine. There's even a signature brand of Callicrate beef, grown nearby in Kansas and sold directly to customers here at a store called Ranch Foods Direct. Several local restaurants serve the extra-luscious, organic, humanely raised beef. (You'll know, because they'll brag about it on the menu. Also see the Shopping chapter.) Burgers are so ubiquitous, we almost didn't include that category. You can find one almost anywhere, but we did give a nod to a few places favored by the locals. Forget the chains—none of them hold a candle to a locally made Colorado beef or bison burger.

But there are also a lot of other local flavors on area menus: bison, trout, Colorado lamb, and other tasty entrees native to the area. Several local restaurants even specialize in exotic meats (or "wild" game).

The strong military influence—soldiers returning from overseas with immigrant brides—has laid the foundation for great German, Japanese, Korean, Vietnamese, Thai, and other ethnic restaurants. And, of course, being in the Southwest, you'll find an inordinate number of Mexican and New Mexican restaurants. But be aware that Mexican regional cuisines represented here can be as far apart as regional American cuisines and vary considerably from one eatery to another. You'll find a number of little *tacqueria* stands around town, some mediocre, some pretty good. A bunch of crepe places have sprung up in the past couple of years—we'll see if they remain or are just (pardon the pun) a flash in the pan.

OVERVIEW

We have the usual suspects among fast-food chains—McDonald's, Burger King, Taco Bell, and such—and the mid-priced chains—Chili's, Carrabba's, and Outback Steakhouse. But you won't find them listed here. If you want to eat the same food you eat at home, why travel? There are so many independent, locally owned restaurants that wander off the predictable culinary path, we focused on them.

We've tried to limit the list of restaurants in this book to those that have a good track record and are known locally for consistently good food. Because there are so many restaurants, and because they come and go with the rise and fall of the economy, this is just a sampling of some pretty dependable local favorites.

This chapter is organized by type of cuisine. But under each one, you'll get an array of price options and of locations in the region (e.g., Downtown, Asian). Most restaurants are minutes away in Colorado Springs or Manitou Springs. Most have decent parking (sometimes acres of it!), but if there's a problem, we'll tell you. On the pricier restaurants, we'd recommend shucking the hiking shorts for a pair of khakis or a skirt. Because it's a tourist town, some restaurants have seasonal hours. Check their websites or call ahead if you want to make sure they're open when you visit.

Unless otherwise noted, addresses refer to Colorado Springs. Colorado law prohibits smoking in restaurants, so that need not be a concern. It also requires restaurants to be wheelchair accessible (including restrooms). There are a few exceptions, and we've noted those.

Some restaurants have patios that are only open seasonally. "Seasonally" means when the weather is nice, which might mean May through October, or much shorter, depending on the whims of Mother Nature.

Price Code

Prices vary wildly from tiny taco stands to the best dining room in the state. You can spend a couple of bucks or a couple hundred bucks.

Assume everyone takes major credit cards unless otherwise specified. The price range includes the average price of entrees only (no appetizers, drinks, or desserts) for two people. Prices generally refer to dinner unless the place is only open for lunch.

$.................less than $10
$$ ....$10 to $25
$$$ ....$25 to $50
$$$$...............$50 to $100
$$$$$..........more than $100

Craftwood Inn, Manitou
Springs, Fine Dining,
$$$$, 65

Dogtooth Coffee, Colorado
Springs, Coffee Shops, $, 59

Edelweiss Restaurant,
Colorado Springs, German,
$$, 66

El Taco Rey, Colorado
Springs, Mexican, $–$$, 69

The Famous Steakhouse,
Colorado Springs, Steak
Houses, $$$$, 71

Fargo's Pizza Company,
Colorado Springs, Pizza,
$–$$, 70

Fratelli Ristorante Italiano,
Colorado Springs, Italian,
$$–$$$, 68

Front Range Barbeque,
Colorado Springs,
Barbecue, $$, 57

Fusion World Cuisine,
Colorado Springs, Asian,
$$$, 55

Gertrude's Restaurant,
Colorado Springs, Fine
Dining, $$$, 64

The Golden Bee,
Colorado Springs (at The
Broadmoor), Pub Fare,
$$, 63

**Jake and Telly's Greek
Taverna,** Colorado Springs,
Greek & Mediterranean,
$$$, 67

La Baguette Bakery Cafe,
Colorado Springs, Breakfast
& Bakeries, $, 57

Little Nepal, Colorado
Springs, Indian, $$–$$$, 68

Luigi's, Colorado Springs,
Italian, $$, 68

MacKenzie's Chop House,
Colorado Springs,
American, $$$, 53

**The Margarita at Pine
Creek,** Colorado Springs,
American, $$$$, 53

Marigold Cafe & Bakery,
Colorado Springs,
American, $$$, 54

Mirch Masala, Colorado
Springs, Indian, $$$, 68

**Mollica's Italian Market &
Deli,** Colorado Springs,
Delis, $$, 60

**Mona Lisa Fondue
Restaurant,** Manitou
Springs, Fine Dining,
$$$$, 65

Nosh, Colorado Springs, Fine
Dining, $$$$, 61

Panino's, Colorado Springs,
Pizza, $–$$, 70

The Penrose Room,
Colorado Springs (at The
Broadmoor), Fine Dining,
$$$$$, 62

The Peppertree Restaurant,
Colorado Springs, Fine
Dining, $$$$, 61

Pikes Perk, Colorado Springs,
Coffee Shops, $, 59

Pizzeria Rustica, Colorado
Springs, Pizza, $$, 71

**Poor Richard's Restaurant
& Rico's Cafe & Wine
Bar,** Colorado Springs,
Vegetarian, $$, 72

Ritz Grill, Colorado Springs,
American, $$$, 53

Saigon Cafe, Colorado
Springs, Asian, $$, 54

Shangri-La, Colorado
Springs, Asian, $$$, 55

Shuga's, Colorado Springs,
Vegetarian, $$, 72

Silver Pond, Colorado
Springs, Asian, $$–$$$, 56

**Slayton's Tejon Street
Grill,** Colorado Springs,
Barbecue, $$, 56

Steaksmith, Colorado
Springs, Steak Houses,
$$$$, 71

Summit, Colorado Springs (at
The Broadmoor), American,
$$$, 62

Swiss Chalet Restaurant,
Woodland Park, Fine
Dining, $$$, 66

The Tavern, Colorado Springs
(at The Broadmoor), Steak
Houses, $$$, 63

Uwe's German Restaurant,
Colorado Springs, German,
$$$, 66

Walter's Bistro, Colorado
Springs, Fine Dining,
$$$$, 61

**Wimberger's Old World
Bakery & Delicatessen,**
Colorado Springs, Breakfast
& Bakeries, $, 58

Wines of Colorado, Colorado
Springs, Burgers, $$, 58

Wooglin's Deli & Cafe,
Colorado Springs, Delis,
$$, 60

AMERICAN

Downtown

MACKENZIE'S CHOP HOUSE $$$
128 S. Tejon St.
(719) 635-3536
www.mackenzieschophouse.com

Located in the lower level of a historic downtown Alamo building, MacKenzie's below-street-level dining seems to insulate it from downtown bustle and creates a cozy cavern-like atmosphere. Even its outdoor patio seems far removed from the city noise. Primarily a steak house that also serves seafood, chicken, and pasta, it has the best bison burger in town—we have to say. Its American cuisine draws business folk from all over downtown for lunch and dinner—lots of deals have undoubtedly been brokered here. They're pretty well known for their Kobe filet, their New York strip, and their surf-and-turf (create your own duo). They also have a rack of lamb. It's one of the few restaurants in town that makes a concerted effort to bring in fresh seafood—king crab legs, lobster, and shrimp. Pair any of these delights with something from their wine list, beer list, or full bar (they're known for their martinis). Also check out their fine liquors—single-malt scotches, aged bourbons, cognacs, and more. Public parking is available on the street at meters and in a nearby parking garage for $1 (located just 1 block east of the restaurant on Nevada Avenue). Business casual is the most likely attire for patrons here and reservations are recommended.

RITZ GRILL $$$
15 S. Tejon St.
(719) 635-8484
www.ritzgrill.com

This hip and trendy downtown American bistro draws the business crowd and anyone else who can find a parking place on popular Tejon Street. It's casual, but you'll also see guys in ties and women in business suits. They have many tasty menu items, but if they ever take the Voodoo Chicken, or Cajun Chicken & Shrimp, or Smoked Salmon Salad off the menu, they'll be in trouble with their regulars. We also love their unique pizzas, like the basil pizza or the Southwestern one that tastes like a giant gourmet taco. Monday night is $14 Steak Night (strip or filet). Want to enter chocolate heaven? Save room for their Chocolate Trio that includes a chocolate-and-espresso pot de crème and chocolate pudding cake with malted Chantilly cream. They are one of downtown's favorite hot spots for live music and a killer happy hour. Besides a full bar, they have a great wine list and 16 beers on draft. Parking on the street can be tough at lunchtime and right after work, but later in the evening and weekends, it loosens up. There's also a large parking garage less than a block away. Don't let that deter you. Ritz Grill opened in 1987 with a striking Art Deco decor, and has never lost its cool vibe.

North

THE MARGARITA AT PINE CREEK $$$$
7350 Pine Creek Rd.
(719) 598-8667
www.margaritaatpinecreek.com

It sounds like a Mexican restaurant, but it isn't—though sometimes there are Mexican-inspired items on the menu. This contemporary casual restaurant is housed in a lovely adobe building that sits on a wooded spot owned by restaurateur Pati Burleson's family for more than 100 years. Since it opened in 1974, it has offered the freshest seasonal menu around. The menu changes weekly and the meals are pretty much prix fixe. Lunch comes with a complimentary pot of pimento-cheese spread and a loaf of fresh-baked wheat bread. Its chef is known for his innovative dishes, but he only prepares maybe half a dozen for each meal. There's always a meat, poultry, fish, or seafood and vegetarian choice. Dinner is $40 for five courses, $34 for three courses, and there's a separate bar menu of nibbles and smaller portions for $8 to $17. They also serve Sunday brunch. They smoke their own salmon, and make sauces, stocks, and bread from scratch. The Southwestern-inspired interior matches the exterior—soft, rounded, rosy adobe walls and lots of nooks for semi-private dining. Two outdoor patios invite diners to enjoy Colorado's fine weather spring through fall, and there's often live music, from jazz to bluegrass and sometimes Celtic music. Some folks just come here after dinner for drinks and music. Dress is upscale casual but they never turn away anyone in a T-shirt and hiking shorts. A private parking lot may overflow onto the grass on busy nights. In the summer, there's a farmers' market on-site. And don't forget to pet the sweet "greeter-dog," Gus.

✳MARIGOLD CAFE & BAKERY   **$$$**
4605 Centennial Blvd.
(719) 599-4776
www.marigoldcafeandbakery.com
The word around town is, if you want a Broadmoor quality meal at half the price, head to Marigold. Serving contemporary American cuisine with a French influence, owners Dominique and Elaine Chavanon are always there, overseeing the kitchen and bakery, respectively. Voted the best power lunch site by local surveys, it's a great place for a sandwich on their excellent homemade

breads, a pizza (big enough for two . . . we like the Greek pie), or a bowl of French onion soup. Salads are crunchy-fresh and include lots of veggies. Dinner entrees come with a bright, crisp side of fresh vegetables, too! And whatever you order, if the creamy scalloped potatoes don't come with it, order them as a side. They may be the best you've ever eaten. Try the lamb (rack or chops) for a real culinary treat, or get anything with a sauce concocted by the chef. His sauces are killer. The beef bourguignon is a customer favorite, too, and sells out every time it's on the daily specials menu. And be sure to check out the excellent wine list. We're not kidding when we say you'll be sorry if you don't save room for dessert. Consider the double chocolate mousse cake, the fruit tart, or napoleon for a to-die-for ending to your meal. No room? Take something to go. Though the food is tops, the atmosphere and dress are casual. This place is so busy it's a good idea to get there early for any meal (and make a reservation at dinner). Closed Sun.

ASIAN

Downtown

SAIGON CAFE   **$$**
20 E. Colorado Ave.
(719) 633-2888
www.coloradosaigoncafe.com
It's not a big restaurant, but if you're downtown and craving a Vietnamese noodle bowl, you'd better get there early. Voted best local Vietnamese restaurant 8 years in a row, Saigon Cafe has been a fixture downtown since 1999 and stays busy with business folk at both lunch and dinner. Their tasty beef noodle soup and other popular noodle bowls fly to tables in an endless parade. We

also love the summer roll and Vietnamese egg rolls. You can get wine or beer, too, but no hard liquor. But who needs that when you have a steaming cup of fragrant tea? Street parking is tight, but there's a pay lot right next door. Closed Sun.

North

AI SUSHI & GRILL $$$
4655 Centennial Blvd.
(719) 266-5858
www.aisushi.us
A shout of welcome greets all guests to the inviting Asian atmosphere of Ai Sushi, located in a strip mall on Centennial Boulevard just north of Garden of the Gods Road. And you'll continue to feel welcome and special during your entire visit. Don't be fooled by the name; they have great sushi, but so much more. Besides a long list of sushi options, they also serve a crispy, light tempura (try the shrimp and vegetable combination), succulent teriyaki chicken, noodle bowls, rice bowls, and all the requisite dishes you expect at a Japanese restaurant. For fun, get a group together and dine at the teppan tables, where the chef prepares your meal to order in front of you. You get a show with dinner! Also try them for a quick and tasty lunch for less than $10 per person. Closed Sun.

FUSION WORLD CUISINE $$$
15910 Jackson Creek Pkwy., Suite 100,
Monument
(719) 488-3900
http://fusionworldcuisine.com
This relative newcomer to the dining scene in the Pikes Peak region has come on with the heat of a fire-breathing dragon. Located in relative obscurity within the Monument Marketplace strip mall, the Asian-inspired

dining is anything but common. Dishes offered run from the traditional won ton and miso soups to some very eclectic choices, such as the Tom Yum Goong soup, a complex seafood concoction reminiscent more of Bangkok than Tokyo or Peking. Entrees cover curry to udon to steak. Especially good is the Chicken Veggie Stir-Fry, made with lemongrass, Thai basil, and a generous amount of veggies, such as asparagus. Also popular is the Beef and Mushroom Stir-Fry, which uses rib eye steak and enoki mushrooms. The staff is open to turning the spice up or down, as requested. The interior design makes a worthy effort at elegant dining, but that isn't really why people walk in the door. The extensive sake and beer lists support whatever tastes are ordered, and a good wine list also is available. This is a good place for groups, families, or couples. Open for lunch and dinner 7 days a week.

*SHANGRI-LA $$$
8850 N. Union Blvd.
(719) 495-1738
Hear that crackle? It's a sizzling seafood combination platter being whisked to your table at Shangri-La. Hot pots and hot plates are a specialty of the house and will get your attention even before you taste the sumptuous dish. This is one of the things that Doug Pua and Ailene Ting brought with them to Shangri-La when they opened it in 2003. Pua, originally from the Philippines, and Ting, who is Taiwanese, met while working at—what else?—a Chinese restaurant. They shared a vision of an upscale Asian restaurant with linen tablecloths, elegant decor, and attentive service. That's what gained them their reputation and a loyal following. Besides their signature "sizzling" dishes, their most unusual dish probably is the walnut

prawns. They're also famous for their delectable crab Rangoon (stuffed wonton) appetizers, which use real crab. All ingredients here are fresh and of the best quality, and every sauce tastes as if it were designed just for that dish. Add to that a tasteful Chinese decor and outstanding service, and it's a place you'll visit again. And if you do, they'll probably remember you by name!

SILVER POND $$–$$$
5670 N. Academy Blvd.
(719) 594-9343
www.bestsilverpondchinese.com
Jack and Jennie Hu specialize in what they call "gourmet Chinese" at their Silver Pond restaurant, which has been a local favorite since it opened in 1996. What sets them apart from many Asian eateries is that the owner also is the chef. Jack does most of the cooking, from hand-shaping the dumplings to crafting special sauces for dishes he concocts. She's Chinese, but grew up in Vietnam, and he hails from Taiwan. Their combined ethnic backgrounds bring a lot of fascinating flavors to their dishes. Customers love the restaurant's elegant black-white-and-red decor, but they love more the avocado-shrimp appetizer, the tender salt-and-pepper calamari, and the scallion pancakes. Favorite dishes include strawberry chicken or scallops and shrimp in the house red garnet sauce or spicy duck in Peking sauce. Everything is made fresh and from scratch and each plate is presented like a work of art. They make egg rolls fresh every day. Nothing is fried twice. They serve brown rice as well as steamed and fried rice and offer a large vegetarian menu. Meats are top quality and well trimmed of fat and they use white meat chicken in most chicken dishes. You won't find lamb in most Asian restaurants, but you will here! Silver Pond doesn't use MSG. And, unlike most Asian restaurants, they have a nice selection of desserts. The restaurant regularly wins "best of" surveys by local media.

South

CHOPSTICKS ASIAN BISTRO $$–$$$
120 E. Cheyenne Mountain Blvd.
(719) 579-9111
www.chopsticksasianbistro.com
This trendy little spot near the Broadmoor, situated in Country Club Corners, serves both traditional Chinese and new Asian cuisine. It's a Zen-inspired retreat that will whisk you away to another culture, even if just for an hour at lunch. Visitors to The Broadmoor and Cheyenne Mountain Resort, looking for something different, feel like they've stumbled on a gem. Locals love it for date nights, for special nights out (say, a birthday or other celebration), and for its Asian fusion cuisine. We're not talking moo goo gai pan here. We're talking Basil Shrimp, Beef Mimosa, Grand Marnier Prawns, and chicken lettuce wraps. Meals can be accompanied by a full array of Asian, domestic, or microbrew beers, as well as what some claim is the best martini in town. Reservations are suggested at both lunch and dinner. After all, it was voted "best Chinese restaurant" the past 4 years in a row by the local newspaper.

BARBECUE
Downtown

SLAYTON'S TEJON STREET GRILL $$
28A S. Tejon St.
(719) 471-2311
www.slaytonsbbq.com
Exposed brick walls and real wood floors hint at the antiquity of this building—one

of the oldest in Colorado Springs. And they set the mood for some good, old-fashioned barbecue, too. Slayton's is a relative newcomer to the Tejon Street dining scene, opening in 2005, but they've quickly earned a reputation for good food and friendly service. They do Kansas City–style 'cue, featuring the usual stuff—baby back ribs, beef brisket, smoked sausage, and pulled pork—all slow-roasted over hickory and apple wood. But we've got to tell you, try the Burnt Ends. Yes, really. They're not burnt at all (so we wonder about the moniker), but the most tender, succulent pieces of meat you've ever laid a fork to . . . in fact, you could probably cut them with a spoon. And save room to share a vanilla rum bread pudding. Yum. On Thursday through Saturday nights, enjoy some cool jazz or hot blues music while you dine.

West

FRONT RANGE BARBEQUE $$
2330 W. Colorado Ave.
(719) 632-2596
www.frbbq.com

Serving Southern, home-style cooking and some of the finest barbecue in town, Front Range's West Side location is a popular spot for lunch or dinner. It's located in an old house in Old Colorado City, with an enclosed outdoor, heated patio that is popular much of the year. They often have live music—mostly bluegrass, country, and folk. Locals hate to tell the tourists about Front Range for fear they won't be able get their own table on busy summer nights. The single most popular item at Front Range is their tender, smoky pork ribs, and regulars rave about their unusual but tasty smoked artichoke appetizer. Homemade sides (beans,

slaw, and such) stand up well against the rich meats. Wash it all down with a microbrew beer on tap. And homemade desserts are worth checking out, especially the rich bread pudding. The Eastside location (4935 Templeton Gap Rd., 719-598-8895) has dine-in facilities, but is primarily a take-out and catering site visited by locals. The Westside only takes reservations for large groups, so get there early if you don't want to wait. The restaurant opened in 2000 and has won local "best of" recognition for barbecue for 10 years running.

BREAKFAST & BAKERIES
Downtown

*LA BAGUETTE BAKERY CAFE $
117 E. Pikes Peak Ave.
(719) 636-5020

The smell of fresh-baked French bread will lure you into La Baguette like a bee to a flower. Crusty rolls, fat loaves of rye, and the quintessential baguette make for good sandwiches or accompaniments to the world's best French onion soup (simmered three full days before serving). Tender, flaky croissants and other pastries make it a favorite local stop in the mornings, too. Many regulars dote on their cheese fondue. A few salads, including an authentic French house salad, daily soup specials (all good), and a few richly outstanding desserts with a European flair complete the simple menu. A sprig of grapes, a wedge of cheese . . . who could ask for more? A glass of wine? Sorry . . . no liquor license. But you can get a great cup of coffee. Closed Sun. A second location is at 2417 West Colorado Ave. (719-577-4818).

ℹ Colorado Springs has several new creperies, but the longtime standby is La Creperie (204 N. Tejon St.). Nab an outside table at this little French bistro in the summer; it sits directly across the street from the Uncle Wilber Fountain. Linger over lunch with a front-row seat to the antics of the kids and the animated musical fountain.

North

BOONZAAIJER'S DUTCH BAKERY $
4935 Centennial Blvd.
(719) 264-0177
www.dutchpastry.com

Don't bother trying to pronounce the name—even employees have a hard time with it, sometimes! Just call it the Dutch Bakery and everyone knows you're talking about the yummy European-style pastries—Danish pinwheels, coffee cakes, muffins, and croissants, all made daily. Want to get fancier? They also make fruit tarts, napoleons, cannolis, éclairs (their single most popular item), and special-occasion cakes. Check out the organic whole wheat or white bread, too.

South

WIMBERGER'S OLD WORLD
   BAKERY & DELICATESSEN $
2321 Bott Ave.
(719) 634-6313
www.wimbergers.com

Started in 1970 by an immigrant German baker, Wimberger's opened its retail store in 1990. You won't find better bread in Germany—from their chewy Kaiser rolls to their flavorful rye bread. Their soft pretzels are a favorite of locals, who go there for the breads but often end up buying deli meats and cheeses, too. They also stock a large variety of German foods, and here's where you can get your German chocolate fix. Several local restaurants and stores also sell their product.

Manitou Springs

ADAM'S MOUNTAIN CAFE $$
934 Manitou Ave.
(719) 685-1430
www.adamsmountain.com

When craving a hearty, homemade breakfast, this is the place locals think about. The whole-grain pancakes and the oatmeal will keep you hiking for hours. In keeping with the restaurant's eclectic approach to food, the huevos rancheros also are a favorite, made with black beans, eggs, and green chile. Also consider the luscious Orange-Almond French Toast, if you're feeling a bit decadent. And be sure to imbibe a cup of organic dark-roast coffee. In the winter months, they serve breakfast all day! (See also Vegetarian category.)

BURGERS

West

WINES OF COLORADO $$
8045 West US 24, Cascade
(719) 684-0900
www.winesofcolorado.com

What better way to while away an afternoon or summer's eve than to sit by a bubbling stream? It's what people imagine when they think of Colorado. Wines of Colorado opened in Cascade in the 1998 and annually snags honors for best alfresco dining in local polls. Sitting at 7,500 feet, at the foot of Pikes Peak and the confluence of Fountain Creek and Cascade Creek, this place is known as a spot where you can sample Colorado's award-winning vintages. It's also famous for its fat, juicy bison burgers and tasty wine burgers, though they have upscale fare, too—such as ahi tuna or smoked prime rib. Choose from the creek-side patio, which seats 50, and the deck, which seats 35. And the best part? You get a complimentary wine tasting!

i A local institution for hamburgers is the Red Top restaurant chain. Though these dinner-plate-sized burgers get a lot of attention from the national media (they're a favorite of food writers Jane and Michael Stern) because they're so big, you get a lot of bun and a thin patty studded with chunks of onion. Still, if you want to wow your friends with a photo of a burger the size of your head, stop by one of their stores.

COFFEE SHOPS

Downtown

DOGTOOTH COFFEE $
505 E. Columbia St.
(719) 632-0125
www.dogtoothcoffee.com
Tucked into an older north-end neighborhood, this cute little shop specializes in coffee blends designed to suit your palate. Like your coffee medium-roast or dark? Light or heavy on the caffeine? They'll come up with the perfect one for you. They have daily coffee specials to try, along with a wide selection of locally prepared pastries, bagels, and cakes. Or go hearty, with egg-and-sausage or egg-and-potato breakfast tacos with fresh, spicy salsa. Their homemade soups (like coconut curry) are becoming famous, and their paninis are perfectly grilled. And yes, dogs are welcome.

PIKES PERK $
14 S. Tejon St.
(719) 635-1600
www.pikesperkcoffee.com
From a distance, you see the sign and think it says Pikes Peak. Then you get closer and realize somebody had an attack of cleverness. It says Pikes Perk. It's frequently voted best local coffee roaster—and most locals like it better than the big coffee chains (you know who we mean). They offer fine air-roasted, fair-trade, and organic coffees from Mexico, Kenya, Sumatra, Guatemala, Peru, and Costa Rica. They also do decaf and flavored coffees, plus terrific Chai and teas. If you fly in or out of Colorado Springs, you also can get their brew at the Colorado Springs Airport; and if you attend concerts or sporting events at the Colorado Springs World Arena or the US Air Force Academy, you'll find them on-site there, too. They also have another location at 5965 N. Academy Blvd. (719-522-1432).

i If you need a caffeine fix, don't worry. Like most cities of any size, there's a Starbucks on every corner (and in bookstores, grocery stores, etc.). For a different brew, try one of the local coffee shops like Pikes Perk.

West

AGIA SOPHIA $
2902 W. Colorado Ave.
(719) 632-3322
www.agiasophiacoffeeshop.com
Modeling itself after the very first coffeehouses in the Western world, which were places where people met to discuss business, politics, culture, and religion, Agia Sophia aspires to inspire that same culture by offering the very best coffee and specialty teas. Try a latte, cappuccino, or espresso.

You also can get pastries, dessert, and a cafe-style lunch. And don't forget it's also a bookstore—satisfy your mind while satisfying your caffeine craving.

DELIS

Downtown

WOOGLIN'S DELI & CAFE $$
823 N. Tejon St.
(719) 578-9443
www.wooglinsdeli.com

What seems to be a holdover from the "health food" trend of the '60s actually opened in 1988 and still serves up some of the best sandwiches in town (and don't hold the sprouts!). Located by Colorado College, there's a heavy student-professor component to its clientele. Don't be surprised to see young people cramming for exams while loading up on the wholesome fuel. Some favorites among longtime patrons include the turkey-avocado and other overstuffed sandwiches on healthful breads, their Reubens and burgers, and their quiches. Sample the tasty house-made baked goods (you must try the carrot cake) with a mug of locally roasted coffee. The restaurant often ranks No. 1 in local surveys for best sandwiches, best deli, and best quesadillas. They serve wine and beer and occasionally offer live music on a weekend evening. There's lots of on-street, metered parking right in front. Closed Sun and major holidays.

North

MOLLICA'S ITALIAN MARKET & DELI $$
985-A Garden of the Gods Rd.
(719) 598-1088
http://mollicas.com

Mollica's not only offers the freshest, finest Italian meats and cheeses around, you also can shop for imported olive oils and other Italian goods in their store. Try their Italian sandwiches and salads, pastas, and especially their homemade sausage from an old family recipe. You can do takeout or dine in, and if you get a chance, sample their fresh-made pizzas, too. It's not totally local (they have delis in a dozen other Colorado cities now), but it's totally good. Closed Sun.

FINE DINING

Downtown

AMUZE AT THE FAC $$$$
30 W. Dale St.
(719) 477-4377
www.csfineartscenter.org

This trendy little bistro opened right inside the Colorado Springs Fine Arts Center in 2010 by owner Bill Sherman, who owned Amuze Bistro in Palmer Lake for two years before that. It's the latest in a series of catered dining operations here, but this one is a real restaurant, with food prepared on-site. And, oh, the food! Think regional Colorado cuisine with a French twist. Local favorites include the Chesapeake Bay blue crab melt-away, vanilla-infused cream of roasted pepper and tomato soup, the crispy polenta, eggplant and goat cheese salad, the bacon-wrapped Wagyu filet mignon, the diver scallops, and mushroom ravioli. In summer, it's the sweetest place in town to have lunch—out on the verandah, high overlooking Monument Valley Park and the Front Range. Indoors, you can enjoy the original 1936 Art Deco interior and murals. It's across the hall from the Art Deco Lounge, where you also can nosh on creative tapas. They have Sunday brunch and jazz on Friday and Saturday nights. Dress is pretty much business attire or business casual at lunch and folks tend to do the same in the evening for apres-work or pre-theater dining. (The theater is right next to it, also inside the FAC.) Closed Mon.

NOSH $$$$
121 S. Tejon St.
(719) 634-6674
www.nosh121.com

The hottest new restaurant in town actually has been around a few years—since 2007—serving new American cuisine. Located near the downtown contemporary art space for the University of Colorado at Colorado Springs, Nosh creates its own works of art—on plates. Serving tapas and "small plates," it's the perfect place for a, well, nosh, after work—or at lunch or dinner! You can order small or large portions, you can do a "flight" of three soups, or put yourself in the chef's hands and let him pick five succulent little nibbles for you. Their most popular dishes feature, if you can believe it, cauliflower and brussels sprouts. Their shrimp bowl and house burger are also crazy popular. They have a full bar, but the house white sangria is the thing to order. Street parking can be tough, but there's a parking garage adjacent and parking is free when you dine at Nosh; they'll validate your ticket. Closed Sun.

South

✳THE BLUE STAR $$$$
1645 S. Tejon St.
(719) 632-1086
www.thebluestar.net

Situated halfway between downtown and The Broadmoor area, The Blue Star has been a fine dining fixture since 1995. If you're looking for innovative, creative takes on classics, this is your spot. Sort of an American twist on Pacific Rim and Mediterranean dishes. The menu changes often, so it's hard to pinpoint a perennial favorite, but foodies who frequent the place love such dishes as the Almond Rosemary Salmon, the Wasabi Mayo Crab Cakes, the Red Bird Chicken Enchiladas, and the Soba Beef Noodle Bowl. They have an extensive wine list (winner of a *Wine Spectator* Award) and an equally impressive beer list. If the fine dining room seems a bit pricey, you can get equally wonderful food in the more casual bar area at a smaller price. Both Blue Star and Nosh, run by the same owner, could fit into any major metro dining scene anywhere. Be sure to make a reservation!

THE PEPPERTREE RESTAURANT $$$$
888 W. Moreno St.
(719) 471-4888
www.peppertreecs.com

Perched on a hill overlooking the city of Colorado Springs, the views here at night are worth the price of dinner. But they've also served upscale American and continental cuisine since 1983 and know many of their regulars by name. The personal service makes the signature pepper steak taste that much better. The atmosphere is very formal and is popular with the Colorado Springs social set. They pride themselves on "tuxedo service," and many dishes are prepared table-side. Beloved by locals are the steak Diane, lobster Thermidor, rack of lamb, and chateaubriand. They sometimes feature other seafood dishes, as well veal specialties. There's a full bar and wine list. Closed Sun.

WALTER'S BISTRO $$$$
146 E. Cheyenne Mountain Blvd.
(719) 630-0201
www.waltersbistrocs.com

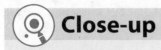 **Close-up**

The Broadmoor

Any time of day, no matter what food you're craving, there's a place to find it at **The Broadmoor** resort hotel complex (1 Lake Ave.; 866-381-8432 or 719-577-5733; www.broadmoor.com/restaurants-colorado-springs.php). With a dozen options, from a confectionary shop to the state's only top-rated restaurant, you'll be able to satisfy your appetite, quench your thirst, or treat your sweet tooth.

Here are the shared basics:

All restaurants offer full bars and parking is by valet or a self-park garage near the main hotel. The Golden Bee does have a small surface parking lot. There are several primary buildings: the 1918 main hotel, Broadmoor South, Broadmoor West, and the International Center. All accept major credit cards, are wheelchair accessible, and take reservations (an excellent idea).

Here's the rundown on its many fine restaurants:

The Penrose Room ($$$$$): Located atop Broadmoor South since it opened in 1961, this is Colorado's only five-star, five-diamond dining establishment. With views of the hotel property and Cheyenne Mountain, you can watch the sun set as you dine on the state's top-rated cuisine. Try the buttery filet mignon, the Lamb Five Ways, or one of their excellent fish dishes, and be sure to dip into the extensive wine list. If you're feeling particularly adventurous and flush, go for the chef's seven-course tasting menu. Impeccable service and more formal dress (coat and tie are requested, but not required) make this the city's most upscale dining room.

✳Charles Court ($$$$): A little less formal than the Penrose Room, you'll nevertheless be impressed with this restaurant, which opened in 1976 on the lake level in Broadmoor West. Its original American cuisine and wines are elegantly served. Regulars love its Maryland Jumbo Lump Crab Cake, the Grilled Rack of Colorado Lamb, and the Bison Tenderloin in a Maytag Crust. There are private dining spaces here, too . . . or, in summer, enjoy alfresco dining by Cheyenne Lake.

Summit ($$$): The newest addition to the hotel's cadre of restaurants opened in 2006, and this American brasserie focuses on seasonal American produce and natural meats, and is situated outside the main hotel for easy community access. Locals love its hangar steak, herb-roasted chicken, and loin of venison, expertly prepared. Check out the stunning glass-enclosed wine turret containing 500 bottles of the nation's best vintages. It also specializes in innovative cocktails (make one up!) and has a much more contemporary design than the other hotel dining rooms. Business casual is the order of the day here, and they even allow "nice" jeans!

Local restaurateur Walter Iser has had several dining venues in Colorado Springs, but his self-named venue in Country Club Corners is the one that has endured. He opened it in 1999 in the Broadmoor area to serve his most loyal, and upscale, clientele. Recently renovated, the elegant decor matches the cuisine he favors. Specialties

The Tavern ($$$): Located on the lobby level of the original main hotel, there are really three dining spaces here: the main Tavern, with Old English decor, including hardwood floors and paneling; the Mayan room, with an Aztec decor and a chance to watch the chef at work; and the Garden Room, an atrium full of plants and flowers. Since 1938, they've been serving steaks and fresh seafood, but their current most popular dishes include the Colorado rainbow trout, honey-mustard glazed salmon, and their famous prime rib. They also serve American Kobe beef.

The Golden Bee ($$): Who else but The Broadmoor would pick up an authentic 19th-century English pub and transport it all the way to Colorado Springs (in 1961)? Quaff one of their famous "yards" of beer—just what it sounds like (and you'd better have long arms!) with some of their pub food, such as fish and chips, shepherd's pie, and bangers with mash. They don't take reservations for dinner; after 2 p.m., it's first come, first served, with only room for 60-some folks in the dining room. It's the old-time honky-tonk piano music that draws folks in and keeps guests singing all night long!

Other venues:

If you can't get into the Bee and you're looking for a truly casual meal, try the **Hotel Bar** on the lake level of the main hotel for heavy hors d'oeuvres, meat-and-cheese plates, and the like. We favor the warm gruyere cheese and spinach dip or the tasty sliders. Sit by the outdoor fireplace on chilly nights.

The newly remodeled **West Lobby Bar** specializes in "small plates" and more upscale noshes, such as an open-faced Duck Confit Sandwich, Korean-style Kobe short-rib skewers, or Indian-spiced "nachos." They offer an extensive list of wines by the glass. Dine in the comfy lobby chairs or alfresco in a secluded outdoor setting.

The main hotel's **Lake Terrace Dining Room,** on the mezzanine level, opened with the hotel in 1918 and is the place to head for breakfast. And on Sunday, it's the place in town for brunch, with more than 100 items from which to choose! Be sure to try the Bananas Foster or the chocolate fountain for dessert. You might need a walk around the lake afterward.

If you're staying at the hotel, you also can dine at the **Golf Club Dining Room** or the **Golf Club Grille** restaurants—both with casual fare but that signature Broadmoor service.

Check out more details about each of these restaurants online.

of the house include pan-roasted Chilean sea bass, sautéed Muscovy duck breast, and a grilled yellow-fin tuna (recommended rare). And the lobster bisque is a classic—as rich as any dessert you could order. The wine list includes varietals from all over the world.

West

GERTRUDE'S RESTAURANT $$$
2625 W. Colorado Ave.
(719) 471-0887
www.gertrudesrestaurant.com

Gertrude's is the quiet constant on the restaurant scene. Open for about 30 years now, people either know and love this place, or they've never heard of it. Those who know about Gertrude's want to keep their secret.

Tucked into a cozy space in Old Colorado City, the surroundings are elegant without being stuffy. Oil paintings by local artists line the walls, and tables with just enough space in-between fill—but don't cram—the tight room. And who cares, because once you're inside, it's like a conversation with a good friend: intimate, simple, and deeply satisfying. Specials are always worth consideration, but mainstays of salmon or steak are sure bets. Vegetarian entrees are noteworthy. Pastas, especially those with seafood, are elegant and tasty. The Mediterranean Seafood Paella is generous, and both smooth and spicy. Desserts are usually scrumptious. Gertrude's offers a full bar and a serviceable wine list, and the waitstaff is knowledgeable about wine-food pairings. Reservations for dinner are highly recommended, especially on the weekends. Open for breakfast, brunch, lunch, and dinner. Closed Mon.

Green Mountain Falls

BLACK BEAR RESTAURANT $$$$
10375 Ute Pass Rd.
(719) 684-9648
www.coloradorestaurantguides.com/blackbear

Chef Victor Matthews was looking for a place to establish his new restaurant in 1999 when he discovered the old Pikes Pub 'n' Grub in Green Mountain Falls. After a $100,000 renovation, he opened the Black Bear, which has earned various awards and accolades every year since. The menu ranges from the a la carte menu, which includes homespun, affordable dishes like chicken fried steak and barbecue, to some extravagant chef's dinners (5 to 12 courses), ranging in price from $55 to $125 per person. Popular with locals is Prime Rib Thursdays, where you can get the succulent cut of beef, with sides, for under $20. The chef/owner specializes in haute cuisine, however, so it's worth a special occasion to splurge on one of the chef's menus once in a while. Serving dinner only. Closed Mon.

Manitou Springs

BRIARHURST MANOR $$$$
404 Manitou Ave.
(719) 685-1864 or (877) 685-1448
www.briarhurstdining.com

The Briarhurst Manor was built by Dr. William A. Bell in 1874 as a summer home. When it burned in 1886, he rebuilt it of stone. It passed through several owners until it was turned into a restaurant in 1975, setting a new standard for fine dining in Manitou Springs. It specializes in well-prepared continental and American cuisine, with unique treatments of everything from beef Wellington to elk tournedos. It specializes in regional Colorado cuisine and for years has been known for its succulent steak Diane.

Meals come with breads and salad, and each entree has a carefully chosen side accompaniment. You'll love the castle-like setting and intimate dining spaces here. It's on the National Register of Historic Places.

CLIFF HOUSE $$$
306 Canon Ave.
(719) 785-2415
www.thecliffhouse.com

You name the award, it's won it. The Cliff House Dining Room can boast about its AAA four-diamond status, its DiRoNA Award, and its Award of Excellence from *Wine Spectator* magazine, among others. Its New American cuisine draws locals, guests, and tourists looking for fine dining in charming Manitou Springs's downtown. Situated in a historic hotel, built in 1874 and totally renovated in the 1990s (see also Accommodations listings), the dining room has Victorian character but strictly avant-garde cuisine. Classics like the chateaubriand, New York steak, or broiled salmon get modern twists from an innovative chef. Check out their extensive and award-winning wine list with more than 700 selections! If that doesn't suit you, they also have a stunning array of vodka and single-malt Scotch offerings. Parking can be difficult in Manitou at certain times of the year, but the Cliff House valets will whisk your car to private parking upon your arrival—for free.

CRAFTWOOD INN $$$$
404 El Paso Blvd.
(719) 685-9000
www.craftwood.com

Originally built as an English Tudor mansion and coppersmith's shop in 1912, the Craftwood Inn has been one of Colorado's premier historic restaurants since 1940. It was serving regional Colorado cuisine before it had a name. Creative, innovative game dishes feature bison, elk, venison, pheasant, wild boar, and antelope. Some favorites? The Rojo Peach Roasted Wild Boar Tenderloin—char-grilled plum-wood-smoked wild boar

with their Sweet Heat Cherry-Peach Chutney—and the Sweet Basil & Butter-Roasted Halibut with Tomato Ginger Relish. Creativity doesn't stop at dessert: If you're adventurous, try the jalapeno white chocolate mousse. You'll either love it or hate it!

MONA LISA FONDUE
RESTAURANT $$$$
733 Manitou Ave.
(719) 685-0277
www.monalisafondue.com

Year after year, since it opened in 1995, the Mona Lisa Fondue Restaurant gets voted as "most romantic" local restaurant (11 times so far). The restaurant, located in a historic building in downtown Manitou, is divided into small cozy rooms and decorated in a very romantic fashion. It's one of those special-occasion places where local couples go for birthdays and anniversaries. Not surprisingly, the Fondue for Two is one of its most popular offerings. This is a four-course fondue meal designed for two people (but can be modified for any size party). It includes a salad; choice of cheese fondue accompanied with fresh breads, fruits, and vegetables for dipping; a meat course (grilled tableside); and a dessert course. The most popular item on the menu, however, is The Traditional, with a choice of flatiron filet, chicken breast, Gulf tiger shrimp, Atlantic salmon, teriyaki filet, a Cajun bratwurst, and some more vegetables to be grilled at the table. There's a seafood and wild game four-course offering, as well. The all-time favorite dessert course is the chocolate fondue with fresh-baked cakes and cookies and fresh fruit to dip. They serve wine and beer only and are open for dinner every night but Monday, when they are closed. Parking can be tight on the street, but there's a public lot a block away.

Woodland Park

SWISS CHALET RESTAURANT $$$
19263 E. US 24
(719) 687-2001
www.swisschaletofwoodlandpark.com

Since 1962, the Swiss Chalet has been *the* place to go for fine dining in Woodland Park, up Ute Pass. Their European and Continental style of cuisine seems to fit the mountain setting, as does its Swiss-style architecture and decor. Its casual fine dining menu includes Chilean sea bass, Zurich-style veal, chateaubriand, and a popular Swiss cheese fondue. A full bar complements any entree. This special occasion restaurant sits right across the highway from Pikes Peak, so you can't miss it.

GERMAN

Downtown

UWE'S GERMAN RESTAURANT $$$
31 Iowa Ave.
(719) 475-1611

A longtime favorite (since 1986) of local German-Americans and other aficionados of German/Austrian cuisine, Uwe's (pronounced Oo-vay's) is tucked away in a small strip mall east of downtown. But it's worth finding, if you love *Jaegerschnitzel,* its single most popular dish! They also have excellent sausages and other schnitzels. Trust them to do authentic side dishes, too—try the sauerkraut or red cabbage. Don't be surprised to hear German being spoken by diners as well as staff. The place is relatively small, so reservations for lunch or dinner are highly recommended . . . probably a day or two in advance. Closed Sun and Mon.

South

EDELWEISS RESTAURANT $$
34 E. Ramona Ave.
(719) 633-2220
www.edelweissrest.com

The sound of an accordion playing "Edelweiss" might be the first thing that draws you in to this stone building that looks like it could have been transported here from the Old Country. Sure enough, on weekend nights, the music is live—and the atmosphere is always friendly. Serving authentic German and other Continental cuisine, Edelweiss has been pleasing schnitzel- and wurst-lovers since 1967. Start off with an imported German beer or wine, to set the stage. Top that with an order of Weiner schnitzel or sauerbraten and you'll be a happy camper. Common side dishes are little German noodle-dumplings called spaetzle, a sweet-and-sour (but mostly sweet) red cabbage. Their German potato salad (comes complimentary on a pre-dinner salad plate) is outstanding. And if they ever take the *rouladen* off the menu, they're in trouble! Other selections include veal Cordon Bleu, a beef filet, and salmon. A favorite with light eaters is their strawberry salad. Fresh, soft Kaiser rolls come with all meals. This is another spot where you don't want to miss dessert. The rich, luscious tortes (Black Forest, chocolate rum, *kirschtorte*) are all homemade and almost too pretty to eat. The strudel's pretty good, too! The casual, family-friendly atmosphere is suited to large groups (taking Grandma out for her birthday) or gatherings (retirement parties), with ample free parking to support such events. Or just stop by for a beer in the Ratskeller downstairs. Reservations are always a good idea, especially on the nights when the accordion player moves from table to table, encouraging diners to join in the singing. Three fireplaces in winter bring the coziness to a new level and the patio in summer re-creates a genuine biergarten.

GREEK & MEDITERRANEAN

North

CASPIAN CAFE $$$
4375 Sinton Rd.
(719) 528-1155
www.caspiancafe.com
This elegantly appointed cafe is modest on the outside, plush on the inside with rich colors, linen tablecloths, and excellent service. And the welcome is always friendly—ladies often get a kiss on the cheek in greeting! Many locals think of it as a Greek restaurant, but it's much more Mediterranean, with an eclectic menu reflecting the cuisines from 15 different countries, including authentic Middle Eastern dishes as well as food from Morocco, Portugal, Turkey, and Spain. Yes, you can get an abundant plate of gyros for lunch (with soft, homemade pita bread), but you also can get their popular avocado, orange, and almond salad. For dinner, the Moroccan chicken and lamb tagine are probably the most sought-after dishes. And if you don't get the Feta Crisps appetizer, you're really missing out on something special. The place really comes alive on Friday and Saturday nights when local belly dancers perform during the peak dinner hour.

West

JAKE AND TELLY'S
   GREEK TAVERNA $$$
2616 W. Colorado Ave.
(719) 633-0604
www.greekdining.com
It's so pleasant on a lovely evening to sit on the second-floor balcony here, listening to the strains of traditional Greek music. Admire the view of Pikes Peak or just watch the world go by in Old Colorado City. Jake and Telly's has been serving Greek and other Mediterranean dishes since 1997, becoming something of a fixture in the historic district. If you'd rather sit inside, you can admire instead the beautiful murals of Greece painted on the walls (and windows and doors). Business folk from the district, locals, and tourists alike appreciate the spacious dining room and the tasty food. At lunch, the gyros are huge! Popular dinner entrees include the Lamb Giouvetsi (slow-roasted lamb shank with orzo), the lamb kebobs (grilled and served with tzaziki sauce and roasted potatoes), and the Chicken Mavrodaphne (pan-seared in a sweet Greek red wine sauce over linguini). And don't forget to try their unusual dolmades (beef and rice wrapped in grape leaves), served with a lemon basil cream sauce. And for something really special, check out the Saganaki, grilled kasseri cheese served flambé! Pair these with your choice from more than 100 wines. Unfortunately, being on the second floor of a historic building, the restaurant is not wheelchair accessible.

i Colorado is a landlocked state. The closest thing we have to fresh seafood is trout (a good choice, if the restaurant serves it). Otherwise, expect to get flash-frozen seafood, which is actually pretty good in most cases! A few restaurants actually fly their own fish in daily.

INDIAN

North

MIRCH MASALA $$$
5047 N. Academy Blvd.
(719) 599-0003
www.mirchmasalaa.com

Need your chicken tikka masala fix? Maybe some Indian-style lamb chops? Since 2003, Mirch Masala has gained a steady following for just such dishes, not to mention a number of vegetable dishes, including saag paneer and various kormas and curries. Most fans of the restaurant say the authentic tandoori dishes are the best. Be sure to try the tasty meat or veggie samosas done in puff pastry for an appetizer. Also try the yogurt-marinated kababs. Regulars always save room for the creamy mango ice cream or mango custard for dessert. A giant Diego Rivera–like mural on the wall intricately depicting the culture and people of India bears close scrutiny. It's fascinating. Local diners regularly name this as one of the city's best Indian food eateries.

South

LITTLE NEPAL $$-$$$
1747 S. 8th St.
(719) 477-6997
www.lnepal.com

Serving north Indian and Nepali food since 2007, this casual little ethnic restaurant has won "best Indian food" three years in a row in local dining surveys. Especially popular are the chicken tikka masala, chicken korma, chicken bhuna, saag paneer, and vegetable korma, accompanied by Chai or a mango lassi. They also have a full bar, wine, and beer. On a weekend night, you might want to make a reservation.

ITALIAN

Downtown

**FRATELLI RISTORANTE
  ITALIANO** $$-$$$
124 N. Nevada Ave.
(719) 575-9571
www.fratelliristorante.com

Located in the downtown historic arts district, Fratelli's is a chef-owned eatery with a European ambience and featuring the works of local artists as part of the decor. Since it opened in 1994, it has drawn business folk from downtown and others from all over the city who like good Italian fare and the downtown setting. House specialties include the handmade gnocchi, veal scaloppini, shrimp Fra Diavolo, Pollo Genovese, and its signature house-made mozzarella cheese. They seek out local meats, produce, and wines, when possible. There's a full bar and a wine list chosen to complement the Italian dishes. There is on-street parking at meters (about $1 an hour) and a parking garage about 2 blocks away. Lunch is moderately priced (about $10) and dinner runs about twice that. Check out the Roman wine bar and its early-bird meal specials and ask about the Italian Social Club that meets the first Tuesday of each month. Closed Sun.

South

LUIGI'S $$
947 S. Tejon St.
(719) 632-7339
www.luigiscoloradosprings.com

For locals looking to nosh on some truly homemade southern Italian classics, Luigi's is the place. All their pasta is homemade, from the lasagna to the signature ravioli to the manicotti. Or try their "new" item, tortellacci—it's only been on the menu 35 years. Other favorites for longtime customers (some of whom have been dining here since the family opened it in 1958) are a trio of chicken dishes—cacciatore, marsala, and parmigiana. You'll also love their succulent homemade sauces, meatballs, and Italian sausage. Stone-baked pizzas and Italian sandwiches round out the menu. They have a senior menu, a children's menu, and, here's a surprise, a gluten-free menu! They have vegetarian offerings, too. Throw in a glass of Chianti, sit at one of the tables laid with a red-checked cloth, and you'll feel like you've taken a mini-trip to Italy. You might have fun checking out the more than 1,000 wine bottles that decorate the place. (Note: They don't take reservations, so get there early if you don't want to wait for a table on busy nights. Or you can call ahead and get on the seating list. And they don't take personal checks, either.) Because it is a very old building, the restrooms may not accommodate some wheelchairs. They serve dinner only and are closed Mon.

MEXICAN

Downtown

EL TACO REY $–$$
330 E. Colorado Ave.
(719) 475-9722
www.eltacorey.com
This little hole-in-the-wall eatery has been delighting Mexican food fans for more than 35 years. Possibly best known for its spicy pork-and-avocado burrito (including a mention in *Sunset* magazine), it serves up some mean green chile. The fried tacos, tamales, and *tres leches* cake have a strong following, too. There's only a couple of tables inside, and a couple of picnic tables outside. If you can't find a seat, get takeout and sample this authentic southern Colorado Mexican food. They don't serve alcohol and are not wheelchair accessible, but they'll come outside and take your order.

i If you're lucky enough to visit a Mexican restaurant that serves green chile, try it! Green chile is a regional concoction of pork (usually), green chiles, onions, garlic, broth, and tomatoes. Servers may ask: "Hot or mild?" If you're not a total wimp, ask for half-and-half. It's hot enough to put a little sweat on your upper lip and make your taste buds stand at attention, but not so intense that it will set your mouth on fire!

SONTERRA GRILL $$$
28 S. Tejon St., Suite B
(719) 471-9222
www.rockymtnrg.com/sonterragrill
Except for the occasional platter of sizzling fajitas whisked from the kitchen, you don't see much tableside cookery at Mexican restaurants. But that's one of the things that makes Sonterra Grill unique. This downtown eatery draws a business crowd at lunch and couples and families at night, and they all enjoy the preparation of guacamole at tableside (customized to their taste!). They also might relish the bananas Foster prepared right next to their table and flamed for their meal's grand finale. Some say the fajitas here are the best in town, but Sonterra Grill doesn't dare take the beef and guacamole enchiladas off the menu, or they'd have a riot on their hands. The colorful, casual atmosphere (check out the cloud ceiling) and some private dining rooms make it a memorable place to dine a deux or with a group. They have a full bar, but try one

of their margaritas. They have more than 30 tequilas and the slushy drink (or on the rocks, if you prefer) is made with all fresh ingredients, not mixers. Open 10 a.m. to 11 p.m. daily; closed Sun.

Take A Food Tour

If you want to get acquainted with some of Colorado Springs's best downtown restaurants, take a **Colorado Springs Food Tour,** hosted by two local women (mother and daughter), who will blend a little local history with samples of food from some of the best restaurants in town.

Your tour will include six or seven local restaurants and may feature anything from crepes to barbecue, pizza to ice cream—depending on the itinerary. The walking tour covers several downtown blocks and is geared for guests 12 and older who appreciate good food and local history. The tours have expanded to Manitou Springs recently, too.

For a current itinerary, prices, and reservations, go online to **www.coloradospringsfoodtours.com.**

PIZZA

Downtown

PANINO'S $–$$
602 N. Tejon St.
(719) 635-7452
www.paninos.com

This Italian favorite has been owned for 35 years by a local hockey family. The original restaurant, this one on Tejon Street, catered to Colorado College students and hockey players. Originally called Pizza Plus, it became famous for its folded pizza sandwiches, called paninos (long before the panini sandwich became popular). Eventually, it changed its name and expanded the menu. They don't stop at sausage and pepperoni, either. You can find a broad variety of paninos and pizzas on the menu, from Philly cheese steak to Mexican style to stir-fry—yes, really. Or make up your own combo—they're game! Hint: Order a side of dipping sauce, because the sandwiches aren't sauced (too messy). Also try their ravioli and lasagna, if you get a chance . . . and don't miss the prime rib on Friday and Saturday nights. A second location is at 1721 S. 8th St. (719-635-1188).

East

FARGO'S PIZZA COMPANY $–$$
2910 E. Platte Ave.
(719) 473-5540
www.fargospizza.com

Families, and especially youth organizations, love Fargo's Pizza Company as much for its ornate, Italianate/Victorian decor as for its fairly mild pizzas. The selection is enormous and the pies are generous in size and with toppings. (They do have one odd quirk: If you order fresh tomatoes on your pizza, they come sliced, raw, on top of the baked pie.) You order at the window, pay, get a number, and go to a table of your choice. Then you watch the carefully placed mirrors all over the various rooms and levels for your number to appear in the glass. They have a great salad bar, too, and pitchers of soda. No table service, so pitchers are a good idea here! It's strictly a family kind of place, so they don't serve alcohol. They have so many different dining areas, seating a total of 500 diners, but it's easy for a Scout troop or a soccer team to hold a party in relative privacy. They've been open since 1973, but the antiques that decorate the place go way back before that!

West

PIZZERIA RUSTICA $$
2527 W. Colorado Ave.
(719) 632-8121
www.pizzeriarustica.com

You'll think you've walked into an authentic Italian trattoria when you enter the doors of Pizzeria Rustica in Old Colorado City. You can smell the wood-fired pizzas baking, and you'll probably want to order a tasty antipasto while you're waiting. They use authentic Italian ingredients—San Marzano tomatoes, Gran Padano Parmesan cheese, and house-made mozzarella. Order a glass of Italian wine, a beer, or other libation to wash it down. And don't forget gelato for dessert! It's fairly new (opened in 2008) and not a really big place, so reservations are a good idea. Hours and days change seasonally, but they're always closed Mon.

STEAK HOUSES

Downtown

THE FAMOUS STEAKHOUSE $$$$
31 N. Tejon St.
(719) 227-7333
www.thefamoussteakhouse.net

This place will remind you of an elegant old Chicago steak house, complete with dark woods and rich red leather booths, discreetly placed ferns and elegant table settings. If you're looking for a fine steak to go with all that ambience, you've come to the right place. They've got it all. They claim to be the only place in Colorado Springs that serves prime-grade beef. They also get tuna flown in from Hawaii, salmon flown in from the Shetland Islands in Scotland, and lobsters from Australia. Also big hits on their menu are the rack of lamb, and for an appetizer, the oysters Rockefeller. Steaks, prime rib, and other entrees come with the classic steak house salad—either a Caesar or a wedge with Maytag blue cheese dressing. Sides, such as a loaded baked potato, sautéed mushrooms, asparagus with hollandaise sauce or creamed spinach, are a la carte. Order up a martini or a fine bottle of wine to accompany your meal and, on most nights, relax to the live piano music. Parking on the street can be difficult, but the city parking garage is right out the back door. Reservations are strongly recommended here.

East

STEAKSMITH $$$$
3802 Maizeland Rd.
(719) 596-9300
www.steaksmith.com

With a name like that, they'd better serve steaks—and good ones, too. In fact, Steaksmith is frequently voted "best steak" in local dining surveys (about 40 times so far) by its faithful fans. They brag about their aged, hand-cut steaks, which they've been grilling since 1981. They also serve fresh seafood, something of a rarity in Colorado Springs. Seafood staples include the classic shrimp cocktail, jumbo shrimp entrees, Canadian scallops, and king crab legs. Hawaiian ono, grilled fresh albacore tuna, and stuffed trout round out the non-meat menu. Meals come with fresh bread and a salad bar. If you have "green" concerns, note that they only buy sustainable products in season. They also buy locally grown produce when available. If you are going for a special occasion, order their rich chocolate fudge cake for your birthday or anniversary before your dinner. Their Sunday brunch includes a carving station, omelet station, and dessert station—you won't go away hungry! For those who imbibe, they have an extensive martini menu, plus wine and beer. Dark woods set the stage indoors, sort of Colorado casual in its ambiance. They do dinner (and Sunday brunch) only and reservations are recommended for this special-occasion restaurant.

VEGETARIAN

Downtown

POOR RICHARD'S RESTAURANT & RICO'S CAFE & WINE BAR $$
322½–324½ N. Tejon St.
(719) 632-7721 or (719) 630-7723
http://poorrichardsdowntown.com
Though well known for its pizza since 1977, this is a true mecca for vegetarians. (OK, you can get meat, too . . . but they shine on their veggie dishes.) Pizzas come with a choice of 30 toppings on house-made dough and sauce. They also have great sandwiches and are known for their fresher than fresh salads, all served with house-made dressings. Daily soup specials also are made here, usually four different choices (plus gazpacho in summer). They also serve a variety of tapas for light eaters. The hummus plate is perfect for a healthful but filling lunch. The chicken pita sandwich on soft flatbread with grilled chicken and a savory sauce is a winner. There's also a limited breakfast menu. Vegans and folks on gluten-free diets can find lots to eat here. Choose from six different dining areas, including a bookstore, a play area for kids, a garden patio, and a "real" restaurant. The clientele is an eclectic mix of high school and college students, downtown business folk, and vegetarians from all over. They serve

32 wines by the glass, 40 beers, and a full cocktail menu. They also offer a choice from 40 different loose-leaf teas, plus homemade pastries and desserts. Everything is natural and pretty much as good for you as it is good. They don't take reservations and street parking can be tight at lunch or right after work on weekdays, so get there early or late for lunch or dinner.

SHUGA'S $$
702 S. Cascade Ave.
(719) 328-1412
www.shugas.com
This cool little cafe located in a 1910 grocery store on the south end of downtown might remind you of some place you'd find in New York or another major metropolis. A flock of origami cranes fly over your head while you dine on such eclectic fare as Mediterranean tapas, Brazilian coconut shrimp soup, grilled Greek (*phelini*) paninis, and super-fresh salads. And don't forget the Double Diablo Chocolate Cake! No, it's not strictly vegetarian, but vegetarians can certainly find more options here than many local restaurants offer. Portions are pleasingly small but big on flavor. Even though it's in an old building, it is wheelchair accessible, and there's ample street parking in the neighborhood. Reservations aren't taken except for groups of six or more (which would almost fill the place!), and they have a full bar to complement the tasty food.

Manitou Springs

ADAM'S MOUNTAIN CAFE $$$
934 Manitou Ave.
(719) 685-1430
www.adamsmountain.com
Located in the restored, historic Manitou Spa building, right on Fountain Creek, this

restaurant is known for its fine vegetarian fare, but meat-eaters shouldn't be discouraged from dining here. They also have fresh seafood and chicken dishes. To say the menu is eclectic is not an exaggeration. Dishes reflect Southwestern, Thai, Japanese, Brazilian, Senegalese, and Italian influences. It's one of the few places in town where you can get a truly vegan meal. At dinner, the Smoked Salmon Enchiladas and cheesy Rural Italian Lasagna are favorites of regular customers. Whole grains and fresh vegetables form the core of the menu, and the restaurant has even received national attention for its food. It's so popular, you'll probably wait in line if you dine here in the summer. Parking in high season in Manitou can be difficult, to say the least. From September through May, however, parking is pretty available and you can get in—sometimes even without a reservation! For 25 years, Adam's has been serving breakfasts, lunches, and dinners that bring people back.

NIGHTLIFE

Once upon a time, the saying here was, "If you want to see some nightlife, go to Denver." That's no longer true. Colorado Springs offers a wide range of evening entertainment, with a full slate of events to rival any city of its size. Two large venues—the Pikes Peak Center downtown and the Colorado Springs World Arena on the south side of the city—fill the bill when it comes to major concerts. Two major college venues offer top-notch shows on a regular basis: Colorado College opened its Cornerstone Arts Center a few years ago and it (along with other venues on campus) offers everything from poetry readings to avant-garde productions, hip and funky music, and much more, all open to the public and many events are free. UCCS has the Dusty Loo Bon Vivant Theatre, home of Theatreworks. All this makes for a packed performing arts calendar.

The trendy bar scene tends to be focused on and around Tejon Street downtown—at least the bars visitors would want to frequent. Those mentioned here tend to have a less-rowdy clientele, but many offer live music, dancing, and general frivolity. For upscale bars, cruise The Broadmoor hotel complex, which has a newly remodeled lobby bar in Broadmoor West, the classy renovated Hotel Bar in the main building, and various other spots scattered throughout the vast property. Dancing? You can dance to live ballroom-style music in the Penrose Room (but then you'd have to drop a couple hundred bucks for dinner) or you can do the cotton-eyed Joe at Cowboys. And there's a wide variety from which to choose in between. If you're looking for a micro-brewed beer, this town has it. If you just want to meet other singles, there also are a few good options. Hookah lounges are the latest craze among the 18 to 30 crowd. Cripple Creek's casinos, where gambling really is the main form of entertainment, also occasionally offer live concerts, too.

OVERVIEW

This chapter offers a wide range of nightlife options, from classy upscale bars to folksy country-western dance clubs, from poetry slams to the singles scene. They are listed by type of venue (bars, cinema, nightclubs, for example). Many of the best bars are also popular local restaurants. When that's the case, we'll tell you when they are crossovers from the Restaurants chapter—but are worth a mention here for their music scene, too. Most local bars get lively for happy hour, and don't close till 2 a.m. The legal drinking age is 21, but a few places accommodate underage guests who want to come hear the music. Addresses are in Colorado Springs unless otherwise noted.

Some places feature local bands as part of their appeal and don't charge extra; others have a cover charge. We'll tell you who charges extra and how much the typical charge is.

i For an overview of local concerts and other nightlife offerings, check out Peak Radar (www.peakradar .com). Also look at the Friday GO! section of the local daily newspaper, *The Gazette*. It lists local as well as Denver events. The weekly *Independent* newspaper also has extensive listings. And look at the KRCC Community Calendar for a multitude of interesting (and often free) events (www.krcc.org), provided by Colorado College's public radio station, KRCC.

BARS

✳THE GOLDEN BEE
1 Lake Ave.
(866) 381-8432 or (719) 577-5776
www.broadmoor.com
Years ago, The Broadmoor imported this quaint 19th-century English pub right from England and they reassembled it here. So it really is authentic. Located outside the main hotel complex, it has a much more relaxed atmosphere and dress code than the hotel's other bars and dining venues. The pub food is decidedly casual, too. Enjoy singing along to the ragtime piano player's tunes, which start up about 8:30 p.m. and go till last call at 1 a.m. There's a camaraderie here that locals love. So raise a pint—or a yard of beer (exactly what it sounds like) and toast the hotel's fun, affordable side. (See also The Broadmoor Close-up in the Restaurants chapter.)

JACK QUINN'S IRISH PUB
21 S. Tejon St.
(719) 385-0766
www.jackquinnspub.com
Ever hear of a bar where the patrons run a race before drinking? Well, that's the deal at Jack Quinn's, a popular downtown watering hole that sponsors a running club. A thousand runners have been known to show up on a Tuesday night to do the 5K run through downtown before ending up at the pub. (OK, you don't have to run, but it's fun!) Typical Irish grub is served, along with imported libations. Irish-themed bands often play live music here, starting about 7 p.m. And we won't even *talk* about what happens here on St. Patrick's Day.

THE LOOP
965 Manitou Ave., Manitou Springs
(719) 685-9344
http://theloopatmanitou.com
Famous for its huge margaritas (they claim the largest in the world), The Loop—a Manitou fixture since 1903—also is known for having the *best* ones in town. Some folks especially like their "Skinny" Margarita, made with pure agave juice, fresh squeezed lime juice, and, of course, tequila. It started out as a wild game restaurant serving bear, venison, elk, and rabbit, among other dishes. Today, it specializes in burgers and burritos. It was called The Loop because the local trolley car system looped around the restaurant before heading back to Colorado Springs. And as far as some locals are concerned, it's still the end of the line when looking for a place to dine.

OLD CHICAGO
118 N. Tejon St.
(719) 634-8812
www.oldchicago.com

Yeah, we know it's a chain, but the downtown version (there are three other locations) doesn't feel like one. And the beer selection alone makes it worth a mention. The food is decent, too. Located in a historic building on Tejon Street (where else?), it feels like a local bar. It has great drink specials and many regular patrons are taking the World Beer Tour. Once they sample all 110 beers, they get their name emblazoned on the Famous Hall of Foam. No prize, just braggin' rights.

✴RED MOUNTAIN BAR AND GRILL
306 Canon Ave., Manitou Springs
(888) 212-7000 or (719) 785-1000
www.thecliffhouse.com
Located in the new $1.7 million addition to the Cliff House hotel, this two-level bar with views of the foothills of the Rockies is an especially nice place to end the day. Plush leather sofas, a marble bar, a cozy fire pit outside, and the views make it a great place to indulge in a creative aperitif or a post-prandial drink. A wine list that features more than 700 choices and a beer list to make you drool provide great options for imbibing. Fun bar food, like buffalo sliders and rattlesnake and rabbit sausage pizzas, reflect the Colorado state of mind.

RICO'S CAFE & WINE BAR
324½ N. Tejon St.
(719) 632-7721
www.poorricharddswebsite.com
Love wine? Love chocolate? Rico's Cafe & Wine Bar offers the best of both worlds and is a favorite with the downtown and Colorado College crowd. It's a hip, but friendly, place to sample wines by the glass and pursue your chocolate passion (eat or drink it). They also have food—pizza, hummus,

salads, and such. Sometimes they have live music, too. (See also Poor Richard's in the Restaurant chapter.)

SODO
527 S. Tejon St.
(719) 314-0420
http://sodonightlife.com
What can we say in a G-rated publication about SODO? Well, it's a singles meat market, proud of it, and recently voted the best place to meet men/women in town. SODO plays up the sexy vibe in its advertising and the thumping beat that emanates from the club most nights. It's not sleazy, though—leather couches and private cabanas give it a rather upscale feel. They play a variety of music, from rap to rock to world music, and have high-tech features, such as full video integration on several large screens that allow for VJ-ing. The club does allow the 18 to 20 crowd, but says it employs systems to prevent underage drinking.

SOUTHSIDE JOHNNY'S
528 S. Tejon St.
(719) 444-8487
www.southsidejohnnys.biz
Despite all the motorcycles parked outside, Southside Johnny's really isn't a "biker bar." It may be a little rough around the edges, but it has lots of room for gatherings large and small. Good parking (a rarity downtown) and good local bands draw customers in for happy hour—and beyond—on a regular basis. The music starts about 7 p.m. and goes till around midnight. They serve decent, if typical, bar food (wings, quesadillas, nachos) that won't knock your socks off, but isn't bad, either. And it's a companionable place—you'll never drink alone.

i Visitors should be aware that the altitude affects your reaction to alcohol. You may find you get a bit tipsy after just one margarita, beer, or glass of wine, though they may not seem to affect you at all at sea level. Pace yourself. Local law enforcement is vigilant regarding DUIs.

SWIRL WINE EMPORIUM
717 Manitou Ave., Manitou Springs
(719) 685-2294
http://swirlwineemporium.com
If it sounds pretentious, it isn't. Swirl is Manitou's hot new wine bar that describes itself thus: "We're a place of jokers, parents, hard workers, artists, flip-flop wearin', mountain watchers, chatterbugs, brew nerds and at the end of the day, always friends." Yeah, it's that kind of place. But the wines and brews are fine and invite you to come back again and again to sample new ones. They're not open late—10 p.m. weeknights and midnight weekends.

TRIPLE NICKEL TAVERN
26 S. Wahsatch Ave.
(719) 477-9555
For punk and rockabilly shows, you can't beat The Triple Nickel Tavern. It's tiny, but a great place for drinks on an off-night and fun for shows on weekends. Owned by a guy who calls himself JJ NOBODY (the bass player for Drag the River and THE NOBODYS) and his family, it's a place where you'll find comfy chairs, cold beverages, and sometimes rowdy conversation—in other words, it's a place where you can go and relax and be yourself.

BREWPUBS

JUDGE BALDWIN'S
4 S. Cascade Ave.
(719) 473-5600 or (719) 955-6291
www.hilton.com
Colorado Springs's first brewpub is located adjacent to the lobby of the Antlers Hilton Hotel downtown. Its 30-foot wooden bar is the focal point of the pub, providing glass windows showcasing the copper-clad brewing equipment. The Judge has seasonal microbrews along with its four popular microbrews on tap daily. The combination of food and drink makes an attractive setting for after-work conversation, watching the big game on its large-screen TVs, or relaxed listening to the live weekend music on Friday nights, usually featured from 6 to 9 p.m., and Saturday nights from 7 to 10 p.m. Weekday happy hours start at 4 p.m. and last till 6 p.m. and their Night Court Happy Hour lasts from 9 to 11 p.m. They normally close at 11 p.m.

PHANTOM CANYON BREWING COMPANY
2 E. Pikes Peak Ave.
(719) 635-2800
www.phantomcanyon.com
You might go here for the hearty pub food, but the beer is the real draw. This local brewery started in a historic 1901 Cheyenne Building downtown and opened its doors in 1993. You can see the brewing process in glass-enclosed cubicles and you can sample their signature brews in flights or by the glass. They usually have 8 or 10 available at any given time. Pure Colorado water and the best malted barley and hops from the American Northwest go into their product, which you can drink immediately,

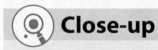

Close-up

Betting on Cripple Creek

OK, gambling isn't strictly a nighttime pursuit, but somehow it feels more natural at night than in the broad daylight! That doesn't stop locals and visitors from heading up to **Cripple Creek** by car or shuttle (see the Getting Here, Getting Around chapter) as soon as the casinos open, however. Legalized gambling was brought back to the feisty old gold camp in 1991. Since then, it has revitalized the local economy while arguably destroying some of the town's historic character. It draws thousands of visitors every year, each one hoping for a big win, of course!

Some of the casinos offer food and entertainment as well; but let's face it, it's the slots and poker tables that draw folks to the celebrated mining town.

Here's a list of some casinos that might be happy to help you spend your money.

All are in downtown Cripple Creek, on the main street of Bennet Avenue, or close by. We list phone numbers and all can be found on one website, **www.cripple-creek colorado.com.** Call the city of Cripple Creek for information on visiting, (877) 858-4653, or check their calendar of events at www.cripple-creek.co.us/Events.aspx.

Brass Ass
(719) 689-2104

Bronco Billy's Casino
(719) 689-2142

Century Casino
(719) 689-0333

Colorado Grande Casino
(719) 689-3517

Double Eagle Hotel Casino
(800) 711-7234

Johnny Nolan's Casino
(719) 689-2080

J.P. McGill's Casino
(719) 689-2104

Midnight Rose Casino
(719) 689-2865

unpasteurized and unfiltered at the proper traditional temperatures. Try the ales, porters, Hefeweizens, and an array of seasonal brews. If you want entertainment while you quaff a cold one, the second floor boasts the most elegant billiard hall in Colorado Springs. The Phantom Canyon Billiard Hall opened in June 1996 and contains 13 pool tables, a jukebox, foosball tables, dart boards, and big-screen TVs. It's a popular destination for both the happy hour crowd and late-night imbibers.

CINEMA

KIMBALL'S PEAK THREE THEATRE
115 E. Pikes Peak Ave.
(719) 447-1945 or (719) 447-1947
www.kimballstwinpeak.com

Two theaters were carved out of a historic old movie house—the Peak Theatre—in downtown in 1994 to create the city's primary venue for independent and art films. It was called Kimball's Twin Peak Theatre. A third theater was added in 2010, thus the name change. If the movie is edgy or controversial, or a small gem with a small draw, this is likely the only place in town you'll see it. It's also the only theater in town where you can get a glass of wine with your movie—the lobby includes a bar as well as the usual popcorn-and-soda snacks. It's been voted best local movie theater 15 years in a row.

CONCERTS

*COLORADO SPRINGS WORLD ARENA
3185 Venetucci Blvd.
(719) 477-2121
www.worldarena.com

This, the largest single venue in the region, is home to Colorado College hockey in season, but also boasts enough seats to host a major concert, such as Cher, Elton John, the Eagles, or Sugarland, among others. It's also the primary venue for such entertainments as ice shows and large-scale events like "Walking with Dinosaurs." The arena was built in 1998 to replace the old, and somewhat decrepit, Broadmoor World Arena, which was razed to make way for an addition to the hotel property. The arena can seat 6,000 to 9,000 people, depending on the event. Though you wouldn't necessarily think an arena would offer a good sound, tell that to anyone who has experienced the Trans-Siberian Orchestra (complete with light show) here!

*PIKES PEAK CENTER
190 S. Cascade Ave.
(719) 520-SHOW (7469)
www.pikespeakcenter.com

The Pikes Peak Center, built in 1988, is the acoustically exceptional home to the Colorado Springs Philharmonic and a touring Broadway series, and also is the perfect place for concerts by such greats as Arlo Guthrie, Michael Bolton, Chris Isaak, or the Judds. Its Studio Bee (named after a longtime patron

of the arts, Bee Vradenburg) hosts local performing groups and bands, often for free. Comedians, choral concerts, dance, and second-tier performers are perfect for this lovely, 1,950-seat hall. (See also The Arts chapter.)

STARGAZERS THEATRE & EVENT CENTER
10 S. Parkside Dr.
(719) 476-2200
www.stargazerstheatre.com

Stargazers is a relatively new addition to the venue scene, opening in its current incarnation in 2009. Though it was originally a movie theater, it now works well as an entertainment venue for concerts, films, comedians, and all kinds of music, from blues and jazz to salsa and classic rock. It seats up to 550 people for concerts.

GLBT HOT SPOTS

BIJOU BAR & GRILL
2510 E. Bijou St.
(719) 473-5718
www.bijoubar.com

The family-run Bijou Bar & Grill is located just east of downtown near an older neighborhood. This gay/lesbian pub offers karaoke, pool tables, theme nights, and Double Jeopardy game nights. Weekends, there are DJ Dance Nights. Open Wed through Sat only.

THE UNDERGROUND
110 N. Nevada Ave.
(719) 578-7771
www.undergroundbars.com

There aren't a lot of nice gay bars in Colorado Springs, but the Underground is probably the best one for a great mix of people, fun events, and decent music. There's

Close-up

B.Y.O.

Maybe you'd rather buy your own beer, wine, or favorite brand of liquor and make your own drinks. There are several really fine liquor stores in Colorado Springs that probably will have whatever you're seeking. Liquor stores now remain open here on Sunday. Here are a couple of places worth checking out. These two always compete in "best of" surveys and alternate taking first and second place!

Cheers Liquor Mart
1105 Circle Dr.
(719) 574-2244
www.cheersliquormart.com
This warehouse of a store has just about anything you can imagine, and pretty good prices, too! With lots of parking, it's close to downtown and easy to access. They have a huge wine selection, imported beers, plus most any hard liquor or liqueur you can imagine. They also do custom gift baskets.

Coaltrain Wine & Spirits
330 W. Uintah St.
(719) 475-9700
www.coaltrainwine.com
Located right at I-25 and near the railroad tracks, this packed retail outlet has an amazing array of 1,000 wines and 350 beers. The parking lot is fairly small, but usually adequate for its come-and-go business. Watch their online calendar for wine-tasting events.

something special going on every night of the week, from karaoke to free pool and poker tournaments. Local polls have voted it the best gay bar in the region 6 years running.

HOOKAH LOUNGES

40 THIEVES HOOKAH LOUNGE
1524 N. Academy Blvd.
(719) 591-8315
http://40thievesonline.com/coloradosprings.html
This franchise in Colorado Springs is large, at 3,000 square feet. It features pool tables, arcade games, DJs, an oxygen bar, and

the smokes. There are karaoke nights and special events like Spookah Hookah around Halloween. They also offer belly dance classes and shows. Oh, yeah, they also sell supplies.

HOOKED ON HOOKAH
6406 N. Academy Blvd.
(719) 886-7107
www.hohstore.com
The first hookah bar in town, Hooked on Hookah is on the north side of town. It has been named by a local paper as "Best Hookah Bar" for a number of years running. The over 18/under 30 crowd in town like

it because of its comfortable, happening atmosphere that keeps happening well into the night. An online store also sells various hookahs and supplies.

NIGHTCLUBS

BLACK SHEEP
2106 E. Platte Ave.
(303) 487-0111
http://blacksheeprocks.com

The Black Sheep has snagged honors as the best local music venue from readers of *The Independent*, the local alternative newspaper, for 5 years running. They feature bands and musicians the over-40 crowd never heard of—like Conor Oberst, Mr. Lif, Gaslight Anthem, Static-X, and Ozomatli. The venue occasionally surprises fans with country acts or alternative hip-hop. They also showcase local bands on Friday nights. All-ages shows and touring acts with national reputations keep its customers entertained. And the owners say eventually they want to feature live music seven nights a week. Cover charges vary by the entertainment. Don't be confused by the phone number—it's for Soda Jerk, a Denver agency that books most of the shows and sells the tickets.

COPPERHEAD ROAD
3330 N. Academy Blvd.
(719) 659-9099
www.thecopperheadroad.com

One of Colorado Springs's newest clubs also is reportedly the wildest! Bartenders (and sometimes customers) tend to hop up on the bar and dance at will. A John Deere tractor helps decorate the place—for no specific reason we can determine—along with a Confederate flag bearing the word: Redneck.

But they serve up live rock and DJ country music on a regular basis and have become one of the most popular new clubs in town. There's a $5 cover after 8 p.m. weekends and occasionally an extra charge for live shows. Be warned: The place gets so packed on weekends that they have security directing parking outside and patrolling the masses inside to stop any trouble before it starts. It's a mob scene, but if you're into that sort of thing, this is the place!

COWBOYS
25 N. Tejon St.
(719) 596-1212
www.worldfamouscowboys.com

Put on your best dancin' boots and practice your Texas two-step if you want to fit right in at Cowboys, a local nightclub that started in 1986 and moved downtown in recent years. Country music—both live and recorded—will get your toes to tappin'. It can get a little rowdy at times, but that's just the way cowboy clubs are. Some nights are concert nights and you'll need tickets, others are just for fun, but there is a $10 cover charge. If you are two-step impaired, they give free Western dance lessons if you get there before 7 p.m. on Sunday. Cowboys doesn't open till 5 p.m. most nights and doesn't answer phones before then. They do list upcoming bands and other events on their website, so you can check those for yourself.

i Parking downtown can be a pain during peak hours, and meters charge $1 an hour. There are several affordable parking garages, though. And you don't have to plug meters after 6 p.m. or on Sunday.

MUSIC

CUCURU ART GALLERY CAFE
2332 W. Colorado Ave.
(719) 520-9900
http://cucurugallerycafe.com

Is it a cafe? A bar? A nightclub? An art gallery? All of that and more. Cucuru is an eclectic jumble of the finer things in life: a good coffee in the morning, surrounded by original, unusual works of art. In the evening, the intimate courtyard comes alive with jazz under the stars. If it's winter, the jazz slides indoors. Or, if it's Tuesday, there's the evening tango lessons, from beginning to expert. The quaint, small space in Old Colorado City refuses to be just one thing to all people, which gives it a subtle but delectable enchantment. Tango on Tuesday (bring your dancing shoes), jazz on Friday and Saturday, and special jazz engagements on some Thursdays and Sundays. Open Tues through Sun.

MOTIF JAZZ BAR
2432 W. Cucharras St.
(719) 635-5635
http://motifwest.com

Cool, urban, hip, sophisticated—these are not descriptions used everywhere in Colorado Springs. But this jazz club, bar, and restaurant (with a tapas-style menu) embraces them all. Motif, like any good club too cool for full-on exposure, is situated behind The Food Designers in Old Colorado City, with an entrance through a gate, into a patio, and finally through big garage doors. Once inside, the vibe is small venue in a big city, with warm, deep colors and high-tech lights. The music is rich and smooth, the martinis are dry, and the food hits a number of high notes, especially the frequent fish specials. The white truffle fries, Salmorejo Shrimp, and beef dishes also are crowd favorites. Open Fri and Sat only.

THE ARTS

When Colorado Springs was founded, it immediately became a haven for high culture in the West—with opera, ballet, classical music, and fine art. Its nickname was "Little London," and it was well deserved. It's said that the famous actress, the beautiful Lillie Langtry, once performed here. Actor Lon Chaney Sr. came from here.

Today, the city still boasts a lively arts and culture scene and draws top performers—from the likes of dancer Mikhail Baryshnikov and Russian cellist Mstislav Rostropovich to contemporary artists like Elton John and The Judds. The beautiful Pikes Peak Center is the perfect venue for Broadway touring companies. Small local theater companies include one at the Colorado Springs Fine Arts Center, one in Manitou Springs, and Theatreworks, a professional company based at the University of Colorado at Colorado Springs, among others. There are choral groups, small musical ensembles, a local dance company, and an exceptional symphony. Classical music found a home here in 1927, with the first professional symphony orchestra (which has been through several incarnations, but has never been abandoned). Dance theater also has had a foothold here for many years, with such famous performers as Martha Graham appearing in local venues. Opera, too, has a small but strong following.

Art has been part of the local culture since the Ute Indians left their mark on the red sandstone rocks of Garden of the Gods. The Broadmoor Art Academy started here in the early 20th century and produced such artists as Boardman Robinson. A lovely Art Deco Fine Arts Center was built in 1936, which has expanded several times into the stunning entity it is today. *Peanuts* comic illustrator Charles Schulz lived here for a time in the early 1950s. Today, in downtown Colorado Springs, you can't turn a corner without coming face to face with a piece of public art. Half the restaurants and banks in town also are art galleries, with the works of local artists decorating the walls (and which usually are for sale). Art galleries and shows fill the "events" columns of the local newspapers and community calendars. There's everything from sculpture to paintings, glasswork to pottery, jewelry to fiber arts, and much more.

OVERVIEW

This chapter is organized by types of arts offerings available—dance, theater, music, and art galleries, for example. Each one includes a website so you can take a look at their current offerings. Considering the quality of what's offered, the prices here are pretty reasonable—and sometimes free. We stuck with tried-and-true art galleries and arts organizations; in this day and age, and with the current economy, things do come

Art on the Streets

Check out the cowboy reading today's newspaper. How about the Pikes Peak Ranger Rider on his horse? Everywhere you look in downtown Colorado Springs, there's public art. That didn't happen by chance.

Thank **Colorado Springs Community Ventures Inc.,** a local nonprofit organization formed by the Downtown Partnership of Colorado Springs in 1997 to support public art. **Art on the Streets,** as it's called, is a yearlong outdoor art exhibit, and was created by the Community Ventures Board in 1998. The first exhibit in 1999 showcased 20 pieces of art, made possible by a generous contribution from its founding sponsor, US Bank. Since then, Nor'wood Development has become a major funder, along with G.E. Johnson Construction and, most recently, the H. Chase Stone Trust. Many businesses, foundations, and individuals also contribute to this popular public art program that relies completely on funding from the private sector. No tax dollars are involved.

Since its inception, Art on the Streets has exhibited more than 180 pieces of art throughout downtown Colorado Springs, with more than 100 regional, national, and international artists participating. Sixteen pieces of sculpture have been purchased through the Art on the Streets program and have been donated to the city for its permanent collection of art downtown. That includes one by the late, local metal sculpture artist Starr Kempf, *Pendulum Clock,* which stands at the Plaza of the Rockies downtown. If you haven't seen his work before, you can't miss it—it's big and impressive!

A walking tour map of the current Art on the Streets exhibition as well as more than 50 additional pieces of public art is available at **www.downtown 80903.com.** As one of the organization's founders, Judy Noyes, always says: "You don't have a world-class community without art in public places."

and go. Many of these entities do not have physical addresses—they don't have the budget for an actual office. You will have to reach them via e-mail or phone, or we included their full mailing address. Street addresses are in Colorado Springs unless otherwise noted. Some also do not have a long-term phone number. The best way to contact them would be via their website, which may have a current, temporary number. We did not include the numerous choral and musical offerings sponsored by local churches—the list is too long! But you can find all those in the various community calendars and events listings noted here.

ART GALLERIES

ARATI ARTISTS GALLERY
2425 W. Colorado Ave.
(719) 636-1901
www.aratiartists.com
At Arati (pronounced AR-ati), one of the city's most established galleries in Old Colorado City, there's an exciting selection of paintings and drawings; sculpture in bronze, clay, and wood; unique jewelry; wood carvings; and

pottery (both fanciful and utilitarian). And check out their gift-able bookmarks and unique greeting cards. This particular shop is a co-op showcasing 20 artists who live in the Pikes Peak region.

BUSINESS OF ART CENTER
513 Manitou Ave., Manitou Springs
(719) 685-1861
www.thebac.org
It's a gallery. It's a studio. It's an events space. The Business of Art Center in Manitou Springs is all this and more. But if you ask the members, they may say that the most critical part of the BAC program for artists are the studio facilities. The BAC has more than 10 studios available 24 hours a day. Beyond providing equipment, which few individual artists could afford, BAC artists are enriched by the interaction with their fellow artists, by classes and other programs that are sponsored here. Visitors are encouraged to observe artists at work in their studios, most of which are open and visible during gallery hours.

COMMONWHEEL ARTISTS CO-OP
102 Canon Ave., Manitou Springs
(719) 685-1008 or (877) 685-1008
www.commonwheel.com
Started in 1974 in historic downtown Manitou Springs, the Commonwheel presents the work of dozens of local and regional artists with gallery shows featuring opening receptions free to the public. In the sales shop, local members offer examples of their creative endeavors, such as pottery, home accessories, photography, paintings, sculpture, and wearable art. Customers love the reasonable prices. It also hosts an annual juried 3-day arts festival with entertainment and kids' activities, in a nearby park. From

about Thanksgiving to New Year's, it also features many special handcrafted gifts appropriate for the holidays.

i For an overview of local arts events, check out Peak Radar (www.peakradar.com), a service provided by the Cultural Office of the Pikes Peak Region (COPPeR). Also look at the Friday GO! section of the local daily newspaper, *The Gazette.* It lists local as well as Denver events. The weekly *Colorado Springs Independent* newspaper also has fairly complete listings of events. Online, look at the KRCC Community Calendar for a multitude of interesting (and often free) events (www.krcc.org), provided by Colorado College's public radio station, KRCC.

HAYDEN HAYS GALLERY
1 Lake Circle
(719) 577-5744
www.haydenhaysgallery.com
Located in the shops at The Broadmoor hotel complex, this is one of the region's finest art galleries. The elegant Hayden Hays Gallery sells collector-quality art, including representational art, by artists of local, regional, national, and international stature. Founded in 1979, the gallery is probably the most high-end store in town. They also will take paintings on consignment and do art evaluations.

HUNTER-WOLFF GALLERY
2510 W. Colorado Ave.
(719) 520-9494
www.hunterwolffgallery.com
The Hunter-Wolff Gallery in Old Colorado City offers a diverse collection of

museum-quality fine art. Focusing on the best Colorado artists, owner Sharon Wolff personally selects the finest works of art by a select group of artists specializing in oil, watercolor, pastel, encaustic, and mixed medium in a wide range of styles including expressionism, impressionism, realism, surrealism, and abstract. Fine bronze sculptures, pottery and ceramics, blown and fused glass, and wearable art jewelry round out the gallery's offerings.

✳I.D.E.A. SPACE
825 N. Cascade Ave.
(719) 227-8263
www.coloradocollege.edu/ideaspace
The InterDisciplinary Experimental Arts (IDEA) Program at Colorado College gave birth to the I.D.E.A. Space, tucked inside the new Cornerstone Arts Center on campus. The program seeks to integrate the visual arts into campus and community life through innovative collaborations, visual art exhibitions, performances, speakers, and events. Exhibitions involve an eclectic range of media, including traditional arts, performance art, and new media. I.D.E.A. Space exhibitions and programs are free and open to the public.

PIKES PEAK COMMUNITY COLLEGE DOWNTOWN STUDIO ART GALLERY
100 W. Pikes Peak Ave.
(719) 502-4040
www.ppcc.edu/departments/art/
ppcc-art-gallery
While preparing its students for careers in art, Pikes Peak Community College also gives them experience in preparing for shows and exhibiting their work. The Downtown Studio Art Gallery not only provides a showcase for students and Art Department faculty, but it also features the work of regional, national, and international artists in critically acclaimed exhibits. Events hosted by the gallery include artist talks, salon discussions, and interdisciplinary performances.

SMOKEBRUSH GALLERY & FOUNDATION FOR THE ARTS
218 W. Colorado Ave., Suite 102
(719) 444-1012
www.smokebrush.org
The name indicates there might be more going on here than art shows, and that's exactly the case. The Smokebrush Gallery & Foundation for the Arts does offer showings by local artists and traveling exhibits of contemporary art with openings the first Friday of each month. But the spaces also are used for yoga classes, concerts, poetry readings, dance performances, and other events. The Smokebrush Foundation also collaborates with nonprofits and area artists to produce public art projects. The Smokebrush Foundation also is the sponsor of the popular Uncle Wilber fountain in Acacia Park. (Also see the Kidstuff chapter.)

TRI-LAKES CENTER FOR THE ARTS
304 Hwy. 105, Palmer Lake
(719) 481-0475
www.trilakesarts.org
In the summer of 1998, artists from the Tri-Lakes area formed a nonprofit foundation and opened the Tri-Lakes Center for the Arts in a donated building in Palmer Lake. The center now offers a variety of programs in both visual and performing arts. Art exhibits are arranged for established, emerging, and student artists at the local, regional, and national levels. Performing artist events include concerts, lectures,

and readings designed to bring in both new and familiar artists who stimulate new interests and ideas. Educational programs are offered for adults and children with a range of abilities and include everything from sculpting and painting to pottery and photography.

UCCS GALLERY OF CONTEMPORARY ART
1420 Austin Bluffs Pkwy.
(719) 255-3504
www.galleryuccs.org
Located both on the campus of the University of Colorado at Colorado Springs and in a downtown studio space (121 S. Tejon St.), the Gallery of Contemporary Art (GOCA) features exhibitions of national and international contemporary art along with related popular programming ranging from lectures to occasional concerts and even films. The campus site opened in 1981 to showcase not only the works of professional artists, but also the endeavors of the faculty and students of the Visual and Performing Arts Department. The downtown location opened in 2010 and features works by local artists as well as international ones. The primary mission of the GOCA is to provide significant contemporary visual art exhibitions, related programming, and forums for discussion on contemporary culture to both the university and to the community of the Pikes Peak region at large. Perhaps more important, GOCA is a social place. Exhibitions are free and refreshments are plentiful at openings and other events. Conversation flows freely, and ideas are always welcome.

ART MUSEUMS

✳COLORADO SPRINGS FINE ARTS CENTER
30 W. Dale St.
(719) 634-5581
www.csfineartscenter.org
Established in 1936, and home to the Taylor Museum, Bemis School of Art, and SaGaJi Theatre, the Colorado Springs Fine Arts Center is a multipurpose facility dedicated to inspiring people through visual and performance arts, as well as education. The newly expanded building features traveling exhibitions, such as Andy Warhol, as well as permanent collections including famous Western artists and Southwestern art (think Remington and Moran) and artifacts. The newest acquisitions include impressive Dale Chihuly glass chandeliers. There's also a kid-friendly tactile gallery, museum shop, a courtyard for events, and spacious education studios. And a gift shop, of course. You can dine in the onsite cafe or have a drink in the Deco Lounge. (Also see Theater listings in this chapter and see the Restaurants chapter.)

MICHAEL GARMAN PRODUCTIONS
2418 W. Colorado Ave.
(719) 471-9391
Local sculptor Michael Garman has spent his life creating sculptures of real people—cowboys and Indians, soldiers and sailors, football quarterbacks and baseball pitchers, bums, hoboes, and working men. His collectible sculptures, and the settings in which he puts them, inspired the birth of *Magic Town*, a fascinating ⅙-scale neighborhood reminiscent of The Bowery or some other downtrodden urban setting. He says he makes "doll houses, but macho dollhouses," and visitors are fascinated by the changing scenes (using moving lights and mirrors).

Note the realistic details, such as a daily newspaper with a real story on the front, about the size of your thumb.

ARTS SCHOOLS

BEMIS SCHOOL OF ART
30 W. Dale St.
(719) 475-2444
www.csfineartscenter.org/education.asp
The Bemis School of Art is an arm of the Colorado Springs Fine Arts Center, and is dedicated to arts education for all ages. Experienced artists and art instructors, large studios, and limited class size create an atmosphere for learning. New sessions begin each January, June, and September and classes range from drawing and painting to photography and pottery-making. (Also see the Kidstuff chapter.)

COLORADO SPRINGS CONSERVATORY
1600 N. Union Blvd.
(719) 577-4556
www.coloradospringsconservatory.org
At the Colorado Springs Conservatory (CSC), kids from preschool to college prep get a thorough education in the arts. Students from middle school through high school enroll in the CORE program, which provides the foundation for a strong comprehensive arts education. The program is based on a classical background in both music and theater, allowing students to understand and explore various artistic styles. CORE programs are non-auditioned and open to all levels of experience. Students are grouped by age and/or proficiency levels. Every student explores arts history, too, and all are eligible for private lessons and tutoring. Students also may audition for the school's COMPANY program, which allows them to execute the skills they have learned.

COTTONWOOD CENTER FOR THE ARTS
427 E. Colorado Ave.
(719) 520-1899
www.cottonwoodcenterforthearts.com
The Cottonwood Center for the Arts is a school, a gallery, and a studio. It offers classes in the classical tradition, including everything from bookbinding to figure drawing. Learn to make jewelry or fiber art. You can even take a yoga class here! The center also has studio space for artists who need a place to work, and space for its students, instructors, and local arts groups to exhibit their works. Opening receptions are held on the last Friday of each month.

CHORAL GROUPS

COLORADO SPRINGS CHILDREN'S CHORALE
P.O. Box 7841
Colorado Springs, CO 80933
(719) 633-3562
www.kidssing.org
The Colorado Springs Children's Chorale is a nationally and internationally recognized youth choir of more than 200 children. Aspiring members, ages 7 to 18, must audition for membership and are then placed in one of five choirs. The Children's Chorale performs more than 100 concerts annually—locally, statewide, nationally, and internationally. The group sponsors an extensive outreach program that includes concerts and workshops in area schools. It also sponsors the All City Boys Choir Festival and two Eastern Plains Youth Choir Festivals annually.

COLORADO SPRINGS CHORALE
P.O. Box 2304
Colorado Springs, CO 80901
(719) 634-3737
www.cschorale.org

The Colorado Springs Chorale, established in 1956, is an adult volunteer community chorus. Membership is determined through auditions, with approximately 120 voices participating. The Chorale performs five concerts per season, usually at the Pikes Peak Center, either independently or with either the Colorado Springs Philharmonic or US Air Force Academy Band. They sing a wide variety of music, but their emphasis is on performing great choral works, in quality venues, with full orchestra.

OUT LOUD: THE COLORADO SPRINGS MEN'S CHORUS
3773 Cherry Creek N. Dr., Suite 575, Denver
(866) 862-9382

Despite its Denver address, this community chorus of the Pikes Peak region is organized to give an opportunity for gay men and their friends to sing together. They use the power of music as a means to foster fellowship and as a vehicle to reach out to the local GLBT community and the community at large. Through song, its 60 or so members act as goodwill ambassadors to present a positive image of the GLBT community. And they're outstanding a capella singers and performers, too!

VELVET HILLS SHOW CHORUS
P.O. Box 7448
Colorado Springs, CO 80933-7448
(719) 630-2525
www.velvethills.org

The award-winning Velvet Hills Show Chorus is a local chapter of Sweet Adelines International. This dynamic, competitive group of women sing a capella four-part barbershop harmony. Their activities include education and performance, and they promote musical excellence.

COLLEGE VENUES

CORNERSTONE ARTS CENTER
825 N. Cascade Ave.
(719) 389-6607
www.coloradocollege.edu/news_events/Cornerstone

Colorado College, the city's oldest institution of higher education, has a number of venues on campus that host plays, poetry readings, author appearances, lectures, music, and more, but the Edith Kinney Gaylord Cornerstone Arts Center is not only the newest, but possibly the most intriguing of its spaces. The 450-seat theater doesn't have a bad view anywhere in the house. The state-of-the-art facility exceeds the standards of most venues—not only here, but nationwide. Performing spaces are not limited to the stage. Opened in 2008, the $33 million facility houses classrooms, offices galleries, and more. If you access the website above, you also can learn about the many other venues on campus and what they are offering. Where else in town would you go to hear the nation's poet laureate?

DUSTY LOO BON VIVANT THEATRE
1420 Austin Bluffs Pkwy.
(719) 255-3232
www.theatreworkscs.org

Located on the campus of the University of Colorado at Colorado Springs, this relatively new venue boasts 150 to 250 seats (depending on the production) and is the home of Theatreworks (see Theater listings), which is one of its primary users. The theater, incidentally, was created in a building formerly occupied by Compassion International, purchased by the university in 2003, and turned into University Hall. The auditorium has been completely renovated into a flexible black-box style of theater.

DANCE

COLORADO SPRINGS DANCE THEATRE
P.O. Box 877
Colorado Springs, CO 80901
(719) 630-7434
www.csdance.org/wp
Colorado Springs Dance Theatre isn't a dance troupe. Instead, its mission is to promote dance in the Pikes Peak Region by presenting world-class concerts that demonstrate a diverse range of dance forms. CSDT nurtures talented young dancers by providing performance opportunities, master classes, and scholarships. Since 1977, they had gotten top performers to come to town, including the Maria Benitez Spanish Dance Company, major ballet companies, and even the incomparable Mikhail Baryshnikov in one of his final public performances.

ORMAO DANCE COMPANY
611 N. Royer St.
(719) 471-9759
www.ormaodance.org
Ormao, in Greek, means "movement with force," and this local nonprofit modern dance company certainly has shown it can move forward. Established in 1990, it presents a contemporary dance repertoire to audiences and also offers classes. Ormao Dance Company often presents collaborative

performances that might include other local entities, such as the Colorado Springs Philharmonic or Smokebrush Readers' Theater.

LITERARY ARTS

PIKES PEAK ROMANCE WRITERS
P.O. Box 62943
Colorado Springs, CO 80962-2943
www.pprw.org
There's a large and successful group of romance writers in the Pikes Peak region—enough so they started their own group. PPRW members regularly meet to exchange writing tips and market news, and to provide support and encouragement to its members. Both published and unpublished writers are members, with the understanding that the focus is on writing romantic fiction. PPRW is a chapter of Romance Writers of America.

PIKES PEAK WRITERS
4164 Austin Bluffs Pkwy., Suite 246
www.ppwc.net
Pikes Peak Writers is a large group of both published and aspiring writers that meets regularly. It provides networking and an educational forum for writers to study the craft of writing via monthly workshops, newsmagazine, seminars, and open critiques. It also sponsors and organizes the annual Pikes Peak Writers Conference, a weekend event that covers all aspects of writing and marketing commercial fiction, including a writing contest. Major authors who have appeared as speakers at the conference include mystery writer Robert Crais, memoir/fiction writer Gus Lee, romance novelist Nora Roberts, and thriller/suspense writers Stephen Coonts and Jeffrey Deaver, among others. (See the Annual Events & Festivals chapter.)

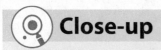 **Close-up**

CC's Summer Festival

When it comes to summer arts festivals, Colorado Springs can rival any of the prestigious mountain towns like Aspen or Vail. Don't believe it? It's true—thanks to **Colorado College.**

Colorado College's annual **Summer Festival of the Arts,** which runs from June through August, features two major festivals; a vocal arts symposium; and a series of world-class film, theater, literary readings, comedy, and art events. The festival program has garnered national prominence and has provided opportunities for performers from around the globe.

The **Summer Music Festival,** held each June, is a teaching festival in which advanced music students study and perform with renowned professional musicians. Also, professional musicians offer a series of concerts. Past highlights have included: a world premiere by New York–based composer and saxophonist Patrick Zimmerli; performances by cellist Bion Tsang, bronze medal winner at the IX International Tchaikovsky Competition and faculty member at the University of Texas; and Jon Nakamatsu, gold medal winner at the X Van Cliburn International Piano Competition. The Summer Music Festival is directed by Susan Grace, a member of the Quattro Mani Piano Duo and a 2005 Grammy nominee.

The **Colorado College Dance Festival** runs from late June to July, and features myriad global dance styles and cultures, with classes open to the public, an "informance" lecture/performance followed by Q&A, a young artists' concert, and faculty gala performances. Students study technical form, range of motion, ballet, yoga, African, hip-hop, dance movement, and therapy. The festival is a celebration of dance from around the world combined with the rich artistic talent found in Colorado Springs. Besides training dancers in diverse dance styles, the goal also is to enlighten and entertain the local community with innovative choreographic works that broaden the audience's understanding and love of dance.

The **Vocal Arts Symposium** in August, led by award-winning singer and teacher Martile Rowland in collaboration with the Opera Theatre of the Rockies, is a 3-week program. World-renowned faculty and students present a series of concerts including opera, jazz, and musical theater. Past program highlights have included scenes from *La Rondine,* by Puccini; *La Gioconda,* by Ponchielli; *The Marriage of Figaro,* by Mozart; *Norma,* by Bellini; and *West Side Story,* by Bernstein.

The festival also hosts a variety of performances and events by local organizations, such as the Shivers Concert Series, Windrider Film Forum, Amateur Pianists International, and the Colorado Springs Guitar Society. And check out the "Enrich Your Life" program, a series of community classes that range from beginning Chinese to art criticism.

Tickets for the annual Summer Festival of the Arts events, many of which are free, can be had by going online to **http://artsfestival.coloradocollege.edu.**

POETRY WEST

P.O. Box 2413
Colorado Springs, CO 80901
www.poetrywest.org

Poetry West nurtures the art of poetry in the Pikes Peak region. For years, it has offered monthly workshops, critique sessions, a writer's salon, and poetry readings to enhance the appreciation of poetry and local poets. The group publishes a poetry journal, *The Eleventh Muse*. The group usually meets the first Saturday of every month at the Worner Center, 902 N. Cascade Ave., on the Colorado College campus. Amateurs are welcome!

LITERARY EVENTS

AUTHOR FEST OF THE ROCKIES

(719) 685-5206
www.authorfestoftherockies.org

Locally published authors come together with those who would like to be published in a weekend event each autumn. Usually held at The Cliff House hotel and conference center, it also includes guest speakers and workshops. Co-sponsored by the Friends of the Manitou Springs Public Library.

i Want to be a writer? The Colorado Springs Fiction Writers Group offers free critique groups at Barnes & Noble stores and other local businesses. You can join at any time at no charge. Check them out online at www.colorado springsfictionwritersgroup.org.

PIKES PEAK WRITERS CONFERENCE

www.ppwc.net

This annual spring event, co-sponsored by the Pikes Peak Library District (719-531-6333 or www.ppld.org), is one of the most prestigious, heavily attended events of its type in Colorado. (See also previous category, Pikes Peak Writers, and the Annual Events & Festivals chapter.)

MUSIC

BLACK ROSE ACOUSTIC SOCIETY

P.O. Box 165
Colorado Springs, CO 80901-0165
www.blackroseacoustic.org/index.htm

Love acoustic music? This group's for you! The Black Rose Acoustic Society is dedicated to the education, performance, enjoyment, and preservation of all types of traditional acoustic music in the Black Forest and Colorado Springs area. The Society holds an open stage event every second Friday of the month at the Black Forest Community Center. There are also weekly jam sessions, private and group lessons, workshops, and special events.

CHAMBER ORCHESTRA OF THE SPRINGS

P.O. Box 7911
Colorado Springs, CO 80933-7911
(719) 633-3649
www.chamberorchestraofthesprings
.org/forhire.html

In 1981, the orchestra now known as the Chamber Orchestra of the Springs began with a small number of players who loved chamber music. It was organized into an orchestra in 1984 by several amateur, semiprofessional, and retired professional musicians wanting to perform serious symphonic music. Originally formed as the Colorado Chamber Orchestra Society, it changed to its current name in 1986. Today, the orchestra performs five concerts per year, accompanying accomplished professional musicians.

*COLORADO SPRINGS PHILHARMONIC

111 S. Tejon St., Suite 102
(719) 575-9632
www.csphilmonic.org

The Colorado Springs Philharmonic is the only professional orchestra in southern Colorado, performing about 40 concerts each year. That includes the seven-concert Classical Masterworks series, the Philharmonic Pops series, a new Vanguard Series featuring 20th-century composers, and "Philharmonic Kids" (a family series). They also present several holiday events, including *The Nutcracker*, with a guest ballet company, Christmas classics, and a New Year's Eve concert. For many years known as the Colorado Springs Symphony, it has had a series of prestigious conductors. In its most recent incarnation, as the Colorado Springs Philharmonic, it has managed to stay alive financially when other similar-sized orchestras around the country have folded. Over the years, its stellar list of guest artists has included such luminaries as the late Mstislav Rostropovich and Joshua Bell.

i New season ticket subscribers to the Colorado Springs Philharmonic get 50 percent off the price for their first season.

COLORADO SPRINGS YOUTH SYMPHONY

1801 N. Howard Ave.
(719) 633-3901
www.csysa.com

If you have a budding young musician in your life, this is the place to direct them. If you want to hear the symphonic stars of tomorrow, come and listen! This comprehensive instrumental music education association has, since 1980, served approximately 450 young musicians, ages 7 to 18, who audition for 6 orchestras and wind ensembles. The organization is nationally and internationally recognized, having placed first at the International Youth Music Festival in Salzburg, Austria.

PIKES PEAK JAZZ AND SWING SOCIETY

P.O. Box 6802
Colorado Springs, CO 80934
www.ppjass.org

Livening up the local music scene is the Pikes Peak Jazz and Swing Society. Its stated mission is "to preserve, support and foster jazz in its various forms; to provide encouragement to jazz musicians in their effort, including providing scholarships for jazz education; to assist members in their knowledge and enjoyment of jazz; to provide a focal point for the exchange of information about jazz and jazz musicians; and to provide a social environment in which to experience jazz." Whew! Sessions are held the second Sunday of every month and feature a variety of music, jamming, and dancing at The Olympian Plaza Reception and Event Center. All activities are open to the public for free or at minimal charge. During the summer, the Jazz and Swing Society and the city parks department host Jazz in the Park, also free and open to the public.

UNITED STATES AIR FORCE ACADEMY BAND

520 Otis St.
(719) 554-BAND (2263)
www.usafacademyband.af.mil

Located on Peterson Air Force Base and consisting of 10 performing units and 72 professional musicians, the Academy Band

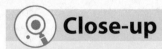 **Close-up**

The "Bee" Factor

Probably no one has been a bigger supporter of the arts in Colorado Springs than the late **Beatrice "Bee" Vradenburg.** It's said she got her nickname not because it was a diminutive of her given name, but because she was always such a busy bee! Vradenburg was born Beatrice White in 1922, in Manhattan, KS, and grew up in Washington, DC. A childhood love of art and music led her to study art history at Oberlin College in Ohio, where she met George Vradenburg Jr. They married in 1942 and four years later, after George's service in World War II, they moved to Colorado Springs, which would remain their home until Bee's death in 2000. George died a few months later.

For five decades, Bee's passion and persistence transformed the cultural climate of Colorado Springs. Those who knew her call it "the Bee factor." Petite but dynamic, she was well known for tackling new projects with gusto and achieving goals others thought impossible.

Under the nearly four decades of leadership Bee provided as general manager of the Colorado Springs Symphony Orchestra, the organization grew from a fledgling music group with an annual budget of $25,000 to a nationally recognized orchestra with a budget of $2 million that always operated in the black. She received a salary for her position—a salary she always donated right back to the symphony. Pianist Van Cliburn and violinist Isaac Stern were family friends and frequent guests in her home.

She also was a major force behind the construction of the $14 million Pikes Peak Center, which opened in 1982 and remains the cultural cornerstone of the city. She "retired" from the symphony in 1990 but remained active in the local arts scene. Among her many other achievements are:

- Founding board member of Performing Arts for Youth Organization (PAYO), which brings performers into public schools and still operates today.

is one of two premier bands in the Air Force. The band maintains a rigorous schedule of national concert tours, performing public concerts and civic and military functions for more than 2.5 million people annually from coast to coast. Audience members can expect to hear a wide variety of musical styles, from fresh, original works composed by the world's most renowned composers to standard and contemporary band tunes, traditional American classics, vocal selections, and patriotic songs—naturally!

OPERA

OPERA THEATRE OF THE ROCKIES
P.O. Box 8110
Colorado Springs, CO 80933
(719) 570-1950
www.operatheatreoftherockies.org

Opera Theater of the Rockies presents memorable opera that spotlights Colorado's top artists. Professional training and opportunities for performance also are provided for emerging artists. The Opera Theatre Goes to School program educates teachers on

- Helped create the Colorado Council on the Arts (CCA), also serving as a member of CCA's first board.

- In the 1970s, launched the Fabulous Fourth celebration in Colorado Springs's Memorial Park, which attracted nearly 100,000 people annually until recently, when the city cut its funding due to economic belt-tightening.

- Created the consortium that produced the acclaimed Broadmoor Christmas Pops on Ice for 17 years, till the old Broadmoor World Arena was torn down.

- Created the Colorado Springs Youth Symphony in 1980. It now serves about 500 children annually.

- Was the senior adviser involved in the creation of Colorado Springs Dance Theatre, the state's only nonprofit presenter exclusively of national and international dance companies.

- A founding board member of Springspree, a citywide festival now in its third decade.

- A founding board member of the nationally acclaimed DaVinci Quartet, now based in Denver.

- A founding board member of Opera Theatre of the Rockies.

In a 1990 article in the *Colorado Springs Gazette* (then *Gazette Telegraph*), conductor Charles Ansbacher said of his friend: "Bee is a brilliant woman, dedicated, unselfish, and a woman who has warmth and generosity of spirit. She has exuded concern for musicians, has an absolutely untiring commitment to the betterment of the community, and a generosity of spirit."

And she had a lot of spunk, our busy, busy Bee.

ways to integrate opera into the classroom curriculum.

ORGANIZATIONS

BEE VRADENBURG FOUNDATION
730 N. Nevada Ave.
(719) 477-0185
www.beevradenburgfoundation.org
The Bee Vradenburg Foundation, named for one of the city's staunchest supporters of the arts, was established in 2001 "to advance (her) vision of a thriving and diverse cultural community by investing in the excellence, innovation and sustainability of the arts in the Pikes Peak region." It sustains existing arts organizations and encourages new ones through its financial endowments. Recent recipients have included the Business of Art Center, Colorado Springs Chorale, the Colorado Springs Fine Arts Center, the Colorado Springs Philharmonic, and the Colorado Springs World Arena.

CULTURAL OFFICE OF THE PIKES PEAK REGION
101 S. Tejon St., Suite 101
(719) 634-2204
www.coppercolo.org
The Cultural Office of the Pikes Peak Region, or COPPeR, is a nonprofit organization, governed by a board of community leaders representing various fields of the arts, nonprofit, public, and business sectors. COPPeR says it "takes a strategic view of the Pikes Peak region to ensure that cultural services reach all people and that the arts are used to positively address issues of economic development, education, tourism, regional branding and civic life." It strives to provide an umbrella service, covering such areas as marketing and communication, data gathering, and advocacy for the arts industry. COPPeR also is the host for the valuable peakradar.com site, which lists just about any arts-related event you can imagine, from church choir concerts to major art exhibits.

EL POMAR FOUNDATION
1661 Mesa Ave.
(719) 577-7000
www.elpomar.org
Established in 1937 by Broadmoor hotel builder Spencer Penrose and his wife, Julie, the foundation has long been a supporter of the arts in the Pikes Peak region. Over the years, it has poured millions of dollars into the arts all over Colorado. Its recipients include Colorado College, the Colorado Springs Fine Arts Center, and numerous local arts organizations (as well as medical services and churches). (See also the Close-up in the History chapter.)

MANITOU SPRINGS ARTS COUNCIL
P.O. Box 61
Manitou Springs, CO 80829
www.manitouspringsartscouncil.org
Established in 2004, the Manitou Springs Arts Council strives to preserve, promote, and pursue collaborations between the arts and the community.

MSAC serves as the umbrella organization for the arts, which are such an integral part of Manitou. It supports visual, performance, holistic, literary, and culinary disciplines. It also helps bring the arts to the local schools and to the public. It works hard to preserve Manitou Springs's heritage as a place for artists to thrive and a community of people who appreciate the arts.

PIKES PEAK ARTS COUNCIL
P.O. Box 1073
Colorado Springs, CO 80901
(719) 475-2465
http://pikespeakartscouncil.org
The stated mission of the Pikes Peak Arts Council is "to serve as advocates for and support the arts and artists in the Pikes Peak Region." Its goals include: to identify, acknowledge, encourage, and advance creative artists from the Pikes Peak Region and assist, promote, and support local arts organizations; to provide greater recognition of local artists; and to distribute an events calendar, brochures, and other materials to the local community. It also aims to produce a cultural assessment of the Pikes Peak Region, documenting the multiple impacts of creative expression, and to produce at least one arts-related event each year to showcase all art forms for the citizens of the Pikes Peak region. Why? Well, they hope to elevate arts appreciation, and create high uniform standards of craftsmanship and artistic integrity, they

say. Lofty goals, but they've done all this and more to support the local arts community.

THEATER

COLORADO SPRINGS FINE ARTS CENTER
30 W. Dale St.
(719) 634-5581
www.csfineartscenter.org
The award-winning resident Colorado Springs Fine Arts Center Theatre Company presents a diverse program of 4 musical productions and 2 plays each season. The recently renovated SaGaJi Theatre, built in 1936 as part of the original arts center, offers historic Art Deco–inspired elegance with state-of-the-art sound and lighting technology. It has been the venue where such greats as the Martha Graham Dance Company have performed. This beautiful, 400-seat theater is now the setting for high-quality productions that range from *Sweeney Todd* to *A Christmas Carol*. The company does them all in style, with clever sets and costumes. A small, fine-dining restaurant in the lobby is the perfect place to have dinner beforehand.

MANITOU ART THEATRE
1367 Pecan St.
(719) 685-4729 or (719) 465-6321
http://themat.org
The MAT was established in 2002 to provide a full-service theatrical venue. It offers classes for all ages, shows for kids, premieres of new plays, and improv in a friendly setting. With just 87 seats but a loyal following, it has managed to grow in recent years without overreaching its abilities. They focus on producing new plays for all ages and have presented 32 new plays for adults and children in their short tenure. They do about 150 performances a year throughout the region. Both talented local actors and professional guest artists have appeared in their productions. Many of their productions have a physical theater component and may feature dance, comedy, improvisation, music, poetry, clowning, and the circus arts. The best thing about the MAT? There isn't a bad seat in the house. The theater is fully wheelchair accessible with dedicated parking and stage-level seating.

PIKES PEAK CENTER
190 S. Cascade Ave.
(719) 520-SHOW (7469)
www.pikespeakcenter.com
This is the obvious choice for Broadway touring companies presenting such productions as *Mamma Mia, Beauty and the Beast, Legally Blonde,* and *Spamalot*. The acoustically wonderful hall makes the sound as clear to the very top row of the top balcony as it is to the folks in front row center! An annual *Nutcracker* ballet and other dance performances also appear here on a regular basis, as well as occasional opera productions. Other groups, such as the Radio City Music Hall Rockettes, have performed here, too.

i Want to participate in some of the fun, local performing arts? Check out the Auditions listings in *The Gazette*'s Friday "Go!" section each week. Local theater companies, musical groups, and others are always looking for new talent!

STAR BAR PLAYERS
P.O. Box 2488
Colorado Springs, CO 80901
(719) 357-5228
www.starbarplayers.org

Founded in 1972 by a group of would-be actors who frequented a local watering hole, the Star Bar, the Star Bar Players is the oldest theater company in Colorado Springs. Their award-winning productions often feature the community's finest actors, of which there are a surprising number. They've had their ups and downs, but recently completed a stellar year of productions in their new digs, the Attitudes Performing Arts Center, 1502–1504 N. Hancock Ave. They do classics like *Waiting for Godot* and quirky new scripts, too. They charge a modest ticket price and, because they feel theater should be for all people, Saturday afternoons are "pay what you can" prices.

THEATREWORKS
1420 Austin Bluffs Pkwy.
(719) 255-3232
www.theatreworkscs.org

Located on the campus of the University of Colorado at Colorado Springs, the relatively new Dusty Loo Bon Vivant Theatre boasts an intimate space—150–250 seats (depending on the production). It is the home of Theatreworks, a professional theater company affiliated with UCCS. Its outstanding productions include an annual tribute to William Shakespeare, both obscure and popular plays, and special events throughout the year. Theatreworks is associated with, but independent from, the university academic theater program responsible for teaching classes, delivering degrees, and mentoring students, among other things.

THIN AIR THEATRE COMPANY
P.O. Box 181
Cripple Creek, CO 80813
(719) 689-6402
http://butteoperahouse.com

A repertory company of paid actors from all over the country—who audition for parts—Thin Air presents one of the oldest forms of theater around, the melodrama. Exactly what it sounds like, the over-the-top, fun, and often funny productions include a lot of audience participation (coached to hiss, boo, and applaud). It's a rollicking good time, especially after the play itself, when the cast presents an olio—a collection of skits, silly songs, and comedy routines reminiscent of vaudeville.

ATTRACTIONS

You can't really say you've visited the Pikes Peak region without ascending Pikes Peak! And no one should miss the stunning red sandstone spires and formations of Garden of the Gods, a city park at the foot of the mountain. The city also is home to the nation's only mountain zoological park, the Cheyenne Mountain Zoo, where you can hop on a Sky Ride that overlooks the zoo and the city below.

The US Olympic Training Center also is here, with world-class athletes in a variety of sports practicing year round. The ProRodeo Hall of Fame honors athletes of the Western kind. The US Air Force Academy also draws hordes of visitors each year to its visitor center and architecturally famous Cadet Chapel.

Nearby towns also offer a grand variety of attractions. Manitou Springs has one of the nation's oldest amusement arcades (got a nickel?), and Cripple Creek, west of Pikes Peak, recalls the area's rich mining history with museums and mine tours. It's also home to the resurrected pastime of legalized gambling (and you'll need more than a nickel).

Cañon City, about an hour southwest of Colorado Springs, has many attractions, including a scenic railroad and the Royal Gorge with its world-famous suspension bridge.

You can see wild animals, or take a wild ride on a river. Hike, bike, and climb to your heart's content. Learn local history and explore a cave. Outdoors stuff rules here, but there are indoor amusements, too.

There truly is something for everyone.

OVERVIEW

This chapter can't possibly include every attraction in the Pikes Peak region—it would take the entire book to do that! We didn't include historic districts such as Old Colorado City and Manitou Springs, or sites such as Colorado College, because they are not single attractions per se, and because they are covered elsewhere in this book. But we've included the well-established and most popular attractions visitors most often want to see (like the zoo), or things they most often want to do (like river rafting). They are divided up by categories (such as museums or natural wonders) and alphabetized after that. There are some museums listed under Historic Sites, because the museum building itself is historic. Addresses are in Colorado Springs unless otherwise noted. Hours for attractions are complicated; they change seasonally and sometimes daily. Check websites or a visitors' guide for current hours of operation. Now pick your pleasure.

ATTRACTIONS

If you can't find enough to keep you busy for a week, you're just not trying!

Price Code

The following price code gives you an idea of what the regular adult admission might be at the following places. Most have children's rates and senior discounts, but the ages vary wildly. Check online or call in advance if you are concerned about the cost. Some are free, and we'll tell you that, too.

$. . . . . less than $5
$$ . . . .$5 to $10
$$$ . . . . $10 to $20
$$$$ . . . . more than $20

ADVENTURES

ACADEMY RIDING STABLES $$$$
4 El Paso Blvd.
(888) 700-0410 or (719) 633-5667
www.academyridingstables.com
Even if you've never been on a horse before, this place will make a cowboy out of you—if just for a day. It's a great way to immerse yourself in the natural splendor and serene landscape of the Garden of the Gods. This is how the first visitors saw it more than a hundred years ago—on horseback. It's a great family outing, and you'll be guided by real cowboys who will point out some of the interesting red rock formations, including the Balanced Rock, Sleeping Giant, Snakehead Rock, Kissing Camels, and Siamese Twins. They'll choose a horse that suits your skill level and you can pick from 1- or 2-hour rides. Horseback rides in the park are available throughout the summer months; from Labor Day through Memorial Day, you can enjoy a perimeter ride (about 3 hours) around the outer edges of the park. They

also offer pony rides for kids ages 2 to 7 (approximately 15 minutes long). The stables are open year-round except on Thanksgiving and Christmas days.

FRONT RANGE CLIMBING
COMPANY $$$$
722 N. 31st St.
(866) 572-3722 or (719) 473-8349
www.frontrangeclimbing.com
You spot them in the Garden of the Gods and on rock walls all over the West: climbers. It's not the world's easiest sport, but here in Colorado Springs, Front Range Climbing Company offers some of the best guided rock climbing in the state. Start with the very basics or build upon your past experience and go to the cutting edge of technical climbing. Climbing classes are offered year round. What about winter, you say? Well, they also offer ice climbing instruction! This is the kind of stuff you read about in adventure magazines—and you can do it here.

River Rafting

River rafting is one of those sports identified with Colorado. You can't do it right here in Colorado Springs, of course—the creeks here are still too small. But you can do it an hour away in the Cañon City area on the mighty Arkansas River. Be aware rafting can be dangerous, so go with a professional outfitter and follow directions. And be prepared to get wet. Here are the names of a few outfitters who will set you up for the thrill ride of your life:

AMERICAN ADVENTURE
EXPEDITIONS $$$$
(800) 288-0675 or (719) 395-2409
www.americanadventure.com

ARKANSAS RIVER TOURS $$$$
(800) 321-4352 or (719) 942-4362
www.arkansasrivertours.com

**BILL DVORAK KAYAK
   AND RAFTING** $$$$
(800) 824-3795
www.dvorakexpeditions.com

**ECHO CANYON RIVER
   EXPEDITIONS** $$$$
(800) 547-3246 or (719) 275-3154
www.raftecho.com

For a full list of outfitters, go online to the Colorado River Outfitters Association website: www.croa.org.

AMUSEMENTS

ARCADE AMUSEMENTS, INC. $
930 Block Manitou Ave., Manitou Springs
(719) 685-9815

The bells and whistles here are all real—and audible. Commonly called the Manitou Arcade, this haven for arcade junkies is scattered among the six buildings behind Patsy's Original Candy Shop on Manitou Avenue. Here, you'll find the original Pac Man game, but that's probably the newest thing there! You'll find pinball machines (some dating back to the 1930s) you can play for a nickel or dime or quarter. There's a Skeeball alley—grab those tickets and trade them in for a cheap souvenir! What can we say? It's fun! The very epitome of cheap thrills. Kids will like it, and adults of a certain age will be hard to pry away. Admission is free. What you'll spend is all the change in your pocket—and maybe a little more.

**IRON SPRINGS CHATEAU
   MELODRAMA** $$$$
444 Ruxton Ave., Manitou Springs
(719) 685-5104 or (719) 685-5572

Boo! Hiss! Hooray! It's one of the few times performers really want the audience to participate in the theatrics. It's called melodrama, and it has been a tradition at the Iron Springs Chateau in Manitou Springs for half a century. The dinner theater experience includes a fried chicken dinner with all the trimmings, served family style. After dinner, the melodrama ensues, complete with a hero, lady in distress, and detestable villain. Puns and other bad jokes rule the script. That's followed by a sing-along and olio (vaudeville-style comedy and skits). It's a family-friendly evening, in all. Don't wear out your voice!

HISTORIC SITES

**✳COLORADO SPRINGS PIONEERS
   MUSEUM** FREE
215 S. Tejon St.
(719) 385-5990
www.springsgov.com

If you're curious to know more about the city you're going to visit, stop at the Colorado Springs Pioneers Museum. You can't miss it. It's the gorgeous 1903 El Paso County Courthouse situated dead center on a full city block downtown. The building itself, rescued from demolition by a local effort, is its own most stunning display. Ornate handiwork unlike anything seen in buildings today will fascinate fans of architecture. A pristinely restored courtroom includes the judge's chambers and glowingly preserved wooden seats and benches. The museum has permanent exhibits that illustrate the city's—and region's—history, and rotating exhibits meant to explore specific aspects of our past (say, the anniversary of Zebulon Pike's sighting of the peak to a display examining our role in World War II). An irreplaceable city history archive resides in the basement. The museum has been in danger of closing due to lack of funds but remains open for now. There is quite a bit of metered on-street parking around the perimeter of the block and there's a parking garage half a block north (where all-day parking is just $1 on Saturday). Closed Sun and Mon.

FLYING W RANCH $$$$
3330 Chuckwagon Rd.
(800) 232-3599
www.flyingw.com
The Flying W Ranch, now surrounded by the city, is a working mountain cattle ranch with an authentic Western village and, incidentally, a Western chuckwagon supper. You go more for the cowboy music and the village than the food—barbecue and beans—and to sit under a starry sky and sing cattle songs. The Flying W Wranglers have recorded a fair amount of early Western music (think Gene Autry, not Toby Keith). During the peak summer season, they serve supper to and entertain more than 1,000 guests a night. An indoor venue is handy if it decides to rain. In summer, there are two seatings: at 5 p.m. and 8 p.m. In winter, they only have one show on Friday and Saturday nights.

GHOST TOWN MUSEUM $$
400 S. 21st St.
(719) 634-0696
www.ghosttownmuseum.com
If you get a rare rainy day in Colorado Springs, you might be looking for something to do indoors. Ghost Town Museum offers a historic look at the life and times of the Old West, from the late 1800s to early 1900s. Established in 1954 inside the cavernous workshop of the old Colorado

Midland Railroad, it includes a blacksmith shop, saloon, general store, livery stable, and Victorian home. Each building is packed with artifacts from the era. There's also an old-timey arcade with games (like a shootin' gallery) and hands-on activities, like panning for gold. Closed Sun.

For More Information . . .

If you plan to visit any of these area attractions, get good, up-to-date information and some great discount coupons from the annual **Official Visitors Guide to Colorado Springs and the Pikes Peak Region.** It's available by writing to: Pikes Peak Country Attractions, 354 Manitou Ave., Manitou Springs, CO 80829, by calling (800) 525-2250, or by going online to www.pikes-peak.com. Information is also available from **Experience Colorado Springs,** 515 S. Cascade Ave., Colorado Springs, CO 80903, by calling (800) 368-4748, or by going online to www.VisitCOS. com. You also can pick up copies of the current visitors' guide at area hotels and attractions.

GLEN EYRIE   FREE–$$$
3820 N. 30th St.
(800) 944-4536 or (719) 634-0808
www.gleneyrie.org
This historic Scottish-style stone castle, built by city founder Gen. William Palmer as his home, has been owned by The Navigators, an international Christian organization, for many years. It was, for a while, closed to the

public. Today, however, visitors can drive the beautifully landscaped grounds (check out the rose garden); hike a challenging, stream-crossing trail on the back of the property; and even make reservations for high tea and a tour. Admission for gawking and hiking is free, but the tea and tour do have a charge. You also can spend the night. (See the Accommodations chapter.)

MANITOU CLIFF DWELLINGS $$
10 Cliff Dwellings Rd., Manitou Springs
(800) 354-9971 or (719) 685-5242
www.cliffdwellingsmuseum.com
OK, so you can't make it down to Mesa Verde National Park on this trip. You can get a small taste of the famous cliff dwellings there if you visit the Manitou Cliff Dwellings site in Manitou Springs. Moved here from a ranch in Southwestern Colorado to protect them from destruction, and preserved under a red sandstone overhang, these authentic Ancestral Puebloan structures were originally built more than 700 years ago. Unlike the ones in the national park, there are no Do Not Touch signs. Visitors may touch and go inside these architectural remnants of an American Indian culture that roamed the Four Corners area of the Southwest from 1200 BC to AD 1300. There's also a replica of a mesa-top structure and a nature walk with well-labeled plants and flowers indigenous to Colorado. Also on-site is a museum dedicated to the native culture of that era. If you use the address above with a GPS unit, it may not work. So try looking for the intersection of Washington Street and US 24.

MCALLISTER HOUSE $
423 N. Cascade Ave.
(719) 635-7925
http://mcallisterhouse.org

In a city where most of the first homes were constructed of wood, Maj. Henry McAllister and his wife, Elizabeth, chose to build theirs of brick. There is a photo of it from 1875 that closely pinpoints the date of its completion. Built by architect George Summers (who also designed Gen. Palmer's Glen Eyrie and the Grace Episcopal Church downtown), it survived a wind storm that demolished many other nearby homes. Some of the woodwork was crafted by carpenter Winfield Scott Stratton, who later made a major gold find and became a millionaire. McAllister lived in the house till his death in 1921. For the next 30 years, it was rented by a woman who used it as a candy and gift shop. When she died, in 1958, it was sold. A few years later, it was acquired by the National Society of the Colonial Dames of America, who restored it and turned it into the museum seen today. Closed Sun, Mon, and the entire month of Jan.

MIRAMONT CASTLE $$
9 Capitol Hill Ave., Manitou Springs
(888) 685-1011 or (719) 685-1011
www.miramontcastle.org
.A Catholic priest born in 1854 in France, Father Jean Baptiste Francolon was the son of a wealthy, aristocratic family. He came to the US in 1878 when he was 24 years old to serve as secretary to the bishop of Sante Fe, NM. In 1892, he came as a missionary priest to Manitou, which was already famous for its healing waters and clean air, in hopes of restoring his failing health. His mother arrived in Manitou from New Mexico in July 1893. He built this mansion for her and filled it with fine furnishings, tapestries, oil paintings, statuary, antique vestments and laces, and native artifacts, exhibiting the family's wealth. In 1900, the pair left Colorado

Springs unexpectedly and for good, taking valuable artwork but leaving the rest. She died a few months later and he died in 1922 in New York. The mansion was vacant until 1904, when the Sisters of Mercy purchased it for the housing of tuberculosis patients. It was sold in 1946 to private owners and eventually was broken up into apartments for rent. In 1976, the Manitou Springs Historical Society was finally able to buy it and restore it to the home it once was. A stunningly enormous fireplace, some original artwork and furnishings, grand architecture, and embellishments make this place worth a tour. If you have time, stop and take a break in the tea room, too. Closed Mon in winter, and on major holidays.

ROCK LEDGE RANCH HISTORIC SITE $$
30th Street at Gateway Road
(719) 578-6777
www.rockledgeranch.com

This living history site, complete with costumed characters on certain days, provides a glimpse into life in the late 1800s and early 1900s in the Pikes Peak region. There are gardens being cultivated, livestock being tended, household chores being performed in the Orchard House, and all the accoutrements of a turn-of-the-century farm that once provided produce to the local hotels. It's a lovely spot, with a barn and a pond and lots of trees and flowers. Open Wed through Sat in summer, and for special events only the rest of the year.

MILITARY

FORT CARSON MUSEUM
Fort Carson Main Gate
(719) 633-2867
http://fortcarsonmuseum.com

We can't tell you a lot about this museum because it is under construction. Ground was broken in 2010. Phase I, with a display of temporary artifacts, will be the first one to open. Phase II will be a larger, permanent historical facility; and not-quite-defined Phase III won't open till 2013. But you can keep an eye on its progress on the website.

UNITED STATES AIR FORCE ACADEMY   FREE
I-25 at North Gate Road (Exit 156 B)
(719) 333-2025
www.usafa.af.mil

Military buffs (and college football fans) won't want to miss a visit to the nation's youngest military academy, the prestigious US Air Force Academy, one of the region's top attractions. A vast complex of buildings and open space, it has an informative visitor center where you learn all about what has happened, and is still happening, here. The 31,600-square-foot Barry Goldwater Visitor's Center contains exhibits, a snack bar, and a gift shop. A one-third-mile paved nature trail east of the facility allows visitors to walk to the architecturally stunning Cadet Chapel. A 14-minute film about the academy experience is shown regularly in the 250-seat theater. During the school year, catch the cadets on parade. If you're in town during an Air Force football game, do your best to get tickets! They put on a good show. Their basketball team and hockey team are top-notch, too. All visitors must show their driver's licenses to the guard and can expect to have their vehicle inspected or other random security measures taken prior to entering the Academy. Visitors who refuse to comply with security measures will not be allowed access on base. Closed to visitors on major holidays.

MUSEUMS

AMERICAN NUMISMATIC ASSOCIATION'S MONEY MUSEUM $
818 N. Cascade Ave.
(719) 632-2646
www.money.org
Who doesn't love money? And to learn all about it, head to the American Numismatic Association's national Money Museum, right next door to Colorado College. Displays at this attraction, the world's largest museum devoted entirely to money, will soon set you straight: It's not all about dollars and cents. Money is intricately entwined with history, culture, science, and art. See rare coins, ancient forms of money, and mistakes made while crafting the stuff. You'll never look at money the same way again. Tours can be scheduled by appointment. Closed Sun and Mon.

EL POMAR CARRIAGE MUSEUM   FREE
10 Lake Circle
(719) 577-7065
www.elpomar.org/what-we-do/
will-rogers-shrine-and-carriage-museum
Right across the street from The Broadmoor hotel, tucked into its new 8,500-square-foot digs inside Broadmoor Hall, is the El Pomar Carriage Museum. This longtime attraction gets most of its visits from hotel guests, but it's open to the public daily and it's free. The museum houses an impressive array of historic carriages, cars, and American memorabilia belonging to Broadmoor founders Spencer and Julie Penrose, who started the museum in 1941. Walk in and take a tour that includes 3 cars from the original Pikes Peak Auto Hill Climb race (from the 1920s), Mrs. Penrose's classic 1928 Cadillac limousine, and a 1906 Renault. There also are 2 carriages

that belonged to former presidents (William Henry Harrison and Chester A. Arthur) and an assortment of harnesses, saddles, and other riding tack. Parking around the hall can be tight, but it is available nearby in the parking garage and the museum will validate your ticket.

MAY NATURAL HISTORY MUSEUM $$
710 Rock Creek Canyon Rd.
(800) 666-3841 or (719) 576-0450
Driving south of Colorado Springs on CO 115, you might spot a gargantuan Hercules beetle perched on a hill right alongside the road. Don't swerve and go into the ditch! It's metal and it's just your signal to take a hard right and enter the amazing world of John May. In 1929, May and his father started exhibiting their fantastic tropical bug and butterfly collection at the Canadian National Exhibition in Toronto. In the 1940s, May built a permanent site to house the collection here in Colorado Springs. At any given time, more than 8,000 of the collection's 100,000 items are on display.

You never knew so many different bugs existed! They range from almost microscopic critters to 10-inch moths from India. And the butterflies are gorgeous. Look up to see the taxidermied bats, too. Shiver. Closed Oct 1 through May 1. Open daily in summer.

i Because afternoon thunderstorms can blow in almost any summer day, it's a good idea to do your outdoors stuff in the morning in case there's a storm in the afternoon. Save the museums for later in the day. That way, weather won't put a damper on your fun!

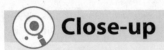

Close-up

Cripple Creek Attractions

Cripple Creek and Victor were the heart of what became known as the "world's greatest gold camp" after gold was discovered here by prospector Bob Womack in 1890. His discovery inspired the last Colorado Gold Rush. Shortly thereafter, W. S. Stratton found the world-famous Independence Mine and although $500 million in gold was eventually mined out of the district, many believe the mother lode has never been found.

By 1900 Cripple Creek and nearby Victor were substantial communities, and in 1903 the towns survived a violent miners' strike. Eventually, the mines played out and the towns began to fade; in fact, they were almost ghost towns at one point. They drew a few weekend tourists to see the melodrama and visit some shops or restaurants, and business was strictly seasonal. Then, in 1991, the state authorized legalized gambling in historic towns, which gave Cripple Creek a shot in the economic arm.

Though the old underground mines were exhausted, open pit mining resumed in 1994 east of Cripple Creek, near Victor. Today, Cripple Creek is currently more of a gambling and tourist town than a ghost town. Casinos now occupy many historic buildings. Casino gambling has been successful in bringing revenue and vitality back into the area. Old attractions have been renovated. New ones have sprung up. It's a great place to spend a day or weekend, even if you don't gamble.

Here are some of its attractions:

Butte Opera House: Need a good laugh? The Thin Air Theatre Company is just the ticket. Or, rather, they have the tickets—to a matinee or evening performance of their latest melodrama. A long-standing Cripple Creek tradition, the crazy theatrics will have you hissing and booing to your heart's content. After the melodrama, the cast changes and presents a vaudeville-style olio with skits and songs and other silly stuff. The opera house is located over the fire station, so performances are occasionally interrupted by the fire siren! 139 Bennett Ave., (719) 689-3247 or (877) 689-6402, www.butteoperahouse.com ($$$)

Cripple Creek Heritage Center: This new, 11,600-square-foot center overlooks the town of Cripple Creek and the Sangre de Cristo mountains beyond. State-of-the-art doesn't begin to describe what awaits visitors here: Multiple hands-on exhibits combine interactive technology with tactile, audio, and video techniques. You'll learn the history of the gold camp in a fun and fascinating way. You also can leave your car here and ride a free shuttle down into town, where parking can be tight on weekends. (877) 858-4653 or (719) 689-3315 (FREE)

Cripple Creek District Museum: The museum complex includes five historic buildings full of railroad history, mining memorabilia, maps, paintings, glass and china, children's toys, furnishings, an assay office, a photograph gallery, Indian artifacts, mineral displays, 2 turn-of-the-century cabins, and 2 Victorian apartments. 5th Street and Bennett Avenue, (719) 689-9540 ($)

Cripple Creek & Victor Narrow Gauge Railroad: The nostalgic whistle of a train will remind you that the early residents of this town got around on the rails, not by car. The historic Cripple Creek & Victor Railroad features a steam locomotive that takes visitors on a narrated winding 4-mile trip through the historic gold mining district. Trains leave the old depot daily from mid-May through mid-October, taking visitors on a trip that includes stops at special points of interest and offers photo opportunities. The track heads south from Cripple Creek, crosses a reconstructed trestle, and stops at a deserted mining town before returning to the depot. 5th Street and Bennett Avenue, (719) 689-2640, www .cripplecreekrailroad.com ($$$)

Mollie Kathleen Gold Mine: Ever wonder what life was like for a gold miner in one of those dark, dank mines? Now you can see for yourself when you take a tour of the Mollie Kathleen. You'll descend 1,000 feet into America's only vertical shaft gold mine. You can view gold veins in their natural state, see them operate some of the machinery it took to extract that gold, and experience what life underground must have been like. Wear a jacket! It's very chilly down there. 9388 CO 67, (719) 689-2466, www.goldminetours.com ($$$)

Outlaws & Lawmen Jail Museum: When a wild and woolly gold camp reaches a population of 50,000 people, there are bound to be a few bad apples in the barrel. Cripple Creek had its share. And the jail was a popular place come Saturday night. The red brick building that served as the Teller County Jail for 90 years is now a museum. Take a look inside the tiny, closet-sized cells and imagine six guys sharing one! Burglars, robbers, highwaymen, and other minor criminals bunked with more serious offenders, including Robert Curry (aka Bob Lee), a member of the "Wild Bunch" gang who was captured after lawmen found him hiding right in town. Check out the cool murals on the walls, too. 126 W. Bennett Ave. (see Information below), (719) 689-6556 ($)

Old Homestead House Museum: It wasn't *exactly* a homestead. More like a brothel. But it was very homey! Nice curtains, lamps, rugs, and furniture made miners feel right cozy. It also was where they found the best prostitutes in town. One madam, named Pearl DeVere, reportedly charged $250 a night—and got it! She also was a noted local philanthropist and loved by many for her kindness. Her funeral was one of the biggest events the town ever had. (719) 689-9090 (see Information, below)

Victor: Unaffected by the resurrection of gambling, the old mining town of Victor remains much as it has for the past century, since gold mining became an endeavor of the rich. Famous radio newscaster Lowell Thomas grew up here, and there's a town museum that bears his name, located in a red brick 1899 hardware store. It's open mostly in summer. Victor Avenue and 3rd Street, (719) 689-5509, www.victorcolorado.com

Information: To find out more about all these attractions in Cripple Creek, call (877) 858-4653. The website, www.visitcripplecreek.com, has additional links to individual attractions as well as general information.

MICHAEL GARMAN MUSEUM & MAGIC TOWN $$

2411 W. Colorado Ave.
(800) 731-3908 or (719) 471-9391
www.michaelgarman.com

Local sculptor Michael Garman has captured the nitty-gritty of the people he sculpts, and captured equally the fancy of collectors and first-timers who see his rough-hewn cowboys, soldiers, and sports heroes. His stuff isn't pretty—but it's pretty engaging. He retired a few years ago, but you still can see and buy his sculptures at his Old Colorado City store/museum. That's free. What's even more fun is to go into the back and see his fantastic mock-up of an urban landscape circa 1930s—complete with hookers, drunks, bums, pool-shooters, poker players, and more. If you look closely, you'll spot the artist himself in this miniature cityscape. Using lights and mirrors, and sometimes holograms, the scenes in some rooms change from time to time (you can be a voyeur and nobody cares!) and if you look down the alleys between buildings you'll see sculpted trash and alley cats. Sort of like visiting the slums without actually having to be there. It's a kick!

WESTERN MUSEUM OF MINING AND INDUSTRY $$

225 N. Gate Blvd.
(800) 752-6558 or (719) 488-0880
www.wmmi.org

They like to brag that this is a museum that *works!* And they're not kidding. Yes, there are artifacts and such displayed, but there's so much more—in the form of actual, working mining equipment. Here's your chance to see the industry that shaped Colorado in action. What started as the 27-acre Museum of the West in 1970 soon changed to its current name in 1972 and has since focused on the rich mining history of the state. They might fire up their 37-ton Corliss Steam Engine, operate the stamp mill, tell you about the rocks you eat, let you try your hand at gold panning (not as easy as it looks), and see how mining families lived in the 1890s. You might even get to dress up like a miner. There's always something going on here, so check the website for special events and activities. Closed Sun.

NATURAL WONDERS

CAVE OF THE WINDS $$$

100 Cave of the Winds Rd.
(719) 685-5444
www.caveofthewinds.com

About 1.8 billion years ago—give or take a few months—Colorado's geology underwent some dramatic changes. The result of that natural upheaval and change was what is today called Cave of the Winds. Discovered by two boys out exploring in 1880, the cave got its name for the winds that whistled through it. That sound disappeared when a front entrance was created. But the stalactites and stalagmites and other formations (even with cheesy colored lighting) are impressive. The mile-long cavern includes a 60-foot-long, 40-foot-wide room with a 35-foot ceiling. You can take the easy, 45-minute walking tour on paved paths or you can get down and dirty with a spelunking adventure that might just activate your latent claustrophobia! In recent years, they've gotten into the geo-venture experience, including flashlight tours. A little bit spooky.

Close-up

✳Garden of the Gods

You won't believe **Garden of the Gods** is just a city park. The dramatic landscape of the 1,400-acre site northwest of downtown is worthy of national monument status, at least! And it's free.

Many visitors wonder, just how did it get its name? The story goes like this: In August 1859 two surveyors started out from Denver to establish a town site, soon to be called Colorado City. While exploring nearby locations, they came upon a beautiful area of sandstone formations. M. S. Beach, who related this incident, suggested that it would be a "capital place for a beer garden" when the country grew up. His companion, Rufus Cable, of a more poetic nature, exclaimed, "Beer Garden! Why it is a fit place for the gods to assemble. We will call it the Garden of the Gods."

Then, in 1879, city founder Gen. William Palmer reportedly urged his friend, Charles Elliott Perkins, the head of the Burlington Railroad, to establish a home in the garden and to build his railroad from Chicago to Colorado Springs. Although the Burlington never reached Colorado Springs, Perkins did purchase 240 acres in what is now the Garden of the Gods for a summer home. He later added to the property but never built on it, preferring to leave this wonderland in its natural state for the enjoyment of the public. Perkins died in 1907 before he made arrangements for the land to become a public park, although it had been open to the public for years. In 1909, Perkins's children, knowing their father's wishes for the site, gave his 480 acres to the City of Colorado Springs as a park "where it shall remain free to the public, where no intoxicating liquors shall be manufactured, sold, or dispensed, where no building or structure shall be erected except those necessary to properly care for, protect, and maintain the area as a public park."

Today, the soaring, interestingly shaped red sandstone rock formations with whimsical or descriptive names (Kissing Camels, Balanced Rock) thrust up through the earth and block out the bluest sky you ever saw. There are few buildings in the park. Roads that once penetrated its interior have been replaced by hiking trails. Rock climbing is allowed with proper equipment. But if you get stuck, there's a hefty fee for rescue. Paved paths thread through the central site, and there are hiking trails and horse trails (check out the nearby Academy Riding Stables, see Adventures in this chapter).

Stop at the visitor center first, both for helpful information and to learn about free daily tours and programs, from bird-watching to wildflower walks. Also catch the movie, which will explain how this geological wonder was formed. If there's time, visit the adjacent, historic Rock Ledge Ranch (see Historic Sites, this chapter) for an insightful local history lesson. The park is open dawn to dusk year-round. Located at 1805 N. 30th St. (at Gateway Road). For more information, contact (719) 634-6666, www.gardenofgods.com (FREE).

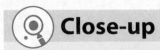

Close-up

✳Pikes Peak: America's Mountain

Pikes Peak. It's called America's Mountain—perhaps the most famous peak in North America, named for (but never climbed by) early explorer Zebulon Pike. Katharine Lee Bates once ascended it and wrote "America the Beautiful," inspired by the views from its 14,110-foot summit. It looms over the city as a stunning landmark, affects its weather, and defines the region. Unlike poor Zeb Pike, you (like half a million other visitors every year) can conquer Pikes Peak. Here are the ways:

By car: You can drive up the Pikes Peak Highway, a well-maintained and paved 19-mile road that rises nearly 8,000 vertical feet from the base to the summit. Driving up the peak is an adventure in itself, and takes several hours for the round trip, depending upon how many times you stop to gawk at the views. Most passenger cars can climb the mountain fine—there are no guardrails but the road is wide enough at most points you don't feel like you're going to pitch off the side if you meet another car. (If you think it's a tense drive, just imagine how those race car drivers feel hitting these curves at as much as 130 mph each June, during the Pikes Peak Hill Climb.)

Coming down, use your lower gears to make the descent easier on your vehicle. By driving slow in the lower gear, you don't have to wear out your brakes on the downhill trip. Despite all these cautions, the drive actually isn't that hard. Just focus on the road instead of the views. How hard can it be? At least 250,000 flatlanders do it every year, according to the Department of Public Works for the City of Colorado Springs (719-385-2489, www.springsgov.com, $$), which manages the highway.

By train: The Manitou & Pikes Peak Cog Railway (515 Ruxton Ave., Manitou Springs, 719-685-5401, $$$$) is the world's highest cog railroad. It offers you a chance to leave the driving to someone else while you look for wildlife, shoot photos, and catch the panoramic views.

It had its start in the late 1880s, when Zalmon Simmons, inventor of the Simmons Beautyrest Mattress Company, rode to the summit of Pikes Peak on a mule. It was a grueling, 2-day trip and the only way to reach the summit in those days. Awed by the scenery but deploring the mode of transportation, he overheard a local hotel owner talking about the possibility of a railway to the top. Simmons agreed to finance the venture.

In 1889, the Manitou & Pike's Peak Railway Company was founded and tracks began to be laid. Six workers died in construction accidents. The spring of 1891 was

FLORISSANT FOSSIL BEDS
NATIONAL MONUMENT $
15807 Teller County Rd., Florissant
(719) 748-3253
www.nps.gov/flfo
You don't have to go all the way to Arizona to see petrified tree stumps. There's a great

collection of them right here, at the Florissant Fossil Beds. Not only that, but more than 1,500 different kinds of fossil insects have been found here, making it one of the most diverse insect fossil sites in the world. Take one of three self-guided tours that are available year-round. Brochures for these a snowy one, and the opening of the line was delayed until June 30, when the first trainload of passengers made its way to the summit.

Spencer Penrose, owner of The Broadmoor hotel, acquired the Railway in 1925 and modernized it. It has continually been upgraded and today the train runs all year round, depending on the depth of snow and weather conditions. Allow half a day for the round trip, including some time on the summit.

On foot: If you're the athletic type, think about hiking up the peak on Barr Trail. Thousands of people do it every year! In fact, each August sees the annual Pikes Peak Marathon, a 26-mile round-trip foot race up the trail and back down, drawing up to 800 runners from all over the world. (FREE)

By bike: Challenge Unlimited (800-798-5954 or 719-633-6399, http://bikithikit .com/PikesPeakByBike.htm, $$$$) offers yet another option. Only a few folks are crazy enough to attempt to ride *up* the peak on a bike. However, you can ride *down* on a bike with this company. Twice a day, May through Oct, weather permitting, you can ride the cog railway up the peak, then bike down with this group of intrepid cyclists. Challenge Unlimited started in 1991. They feed you breakfast, take you up the mountain in a van, supply hats, coats, mittens, and 27-speed mountain bikes, then guide the group down the winding highway to the bottom. It takes about 2½ hours. They claim you need not be an expert rider to do the trip. Use your own judgment on that!

Cautions: However you do it, pack a jacket and hat; no matter how warm it is in the city below, it will be chilly and windy on the peak. There's been snow on the peak every month of the year. We recommend the morning for ascending the peak by whatever means you choose—storms can brew up quickly in the afternoons on some summer days. Once you reach the top, take a few minutes to visit the Summit House, which serves its famous doughnuts. There's a great gift shop, too. Surprise.

Note: If you happen to be around on New Year's Eve, catch the fireworks on the top of Pikes Peak. Each year, the AdAmAn Club (so called because they add a member each year), a group of intrepid local climbers, ascend the peak on foot, regardless of the weather and depth of snow, and set off fireworks. It's a sight to behold—and photograph, if you can!

tours are available at the visitor center desk. The trails include: the Petrified Forest Walk, a 1-mile path that passes through massive petrified redwood stumps; the Ponderosa Loop Trail, a half-mile loop that takes you through a modern Ponderosa pine forest; and a tour of the grounds of the historic 1878 Hornbek Homestead, located a mile north of the visitor center. There also are more than 14 miles of hiking trails in the monument. Most wind through hills covered with pines, aspens, and Douglas firs. Some of the trails go through riparian areas. When there's enough snow in winter, the area's gentle meadows, hills, and trails can be a great place to snowshoe or cross-country ski. You'll have to bring your own, though. They don't have equipment. Same goes for horseback riding. It's permitted on a limited basis, but you have to bring your own horse.

ROYAL GORGE BRIDGE
AND PARK $$$$
4218 CR 3A, Cañon City
(888) 333-5597 or (719) 275-7507
www.royalgorgebridge.com

Records show that Spanish missionaries visited the Royal Gorge area as early as 1642. Fur traders and trappers subsequently visited the region during the 1700s. And in 1806, explorer Zeb Pike established a camp at the eastern portals of the Gorge and sent a scouting party to explore the canyon.

Today, the area surrounding the gorge is privately owned. There's no way to see the famous attraction without forking over an admission fee, so go ahead and do it. It's a fun place to spend a day. The world's highest suspension bridge, completed in 1929, sways over the 1,200-foot-deep chasm, making some folks queasy and others exhilarated. You can walk or drive across the 1,260-foot bridge (which is a generous 18 feet wide). If you choose to ride America's longest single-span aerial tram, you might want to know it cost $350,000 when it was built in 1968 and it traverses 2,200 feet from rim to rim. It only goes about 11 miles an hour, so you get a good look down at the gorge on your way across. Don't worry. For safety's sake, wind-warning gauges are working at all times and the tram will not operate during severe weather or gusty winds. Visitors also can board the 1930 incline rail that drops 1,550 feet from the rim to the bottom of the

gorge. All three of these are listed on the National Historic Register.

If you want a tame approach to your visit, you can take one of the new mule rides or perch atop a miniature train—both go to the rim. But if you want a real thrill, check out the Skycoaster! Built in 2003, we can only liken it to being shot out over the chasm at 50 miles an hour, sort of like being flung from a giant slingshot. Snaking through the bottom of the gorge is the churning Arkansas River, where you might spot the bright dots of whitewater rafts bobbing along. To try that exciting experience, check out the local outfitters (see Adventures, this chapter). The Royal Gorge Route Railroad (see next listing) runs through the canyon below.

ROYAL GORGE ROUTE
RAILROAD $$$$
401 Water St., Cañon City
(888) RAILS-4U
www.royalgorgeroute.com

The Royal Gorge wasn't always a peaceful place. In 1877, when silver was discovered on the upper waters of the Arkansas River, it sparked a controversy between two competing railroads: the Rio Grande and the Santa Fe. Both wanted the rights to build the new freight railroad to carry the ore down from the mountains. From dynamiting competitor's railway efforts to exchanging gunshots, the Royal Gorge War eventually evolved into a 6-month court battle. The Santa Fe was unhappy with those results and hired legendary gunfighter and US Marshal Bat Masterson and part of his Kansas posse to help protect their crew and materials, while the Rio Grande countered with a 200-man posse led by former Gov. A. C. Hunt. The Rio Grande railroad eventually won out. Today, the only trains traversing the tricky railbed are carrying tourists. The relatively short ride offers a different perspective on the canyon, and you can have lunch or dinner while you're riding, if you like. They also have mystery trains, a Santa Express, and other special train rides throughout the year.

SEVEN FALLS $$
2850 S. Cheyenne Cañon Rd.
(719) 632-0752
www.sevenfalls.com
The falls, which drop 181 feet from canyon rim to the floor, were part of a homestead in 1872, later sold to the Colorado Springs Land Company and then, in 1885, to James Hull, an early environmentalist who thought the best use of the site was not development, but tourism. He installed a gate at the canyon's entrance and created one of Colorado Springs's first tourist attractions. Visitors came by horse and by carriage to view the site and climb the wooden stairs built alongside the waterfall. Today, visitors come in cars and can ride an elevator up to view the falls—or they still can climb the modernized 224-step staircase. Be on the lookout for hordes of chipmunks around the visitor center and gift shop. They're cute but may carry diseases, so don't feed or pet them! Also look for American dippers (also called water ouzels) plunging into the stream in search of food (insects and larvae), and watch the feeders for hummingbirds.

SPORTS

PRORODEO HALL OF FAME
& MUSEUM OF THE AMERICAN
COWBOY $$
101 Pro Rodeo Dr.
(719) 528-4764
www.prorodeohalloffame.com/joomla

America's original sport—rodeo—is showcased at the ProRodeo Hall of Fame and Museum of the American Cowboy. The Hall, established in 1979, is located adjacent to the national headquarters of the Professional Rodeo Cowboys Association (PRCA). Check out the larger-than-life bronze statue of famous rodeo cowboy Casey Tibbs riding Necktie right in front of the museum. Rodeo's history, dating back to cattle drives and ranch work, is well illustrated in a video shown every 30 minutes. Visitors also get to see the evolution of gear, equipment, and clothing, explained in a guided tour of the Heritage Hall portion of the museum. Exhibits featuring memorabilia from more than 160 inductees fill the Hall of Champions and include everything from Joe Beaver's first saddle and boots to Descent's silver halters. It's interactive, too. A touch-screen kiosk features highlights from the previous year's Wrangler National Finals and clips from each world champion. You'll also find a few live animals on-site, to help visitors imagine what it's like to be a cowboy. And be sure to scope out the excellent art collection, too. If you like the museum and happen to be in town during the annual Pikes Peak or Bust Rodeo, don't miss it! Closed Mon and Tues in winter.

US OLYMPIC TRAINING CENTER   FREE
1750 E. Boulder St.
(719) 866-4618
www.teamusa.org/about-usoc/u-s-olympic-training-center-colorado-springs
Visitors' heads tend to turn as recognizable Olympic athletes stroll by their tour group at the US Olympic Training Center, a unique attraction just out of downtown Colorado Springs. It might be a wrestler, a speed

skater, a cyclist, or a swimmer—they all come here to live and train at high altitude to improve their performance. The Olympic complex, located on a former air force base, includes dorms and a dining hall for the athletes. The $23 million facility opened in 1996–97 and serves nearly 600 coaches and athletes who are in training. There are state-of-the-art medical and sports science centers. Free daily tours offer insight into how these young athletes live and what it takes to become a world-class competitor. Check out the cool museum, too. It'll bring back memories of Olympics past.

WORLD FIGURE SKATING
HALL OF FAME $
20 1st St.
(719) 635-5200
www.worldskatingmuseum.org
Started in 1965 by popular demand—people kept dropping off memorabilia at the US Figure Skating headquarters in Massachusetts—the museum moved to Colorado Springs in 1979 when the headquarters also moved here. Stuff kept coming, and eventually they had to create display space for it. This "accidental museum" now is the international repository for the figure skating world. It includes thousands of photographs, more than 3,500 items of memorabilia (including gold medals and costumes) from such famous skaters as Sonja Henie, Scott Hamilton, Dick Button, Kristi Yamaguchi, and Katarina Witt. Anything you ever wanted to know about figure skating and skaters is probably tucked away in its archives. Located on the grounds of The Broadmoor hotel complex, it's open Tues through Fri only.

WILDLIFE & ZOOS

✳CHEYENNE MOUNTAIN ZOO $$$
4250 Cheyenne Mountain Zoo Rd.
(719) 633-9925
www.cmzoo.org
You just haven't lived until you've had a giraffe wrap his soft, prehensile tongue around your hand in search of a cracker. That's just one experience you can write home about after you visit the nation's highest and only mountain zoo. The 145-acre park sits at 7,000 feet on the east face of Cheyenne Mountain at the end of a winding road behind The Broadmoor hotel. Head first to the African Safari exhibit, where you'll buy and hand-feed crackers to the giraffes at head-height (and have the aforementioned experience). Kids love this! Adults, too. These tall, gentle giants (the largest breeding herd in the country) accept the crackers with quiet dignity. And don't miss the Rocky Mountain Wild exhibit, where you almost always see mountain lions up close (through glass, not bars), plus grizzly bears (you might see them catch trout right in front of you), and a resident moose, who munches on branches and hangs out with wild turkeys all day. You'll also see African lions, Asian tigers, Mexican wolves, and lots of primates among the 150 or so species represented here. Don't forget to ride the antique wooden carousel. For an overview of the zoo and city beyond, hop on the Sky Ride. If you have a few extra minutes, drive on up to the Will Rogers Shrine of the Sun, above the zoo on the mountain. This stone monument honors the famous cowboy humorist, who died in a plane crash in 1935 and who was a friend of the Penroses, who built The Broadmoor hotel. Even if you don't visit, you'll hear the chimes from the tower every 15 minutes. If you do visit, it's included in your zoo

admission. And the view of Colorado Springs and the vast plains beyond is incredible.

i If visiting during the winter holidays, check out the Cheyenne Mountain Zoo's annual light display, one of the few occasions the attraction remains open after dark. And Seven Falls presents an amazing array of lights, with admission fees going to charity.

COLORADO WOLF AND WILDLIFE CENTER $$
Teller CR 42/Twin Rocks Road, Divide
(719) 687-9742
www.wolfeducation.org
Spend an hour with the wolves. And foxes, coyotes, and mixed breeds. This sanctuary located in the forest outside of Divide has given shelter to these wild creatures which, for whatever reason, have been abandoned. Some didn't "perform" properly in movies; others represent failed attempts at raising pets. Meet Koda, Micah, Nakai, and many others, and learn their stories. Each has its own spacious enclosure. All tours are by reservation only and your GPS won't get you there, so call to set up a tour and then follow the directions you are given (or get them online). Arrangements can be made for a one-on-one wolf encounter or for special photography sessions, too. All proceeds from admissions go to support the center.

SERENITY SPRINGS WILDLIFE CENTER $$
24615 Scott Rd., Calhan
(719) 347-9200
www.serenityspringswildlife.org
It started out as a big-cat rescue site on the plains near Calhan, east of Colorado Springs. More than 100 cats—lions, tigers, panthers, cougars, lynxes, and others—have found refuge here. Tours last about an hour and are available by appointment only and must be arranged in advance. You'll hear the story of each animal at the center—some sad, some strange, some almost unbelievable. Some of the animals are more socialized than others, so not every critter there is on view. But you'll see dozens and dozens of them and empathize with their plights. The tour is on a flat path, but a golf cart is available for anyone who can't walk for an hour. It's quite a drive from the Springs (nearly an hour) but worth the trip for animal lovers.

KIDSTUFF

Tourists love the Pikes Peak region for the scenery and attractions, and that makes it easy for parents. Any time of year, there is more to choose from than the usual suspects when talking activities for kids.

First, Colorado Springs has more than its fair share of arcades, from laser tag to bumper cars. There are also great attractions, including a world-class zoo, cave exploring, visits to Santa, and trips on a narrow-gauge railroad.

The natural world is a big draw here, too, with a number of terrific nature centers catering to programs and activities for kids. Whether it's about bugs, butterflies, or dinosaurs, kids can really get into it in Colorado Springs. For those who'd rather do than see, there also are places to get your hands dirty picking apples or discovering urban farming.

For the artsy types, singing, dance, and art programs are available throughout the region. Or for those who'd rather expend muscle energy, kids can ski in the winter, run in the many parks in the summer, or skate on just about any surface any time of year. There's something for every kid, every budget, and every season. So whether you've lived here for a lifetime or are just visiting for a quick weekend, pack up the kids and head out on a treasure hunt of great things to do in Colorado Springs and beyond.

Price Code

The following price code gives you an idea of what the regular children's admission might be at the following places. Check online or call in advance if you are concerned about the cost. Some are free, and we'll tell you that, too.

$ . . . . less than $5
$$ . . . . $5 to $10
$$$ . . . . $10 to $20
$$$$ . . . . more than $20

HOW AMUSING!

Apparently we're easily amused in Colorado Springs because we have more than our fair share of amusement-type businesses. Most are indoors, so even if it's cold and snowy, when cabin fever hits we can always load up the kids and get out of the house. For those who go catatonic at flashing lights and high-volume jingles, a few of the listed items are of the more natural, fresh-air variety. No matter what your taste, there's something here your kid will love.

✳HAPPY APPLE FARM FREE
1190 1st St., Penrose
(719) 372-6300
www.happyapplefarm.com
From July through October, this you-pick-it farm offers a fabulous day. Located in Penrose about 45 minutes south of Colorado Springs off CO 115, the souvenirs taste pretty

good, too! Depending on the season and weather during the growing season, you can pick gooseberries, raspberries, blackberries, pumpkins, pears, and, of course, apples. There's no charge to get onto the grounds, and there's a free tractor ride out to the fields and orchard (it's not that far, but going out by tractor is half the fun). The by-the-pound cost of the fruit you've picked is more than reasonable. At the end of your harvest, the country store sells fresh apple or pumpkin pie, fresh-pressed apple cider, cheeses, olives, deli foods, jams, and blackberry cobbler. Fresh chilies are roasted on-site in the fall, and the owner runs an apple-smoked barbecue of brisket, turkey legs, and hot dogs on the weekends.

IT'Z FAMILY FOOD & FUN $$
3035 New Center Point
(719) 623-1550
www.itzusa.com/colorado
This is a national company with one location on the east side of Colorado Springs. It's the kind of loud, raucous fun that can be just the ticket for a snowy day or birthday party. Besides the kid-friendly food like pizza, IT'Z has thrill rides such as bumper cars, games (Dance Dance Revolution and Guitar Hero), a full arcade, and bowling. There's free Wi-Fi for the adults who might want to work while the kids play, and a party planner can make throwing a party an easy task—and the mess isn't in your house.

LASER QUEST $$$
1605 N. Academy Blvd.
(719) 570-1115
www.laserquest.com
Run by another national company, Laser Quest is housed in a large building that used to be a movie theater. The two-story laser

tag space has lots of corners and angles that make hitting a challenge. This is a terrific place for multi-age family time as the younger kids might find accuracy a problem, but their smaller size (i.e., smaller target) gives them an advantage. Young adults tend to claim Laser Quest as their own in the evenings.

i Focus on the Family headquarters, at Briargate Parkway and Explorer Drive, is open to the public and features an elaborate indoor play place with a three-story corkscrew slide. A soda shop in the basement tempts with sweet treats.

LI'L BIGG'S $$
5944 Stetson Hills Blvd.
(719) 884-6838
www.becooldoright.com
The little brother of Mr. Bigg's (see next entry), Li'l Bigg's is the indoor amusement place that won't intimidate the younger crowd. The big draw is the inflatable area, but there's also a pint-sized arcade and kid-friendly food, such as pizza. Birthday parties can be booked as well.

✱MR. BIGG'S FAMILY FUN CENTER $$$
5825 Mark Dabling Blvd.
(719) 955-7220
www.becooldoright.com
Mr. Bigg's is—duh—really big (although the name comes from the owner, not the size). The 3-acre complex is locally owned and houses every kind of indoor amusement a kid (of any age) could want. Mr. Bigg's has go-karts, laser tag, bumper cars, minigolf, and bowling. The arcade is full of the latest zapping, zooming games and there's a full-size Battle Tech cockpit. For those with

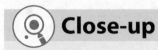 **Close-up**

Venetucci Farm

5210 S. US 85
(719) 389-1251
www.ppcf.org/venetuccci

Generations of Pikes Peak area children have known a man who had a heart of gold, smiled with a twinkle in his eye, gave out free gifts once a year, and went by the name of Nick. Not as in Claus, as in Venetucci. And we're talking pumpkins.

The Venetucci family established an urban farm in south Colorado Springs in 1936. They grew sweet corn, alfalfa, asparagus—and pumpkins. Sometime in the '50s, **Nick Venetucci** started giving away pumpkins to local kids every October. The tradition grew and continued for more than 50 years, and he became known as **"the pumpkin man."** School groups would schedule field trips, families would stop by, and locals would plan on going to **"the pumpkin farm"** months in advance. Each child could go out into the acres of pumpkin fields and pick the one pumpkin that was perfect for him or her, no charge. Over the years, tall kids with tiny pumpkins and scrawny kids with humongous gourds would tromp out of the fields, a jack-o-lantern grin on their faces. There was no one quite so loved as Mr. Venetucci in October.

Nick has since passed on, and the farm is now run by the Pikes Peak Community Foundation as a way to provide locals with healthy food and experiences as well as volunteer opportunities. The farm grows more than 100 varieties of chemical-free vegetables and herbs and is home to pastured hogs, grass-fed beef, and a large flock of laying hens. Education classes are held for both individuals and groups, and there's also a farm tour available and a junior farmhands program for kids in the summer. To schedule, contact drudin@ppcf.org or call (719) 389-1251, ext. 112.

And the pumpkins? The farm still offers a free pumpkins for kids program. Because the fields lay fallow for a number of years after Nick's death, the farm doesn't currently support the acres and acres of pumpkins of years past. But, some are grown every year, and each year more pumpkins can be planted. Currently the free pumpkin giveaway is for scheduled, pre-K through first grade school groups only.

Nick still lives on in a bronze sculpture downtown just west of the Pioneers Museum. He's in a pumpkin field, surrounded by smiling children on a great pumpkin search. The best time to see the artwork is in the fall, when the planter surrounding the sculpture is ripe with a real patch of the glowing orange orbs that helped make Mr. Venetucci southern Colorado's very special pumpkin man.

more energy, the inflatable area and bounce houses are enough to keep even Tigger happy. Little Bigg Town is an imagination play zone with 16 shops where little ones can pretend to join the police force, bake a cake, fix a car, or hit the beauty salon. Food ranges from pizza to salads to burgers, and birthday parties are popular and should be booked well in advance. Passes can be purchased based on hourly increments or as an all-day pass.

**✷NORTH POLE/SANTA'S
  WORKSHOP** $$$
5050 Pikes Peak Hwy., Cascade
(719) 684-9432
www.santas-colo.com
This retro amusement park with a Christmas theme was established in 1956. Hugging the ankles of Pikes Peak, the quaint layout really does look like a magical winter wonderland, so it's no surprise *USA Today* has listed it as one of the nation's top 10 places for grandparents to take grandkids. Children and their adults flock here to meet Santa Claus, touch the "North Pole" (frozen any time of year), and pet the resident reindeer. They also may take a sky ride, twirl on the whirligig, take a turn on the big Ferris wheel, see a magic show, or brave the haunted house. You can do a little Christmas shopping, even in July! This really is a place for kids 12 and younger—teens will think it's "lame."

COOL MUSEUMS

Listed here are some of the very cool museums (really!), historic sites, and other attractions that will get your kids out of the house and into the car faster than they can find their shoes. Just don't tell them that most of these are a little bit educational. Shhh . . . your secret's safe with us!

**ROCKY MOUNTAIN DINOSAUR
  RESOURCE CENTER** $$
201 S. Fairview St., Woodland Park
(719) 686-1820
www.rmdrc.com
Just a short drive up Ute Pass from Colorado Springs, the Dinosaur Resource Center sits on the main drag in Woodland Park. You can't miss it—a palm tree towers out front. In a Colorado mountain town, especially under the white blanket of winter, a palm tree is just a little out of the ordinary. Unusual too is what goes on inside the 20,000-square-foot building. There are more than 30 life-sized dinosaur specimens (mostly skeletons) and, better yet, a working paleontology lab. Kids can watch scientists working on the latest discoveries and even feel dinosaur poop. There's stuff to keep the kids moving, like a station to build a new species of dinosaur out of magnets and a small dinosaur dig site. A small theater shows entertaining but scientific films, and there is a store for dino trinkets.

i Kids love to pan for gold at the Garden of the Gods Trading Post. Only $6 for all the goods for one child or $10 for two kids, little gold miners have easy access to the low trough, where they sift through a pail of sand for rocks, minerals, and fool's gold.

SIMPICH SHOWCASE $$
2413 W. Colorado Ave.
(719) 465-2492
www.simpich.com
Simpich Showcase has been in Old Colorado City for decades, and yet it's like an underground find. Quaint and entertaining, the cottage-like building actually houses three things: a theater, museum, and gallery. The theater is an intimate space—and one of the only performance venues in the US—dedicated to string puppet productions. Shows feature classics such as *Aesop, The Secret Garden,* and seasonal favorites on an oft-changed bill. The museum features rotating exhibits of the marionettes from the Simpich performances, each displayed in detailed settings. The puppets are quite amazing; all handmade, intricate

pieces created by doll artists Jan and Bob Simpich and staff. The gallery showcases Bob Simpich's oil paintings. In this day of in-your-face entertainment, a Simpich day is a sweet retreat.

i Let your dreams take flight by viewing the full-sized airplanes at the US Air Force Academy. From big bombers to sleek jets, decommissioned flyers are all around the grounds. A parking area is at each plane, so kids can run around and touch them.

STARSMORE DISCOVERY CENTER FREE
2120 S. Cheyenne Cañon Rd.
(719) 385-6086
www.springsgov.com

The lovely stone building at the mouth of Cheyenne Cañon used to be owned by the Starsmore family—and thus the name of this wonderful resource for kids of all ages. The center gives out free maps and information on the cañon, has some interesting (and sometimes scary!) dioramas of local wildlife, features hands-on nature exhibits, and sells books and more. The programs over the spring, summer, and fall run from tipi raising to junior rangers ($–$$ for certain events). Every May the center is home to the Hummingbird Festival, a full day of bird lore, face painting, bird-feeder making, and amazing facts about those fast little flyers. Starsmore is generally open Tues through Sun, but is both season and volunteer dependent, so call before visiting. (Also see the entry on North Cheyenne Cañon in the Parks chapter.)

ARTS & CRAFTS

Sometimes, a good book or artist's pad is the best activity around. There are plenty of places to let loose with some creative energy in the Pikes Peak region, either for an hour or on a scheduled basis.

BEMIS SCHOOL OF ART FREE–$$$$
818 Pelham Place
(719) 475-2444
www.csfineartscenter.org/education.asp

As part of the Fine Arts Center, Bemis has been the go-to art school in town for decades. The funky building is perfect for getting kids (and teens and adults) dirty with paint, clay, ink, and chalk. Classes are clearly marked for age groups and include some real doozies, such as Outside the Lines and Pottery Wow! Class fees are discounted for Fine Arts Center members. Bemis also sponsors free Family Adventure Days once a month, where for 2 hours on a Saturday parents and kids can experience something completely different, such as crafting Mexican maracas or painting on Japanese silk. (See also The Arts chapter.)

COLORADO SPRINGS CHILDREN'S
CHORALE $$$$
(719) 633-3562
www.kidssing.org

This nonprofit has grown from a small civic children's choir in the late '70s to five choirs featuring nearly 200 kids aged 8 to 18 from across the Pikes Peak region. The preparatory choir, concert choir, touring choir, and high school ensemble perform year-round at many locations within the Pikes Peak region as well as internationally. They have won gold medals at international competitions and have been to Japan five times. Auditions

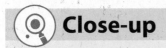

Imagination Celebration

1515 N. Academy Blvd., # 200
(719) 597-3344

Squeeze your eyes shut and imagine a community brimming with the arts in its schools, in neighborhood centers, in shopping malls, and in parks. Music, theater, dance, painting, sculpture, poetry, folk art, literature. People using their imaginations and people applauding the imaginations of others.

Now, open your eyes and see how **Imagination Celebration** at Colorado Springs has brought this image to life! Since 1986, Imagination Celebration has produced, presented, and promoted programs that have nourished, educated, and entertained thousands and thousands of children, teens, and adults.

Imagination Celebration, part of the Kennedy Center Imagination Celebration, is alive and well because there is more to life than tests, work, and video games! Imagination Celebration has forged partnerships with arts, science, and cultural organizations (local, regional, and national), schools, businesses, and government agencies. The common cause of all these partnerships is to ensure that every child grows up rich in the creative experiences of the arts, while keeping an eye on the 21st century learning skills for "STEAM" (Science, Technology, Engineering, Arts, and Math). The region has a wealth of talent in all of these criteria—and Imagination Celebration gives it a that needed showcase or an opportunity to bloom.

There are two community centers for creative engagement run by the Imagination Celebration, both housed in The Citadel mall. **Celebration Place** is the more intimate of the two spaces, affording live performances, art exhibits, and dance and movement classes. **Imagination Space** provides 20,000 square feet of space in which to play, explore, relax, reflect, and observe. There are daily hands-on activities of tinkering, dancing, sculpting, reading, robotics, and storytelling—all opportunities to give your child's imagination some space! Free admission and all ages welcome!

A showcase for the innovation and creativity of the Pikes Peak region is the fall festival *What If! Festival for Innovation and Imagination.* Attendees to this annual fall festival (second Sat in Sept) experience the breadth and depth of creativity/innovation in this region through interactive presentations, hands-on demonstrations, exhibitions, and performances. This "coming together" of arts and technology, right-brainers and left-brainers, occurs throughout the festival's 6-block downtown Colorado Springs location.

Perhaps the scope of Imagination Celebration is best summed up by the child expert, Kermit the Frog. "Yeah, well, I've got a dream too. But it's about singing and dancing and making people happy. That's the kind of dream that gets better the more people you share it with. And, well, I've found a whole bunch of friends who have the same dream. And it kind of makes us like a family."

are required, and tuition is charged. Even with its esteemed reputation, the chorale is best known for the kids' touching performances at smaller meetings and events, such as at nursing homes and civic events. (See also The Arts chapter.)

Paint Your Own Pottery

Need a special platter from junior to grandma at Christmas? Want to document your kid's artwork with more than macaroni and construction paper? Just want to spend a few hours sitting next to your kid doing something fun? All these reasons plus birthday parties and more are what keep the we-supply/you-paint pottery stores in business. $$–$$$$

Artful Adventures
3586-C Hartsel Dr.
(719) 264-6767
www.artful-adventures.com

Brush Strokes
808 Village Center Dr.
(719) 219-1880
www.brushstrokesceramicstudio.com

Puttin' on the Paint
2616 W. Colorado Ave., Suite 21
(719) 633-5330

PERFORMING ARTS FOR YOUTH ORGANIZATION (PAYO)
(719) 634-4300
www.payo.org
PAYO is a nonprofit organization that provides a variety of high-quality, multicultural, arts-in-education programs in the areas of music, storytelling, dance, magic, and drama for children in all public, private, and independent schools and community and youth centers in the Pikes Peak region. Formed in 1969 when budget cuts hit the arts programs in local schools, PAYO is still an important cog in the local art wheel, reaching several thousand youth annually. Schools or private groups can book performers such as Art Guffaw, who brings painting and drawing to life through original puppetry, magic, juggling, mime, and comedy, or the Sound Ideas program, which uses exotic musical instruments (khaen, didgeridoo, angklungs) for lessons in geography, social studies, and local customs. PAYO does charge for its performances but tries to keep these fees low through active fund-raising.

PIKES PEAK LIBRARY DISTRICT   FREE
(719) 531-6333
www.ppld.org
The Pikes Peak Library is the bomb. The 13 libraries plus mobile library have events and resources for kids from infants to teens. There are traditional story times, bilingual story times, and snuggle up evening story times. Furry friends lend a soft ear to reluctant readers in the Paws to Read program. Homework help is available on any subject imaginable, and there are clubs for chess, American Girl books, improv groups, and more. In the fall the popular Stories in the Dark bring out the brave, and family events such as American Indian drumming or crafting a storm trooper light saber are scheduled regularly. These are not the tiptoe libraries of stereotype, but hopping community centers especially friendly to children and their taller friends.

RUN IT OFF!

Sometimes, kids just need to move. Let loose. Blow off some steam. This listing includes some spontaneous activities as well as some sports opportunities targeted to the under 18 crowd.

AMERICA THE BEAUTIFUL PARK   FREE
126 Cimino Dr.
www.springsgov.com
Aside from the big state and federal parks, Colorado Springs has a lot of neighborhood parks for kids to get rid of energy. This one stands out because of the cool playground and impressive fountain.

Located near I-25 downtown, America the Beautiful Park is a 30-acre wonder. Established through both state and private funding, the park features a big green space, lots of easy parking, and The Continuum–Julie Penrose Fountain. Meant to convey the life-giving movement of water between the atmosphere and earth, the large, circular fountain drops water down inside a circle. Kids love to wade in the base in the summer when the water is running. Next to the fountain is one awesome playground. The 15,000-square-foot space includes access for the disabled, hammocks, spinner bowls, and turntables. And then there are "the quirks," interactive pieces of art created by local elementary school kids. The child who plays here can be sure to have a quirky, crazy, and just plain amazing day.

BOMBERS $$$$
Breckenridge Resort
(888) LRN-2SKI or (970) 453-3272
www.breckenridge.com/ski-and-ride-school/specialty-programs/ski-and-snowboard-bombers.aspx
Many Pikes Peak region kids learn to ski or snowboard through the Breckenridge Bombers program. Yes, it's a long drive. Yes, it's pricey. But yes, your kids become really good skiers and/or snowboarders. If it's important to you as a Colorado local to have the whole family comfortable with the slopes, Bombers is the (lift) ticket. The multi-week program, which has been schussing away for 22 years, pairs kids with the same instructor and class (based on age and ability) every weekend through the winter months. There are three types of bomber programs: All-Mountain Bombers teaches the full range of mountain pastimes with themed days such as Race Day or Safety Day; Freestyle Bombers (otherwise known as park and pipe) focuses on tricks for both natural slopes and terrain parks; and Pee Wee Bombers is for 3-year-olds. For more information, including registration information, e-mail brskischoolprograms@vailresorts.com and put "Bombers" as the subject line. You'll be automatically added to the program's distribution list.

i When heading to America the Beautiful Park, make sure your kids are wearing play clothes and shoes and socks that slip off. You might not plan for your kids to splash in the fountain, but if the water's running and other kids are in it, you know yours will be too!

CHAPEL HILLS MALL   FREE
N. Academy at Briargate Blvd.
www.chapelhillsmall.com
In the Chapel Hills Mall (see the Shopping chapter) is a cartoon-like, injury-proof play space designed to let kids run off, climb off, slide off all that excess energy—and give

parents a place to sit and watch while they're doing it. It gets crowded, but the kids don't seem to mind at all. The more the merrier! It's free and open during mall hours. Located on the lower level just outside of Sears and Borders Books.

CITY OF COLORADO SPRINGS
YOUTH SPORTS $$–$$$$
1315 E. Pikes Peak Ave.
(719) 385-5981
www.springsgov.com

Youth sports and other programs are run by the City of Colorado Springs. They are recreational, developmental leagues that use volunteer coaches and are held on the grounds of city parks. Those in the know sign up early so they can have their first choice of practice site. City youth sports include football, soccer, T-ball, baseball, and softball.

Baseball

In springtime, kids play ball—lots of it, from T-ball to baseball. By high school, the many strong youth programs provide experienced ball players who've grown to love the game. The main reason to choose one club over another for young children is location since they're all excellent programs. Once a kid gets into serious play, either of the two Little League clubs are your best bet.

ACADEMY LITTLE LEAGUE $$$$
www.academylittleleague.com

CITY OF COLORADO SPRINGS
YOUTH SPORTS $$$$
1315 E. Pikes Peak Ave.
(719) 385-5981
www.springsgov.com

COLORADO SPRINGS
LITTLE LEAGUE $$$$
www.eteamz.com/csll

Gymnastics

Gymnastics is very popular with the preschool and elementary set in Colorado Springs, which probably explains why the pool of more accomplished and committed youth gymnasts is so strong in the area. **Aerials Gymnastics** has a number of locations in strategic corners of the Pikes Peak region, and it supports both the beginner and the serious competitor. **Stars,** located in north downtown, caters to a similar crowd. **ArtSports** is focused on tumbling and trampoline and boasts "the world's largest trampoline gymnastics center" with 32 tramps. **Kinetic Gymnastics** is a good choice for those on the south end of town for everything from gymnastics to cheerleading.

AERIALS GYMNASTICS
1459 Woolsey Heights (east location)
(719) 550-9209

3536 Hartsel Dr. (north location)
(719) 260-1893

1789 S. 8th St. (south location)
(719) 578-1006
www.coloradoaerials.com

ARTSPORTS WORLD
780 Vondelpark Dr.
(719) 531-5867
www.artsportsworld.com

KINETIC GYMNASTICS
30 Widefield Blvd. E.
(719) 391-8295
www.kineticgymnastics.com

STARS NATIONAL GYMNASTIC VILLAGE
3870 Mallow Rd.
(719) 598-6863
http://starsngv.com

Ice Hockey

COLORADO SPRINGS AMATEUR HOCKEY ASSOCIATION $$$$
http://csaha.com

Coloradoans love hockey. So it's probably no surprise that the most organized youth sport in the region is ice hockey, with one-stop shopping at Colorado Springs Amateur Hockey Association (CSAHA). From mini-mites to the AAA Pikes Peak Miners team, CSAHA offers it all. The group's goal is for every child, girl or boy, to receive great coaching, advanced training methods, and lots of ice time, and in general they score in this effort. From house leagues to travel programs, CSAHA reaches every hockey kid at any level. The website is an easy place to follow practice and game times at all the local rinks, and sports shops often work with CSAHA for equipment discounts. And with a no-checking policy for recreational players, the only hard hit is that inevitable 5 a.m. ice time.

Ice Skating

(See the Sports & Recreation chapter on p. 164.)

i Almost every local kid wants to play ice hockey. Do them a favor and sign them up for one of the Learn to Skate classes first. Both Sertich and the World Arena (see the Sports & Recreation chapter) have great inexpensive beginner classes for every age.

Inline & Roller Skating

Kids in our area love skating of all kinds, so roller and inline skating are as strong as ice skating. On any sunny day you'll find casual games of street hockey happening in neighborhoods and parks (see the Sports & Recreation chapter for a listing of all skate parks). Roller rinks are popular places for birthday parties, school fund-raisers, and just plain good times with friends and family.

i If your kids are skiing or snowboarding, don't forget the goggles. Sun glare off the snow at high altitude can really hurt and even damage the eyes. Goggles can be expensive, but try Play It Again Sports (www.playitagainsports.com) for gently used deals.

SKATE CITY $
1920 N. Academy Blvd.
(719) 597-6066
www.skatecitycolorado.com

These popular roller skating rinks host everything from school nights to birthday parties—a second Skate City is located at 4575 Austin Bluffs Pkwy. (719-591-1016). Each also host a number of public skating times, inline hockey leagues, classes, fund-raisers, private parties, and special events. The music is loud and rocking (but family friendly) and there's a snack bar, pro shop, and rentals. Free Wi-Fi is available for any parents who'd rather watch—but you know you'd rather be doing the hokey-pokey! (Also see the Inline Hockey entry in the Sports & Recreation chapter.)

Lacrosse

It wasn't long ago that lacrosse was the sport where people asked, "What is that?"

Not so anymore. Youth lacrosse leagues are growing in popularity, and many of the high schools now front both boys and girls varsity and junior varsity teams. You want your kid to play the sport that's on the rise in the region? Lacrosse is for you.

PATRIOT LACROSSE CLUB $$$$
www.patriotlax.org

Miniature Golf

Putt-putt golf is a great way to spend an hour or two—everybody's a kid on a miniature golf course! **Glow Golf** and **Mr. Bigg's** are indoors and can bring sunshine into any snowy day. Of the three outdoor courses, **Academy Miniature Golf** is a hilly challenge with a great waterfall, **Adventure Miniature Golf** has goofy, huge obstacles like an elephant and a pirate, and **Hitt's** features three 18-hole courses for lots of variety. It's also the best deal in town, charging only $2 per person per round.

ACADEMY MINIATURE GOLF $–$$
1825 Dominion Way
(719) 260-1367
www.academyminigolf.com

**ADVENTURE MINIATURE GOLF
& BATTING CAGES** $–$$
6550 Corporate Dr.
(719) 528-5430
http://adventuregolfandbattingcages
.com

GLOW GOLF $–$$
750 Citadel Dr. E., #2072
(719) 597-2720
www.opryglowgolf.com

HITT'S MINIATURE GOLF $–$$
3402 N. Academy Blvd.
(719) 591-1146

MR. BIGG'S FAMILY FUN CENTER $–$$
5825 Mark Dabling Blvd.
(719) 955-7220
www.becooldoright.com

Paintball

Older kids, like those in middle and high school, tend to love paintball. The actual hits can sting more than you might expect, but the paint-covered kids who finish a game don't seem to care. All's fair in paintball war!

DRAGONMANS $$$$
1200 Dragon Man Dr.
(719) 683-2200
http://dragonmans.com

Rock Climbing

You'd think the reason to rock climb indoors is to learn enough to go outside—but that's not really the case. Indoor rock climbing has a serious fan base, and the local climbing centers even field teams and competitions for indoor climbing only. That said, all the indoor gyms are a great place to start climbing, and all offer instruction if needed.

CITY ROCK $$$
21 N. Nevada Ave.
(719) 634-9099
www.climbcityrock.com

**FRONT RANGE CLIMBING
COMPANY** $$$
722 N. 31st St.
(866) 572-3722 or (719) 473-8349
www.frontrangeclimbing.com

Sledding Hills

It's a cold state's greatest gift to children of all ages: Snow Day! When this happens, kids love to spend the currency of their free day flying down local hills. It doesn't usually last long, but when we get good sledding days, there's just about nothing better—especially when followed up with hot chocolate, popcorn, and an afternoon movie at home. Last thought—watch out for trees!

A few of the top spots:

Bear Creek Regional Park
South, off 21st St. and Argus Rd.

Cottonwood Creek Park
North, corner of Dublin Blvd. and Range-wood Dr.

Fine Arts Center
Downtown, hill that slopes west of the building at 30 W. Dale St.

Howbert Elementary School
West, hill behind the school at 30th St. and Water St.

Iron Springs Chateau
Manitou Springs, hill behind at 444 Ruxton Ave.

Meadow Wood Park
Woodland Park, north on CO 67 to Ever-green Heights Dr. (left)

Monument Valley Park
Downtown, where Fontanero St. ends

Quail Lake Park
South, 915 Cheyenne Mountain Blvd.

Rockrimmon Hill
North, near the Safeway at 840 Village Center Dr.

Toboggan Hill
Monument, corner of Deer Creek Rd. and Toboggan Hill Rd.

Woodstone Park
North, off W. Woodmen Rd., on Carlson Dr.

SPORT CLIMBING CENTER OF COLORADO SPRINGS $$$
4650 Northpark Dr.
(719) 260-1050
www.sportclimbcs.com

Skateboard Parks

(See the Sports & Recreation chapter on p. 164.)

i You don't have to go to a sporting goods store for sleds. Starting around December, look for sturdy but inexpensive plastic sleds at King Soopers and other grocery stores as well as at most discount stores.

Soccer

Soccer is big in the Pikes Peak region—as in, BIG. Almost every kid is on a soccer team at least once, and by high school soccer is serious competition. Also, some of the biggest soccer tournaments in the country are held here (see the Annual Events & Festivals chapter on p. 194). Where a family goes for their soccer fix has a lot to do with location and level of competition desired. Suffice to say, anything your family wants can be found at one—or many—of the soccer groups.

CITY OF COLORADO SPRINGS
   YOUTH SPORTS $$$$
1315 E. Pikes Peak Ave.
(719) 385-5981
www.springsgov.com

COLORADO SPRINGS
   SPORTS CENTER $$$$
2450 Canada Dr.
(719) 637-3695
www.letsplaysoccer.com/main/locations/
coloradosprings

This indoor facility is owned by a national firm, and the kids programs include leagues. Their Lil' Kickers program, which is for kiddos 18 months up to 9 years, introduces the concept of soccer in a non-competitive play.

PRIDE SOCCER $$$$
2660 Vickers Dr.
(719) 597-6700
www.pridesoccer.info

Pride is a private, nonprofit soccer club started by parents. Now it hosts youth ages 4 to 18 in developmental, intermediate, and competitive soccer. They also run tournaments and camps. Open to boys and girls.

YMCA OF THE PIKES PEAK
   REGION $$$$
316 N. Tejon St.
(719) 471-9790
http://ppymca.org

Water Fun

*UNCLE WILBER FOUNTAIN
Bijou and Tejon Streets
(719) 385-6504
http://unclewilberfountain.org

There's a funny man with a tuba downtown. Kids love to do a happy dance around his ankles. Don't worry, our tuba man is not an odd duck, but rather the endearing Uncle Wilber, as in Uncle Wilber Fountain. Opened in 2001, the whimsical, kinetic water sculpture first appears as a colorful, free form mosaic. Then, about every half hour, the top rises to show Uncle Wilber playing his tuba with his trusty dog always by his side. There are 52 pop jets, more than 200 streams of unpredictable water, dozens of fiber optic lights, changing tunes, and a water-themed riddle that, when the fountain is up, is accessible only to those beneath the waterfall cascading from the good uncle's sky-blue dome. The weird and wonderful fountain, a gift to the city from local art forces Kat and Bob Tudor, runs in the summer. Bring the little ones ready to get wet, and plan to stay a while. On a hot day, there's no

---

Moms Club

Stay-at-home moms don't need to feel isolated or lacking in adult conversation. The national nonprofit **MOMS Club** has community chapters in Colorado Springs for the west, east, north, northwest, and northeast areas of town. There's also a group in Monument. The support group for at-home moms has organized weekly events, playgroups for kids of all ages, community service projects, and special interest groups such as scrapbooking and book clubs. They also offer a support network when spouses are out of town and meal delivery to new moms. For more information, go to www.momsclub.org.

more happening spot than at Uncle Wilber's feet. There's also a playground adjacent to our tuba-playing good uncle. (See the Parks chapter for more information on Acacia Park.)

I'M HUNGRY!

It's true of everyone, but especially kids: When they're hungry, they can be little monsters. Sometimes it's hard to both tame the beast and have a good time dining out. These are a few of the kid-friendly dining options.

FARGO'S PIZZA COMPANY $$
2910 E. Platte Ave.
(719) 473-5540
www.fargospizza.com
Opened in 1973, this looks like a Victorian establishment in Little Italy. Confused? Don't be. It's a fun mix of time, culture, and food that now serves as a great place to hold a team after-season party, a big family get together, or a festive night out for a small family. The building is two stories and 14,000 square feet. So although it can feel a little cavernous, it also can hold a lot of groups at once. The food is passable, but that's not why people come here. Think themed restaurant in Fantasyland and you get the picture. There's plenty of parking out front. (See also the Restaurants chapter.)

GIUSEPPE'S OLD DEPOT
RESTAURANT $$$
10 S. Sierra Madre St.
(719) 635-3111
www.giuseppesdepot.com
Make no mistake—it's what goes on outside this downtown restaurant that draws the kids, time and again. Located in the historic Denver & Rio Grande train depot, the long-time restaurant is set right next to the tracks.

Big, west-facing picture windows look out on the trains as they inch or race by at all times of the day. Kids LOVE this place. Parents like it because you can get a decent meal (salads, pizza, pasta, steaks) and a beer or a glass of wine. A renowned local chef took over recently, and time will tell if he's able to move the fare up from the caboose to first class. In the meantime, children (and train buffs of all ages) still beg to go back to "the train station." All aboard!

The Gazette's monthly magazine for parents, *Pikes Peak Parent,* has a website that lists upcoming events, blogs by local moms, deals for families, archives of the printed version of the magazine, and more: www.pikespeakparent.com.

JOSH & JOHN'S ICE CREAMS $–$$
111 E. Pikes Peak Ave.
(719) 632-0299
http://web.me.com/joshandjohns
What kid doesn't love going out for ice cream? From toddler to grandparent, all kids-at-heart crave a good cone every once in a while, and these are good cones (or cups) extraordinaire. The all-natural, hormone-free desserts (some even lactose free) are sold out of a whimsical, wide store downtown. Hundreds of flavors rotate on the menu, some the usual (Dutch chocolate, Rocky Mountain road) and some more exotic (carrot cake, yellow cake cookie dough, ginger-snap molasses). A core of popular flavors is always available, such as Almond Joy, oatmeal cookie, and root beer float. You can sign up on the web for e-mail updates on daily flavors, and by signing up you get one free scoop. They offer a fun "icecreamometer," a punch card that gains punches the colder

and wetter it is outside. With kiddie cones under a dollar, how can you resist?

PATSY'S CANDY $-$$
1540 S. 21st St.
(719) 633-7215, (866) 3-PATSYS (372-8797)
www.patsyscandies.com

Patsy's is a cute, old-time candy shop in a very "wild west" building. Since they've been making candy for more than 100 years, it seems to fit. Of course kids love candy of any kind, but Patsy's is old-world, artisan chocolate that adults crave as well. Very popular as gifts in the holiday season (you choose the contents, they'll ship the box), Patsy's makes to-die-for truffles of every imaginable flavor, salt water taffy, rum cherry cordials, and their Patsy's Pride of the Rockies Almond Toffee. They also sell flavored popcorn and more. Most fun of all? Get on one of the chocolate and candy factory tours and watch that taffy getting stretched and folded, or see that warm chocolate swirl into shape. Tours are held twice daily on weekdays in the summer.

POOR RICHARD'S,
THE RESTAURANT $$
324½ N. Tejon St.
(719) 632-7721
http://poorrichardsdowntown.com

Part of the Poor Richard's four-store complex, the restaurant is not just for kids. But, the back room has an awesome castle structure and play place. Don't think McDonald's though—the only thing similar is the suggestion of play place and food in the same room. Poor Richard's castle and surrounding play area is a whimsical, original, artistic take on a kid's area. The food features hand-tossed, New York–style pizza and fresh salads topped with choices like portobello mushrooms and steamed broccoli. Poor Richard's prides itself on the organic, fresh, healthy alternatives, so there's no guilt in a play date here. In summer, the shaded back patio is also open. Don't miss the toy store in the connected retail shop (see the Shopping chapter). (See also the Restaurants chapter.)

SQUEAK SODA SHOP $$
812 Village Center Dr.
(719) 265-4677
http://squeaksodashop.com

This is a franchise, but it doesn't feel cookie-cutter. Squeak is for kids and adults in touch with their inner child. The wild, colorful, happy little shop is tucked into a shopping center in the Rockrimmon neighborhood. The soda fountain drinks come in no less than 70 flavors, custom-labeled bottles can be made for your special occasion (you even pick the flavor inside), and ice cream floats are thick and rich. There's also candy, coffee, tea, shaved ice, and hot chocolate. What's not for a kid to love? Birthday parties can be arranged.

PARKS

In our parks, Colorado Springs is rich indeed. There is an average of 35 acres of park for every 1,000 people living in El Paso County, which is 40 percent higher than the national average—not that we're bragging or anything! This includes 136 neighborhood parks, plus regional, community, and state parks, as well as open spaces and trails. Within the city limits alone, we have 9,000 acres of parks and 500 acres of trails.

The Pikes Peak region does have the classic green expanse of lawns, in particular at the large Memorial Park, Cottonwood Creek Park, and Bear Creek Park. But we also have every park activity—and corresponding facility for it. There are open spaces with hiking trails and regional parks with pavilions for gatherings. There are parks with courts for tennis, sand volleyball, inline skating, and basketball. There are community parks with baseball fields, neighborhood parks with playgrounds, city parks with glorious, bubbling fountains, and state parks with serene, natural vegetation. In our parks you can swim, skate, jump, climb, and dig. It's fair to say that to know the people of Colorado Springs, you have to spend at least some time hanging out in our parks.

OVERVIEW

This chapter lists many of our biggest, best, most important parks, whether managed by the city, county, or state. There are, of course, dozens more. This doesn't mean those not listed here aren't good—sometimes those smaller, personal park experiences are just the ticket. Also, most parks listed here are on the north, west, or southern part of the city, probably because as you go east, the land flattens out and becomes more prairie—beautiful in its own way, but less likely to be designated a park. This does make it easy to tell where you are, though. Locals say you always know where you are because if you see mountains, you're looking west. For those directionally challenged, this can be a real help!

A note about city parks: Colorado Springs, like all cities in the US, has found funds short in recent years. Parks have

suffered a bit, and visitors found bathrooms locked and trash cans not serviced. These services will be available again when funds permit, as early as summer 2011. The county had these troubles earlier than the city and has now been able to keep restrooms open (other than in winter months, when they're normally closed anyway). The state restrooms remain open.

And the trails, open spaces, and parks, they too remain open, glorious and just waiting for our citizens and visitors to spend many an active, invigorating day. So read fast and get out there to hike, bike, or visit in the parks, open spaces, trails, and natural wonders of the Pikes Peak region.

Unless noted with the word "Fee," all parks are free. Renting spaces, such as pavilions, or using facilities such as pools can incur a fee as well.

PARKS

ACACIA PARK & UNCLE WILBER FOUNTAIN
Bijou and Tejon Streets
(719) 385-5940
www.springsgov.com
Acacia Park, located in the heart of downtown, is the city's first park, donated by General Palmer in 1871. Today it is a mecca for high school students at lunchtime (Palmer High School is across the street); children and families who flock to the Uncle Wilber Fountain in the summer; and shoppers, diners, and business folks who want a few minutes' respite under a cool tree. There is a band shell that is used often by music groups and a playground. (For more detailed information on the Uncle Wilber Fountain, see the Kidstuff chapter.)

AIKEN CANYON NATURAL AREA
South of Colorado Springs on CO 115
(303) 866-3454 or (303) 444-2950
http://parks.state.co.us/
SiteCollectionImages/parks/Programs/
CNAP/AikenCanyon.pdf
The 1,621-acre Aiken Canyon Natural Area includes the largest intact foothills ecosystem on the Front Range. In 1991, the Nature Conservancy signed a 99-year conservation lease, giving it exclusive right to manage the state-owned land. The area contains one woodland and two foothills shrub-land plant communities of special interest. Aiken Canyon also contains an unusual diversity and concentration of wildlife. Mountain lions, black bears, wild turkeys, elk, mule deer, and an abundance

of migratory birds live in or visit in the area. You might also spot Colorado nuthatches (three species), Cooper's hawks, golden eagles, hairy and downy woodpeckers, northern harriers, prairie falcons, and sharp-shinned hawks. In summer, the prairie grasses and wildflowers lure countless butterflies. The ponderosa pines and Douglas firs along the streams and on the rugged canyon walls have not been logged, unlike most of the Front Range. In this life zone between the plains and mountains, dramatic red spires and rocky outcrops collide with rich green flora. Named after ornithologist Charles Aiken, this is a great destination for birders; more than 100 species have been seen. Aiken, a US surveyor, taxidermist, and collector, first surveyed this region in the 1870s. The preserve is open year-round, dawn to dusk, on Sat, Sun, and Mon only. The wildlife gets a respite from visitors the remainder of the week. Some school programs are scheduled. The innovative straw-bale construction Field Station and Visitor Center is open 10 a.m. to 3 p.m. those days, from Memorial Day to Labor Day. During the rest of the year, it's open on Sun only. Hike the well-maintained, 4-mile-loop trail that begins at the entrance. An additional ¾-mile trail branches off from the loop and makes its way through the canyon. Interpretive signs highlight important features along the trail. Dress for the occasion. You will encounter rocky areas with low brush and cactus, and maybe even a rattlesnake or two, so wear sturdy leather boots. Leave Fido at home—pets are not allowed, even on a leash. Camping is not permitted here. To get here, take CO 115 south from Colorado Springs, about 16 miles from downtown. Look for Turkey Canyon Ranch Road (located 0.1 mile south of milepost 32) and turn right (west) and drive 200 yards to the preserve parking area.

AMERICA THE BEAUTIFUL PARK
126 Cimino Dr.
(719) 385-5940
www.springsgov.com
This new city park sports a lovely, impressive fountain, a wide grassy area, walking paths, a picnic pavilion, and an innovative playground. Set just west of downtown (you can see it from I-25), this is a great place to enjoy a bag lunch or a play date or to scope out the Farm and Art Market on Wednesday in the summer and fall. (More detailed information is in the Kidstuff and Shopping chapters.)

BEAR CREEK REGIONAL PARK
21st Street and Argus Boulevard
(719) 520-6375
http://adm.elpasoco.com/Parks/
Documents/BCRPHandout.pdf
This popular, sprawling, always-green park lies on the west side of town in the Skyway/Broadmoor area. The fields are almost always busy with soccer, rugby, football, or lacrosse games, both pick-up and team. There are 8 pavilions of various sizes, the largest of which can seat up to 150 people. Each pavilion has tables and grills and some have an electrical outlet. On spring, summer, and fall weekends, the pavilions are busy with family parties, group events, reunions and more (so book ahead of time if you need one of the bigger pavilions). There are restrooms, 2 playgrounds, 2 sand volleyball courts (bring your own net and ball), 4 horseshoe pits (bring your own 'shoes), 8 tennis courts with lights, an archery range, an exercise course, a basketball court, and

small picnic areas. You can see why this park is so popular!

Nature Centers

There are two excellent nature centers in the Pikes Peak region. Both are run by El Paso County and offer interpretive programs, classes, special events, guided and self-guided tours, presentations, trails, and more. Some of the programs in the past have included "Bear Necessities," "Free Star Gazing," and "Pajamas in the Park: Going Batty." The **Bear Creek** center is in the foothills and features a prairie-to-peaks landscape, while the **Fountain Creek** center lies in the Cattail Marsh Wildlife Area. The regional trails are open to hiking, horseback riding, and pets on a leash. Both nature centers are free and open Wed through Sat.

Bear Creek Nature Center
245 Bear Creek Rd.
(719) 520-6387
http://adm.elpasoco.com/Parks/Pages/
BearCreekNatureCenter.aspx

Fountain Creek Nature Center
320 Pepper Grass Lane, Fountain
(719) 520-6745
http://adm.elpasoco.com/Parks/Pages/
FountainCreekNatureCenter.aspx

CHEYENNE MOUNTAIN
STATE PARK   FEE
410 JL Ranch Heights
(719) 576-2016
http://parks.state.co.us/Parks/
CheyenneMountain

The newest state park covers a vast 1,680 acres, going from rolling prairie up to peaks. Located on the southern end of Colorado Springs just opposite Fort Carson Gate 1, Cheyenne Mountain State Park underwent years of careful planning before opening in 2006. The park, the largest in El Paso County, offers year-round hiking, biking, camping, wildlife viewing, a visitor center, and facilities for group events.

This park offers the classic Colorado experience. Near the entrance is a mosaic of Great Plains grassland and oak shrubs, but as the park climbs to peaks in the west, there are classic ponderosa pine and Douglas fir forests. In between are varying grass species, mushrooms, northern-most wild grapes, and some of the largest strands of plum in Colorado Springs. The wildlife is just as diverse, including deer, elk, black bears, mountain lion, red foxes, bobcats, and badgers. Wild turkeys roam the grounds while red-tail hawks and golden eagles soar above.

The best way to experience the park is with time on your hands and a bike or hiking shoes. There are 16 trails covering more than 20 miles, from easy, short jaunts to long, more difficult routes. A number of suggested hikes with maps are available on the website (also see the Hiking section in the Sports & Recreation chapter). Leave Fido at home, though, as pets and horses, are not permitted on the trails—and neither is smoking—in an effort to protect the fragile ecosystems.

Geocaching, a popular GPS-inspired treasure hunting activity, is another great way to explore the park's trails and generous open space. There are several caches hidden in the park, and clues to hidden cache locations are posted at www.geocaching .com. GPS units are available for rental at the park visitor center. They even offer GPS/ Geocaching instructional programs for those who want to start the hobby. Check the park calendar of events (on the website) for the next session.

Evening programs and naturalist-guided hikes are led regularly in the summer and occasionally in the fall, winter, and spring. Programs include the new Junior Ranger program, children's activities, wildlife information, and more. Some past sessions have covered "Munching Mouthparts" (the construction of a large-scale model working grasshopper's mouth), "Rattlesnakes!" and "Star Trekking." You can sign up as an individual, or schedule a special group activity. Check the visitor center calendar, or call to make a special group appointment. When at the visitor center, also pick up the wildlife and birds checklists.

For those who want to picnic, there are 41 day-use picnic sites (available first come, first served), complete with table, grill, and peak to prairie views.

If a group event is in your future, there are 2 outdoor facilities. The Prairie Skipper, which accommodates up to 200 people, is a pavilion with electric service, picnic tables, restrooms, activity area, and parking for 85 vehicles. Prairie Falcon Event Facility is an outdoor amphitheater with rock-step seating that overlooks green open space (hint: great for weddings!). It holds up to 200 people and is open May through Oct. Both require advance reservations and a fee. Check the website for the "group facilities" link for more information.

Camping also is available (see the Camping section in the Sports & Recreation chapter as well as the Accommodations chapter).

Park passes are $7 daily per vehicle, or you can purchase an annual pass for $70, although Colorado seniors pay only $35.

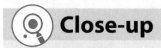

Close-up

Dog Parks

We do love our dogs here in the Springs. Why else would Colorado Springs be ranked No. 1 by *Forbes* for "America's Most Pet-Friendly City" as well as No. 1 by *Men's Health* for "Best Cities for Dogs." You could say we've gone to the dogs—and you'd be right!

With all this animal love, you know we have places for our best friends to play. There are three dog runs—hiking areas where dogs are allowed off-leash if kept under control. They are at **Garden of the Gods Park**, east of Rock Ledge Ranch and south of Gateway Road; **Red Rock Canyon Open Space**, on the designated Dog Loop Trail south of the main parking lot; and at **Palmer Park** at the Yucca Flats.

The city also has four distinct dog parks—fenced areas where dogs are allowed off-leash if kept under control (but watch out for your dog as some people think "under control" means anything goes). Each of these parks has definite advantages, and they are conveniently located across the city.

The big dog in parks is the **Bear Creek Dog Park**, off 21st Street at Rio Grande. Your dog can run free in the 25 acres of hills, trees, and a mountain creek. There is also a 2-acre small dog area with benches and tables. Water is usually available (jugs are left for people to bring home and replenish on their next visit). The terrain has an elevation change of up to 100 feet, and the many areas of bushes and high grass give dogs lots of romping room. Bear Creek is on the west side of the city.

Cheyenne Meadows Dog Park, off Charmwood Drive and Canoe Creek Drive, is a bit bare bones (pardon the pun). There is a bench and no water for dogs or separate small dog area. It is the most southern dog park in the city.

Palmer Park Dog Park, found 0.3 miles into the park from the Maizeland Road entrance, is small but serviceable. There is a larger area for big dogs and a miniature space for the small dog area. Wood chips are sometimes fresh in the small dog area. There are no trees or other vegetation, but the dogs don't seem to have a bone to pick with the frugal surroundings. This is the eastern-most dog park in the city.

Rampart Dog Park is tucked behind Rampart High School, just east of the base-ball diamond. Originally built as a project for an Eagle Scout award, this is a large space with a few trees and big logs. It can be very dusty or, in spring, muddy. There is no small dog area. This is the city's most northern dog park.

All dog parks require (by city ordinance) owners to pick up what their dogs leave behind, and there are plenty of collection points for donated dispenser bags if you've forgotten your own.

Open year-round, 24 hours a day with a quiet time between 10 p.m. and 6 a.m.

To reach the park, drive south on I-25 to exit 135 at South Academy Boulevard. Go west (right) past Pikes Peak Community College. At CO 115, turn left (south). At the first stop light, turn right (Fort Carson Gate 1 will be directly across the street). Go west and follow the road into the park.

COTTONWOOOD CREEK PARK
7040 Rangewood Dr.
(719) 385-5940
www.springsgov.com

This is one of the big community parks in Colorado Springs. First, the Cottonwood Creek Recreation Center is located here, complete with indoor pool and fitness center. The 77-acre park features picnic tables, playground, 4 soccer fields, 3 softball/baseball fields, tennis courts, an inline hockey court, a disc golf course, walking and running paths, and, in winter, prime sledding hills. The city's website (listed above) has complete maps of the park, a detailed disc golf course layout showing tee box and primary and alternate basket locations, and distances for various trail loop distances. Find the park at the corner of Dublin Boulevard and Rangewood Drive in the northeast part of the city. (See also the Sports & Recreation chapter for more details on the various activities accommodated at the park.)

Questions?

If you're curious about a park, or just want specific information, these are the three main agencies that manage the parks in our region:

City of Colorado Springs (719-385-5940, www.springsgov.com)

El Paso County (719-520-7276, www.elpasoco.com/parks.asp)

Colorado State Parks (303-470-1144, www.parks.state.co.us)

ELEVEN MILE STATE PARK   **FEE**
CR 92, near Lake George
(719) 748-3863
http://parks.state.co.us/Parks/ElevenMile

Eleven Mile is a big chunk of Colorado: a large, high altitude (8,600 feet above sea level) reservoir for boating and fishing, miles of hiking and biking trails, secluded canyons, and remote hillsides. Even on hot summer weekends, crowds are rare.

The dam that made the reservoir was finished in 1932, and is today owned by the Denver Water Department. As one of seven reservoirs for Denver's drinking water, there are strict regulations to protect against pollution. This poses some barriers for the recreational user, but more than that has created a pristine space of land and water that is perfect for a weekend in the mountains.

Fishing is perhaps the biggest draw, with the popular catch of brown, cutthroat, and rainbow trout, as well as northern pike. The lake is one of a very few in Colorado stocked with kokanee salmon. (See Fishing in the Sports & Recreation chapter for more detailed information.) Boating is also a big draw, including kayaking, canoeing, sailing, and motor boating. Keep your toes in the boat and on shore, though: Because of the human water supply issue, you can't swim, scuba dive, water-ski, or even wade. Sailboarding is allowed all summer, although the high mountain winds make it a challenge even for the most experienced of sailboarders. If you need to rent boating and/or fishing equipment, **11 Mile Marina** (719-748-0317, 877-725-3172, www.11milesports.com) is located on the north shore of the reservoir and rents boats (pontoon, fishing, power, and canoe), boat slips, and mooring buoys.

For landlubbers, Eleven Mile has scenic hiking and biking trails in the Coyote Ridge/Backcountry area. There also is a self-guided nature trail and an orienteering trail. Brochures for both are available at the park office. While you're out in the woods, watch for every kind of bird from songbirds and raptors to waterfowl and shorebirds. The rare bald eagle, American peregrine falcon, and white pelican also might be spotted. (Download a PDF of Eleven Mile's Bird List under the "Publications" link on the website.) There also are 15 picnic sites and a playground, if you're just out enjoying the day.

If you want to make it a weekend, there are 349 campsites, from basic and secluded sites to electric or lakeshore sites. Or, there are 25 secluded backcountry sites for the more adventurous campers. (See Camping in the Sports & Recreation chapter for more detailed information.)

In the fall, hunt for everything from elk and bear to mallards and gadwalls. (Go to the park's website for more information about hunting in the area; or for general season dates and regulations, go to the Colorado Division of Wildlife's hunting webpage at http://wildlife.state.co.us/Hunting.)

This high-altitude park doesn't take a vacation when the snow comes. In fact, winter is almost as active as summer, with cross-country skiing on the open meadows and, when the water freezes solid, on the lake. Ice skaters also enjoy the hard surface. Snowshoers find the park a virtual paradise. But the biggest crowds in winter are hearty ice fishermen. Those who leave with a fish story catch kokanee, trout, and pike all winter long. Ice boating is not currently allowed on the lake.

Eleven Mile has numerous education programs each summer, presented by Great Outdoors Colorado (GOCO) Interpreters. (See the website's calendar for upcoming programs.) There's also a Junior Rangers program for those budding outdoors kids, ages 6 to 12. Those who've completed the Eleven Mile Junior Ranger activity book can receive certificates in a ceremony held on Sunday mornings.

To get to Eleven Mile, head west out of Colorado Springs on US 24. One mile past the small town of Lake George, turn left (south) on CR 90 and drive for 6 miles to CR 92. Continue south on CR 92 for 5 miles to the park.

The park is open 24 hours a day for camping and fishing, and the office is open daily. Fees are $7 per vehicle for a daily pass, or an annual pass is $70 (discounts available for Colorado seniors).

FOUNTAIN CREEK REGIONAL PARK
Duckwood Road and US 85/87, Fountain (719) 520-6375
http://adm.elpasoco.com/Parks/Documents/FCRPHandout.pdf

This quiet jewel of a park has trails, ponds, a creek, and more in a serene shortgrass prairie. There are open areas in the Cottonwood Meadows and playing fields and pavilions at the Duckwood Active Use Area, but this park is more the dense, introspective, tranquil variety. The Fountain Creek Nature Center (see box on p. 133) sits about center of the park, and its Cattail Marsh Wildlife Area is a quiet preserve for wildlife. A stroll through these wide, easy trails is a walk in bird land, with lizards, toads, frogs, beavers, muskrats, and arthropods sharing the habitat. At the north end of the park is Willow Springs Ponds, a favorite fishing hole on the weekends. The south end of the park is home to Hanson Nature Park. If you'd rather use the park for more active pursuits than wildlife and plant appreciation, there are 6 pavilions, one of which seats 100 people. Each pavilion has grills and an electrical outlet. There also are 2 volleyball courts (bring net and ball), a basketball court, 2 horseshoe pits (bring 'shoes), water, and restrooms.

FOX RUN REGIONAL PARK
On Stella Drive
(719) 520-6375
http://adm.elpasoco.com/Parks/
Documents/FRRP_Brochure.pdf

Fox Run is in the Black Forest area. The open meadows, gazebo, lake, forest, and playground make this a perfect place for a family gathering or just a day spent outside. The Oak Meadows area has 3 picnic pavilions, each with seating for 50 people at 7 tables, grills, and electrical outlets. There also are restrooms, a sand volleyball court (bring your own net and ball), and a horseshoe pit (bring you own 'shoes). The Pine Meadows area has 2 similar pavilions, each with lighting. The gazebo at Aspen Lake seats about 20 and can be reserved for weddings and other ceremonies. There are a few trails, but mainly this is a park for picnics and relaxing. Open year-round. North of Colorado Springs, exit I-25 at Baptist Road and go east. Take a right on Roller Coaster Road. Turn right again on Stella Road and turn right into the main entrance.

✳GARDEN OF THE GODS PARK
1805 N. 30th St.
(719) 634-6666
www.gardenofgods.com

This towering, bright, truly amazing park of rock formations, vegetation, and wildlife is one of our city's best-known attractions. (See the Attractions chapter for detailed information.) The city-owned, 1,400-acre park has a visitor and nature center and has been recognized by the Department of the Interior as "a nationally-significant natural area." It offers towering sandstone formations, a wonderful view of Pikes Peak, paved and unpaved hiking paths, the Rock Ledge Ranch Historic Site, and a living history museum, among other amenities. Placed on the National Register for Historic Places in 1971, Garden of the Gods is one of the jewels of our community and NOT to be missed, even if you only have time to drive the loop through the park.

A short note for those adventurous types: Every year a good number of tourists are tempted to climb the rocks. They are deceiving and can be extremely hard to climb up and get down. Climbers must first register at the Garden of the Gods Visitor and Nature Center, and technical climbing is permitted only on established routes in groups of two or more. All other climbing or rock scrambling past 10 feet high is illegal and will get you a big fine or even jail time. Sadly, there's almost always a death or two every summer as tourists ignore these rules, get too far up, and fall. We like our visitors to leave happy and alive—please respect this park and its rules. (See more detailed climbing information in the Sports & Recreation chapter under Climbing.)

MEMORIAL PARK
1605 E. Pikes Peak Ave.
(719) 385-5940
www.springsgov.com

If Colorado Springs had a "Central Park," this would be it. Located just east of downtown, the sprawling, almost 200 acres has a little bit of everything. It's also the location of many events and happenings, most notably the Labor Day weekend hot-air balloon festival (see the Annual Events & Festivals chapter). On a day-to-day basis, the park is home to the city's Parks and Recreations sports division offices, 3 baseball/softball fields, 15 football/soccer fields, 15 tennis courts at the

Tennis Center, picnic shelters, a large group picnic area, multi-play court, and horseshoe courts (bring your own 'shoes). There are 3 playgrounds, including the Phil Long/Denver Broncos Community Playground with ADA accessibility. There is the Colorado Springs Recreation Center, with pool and fitness center, near a Veterans Memorial. The Fireman's Memorial is on the other side of the park (see the Annual Events & Festivals chapter). Prospect Lake sits on the south border of the park, and it includes a bath house, swimming beach, boating for both motorized and non-motorized watercraft, water-skiing, boat rental (paddle, row, sail, and canoe), and 2 fishing areas (one with a wheelchair-accessible fishing dock). For those who like their water frozen, Memorial also is home to Sertich Ice Center with public ice skating and lessons. For those who don't want water at all, there is the world-class bike racing track 7-Eleven US Olympic Training Center Velodrome. Built in 1982 in preparation for the 1984 Olympics in Los Angeles, the 333.3 meter track with a 33-degree banking is popular with riders for its speed. You must be a member of USA Cycling to train and/or race on the track, although many events are open to public spectators. And finally, the city's newest, sickest skate park is next to Sertich Memorial Park and can be seen at numerous intersections along Pikes Peak Avenue, starting from the west side at South Hancock Avenue. (See the Sports & Recreation chapter for details on the sporting activities listed above.)

✳MONUMENT VALLEY PARK
170 W. Cache La Poudre St.
(719) 385-5940
www.springsgov.com

This lovely park—it stretches a few miles along Monument Creek downtown—was one of General Palmer's most treasured gifts to the people of Colorado Springs. Today, Monument Valley Park is one of the community's most traveled green areas. Joggers, cyclists, mothers with strollers, and couples hand-in-hand travel the trails while others have picnics, play tennis, swim, or use the sports fields. The 153-acre expanse houses the City Greenhouse as well as the Horticultural Art Society Demonstration Gardens, where native and regional plants are tagged in both English and Braille. (If you're here in the spring, the annual plant sale at the Demonstration Garden is a local delight. For dates and information, call 719-357-9427 or see http://hasgardens.org.) There is a formal garden gracing the southern edge of the park, and a Heritage Garden and Pinetum are north of the Demonstration Garden. For the more active lot, there are baseball/softball fields; a soccer field; a substantial playground; a 4.3-mile trail for walkers, runners, and cyclists; and a 1-mile fitness trail. An interesting geologic column is part of the park. There are also tennis courts, basketball courts, a sand volleyball area, 2 fishing ponds, and large and small picnic areas.

A roomy parking lot can be found across the street from the Demonstration Garden at Glen Avenue and Cache La Poudre, or the park can be accessed from Monroe Street and Wood Avenue on the north, or by W. Bijou Street and Sierra Madre Street at the south end of the park.

MUELLER STATE PARK   **FEE**
21045 Highway 67 S., Divide
(719) 687-2366
http://parks.state.co.us/Parks/Mueller

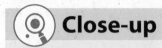 **Close-up**

Wildlife Among Us

The Pikes Peak region lies at the base of the famous mountain, along the foothills of the Rockies. It stands to reason that wildlife lives up there. It also follows that they don't know where the city limits lie and tend to wander down to check things out.

It's not uncommon to see foxes, coyotes, raccoons, skunks, rabbits, squirrels, and other small animals. It's also not uncommon to lose your summer garden to a doe and her fawns, or to drive around a curve and see a six-point buck standing in the middle of the road. Bears also like the forage they find in neighborhood trash cans and birdfeeders. A few years ago, there even was a moose that made his home in Monument Valley Park for several months!

When visiting the area, be aware that wildlife is everywhere. On a day hike in any city or county park, visitors have encountered everything from ground squirrels to mountain lions. At some of the state parks, you're likely to see black bear or elk. Here are some tips for dealing with the critters:

- **Never approach wildlife.** They're called that for a reason. Their behavior is unpredictable.

- **Never try to feed wildlife.** They can't always differentiate the food from the source, and it makes them too tame and more likely to interact with humans. When that happens, they often must be euthanized.

- **Don't leave food or trash where they can get into it.** If you live here, don't put out your trash until the morning of pick up, and put caps on chimneys to keep raccoons and squirrels out.

- **If you encounter a bear or mountain lion, stay calm.** (Yes, we know, easier said than done.) Chances are they don't want to be near you any more than you want to be near them. Stop, then back away slowly. Open your jacket or wave your arms to appear larger than you are. Don't turn and run—that makes you prey. Carry a sturdy walking stick and use if necessary. They often retreat when they encounter resistance.

- **A word about rattlesnakes: Yes, they live here.** Wear boots when hiking and carry a walking stick. Be alert. They like to sun themselves on rocks. If you get bitten, do not use a tourniquet or try to suck the poison out of the wound. Get your cell phone and call a doctor or hospital emergency room and then, if you can, drive there!

You want to see wildlife? Go to Mueller. The 5,121-acre park, with 50 miles of trails, is home to elk, black bears, mountain lions, and mule deer. There is so much activity, pets are not permitted on the trails or in the backcountry, and one area of the park is off limits in June for elk calving. There are more than 115 species of birds, including golden eagles, red-tailed hawks, and Clark's nutcrackers. It is awe-inspiring in its beauty, with mixed coniferous and aspen forest, rock outcroppings, grassland, and wetlands. There are homesteads from early pioneers. From pines to meadows, Mueller is what one pictures when thinking of classic Colorado.

Hiking and biking are extremely popular here, but visitors also can ride horses. You need to bring your own horse, and out of the 50 miles of trails, 19 are designated for riding horses or bikes. The visitor center and website list a number of short, family-friendly hikes of less than 1 mile. There also are 132 campsites, with many open for winter camping, and there are 3 cabins available year round (see Camping in the Sports & Recreation chapter). Snowshoeing, cross-country skiing, and sledding/tubing are also popular here in the winter.

If a simple day hike and picnic are in your plans, Mueller offers 41 wooded, scenic picnic sites (table and grill) scattered among conifer and aspen forests, some with views of the surrounding peaks. A few sites also are near restrooms and drinking water, and all are on a first-come basis.

In the fall, Mueller is a choice hunting spot. The Dome Rock State Wildlife Area (http://wildlife.state.co.us/LandWater/StateWildlifeAreas) adjoins Mueller, with 800 acres designated for hunting during season in the fall. Three trails from Mueller access the hunting area.

In the summer, naturalists lead hikes, and there are other educational activities and programs throughout the year. Check the calendar on the website or stop in the visitor center to see what's up during your visit. And don't forget your camera!

The park is open year-round, and the visitor center is open Wed through Sun. Park passes are $7 daily per vehicle, or you can purchase an annual pass for $70, although Colorado seniors pay only $35. You can get to Mueller by going west out of Colorado Springs on US 24. At Divide, turn left on CO 67 South for 3.5 miles to the park entrance.

✳NORTH CHEYENNE CAÑON PARK
Cheyenne Mountain Boulevard
(719) 385-5940
www.springsgov.com

Managed by the City of Colorado Springs, North Cheyenne Cañon is a full forest ecosystem right here in the city. The canyon itself is 1,000 feet deep and cut into 1.5 billion-year-old granite. The swift, clear North Cheyenne Creek runs through the spine of the 1,600-acre park, providing an ideal habitat for diverse plant life and such large animals as black bears, mountain lions, and mule deer. The little birds that love water, such as the broad-tailed hummingbird and kingfisher, also make a happy home here.

You don't have to remember all this, though, because as you enter the park you can stop at the **Starsmore Discovery Center** (719-385-6086). Each year, more than 450,000 people visit this unique City of Colorado Springs center, especially active in the summer with programs and festivals such as the annual Hummingbird Festival in May. At Starsmore you can pick up free canyon maps, see the critters outside the bird-watching window, see authentic dioramas, and explore hands-on nature exhibits. Books, videos, and hummingbird feeders are on sale, and past programs offered include a "Tipi Raising & Ute Heritage Workshop."

The **Helen Hunt Falls Visitor Center** (719-633-5701 in summer or 719-385-6086 during the school year) is a quick drive up the canyon. Visitors find exhibits, scheduled hikes and walks, and informative staff and volunteers on-site. There's also a gift shop with Colorado scenic guides and history books, maps, nature books, videos, gift items, and drinks. The stars, though, are the falls and trailheads accessed from this spot. You can find a trail map at www.springs gov.com, and also see the Hiking entry in the Sports & Recreation chapter for more detailed information. Note that the visitor center is normally closed in the winter months.

✳PAINT MINES INTERPRETIVE PARK
On Paint Mines Road, eastern El Paso County
(719) 520-6375
http://adm.elpasoco.com/Parks/
Documents/StoryofthePaintMines.pdf

When it comes to parks, Paint Mines is a whole 'nother thing. Hoodoos, spires, little caves, and mushroom-capped rock formations in shades of ochre, rose, rust, and gold cover the moonscape-like park. Archeologists say humans visited here 9,000 years ago, and the towering colored clays, deposited 55 million years ago, were used to make pottery. Many of the plants in the 750-acre park were used in native ceremonies.

Wildflowers, from startling orange paintbrush to fragrant snowy spirea, flourish in the undulations of the soil. Butterflies flutter around, and you'll see countless birds—from hunting hawks to darting swallows. Depending upon which trail you choose (don't worry, it's all a big loop—you won't get lost), you meander alongside a riparian area rife with red-winged blackbirds, or you head over a rise and right down into the rocky canyons. Many trails are dead-ends in the hiking sense, but revelations to the explorer's eye. In all, you can hike up to 4 miles and it will take about 2 hours, with stops to gawk and

wonder and shoot photos. Take a moment to share the shelter of a shady rock with a lizard (they're not too territorial). If you're quiet, you may spot a fox, a deer, or even a pronghorn. Walking is easy in many places, slightly steeper in others. (See also Hiking in the Sports & Recreation chapter.) You'll be tempted, but you're not supposed to climb on the soft, crumbly rock.

Don't be surprised if yours is the only car there (on a weekday) or one of just a handful (on weekends). Go early in warm weather, when the day still is cool. Wear sunscreen and good walking shoes; pack water and your camera.

The Paint Mines are open dawn to dusk daily. To drive there, go east on US 24 about 35 miles to Calhan. Turn south (right) on Yoder Road/Calhan Highway. Turn east (left) on Paint Mine Road, and follow the signs.

PALMER PARK
3650 Maizeland Rd.
(719) 385-5940
www.springsgov.com

Palmer Park is a great expanse of a park—730 acres that lie east of downtown. It has open fields, steep cliffs, hoodoos (tall rock spires), and great views of Pikes Peak. A favorite of hikers and joggers, it's convenient to those on the east side of town. Palmer Park has 2 baseball/softball fields, a big playground (worth a drive), a football/soccer field, 3 volleyball courts (bring your own ball), a dog park (see the Close-Up on Dog Parks in this chapter), and horse stables (lessons and boarding, 719-634-4173). There are scenic overlooks from a drive through the park, picnic spots for large and small groups, a botanical reserve, and the Seven Castles geological point of interest. There also are more than 25 miles of trails for hikers, cyclists, joggers, and equestrians (see the Hiking and Cycling sections of the Sports & Recreation chapter).

Palmer Park can be accessed either off Maizeland Road just west of the intersection of Maizeland Road and North Academy Boulevard, or off of Austin Bluffs Parkway west of its intersection with North Academy Boulevard.

QUAIL LAKE
915 Cheyenne Mountain Blvd.
(719) 385-5940
www.springsgov.com
This 113-acre park is most identified by its lake. Good for fishing and non-motorized boating, Quail is a bit of serenity in the middle of the city. A fitness trail is 1 mile long, there are 2 sand volleyball courts (bring your own ball), a basketball court, picnic areas, and a large group shelter and, when it snows, a very respectable sledding hill. Quail can be reached on East Cheyenne Mountain Boulevard just east of CO 115.

RED ROCK CANYON OPEN SPACE
3615 W. High St.
(719) 385-5940
www.springsgov.com
This old quarry, ideally situated near Fountain Creek, saw man as early as 7000 BC. Today the 785-acre park is one of the newest open spaces within the city, and one of the most striking. More than 100 million years ago, geologic upheaval pushed the red limestone strata up, creating great red parallel ridges. The gentle upslope of the area is perfect for hiking, climbing, cycling, horseback riding, and having a leisurely picnic (see detailed information in the Sports & Recreation chapter). There also is a dog run area (see Close-up on Dog Parks

in this chapter). Red Rock Canyon can be reached off US 24 just west of 31st Street. Go south onto Ridge Road and find the parking lot at the end of the road. An additional parking lot is off South 31st Street and Ore Mill Road; this space has horse trailer parking.

SPINNEY MOUNTAIN STATE PARK   FEE
CR 59, west of Wilkerson Pass
(719) 748-3401
http://parks.state.co.us/Parks/
SpinneyMountain
Spinney Reservoir is just west of Eleven Mile (see listing in this chapter), but because of topography, you have to travel into South Park to reach it. Most of Spinney's services are available at the Eleven Mile park office. Its isolation and fishing are the draw. To anglers, this reservoir is a legend where they enjoy shoreline, fly, belly boat, or trolling fishing in a peaceful setting. Besides the gold-medal fishing, visitors enjoy bird watching, or boaters can explore the 2,500 surface-acre expanse of water. There are 2 boat ramps, depending on water level. Be aware that all boats, including belly boats and float tubes, are inspected for zebra and quagga mussels prior to launch. There are some picnic sites with tables and grills. Given its remote, high-altitude location, Spinney is open seasonally from ice-off to ice-on, usually mid-April through mid-November when it's open from just before sunrise to just after sunset.

Park passes are $7 daily per vehicle, or you can purchase an annual pass for $70, although Colorado seniors pay only $35. Travel west on US 24 past Lake George and over Wilkerson Pass (about 55 miles from Colorado Springs). Turn south on Park CR

23 and drive 2.8 miles to CR 59. Turn right and continue another 1.1 miles to the park entrance (where the asphalt ends).

UTE VALLEY PARK
1705 Vindicator Dr.
(719) 385-5940
www.springsgov.com

Ute Valley is one of those places that can be seconds from your home or hotel and take you into the wild almost instantly. There are 338 acres of hiking and mountain biking trails over rocky cliffs and canyons and a wetland area. Due to the rocks, canyons, caves, water, and good sunlight, there is abundant wildlife. (The middle school to the east of the park isn't really joking by naming their annual cross country competition "Rattlesnake Run.") To reach Ute Valley, go east on Vindicator Drive from Centennial Boulevard. The entrance to the parking lot is on the right.

SPORTS & RECREATION

Colorado Springs has been ranked No. 1 by *Outside* magazine as "Best Town." *Men's Fitness* has ranked the city No. 2 for "Fittest City in America" and No. 3 for "Top Sports Town." With other accolades by the dozen, including a number of publications listing the city somewhere in the top 10 for "Best City to Live, Work, and Play," you know that when it comes to sports and recreation, there's something to talk about.

First, there's the no-brainer category: gorgeous golf courses, easy access to scenic hiking trails, tennis courts all over town, lush soccer fields, and smooth ice hockey rinks. The depth of the Pikes Peak region's athletic interests, though, becomes clear with all the secondary things to do, from disc golf courses to geocaches, from hot skate parks to cool wave pools. There are horses and bikes to ride, ropes and rocks to climb, footballs to throw, lanes to bowl, sand volleyball courts to spike, and gold-medal fish to catch. For those who'd rather watch, top-level college hockey and football are two of the biggest draws in the state. Perhaps the easiest way to explain how much sports and recreation fit into the civic soul is to ask, what isn't here? The answer . . . wait, still thinking.

OVERVIEW

This chapter lists all forms of sports and recreation, first from the participation viewpoint and then from the spectator seat. There's a lot of cross-over of information, especially with the Parks chapter, so we let you know when you can find more information elsewhere. Go by this very loose guideline: You want the place, look in the Parks chapter. You want the activity, look in the main section of this chapter. You want to watch, look in the Spectator Sports section of this chapter. Most of all, know that there's no reason to sit around doing nothing because there are tons of activities in Colorado Springs.

Price Code

The following price code gives an idea of what the regular adult admission or fees might be at the following sports and recreation facilities as well as sporting events. If it's a freebie, we'll let you know.

$ . . . . less than $5
$$ . . . . $5 to $10
$$$ . . . . $10 to $20
$$$$ . . . . more than $20

SPORTS & RECREATION ACTIVITIES

Basketball

There are a number of ways to shoot some hoops in the Springs. First, there are more than 50 neighborhood parks with basketball courts. If you want something organized, check out the adult and youth sports programs with the **City of Colorado Springs Sports Office** (719-385-5981, www.springs gov.com). The programs change throughout the year, so check the link for the current programs. Also, basketball is quite active at the local **YMCAs** (see the Health and Wellness chapter). Courts in the parks are free, but joining any of the available teams and leagues costs a fee of about $65.

i Most bowling alleys host full leagues, so call before showing up, especially at night. They're happy to tell you if any lanes are open for walk-in players.

Bowling

There are bowling alleys in all corners of town, and they're all hopping. Leagues can make it difficult to get a lane when you want, so be sure to call before you go. Most have grills or snack bars and also run deals that include games, shoes, and snacks. Prices can vary depending on time of day.

BEAR CREEK LANES $-$$$
1232 S. 21st St.
(719) 634-6719

BRUNSWICK ZONE CIRCLE $-$$$
999 N. Circle Dr.
(719) 596-5257
www.bowlbrunswick.com

CLASSIC 300 LANES $-$$$
1867 N. Circle Dr.
(719) 632-4636

MR. BIGGS FAMILY FUN CENTER $-$$$
5825 Mark Dabling Blvd.
(719) 955-7220
www.becooldoright.com

HARMONY BOWL $-$$$
3845 N. Academy Blvd.
(719) 591-1000

KING PIN LANES $-$$$
3410 N. Academy Blvd.
(719) 574-0820

PEAK BOWLING CENTER $-$$$
2861 N. Prospect St.
(719) 636-5193
www.peakbowl.com

BMX Biking

See the Skateboarding section in this chapter for detailed information on two areas that attract BMX bikers: **Memorial Park Skate Park** and the **Gossage Youth Sports Complex** skate park and adjacent BMX area. Also, **Rampart Park** has a BMX track (8270 Lexington Dr.; access parking lot from Lexington Drive north of Rampart High School). Free admission at all parks.

i In Colorado, helmet hair is all the rage—from little tykes to Olympic athletes, cyclists always sport the smart gear. Don't leave home without one!

Camping

There's nothing quite like sleeping out under the stars, or even in a tent or RV that's far away from civilization. Finding a place to do that in the Pikes Peak region is pretty easy—more than one-third of Colorado's land is owned by the public and available for public use. If you're unsure where these areas are, check with the three agencies that manage the land: **Bureau of Land Management** (www.blm.gov), the **US Forest Service** (www.fs.usda.gov), and the **National Park Service** (www.nps.gov).

The US Forest Service also has a good web page on camping within Colorado at www.fs.fed.us/r2/recreation/camping. This site allows you access to maps of all the nearby national forests and a complete listing of all campgrounds, including directions and fees.

Perhaps even easier is to plan on camping at one of the state parks within our region. Each offers views, services, and various amenities to make camping a stellar experience.

CHEYENNE MOUNTAIN
STATE PARK $$$–$$$$
410 JL Ranch Heights
(719) 576-2016
http://parks.state.co.us/Parks/CheyenneMountain

This plains-to-peak park is still within the city limits and yet so far away. (See full entry in the Parks chapter.) There are 61 gorgeous campsites, most with a paved parking area, grill ring/fire pit, 10-foot-by-10-foot tent pad, picnic table, and panoramic views of Colorado Springs and Cheyenne Mountain. Most campsites (51) are full-service ($24/night), with water, electrical, and sewer hookups for RV campers. Tent campers also may use these RV sites, but there are 10 unique walk-in sites among the scrub oak, reserved for tents only ($16/night). A nearby camper-services building is where you get permits and park information, and find flush toilets, coin-operated showers, and a coin-operated laundry room. There's also an activity room, and a camp store that sells everything from books and souvenirs to snacks and camping necessities. Playgrounds, additional

restrooms, a beautiful amphitheater, and easy trail access are also available from the campgrounds. Reservations are strongly recommended, handled through the Colorado State Park's reservation system (800-678-2267, www.parks.state.co.us). Group camping also is available through the local office (719-576-2016). Reservations can be made 6 months in advance and are open for the summer beginning mid-Apr. For self-service at the park, be prepared to pay with cash or a check, and know you can only purchase one night at a time.

ELEVEN MILE STATE PARK $$$–$$$$
CR 92, near Lake George
(719) 748-3863
http://parks.state.co.us/Parks/ElevenMile

This lake-based park is home to some of the best fishing in Colorado (see full entry in the Parks chapter, and see the Fishing entry in this chapter). Eleven Mile offers 9 campgrounds with a variety of facilities, and there are 25 secluded backcountry sites as well. Most are open year-round. A detailed campground map can be found on the website, but here's a general summary. The only electrical sites are nestled among trees and rocky outcrops at Rocky Ridge. The North Shore and Witchers Cove campground offer open lakeshore views and access to boat ramps (this is a good choice for fishermen). The Stoll Mountain, Howbert Point, Lazy Boy, Rocking Chair, and Cross Creek campgrounds offer lakeshore sites, seclusion, and few crowds but can be more exposed to weather. The sites with electrical hookups are $20/night and the non-electric sites are $16/night. A camper-services building (also the park office and main entrance station) contains flush toilets, coin-operated showers, coin-operated laundry facilities, a bookstore, and several interpretive displays. (The toilets, showers, and laundry facilities are closed from Oct to May.) Reservations can be made through the Colorado State Park's reservation system (800-678-2267, www.parks.state .co.us).

> ℹ **Mountain streams look crystal clear, but don't drink the water! Millions of microorganisms are present and can make you very sick. Always pack in your water supply.**

MUELLER STATE PARK $$$–$$$$
21045 CO 67 S., Divide
(719) 687-2366
http://parks.state.co.us/Parks/Mueller

Mueller is the classic Colorado vista of mountains, meadows, and forests (see the full entry in the Parks chapter). Mueller's campground, with 132 campsites for motor homes, trailers, and tents, is located in picturesque spruce, fir, pine, and aspen trees with an awe-inspiring view of the surrounding peaks. Sites for RVs or tent-electrical capabilities are $22/night and walk-in tent sites—all with tent pads—are $18/night. There is a camper-services building with modern restrooms, coin-operated showers, and coin laundry. In addition, water hydrants and vault toilets are located throughout the campground.

Winter camping your thing? Mueller has 17 electrical sites that stay open Oct through May for $20/night on a first come, first served basis, and the modern bathrooms and vault toilets stay open during the winter camping season.

If you'd rather "camp" in a more comfortable, cozy style, Mueller has 3 modern cabins nestled in secluded alpine meadows. They each feature log construction, fully equipped kitchen and bath, indoor gas fireplace,

furniture, outdoor deck with gas barbeque, and amazing views. The cabins are either a 2-bedroom ($140/night), 3-bedroom ($200/ night), or 4-bedroom ($260/night).

Pets are welcome in the campground and picnic areas, but they have to be on leash at all times. Pets are not allowed on the trails or in the backcountry. Since this is serious bear country, all trash and food should be put away except when you're eating. Individual campsites can be reserved through the Colorado State Park's reservation system (800-678-2267, www.parks.state .co.us), but the group campground needs to be reserved locally (719-687-2366). The campsites can start being reserved mid-May through mid-October and are available up to 6 months in advance.

Climbing

Outdoor adventure doesn't get more thrilling than climbing. With our stunning rock formations and steep mountain canyons, Colorado Springs has an excellent selection of climbing hot spots. And, as a sideline of the outdoor activity, there are a number of indoor climbing gyms in the area (see the Kidstuff chapter for a full listing, and also see climbing information in the Attractions chapter).

Every year, more than 2,500 climbers get a free annual permit to technical climb the ancient sandstone and conglomerate rocks in our area. The climbing is regulated to protect both the rocks and the climbers, and any technical climber, regardless of age, needs to register for climbs anywhere in the city at the **Garden of the Gods Visitor Center** (1805 N. 30th St., 719-219-0108).

Technical climbing is permitted in the **Garden of the Gods, Red Rock Canyon Open Space, North Cheyenne Cañon,** and

Ute Valley Park (see full entries on each of these in the Parks chapter). Garden of the Gods and Red Rock Canyon are particularly popular climbs. Red Rock Canyon also has the good fortune to have a Friends of Red Rock Canyon group involved in its development, and climbing information can be found at its website, www.redrockcanyon openspace.org. With 85 climbing routes with difficulties ranging from 4th Class to 5.13, Red Rock offers a challenge to almost any climber.

A number of **climbing guidelines** need to be noted (find the complete list on the city's website, www.springsgov.com. First, technical climbing is permitted only when there are at least two climbers using proper equipment. Rock scrambling (climbing a rock formation more than 10 feet above its base without proper equipment) is definitely not allowed. This is what gets most tourists in trouble at Garden of the Gods and other area parks. Believe us—it is hard to get down. Also, if you have to be rescued, you'll probably incur both a fine and a written offense.

Bouldering (climbing smaller rocks only up to 10 feet) is permitted except in the Garden of the Gods on certain rocks. Sport rappelling (hiking to the top of a rock and rappelling down) is only allowed in North Cheyenne Cañon. Otherwise, you have to climb up the rock to be able to rappel down. Also, don't put in anything permanent in the rocks, such as pitons, expansion bolts, and the like.

You're best bet is to register at the Garden of the Gods Visitor Center, get maps while there, and make sure to read all the rules and regulations on the city's website. It's the only way the city can keep climbing available and safe.

We've been talking rock climbing, but there also is limited **ice climbing** available in the winter in North Cheyenne Cañon. Silver Cascade Falls (see the Hiking section in this chapter) is just a few minutes walk from the Helen Hunt Falls Visitors Center, while Hully Gully takes more commitment to reach, off Old Stage Road. If interested in ice climbing, a good first stop is at **Front Range Climbing** (719-473-8349, www.front rangeclimbing.com; see the Attractions and Kidstuff chapters).

One additional resource is **Mountain Chalet** (719-633-0732 and 800-346-7044, www.mtnchalet.com; see the Shopping chapter). They'll have the tools, maps, and resources needed for any climbing adventure. And they love to talk climbing, so everybody's happy.

Cycling

For many in the Pikes Peak region, road and/ or mountain biking is not just an activity, it's a lifestyle. Great trails and asphalt can be found in every direction, and for the serious rider or professional, our high altitude makes for excellent training. There are so many places to cycle, in fact, we can't begin to list them all here. Instead, we'll give a very brief list of suggested rides and shortcuts to finding more obscure trails and roads. All trails and roads allow free access unless they're in a state park, which requires a small fee or an annual parks pass (about $70 per year).

For road cyclists, one of the more scenic rides is through the **Garden of the Gods Park** (see the Parks chapter as well as the Attractions chapter). A bit more demanding are the roads within the **US Air Force Academy** (see the Attractions and Education & Child Care chapters). The roads are smooth and wide with long, loopy hills. Be sure to tuck identification into a pocket as you might be asked for it on the Academy grounds. **North Cheyenne Cañon** (see the Parks chapter) is a steep climb up and sure to make your legs and lungs burn. The ride down, though, is a gas.

For mountain biking, the **Falcon Trail** on the grounds of the US Air Force Academy can't be beat. Beginners can handle it (mostly) and advanced to expert riders find constant challenges. This trail can be accessed from the **Santa Fe Trail,** which runs north to south from Monument well down past Fountain. If logging miles is your goal, this is a good place to start. **Palmer Park** (see the Parks chapter) has numerous trails, some quite difficult while others are more accommodating. **Red Rock Canyon Open Space** (see the Parks chapter) has a number of bike trails, as well as ways to connect with other destinations in the West Side and Manitou Springs areas. **Cheyenne Mountain State Park** (see the Parks chapter) has great trails with some challenging elevation changes, and with open areas, the direct sun melts snowfall faster than in areas with denser tree cover, such as the US Air Force Academy.

For anyone who wants more selection or more detailed directions, stop into any of the good bike shops in town (see the Shopping chapter). There are a number of excellent maps specifically for cycling, and the bike shops will carry all or, at the very least, a few of these. The *Pikes Peak Atlas* ($13.95, www.pikes-peak-atlas.com) by Robert Ormes and Robert Houdek is legendary to locals. The two men, one who has since passed away, did this by hand. It is revised about once a decade. Good news for you, it was just revised, so until about 2015 it will be pretty close to perfect. The large, foldout

map lists all of the trails on one map. If you only want to view the map and not buy it, go into Criterium Bicycles (719-599-0149, http://criterium.com) and, just inside the entrance, view the full map mounted on the wall to your right.

Also recommended is the book *Mountain Biking Colorado Springs, 2nd: A Guide to the Pikes Peak Region's Greatest Off-Road Bicycle Rides* by David Crowell at $10.95. This book lists trails in detail, with each trail getting its own map, directions, and description. (Full disclosure: The publisher for this *Insiders' Guide* is the same publisher of the mountain biking book—which we didn't realize when the guy at the bike shop pushed it across the counter as the first good example of what to buy for a bike trail resource. True story.)

Also recommended is Jim Fladland's *Colorado Springs Trails Network Map* for $5.99. Slim enough to fit in a pocket, this book is an easy take-along on a ride. Another slim Jim is MacVan's *Colorado Springs Trail Map & Guide* for $6.95. The MacVan map books come in a number of versions, each with a few choice destinations, so whichever book you buy will fit easily in a pocket.

If you want one complete map for a certain area, **Western Maps** (www.westernmaps.us) is the thing at $6.99 per map. Each map is an individual area, such as Palmer Park, in an 8½-inch by 11-inch brochure. Every trail is noted with topographic detail, there are photos for easy identification of trails and sights, and new maps are produced constantly.

For those who don't want to buy anything or go to any stores, an easy shortcut is at the website run by the **Trails and Open Space Coalition.** The following link will get you information and directions to all the region's popular trails: www.trailsandopen spaces.org/popular-trails.

> **i** All cyclists want cool, dry air, which in Colorado means morning. No matter how hot a summer day gets, in Colorado the dawn almost always breaks cool and clear. In winter, give the sun a few hours to melt the snow and ice and you can generally get in at least a short ride.

Disc Golf

The outdoorsy flavor to the Colorado Springs community translates into a number of challenging disc golf courses. Although there are a few private disc courses as well, this list is only of those courses that are free and open to the public. You might also check out two online sources of disc golf information for the area. The first, **Pikes Peak Flying Disc Club** (www.ppfdc.com), is a local group that has an active listing and discussion of disc golf in the area. By joining that group, you can also gain access to a particularly demanding private course. The second site can lead you to courses both in the Pikes Peak region and beyond. At **Disc Golf Course Review** (www.dgcoursereview.com), plug in a city or zip code and listings, ratings, and reviews of nearby courses are displayed.

COTTONWOOD CREEK PARK

This city-run park (see the Parks chapter) is a multi-use space, but the entire west end is dedicated to the disc golf course. A full map of the course can be found at www.springsgov.com/units/parksrec/maps/pdf maps/cwood_pg1.pdf. The course is a mix of open and wooded fairways and, at 6,300 feet, has some nice elevation changes. There are both primary and alternate pin placements for good course variety. The 18-hole course carries a pro par of 54 and an amateur par of 72 with the longest configuration of the course at 5,275 feet. The tees are concrete. To reach Cottonwood Creek, find the park at the intersection of Dublin Boulevard and Rangewood Drive in the northeast part of the city. From Dublin, turn onto Montarbor Drive as it follows the park to the west. The disc golf is at the end of the park.

TURKEY CREEK DISC GOLF COURSE

Located on the Turkey Creek Ranch, which is run by Fort Carson, this course is host to the Jive Turkey Shootout in the fall. With 18 holes of hilly and moderately wooded terrain, Turkey Creek is long (9,425-foot course length) with some open holes as well as treed pin placements. High grass can make for lost discs, although the Army has been known to mow prior to tournaments. Wind can be brutal on accuracy. Because of the remote location, protected lands, mountain views, and wild turkeys walking through, this can be an idyllic course. A practice basket also is available. Because this is a military recreation area, there are certain rules. First, check in before playing. Also, stay away from the big white house behind the basketball courts as well as a fenced-off triangle between holes 8, 9, and 10. There was a fire in the area in the recent past, so the nonsmoking rule is one that's taken quite seriously. To reach Turkey Creek, head south on CO 115, 8.3 miles south of Fort Carson's Gate 5. Turn left onto Turkey Creek Lane—the ranch is well marked and easy to find. For any questions, call the Turkey Creek staff at (719) 526-3905. Note that the ranch is closed in the winter.

WIDEFIELD PARK

This El Paso County park and disc golf course is quite popular and is the home to a number of tournaments. A detailed map of the course is available at http://adm.elpasoco .com/Parks/Documents/WFCP_frisbeegolf .pdf. The mature trees and brook that runs through the course make it one of the most beautiful in the area, particularly in summer and fall. There are homes nearby, so be respectful if your disc goes onto private property. With concrete tees and 18 holes, this has a longest course length of 7,208 feet. Par is 54. Widefield Park is located south on I-25 to the South Academy Boulevard exit. Go east (left) and then turn south on US 85/87. Go 3 miles to Fontaine Boulevard and take a left. After 1.5 miles you'll come to Drury Lane; take a right. Parking is on the right.

Downhill Skiing & Snowboarding

Yes, we're near the mountains, but no, Colorado Springs is not really close to a ski area. Driving fast, the nearest is a good 2 hours away. To those avid, passionate souls who live all summer for the first snowflakes of winter and the first opening days at ski areas, close proximity is a minor detail. People who like to ski tend to be a little . . . avid. That said, we really can't leave skiing out of a recreations section!

First, check out the Day Trips & Getaways chapter in this book. There's a lot of info on the major players such as Vail, Breckenridge, Aspen, Crested Butte, and more, including contact info for the mountains as well as dining, lodging, and other activities. People in Colorado Springs tend to hit Breckenridge pretty consistently. Of the big areas, it also is the closest. Keystone and Copper

Mountains also are popular downhill day-trip destinations.

Locals also have a soft spot for **Monarch Mountain** (888-996-7669 and 719-530-5000, www.skimonarch.com, $41 to $56/day). Especially good for families on a budget and new skiers, this longtime mountain—it first opened in 1939—has a quaint main lodge, 800 skiable acres, 63 trails, and 5 lifts. There's a good ski school (not the behemoth operation you'll find at the premier mountains), snowcat tours for backcountry skiing, a sport shop (handy if your kid dropped goggles back in your driveway), terrain parks, and a free parking lot right at the base; you are allowed to bring in a bag lunch and there's a decent bar right above the base lifts. Did we mention it's also less expensive than the big hills? And at almost 11,000 feet at the base, they usually get more than 350 inches of snow a year—and it's all natural. The 2½-hour drive from Colorado Springs starts south on CO 115. After you pass the town of Penrose, turn west onto US 50 and go about 85 miles. Monarch will be on your right, just below Monarch Pass.

Ski Cooper/Chicago Ridge (719-486-2277, www.skicooper.com, $31 to 42/day) is another good choice for families. It's a 3-hour drive, but the price is about the lowest in the state—Ski Cooper is generally less than half the cost of the big mountains like nearby Vail. With 2,400 skiable acres and 3 lifts (plus 1 pony lift), Ski Cooper is a great place for the beginner or intermediate skier. The more advanced skier will only be happy at Ski Cooper for a few hours, but Chicago Ridge snowcat tours, available to 12 people each day, will keep those expert skiers and snowboarders up to their knees in powder. Chicago Ridge reservations can be made via the Ski Cooper contact info. To reach Ski

Cooper/Chicago Ridge, head west on US 24 for about 110 miles. The entrance to the area will be on your right just before you reach the town of Leadville.

For those who want the elite ski areas, there are still ways to save some coin. First rent equipment in Colorado Springs. **The Ski Shop** (719-636-3355, www.theskishop inc.com, see the Shopping chapter) will make sure you have quality, comfortable equipment. There are other smaller ski rental shops and the big sporting-goods stores, such as Sports Authority, also rent equipment for both skiing and snowboarding. For discount lift tickets, go to the big box sports stores, King Soopers markets, or the websites for many ski areas.

Also check out **Colorado Ski Country USA** (www.coloradoski.com). They offer a number of discounts, including a free season pass for all Colorado fifth-graders. Many residents also find they save hundreds by buying season passes such as the **Colorado Pass** (www.coloradopass.com), which is about $480 and good for unlimited access to Breckenridge, Keystone, and Arapahoe Basin with no restrictions as well as 10 restricted days at Vail and Beaver Creek. With 1-day lift prices in the area of $80 (and sometimes much more) when purchased at the mountain the morning of skiing, all of the above can save serious money at the end of a ski season.

Fishing

Fishing in the mountain streams and lakes is one of the most popular activities in the area, probably because we have such an abundance of good fishing spots. Don't forget your Colorado fishing license ($9 per day or $26 per year), which can be bought at all area sporting goods stores, Wal-Mart, Kmart,

and others. For a full list of where to buy a license or more fishing information, contact the Colorado Division of Wildlife (719-227-5200, http://wildlife.state.co.us/Fishing).

Eleven Mile (see the Parks chapter) sees brown, cutthroat, and rainbow trout as well as northern pike. It's also one of the few lakes in Colorado stocked with kokanee salmon, and carp are plentiful in the shallow bays and inlets for bow fishermen. Yellow perch and smallmouth bass have also been caught at Eleven Mile. And then there are the tournaments, with ice fishing tournaments monthly in winter, the spring No Name Tournament is usually the weekend after Mother's Day and the fall pike event is usually the weekend after Labor Day weekend. (Check the park's calendar on the website for more detailed and current information.) All fishing is flies and lures only and is catch-and-release within 100 feet of the mouth of the inlet, and fishing is prohibited in the restricted area near the dam on the east end of the reservoir. Trout daily bag/possession limit is four fish, with no more than two 16 inches or longer. Kokanee salmon daily bag/possession limit is 10 fish at all times of the year, and northern pike has no bag/possession limit. Colorado has been hit hard by zebra mussels, so fishermen should clean the hull of their vessel, drain any water including from live wells and ballast tanks, dry the vessel, inspect all surfaces, and remove any plant or animal material.

The **South Platte River** just below Eleven Mile's dam has seen improvements in recent years, including the placement of natural in-stream structures to enhance the habitat. The stable flows and absence of whirling disease have created a popular fishery. Regulations are catch-and-release and artificial lure only. The South Platte also is popular between Eleven Mile and Spinney Reservoirs (called by some the "Dream Stream"). Last, you can't talk about the South Platte without mentioning the town of **Deckers** (from Woodland Park, travel about a half hour on CO 67). The South Platte has a number of access points along a 20-mile stretch here. Stop at the fly shop in town (the town has a total of about three buildings, you can't miss it) to get news on the most active fishing spots. Anglers regularly haul in good-sized brown and rainbow trout.

Spinney Mountain Reservoir (see the Parks chapter) is an especially well-liked fishing spot. Opening day tends to bring out a big, excited crowd. (Check the park's website for detailed open/closed months and other fishing information.)

Another place you'll find anglers is on the north side of Pikes Peak at **North Catamount Reservoir,** where you'll mainly run into fly fishermen, and **South Catamount and Crystal Reservoirs,** where you'll find shore fishing and those in small boats. You'll reach these reservoirs off the Pikes Peak Highway. The charge for this toll road varies by time of year and number of people in the car (see www.springsgov.com). North Catamount is restricted to flies and lures, but other methods are allowed at South Catamount and Crystal. The bag/possession limit for mackinaw is two.

If you're up for a drive, the **Arkansas River** near the town of Salida, about 2 hours south and west on two-lane highways, is a strong draw. **Antero Reservoir** (www.denverwater.org/Recreation/Antero) also is a bit of a hike out past South Park. At almost 9,000 feet, it gets cold in the winter, which is just perfect for the annual Bob Taylor Memorial Ice Fishing Tournament, usually held in January.

Football

Football is quite popular in Colorado Springs, and most middle and high schools run active programs. For adults and youth younger than middle school, football is best found through the **City of Colorado Springs Sports Office** (719-385-5981, www.springsgov.com. Football programs run both by the city and the schools charge fees, starting at about $65.

Golf

The Pikes Peak region has a generous share of scenic, challenging golf courses. Some offer a plains landscape, with links-style golf on open fairways. Others are tucked into the foothills or mountains and have tight doglegs and heavy woods on all sides. Golf in the region is accommodating to both the touring pro and the weekend duffer, and the occasional wandering wild turkeys or black bears put a new slant on the meaning of hazard. There are a number of amazing golf courses that are either country clubs or military (the Air Force Academy has two of the best in the state), but those are closed to the average Joe. Still, those available to the public (listed here) are tremendous courses that people travel miles to play. Keep in mind that Colorado's varied seasons make for all types of play.

The range of costs for green fees spans 9- and 18-hole play, the less expensive fall/winter rates as well as the high season rates of spring and summer. Choosing to play late in the day also can be a real cost savings, especially at the exclusive courses. Fore!

THE BROADMOOR GOLF CLUB
1 Lake Ave.
(719) 577-5790
www.broadmoor.com/luxury-golf-resorts.php

With three 18-hole championship golf courses and the home of the 2011 US Women's Open (among other recent major events), The Broadmoor holds the green jacket of courses in the region. Unfortunately, you must be a member (or member's guest), guest of the resort, or part of an organized group to play. That said, those who play here always have a memorable round of golf. The professional championships are played on the East Course, but many find the hilly, picturesque Mountain Course the greatest challenge due to topography and outlying vegetation. Green fees run from $75 to $230, and prior to 3 p.m. players are required to take a cart or caddie. No push carts are permitted. Clubs are available for rent. Dress is strict golf attire, with collared shirts, no jeans allowed, shorts of Bermuda length, and spikes required. There are lessons available, a host of restaurants, grills, and beverage carts available, a pro shop, and more.

CHEROKEE RIDGE GOLF COURSE
1850 Tuskagee Place
(719) 597-2637
www.cherokeeridgegolfcourse.com

Cherokee Ridge is the most low-key course in town—which doesn't mean it's not a great day of golf. Families come here with kids just learning, and seasoned amateurs like the casual atmosphere. There is a par 3 9-hole course and a regulation 9-hole course. Both courses are sloped and open, and there's also a driving range and putting green. Green fees run from $7 to $28 (kids

and seniors get a discount), with cart and push carts for rent and walking allowed (most walk here). Lessons and leagues are available. No dress code.

CHEYENNE SHADOWS
Building 7800, Titus Blvd., Fort Carson
(719) 526-4102
www.mwrfortcarson.com/cheyenne-shadows-golf-club.php

On the base of the Army's Fort Carson, Cheyenne Shadows is open to the public. The 18-hole course offers rolling terrain that gets challenging off the fairways. This course can be compared to a good municipal course. Green fees range from $16 to $30, push and electric carts are available for rent, and walking is allowed. The dress code is relaxed: no cut-offs and no plain white T-shirts (to the Army, those are considered underwear). The public must access the course from Gate 1, off CO 115, and have identification and vehicle registration and insurance information handy.

COUNTRY CLUB OF COLORADO
125 Clubhouse Dr.
(719) 538-4095
www.ccofcolorado.com/golf.html

This is a country club but also is available to guests of the Cheyenne Mountain Resort (see the Accommodations chapter). This 18-hole Pete Dye golf course is set in a stunning valley, surrounded by mountains, a lake, and hills. The rolling course has broad greens and it can be a more user-friendly course than most to those who've never played it. Water is a factor on 5 of the back 9 holes and watch out for numerous bunkers throughout the course. Putting greens, chipping areas, and lessons are available. The cost ranges from about $60 (as guest of a member) to $100 (resort guest green fee). Carts are available for an additional fee, but golfers may walk. Shirts with collars and sleeves are required, and no denim is allowed.

THE DIVIDE AT KINGS DEER
19255 Royal Troon Dr., Monument
(719) 481-1518
www.kingsdeergolfclub.com
Kings Deer, a semi-private club that allows the public, sits at 7,400 feet above sea level and has been likened to Scottish courses—rolling hills, high grasslands, open space, and wetlands. With views of Pikes Peak and the Front Range from nearly every hole on the course, this is one majestic spot that offers something for every ability level. Opened in 1999, this 18-hole course can be very challenging, with narrow fairways and a layout that can be trouble. Green fees are $8 to $45, and carts are available for an additional fee (and are required for non-members on weekends and holidays). Shirts with collars are required, and jeans are allowed if not torn. Shorts are allowed, but not cutoffs. There is a clubhouse and restaurant, golf shop, putting and chipping area, large elevated practice range, and an indoor video teaching area.

GARDEN OF THE GODS CLUB
3320 Mesa Rd.
(719) 636-2520
www.gardenofthegodsclub.com/club_amenities/golf/index.php
This is one of the more posh private clubs in town, but by staying at The Lodge you can play this spectacular course (see the Accommodations chapter). You may also play as the guest of a member. The 27-hole course (configured in three 9-hole courses)

features bunkered greens, pines, and probably the best view of Garden of the Gods and Pikes Peak in town. Well laid out and maintained, Garden of the Gods Club provides a challenging game. Green fees run $75 to $125, cart included although walking is allowed. There is a driving range and practice facilities, pros available for lessons, an award-winning pro shop, and many dining options. Dress is traditional country club golf attire, including Bermuda-length shorts and tucked-in, collared shirts.

GLENEAGLE GOLF CLUB
345 Mission Hill Way
(303) 488-0900
www.gleneaglegolfclub.com
This private club is also open to the public. The 18-hole course offers something for everyone, with open, flat holes as well as blind shots. With a beautiful view of the Front Range and US Air Force Academy, Gleneagle winds in and out of homes and trees. Green fees range from $11 to $30, and carts are available for an additional fee. There is a pro shop, restaurant, and lessons are available, and standard golf attire is requested.

✳GOLF CLUB AT BEAR DANCE
6630 Bear Dance Rd., Larkspur
(303) 681-4653
www.beardancegolf.com
Bear Dance is just a smidge north of the Pikes Peak region, but it is a local secret of sorts—open to the public, Bear Dance is the home of the Colorado Section of the Professional Golf Association (PGA). The 18-hole course is designed for championship play and is absolutely magnificent. The challenging course is almost 8,000 yards in layout, with dramatic elevation changes, tree-lined fairways, dramatic water features,

and stunning views. Green fees range from $40 to $109, and there is a pro shop and restaurant. Standard golf attire is required, including no denim allowed. A PGA Master Professional is available for lessons.

i If you want to try and walk-on at a golf course, the best bets are Cherokee Ridge, Cheyenne Shadows, Gleneagle, and Valley Hi Golf Courses.

PATTY JEWETT GOLF COURSE
900 E. Espanola St.
(719) 385-6934
www.springsgov.com
Patty Jewett is the third oldest public course west of the Mississippi. As you drive in through a canopy of stately trees, watch for the foxes that live in the lush area. There are 27 holes of play, one 18-hole course, and one 9-hole course. It is well-maintained and laid out, with a bit more challenge than expected for a municipal course. With spectacular views of Pikes Peak, Patty Jewett is a jewel for the city. Tee times can be booked up to 7 days in advance (and are highly suggested). The green fees run from $14 to $30. Rolling carts and push carts can also be rented for an additional fee, or you may walk. There is no dress code. There's a nice bar and grill with a stunning view of the Front Range, a driving range, and pro shop. Lessons and leagues also are available.

PINE CREEK GOLF CLUB
9850 Divot Trail
(719) 594-9999
www.pinecreekgc.com
This 18-hole course rolls and dips through the northern Pine Creek neighborhood drainage area and can be quite challenging. With upscale homes surrounding the course

and glorious views of Pikes Peak and the US Air Force Academy, this is one of the more scenic courses around. Green fees are $20 to $44, and driving carts are available for an additional fee. Walking is allowed, and the usual golf dress code of collared shirt and jeans in good repair applies. There is a pro shop, restaurant, and driving range, and lessons are available.

SHINING MOUNTAIN GOLF CLUB
100 Shining Mountain Dr.,
Woodland Park
(719) 687-7587
www.shiningmountaingolfclub.com
At 8,500 feet above sea level, the 18-hole Shining Mountain is located just outside of Woodland Park. As a true mountain course that rolls and climbs through pine forests and mountain valleys, it can be quite unforgiving if you get out of the fairways. Carts are recommended as the distance between holes is sometimes great. Green fees are $25 to $59, with rolling cart and push cart rental extra (rolling carts must be used at certain times). Standard golf dress code of collared shirt and jeans allowed if not ragged applies. There's a pro shop, restaurant, and lessons available.

SPRINGS RANCH GOLF CLUB
3525 Tutt Blvd.
(719) 573-4863, (800) 485-9771
www.springsranchgolfclub.com
Springs Ranch lies east of Powers Boulevard and is open and scenic, with wide views of the Front Range. The rolling hills and creek basin make this 18-hole course a surprisingly challenging game, with a lot to offer in terms of shot-making decisions. Green fees are $17 to $52, and rolling and push carts are available for rental. Walking is allowed. Driving

range, lessons, leagues, tournaments, restaurant, and pro shop are available. Punch cards and other passes give regular, local players a range of discounts.

VALLEY HI GOLF COURSE
610 S. Chelton Rd.
(719) 385-6911
www.valleyhigolfcourse.com

The second municipal course in the city, Valley Hi is an 18-hole course that appears flat and innocuous but can be surprising. Challenging bunkers and tall, mature trees line the fairways. Green fees are $14 to $30, and both push carts and riding carts are available for rent. You may walk. Lessons and leagues are offered, and there's a pro shop and the Caddy Shack restaurant.

Hiking

What's more Colorado than hiking? There are full books of information on hiking in this region, so this is just an overview of what's available—and it's a lot. From stunning plains to majestic peak-to-peak views, hiking in the Pikes Peak region is fantastic.

We'll list here trails for the easy, moderate, and difficult hike. As a note, it's suggested that those not familiar with trails go with a guide on the moderate and difficult trails for the first time. Some trails can be as big a challenge to follow as to hike! If you don't know a knowledgeable local who can guide you, **Gravity Play** (719-531-7510 and 800-984-9068, www.gravityplayadventures .com) is a longtime and well-respected outdoor adventure guide. They'll also take you rock climbing. Also, the **Friends of Cheyenne Cañon** (www.tfocc.org) has plans to offer guided hikes by volunteers, so check with them as well.

For trail maps, directions, and information on all the following hikes, first try the free online maps (see box). If you'd rather have all the maps at your fingertips at all times, local sports stores sell a number of good books and maps. See the Cycling section of this chapter for a complete listing; other hiking-specific books are available at area stores as well.

Easy Hikes

Easy hikes are those that require limited fitness and skills, are on trails with little elevation change, and are a short length. The first we like is the **Palmer Trail in the Garden of the Gods.** This trail gives a good flavor of hiking without being overwhelming, and the views down into the Garden are stupendous. The **Contemplative Trail at Red Rocks Open Space** also is an excellent introduction to hiking as you travel in and out of majestic rocks and end with a glorious view north. This is a trail on which you're more likely to see wildlife such as bears and mountain lions than in Garden of the Gods. In this same area is the recommended **Paul Intemann Memorial Trail.**

Paint Mines Interpretive Park (see the Parks chapter), the **Sundance Trail in Cheyenne Mountain State Park** (see the Parks chapter), and **Palmer Lake Reservoir** and **Spruce Mountain** (especially lovely views on this trail) in Monument are also great, easy day hikes.

A favorite is the **Seven Bridges** trail in Pike National Forest. It's quick (45 minutes in, 45 minutes back) and forested. Although not long on views, there are wildflowers in summer and you almost always hear gurgling water. Waterfalls sparkle throughout.

The Cheyenne Cañon area has a number of easy, good hikes, including the **Lower**

Columbine, **Silver Cascade Falls,** and **Mount Cutler** trails. Mount Cutler ends at a peak with city views, so it gives visitors a great vista and a feeling of accomplishment.

South of town, the **Aiken Canyon Natural Area** (see the Parks chapter) has an easy loop trail that travels through a diverse ecosystem and is of special interest to bird lovers.

Finally, the **Devil's Head Ranger Station** is exactly that: You climb stairs up an old forest ranger lookout. Your thighs might burn, but the views are 360 degrees.

Hiking Poles: The Serious Tool

Often given a bad rap as being wimpy, hiking poles are a serious tool for very un-wimpy hikers. Poles give stability, keep hands from swelling, let snakes know you're around (the vibration of planting the pole lets them know to skedaddle), can be used as a weapon (bears and mountain lions are no wimpy joke), provide a great workout for the upper body, and save knees going downhill. Poles can be purchased at sports stores or even Target or Wal-Mart. Or, find a good stick or two. Collapsible poles are nice, though, as they can be easily stored when traversing scree fields or boulders.

Moderate Hikes

Moderate hikes require some fitness and skills and give a physical challenge. The trails usually have moderate elevation change (generally 500 feet to 2,000 feet) and are anywhere from 3 to 8 miles in length. A favorite here is **Saint Mary's Falls** in the Pike National Forest. This wanders by a creek and then climbs up over a waterfall. The last 0.2 mile is steep and somewhat scary but worth the view. Bring lunch and relax at the top. The **Mt. Rosa Trail** (Zebulon Pike's route) also is a good one in this area.

Cheyenne Cañon's **Mid/Upper Columbine** trail is nice, and the easier Seven Bridges trail combined with **Jones Park** (big boulders and scree) is a challenging but rewarding hike. **Waldo Canyon** also is a local favorite, with sunny and wooded spots, and plenty of up and down. It can get crowded on the weekends.

Near Divide, **The Crags** is a classic area hike, and **Pancake Rocks/Horsethief Falls** are bright with fall colors and a killer view of Cripple Creek and Divide. Those rocks—yep, just like pancakes and steep all the way up.

Mount Herman in Monument also is recommended. Just south is **Stanley Canyon,** which is on the grounds of the US Air Force Academy, so bring some identification.

Another trail you need identification for is Glen Eyrie's **The Punch Bowls.** It starts on wooden bridges and moves to a lot of climbing up and down rocks. The Punch Bowls themselves, at the end of the hike, are filled with very cold water, but local teens think it's fun to swim there. To do The Punch Bowls, you need to reserve online at www.gleneyrie.org/hiking. After completing the reservation, print out your confirmation form as well as a release form, and bring those along with your photo identification to the guard at the Glen Eyrie gate. You are allowed a maximum of eight people and four cars per reservation and can only reserve a spot once a month.

Difficult Hikes

Difficult hikes require a high degree of fitness and skills and definitely bring a physical challenge. Beginners should NOT hike here. Difficult trails have high to extreme elevation change (usually more than 2,000 feet) and/or are more than 8 miles long. The first is a classic: **Barr Trail,** up Pikes Peak. Starting in woods and ending above 14,000 feet, this trail is deceiving. Conquer it with respect—or you will, at least, respect it when you're done!

Also steeped in local lore is **The Incline.** Yes, it is illegal. Yes, it is sometimes so heavy with foot traffic you might feel like you're on an L.A. freeway. The up to 68 percent grade is the draw here, and the views and camaraderie can be nice, too. The Incline, which was once an old cable car route and now is simply railroad ties in a straight line up to the top of Mount Manitou, has been called Stairmaster on a mountain—you get the idea.

Similar to The Incline is **Eagle Peak** on the US Air Force Academy (so bring identification). The cadets would love to keep this spectacular hike a secret, but too late. The trail is more shaded than its counterpart, and while The Incline is 2,000 feet up and 1 mile, this is 2,000 feet up and 3 miles. The last half mile of Eagle Peak is really steep. You also walk on loose boulders, just to up the challenge. The view from the top is an amazing sight, though, and worth the difficult climb. This, particularly, is a trail where you could use a guide: Cadets have painted white and blue spots along to the way to show the trail, which covers some tight wedged areas. The spots can be hard to see—sometimes on rocks or trees, sometimes on the ground. Also, a bigger person couldn't fit through some of the wedges. Think carefully about this one!

Cheyenne Cañon's **Mount Muscoco** is another tough trail to follow, but the saying is, it's like finding lost car keys—eventually you find them! The trail offers gorgeous views of Seven Falls and the Will Rogers Shrine.

For those wanting to cut their teeth on one of Colorado's 53 Fourteeners (mountains above 14,000 feet), **Mount Democrat** is a good choice. About a 2-hour drive from Colorado Springs, it is ranked No. 28 in elevation, but you can park 2 miles from the summit. Still, with the basic calculation of 1 hour hiking for every mile at this altitude, this is still a 4- or 5-hour hike. Go early in the morning as you want to be down by noon or 1 p.m. at the latest—Colorado's thunderstorms are wicked and quite dangerous above treeline.

Free Online Trail Maps

Some of the best trail maps are found free online. Our favorite is **www.e-trailmaps.com.** It begins with a nice description of the trail, then runs down a list of trail uses, length, elevation changes, difficulty, and more. Page 2 shows two good topographic maps, one bird's-eye view, one horizontal. Page 3 details trailhead directions, a waypoint log, geocache info, and other trails accessible from this trail.

If this site doesn't have the trail you want (some are still not on this site), look also at **www .outtherecolorado.com** and **www .gettingoutsideagain.com.**

Day Hike Checklist

- 1 liter of water (minimum)
- 2+ energy bars
- Sunscreen

- Sunglasses
- Hat
- Bandages or moleskin

Also smart to have:
- 1 extra pair socks
- Hiking poles
- Map
- Compass
- Small knife
- Pen and notebook
- Camera

- Insect repellant
- Hand wipes
- Gloves
- Handkerchief
- Lunch
- Toilet paper and baggy (leave nothing behind . . .)
- Rain poncho

Martial Arts

The martial arts community is strong in Colorado Springs, with hundreds of studios and schools across the city. And they're not just one type of practice: There's karate, mixed martial arts, and even Brazilian Capoeira. With such a strong base, we'll list a few of the top-level, larger programs that have been here for a number of years and have proven, quality instructors. Most studios run discounted introductory prices or free classes to start and then charge a monthly or program fee after that.

Aikido
PIKES PEAK AIKIDO $$$$
3425 Van Teylingen Dr.
(719) 574-7420
www.pikespeakaikido.com

Judo
**USA JUDO, OLYMPIC TRAINING
  CENTER JUDO CLUB** $$$–$$$$
One Olympic Plaza
(719) 866-4730
www.usjudo.org

Karate/Kobudo
**ALL OKINAWA KARATE
  & KOBUDO** $$$$
1795 Jet Stream Dr., Suite 106
(719) 232-1882
http://allokinawakarate.com

**JAY HAYNES FAMILY KARATE
  CENTER** $$$$
3617 Betty Dr.
(719) 574-7557
www.familykaratecenter.com

**UNITED STATES KARATE
  ACADEMY** $$$$

1769 S. 8th St.

1808 Woodmoor Dr., Monument

207-A Rockrimmon Blvd.

5245 Galley Rd.
(719) 388-2020
http://unitedstateskarateacademy.com

Kempo
**UNIVERSAL KEMPO KARATE
  SCHOOLS** $$$–$$$$
(More than 20 schools in town. See
website for all locations.)
(719) 598-6046
www.kempocolorado.com

Kung Fu
SHORIN KUNG FU $$$–$$$$
955 Garden of the Gods Rd.
(719) 268-9560
http://shorinkungfu.com

Mixed Martial Arts
THE DEFENSE INSTITUTE $$–$$$$
4438 Austin Bluffs Pkwy.
(719) 630-8373

2370 S. Academy Blvd.
(719) 392-1380
http://defenseinstitute.com

Taekwondo
US TAEKWONDO CENTER $$$–$$$$
1316 N. Academy Blvd.
(719) 574-8782

16328 Jackson Creek Pkwy., Monument
(719) 488-4321

6217 Lehman Dr.
(719) 598-8000
http://martialartscoloradosprings.com

Running

There's a reason magazines like *Men's Health* rank Colorado Springs high in "Fittest City in America," and a big chunk of that reason has to do with running. Coloradoans love to run. You almost can't go down any street without seeing a runner (or cyclist or walker), and that doesn't even touch the activity on the wide trails.

Given all the fleet feet, there's ample opportunity for runners to find a good route or join in a group run. One of the most popular runs is on the **Santa Fe Trail,** otherwise known as the **Pikes Peak Greenway.** This 30-mile, north-to-south route starts in Palmer Lake and runs all the way south to Fountain. There also are ways to connect to other trails from it. It is wide, mostly packed dirt but sometimes asphalt. It runs next to a creek, through dense forest, in open fields, and up and down hills. Because it is so well-developed and popular, maps can be found in many places, such as at the City of Colorado Springs's website, www .springsgov.com/units/parksrec/maps/mpp grnwya.htm. This is a good map because it shows the whole trail and also links to more detailed, smaller sections. If you don't want to bother with a map, the trail runs through Monument Valley Park downtown (see the Parks chapter). Just pick a direction and start running.

If you'd rather join with others, not a problem. **Colorado Springs Running Company** (719-635-3833, www.corunco.com; see the Shopping chapter) sponsors social runs from their store on Wednesday at 6 p.m. and Friday at 7 a.m. The group welcomes all ability levels, and usually runs through Monument Valley Park for anywhere from 45 minutes to 1½ hours.

For the ultra runner, **The Incline Club** (www.inclineclub.com) is the group for you. Started by Matt Carpenter, a local running legend given his frequent winning of the Pikes Peak Marathon (see the Annual Events & Festivals chapter), this club is for the serious runner. Many of the group members (it's free—you just sign up online at the website) are in training for the Pikes Peak Ascent and Marathon or for other high-altitude, ultra races. They meet on Sunday mornings in Memorial Park in Manitou Springs and go for long runs. During the summer months, they also meet for "quality hill sessions" on Thursday evenings. Although they've taken the name of The Incline (a popular although legally ambiguous trail on an abandoned cable car route outside of Manitou Springs), the group does not necessarily run The Incline (see the Hiking section of this chapter). Now they use the dictionary's definition of incline to describe themselves: to deviate from the horizontal. The Incline Club's website also has a few maps of the most popular runs in the area.

If you're a more solitary soul, the local running and biking stores stock a number of decent trail maps. See the Cycling section of this chapter for a full list, but for runners the most popular is probably the small MacVan map, *Colorado Springs Trail Map & Guide* for $6.95.

And if you're the opposite of the solitary soul, you might enjoy the **Jack Quinn's Running Club,** a drinking party for people with a running problem (see the Nightlife chapter). Held every Tuesday evening downtown, the large group—up to thousands—ends a very social run for all ability levels at Jack Quinn's Irish Pub for a pint . . . or two.

Skateboarding

CITY OF COLORADO SPRINGS PARKS   FREE
(719) 385-5940
www.springsgov.com
Colorado Springs has two big skateboard parks and a few choice grinding areas at neighborhood parks around the city. All of the skateboard parks are managed by the City of Colorado Springs.

The biggest, newest skateboard park is at **Memorial Park** (see the Parks chapter), next to Sertich Ice Arena at the corner of E. Pikes Peak Avenue and S. Union Boulevard. It is a destination skate park, with 40,000 square feet of competition-size skate area. The park was designed and constructed by the world-renowned skate park design firm Team Pain. It is three times the size of other skate parks in Colorado Springs and is the second largest skate park in Colorado. This state-of-the-art park includes features such as bowls, a street course, backyard-style pool, and a one-of-a-kind hole-in-the-wall. There is also an events plaza with a picnic pavilion and natural boulders for spectator seating. Because of its multi-use design, this park also is a draw to inline skaters and BMX bikers. You want to see what's going on there in real time? Check out the four web cams, refreshed every 60 seconds, at www.springsgov.com.

The other larger skate park in town is at the **Gossage Youth Sports Complex** (3950 Mark Dabling Blvd., north of Fillmore Street and south of Garden of the Gods Road). Right next to it is a BMX park with some decent dirt hills.

Smaller skate parks can be found around the city at:
- **Gold Camp Park,** 1536 Gold Spike Terrace

- **Laura Gilpin Park,** 7415 Kettle Drum St.
- **Prairie Grass,** 710 Chapman Dr.
- **Stetson Hills Park,** 4870 Jedediah Smith Rd.
- **John Stone Park,** 4017 Family Place
- **Wilson Ranch Park,** 2335 Allegheny Dr.

Skating—Ice Rinks

We do love to ice skate here—figure, hockey, speed, short track, or just plain goofing off. With Olympic and elite athletes of every winter sport living and training in our city, as well as all the youth and adults who love to skate, there's a huge demand for time at the rinks. Here's the lowdown of each of the frozen sheets open to the public; there's also a rink at the US Air Force Academy, but it is only open to the public as spectators. Prices range from modest fees for public skate times to more expensive classes, programs, and leagues.

HONNEN ICE RINK $–$$$$
44 W. Cache La Poudre St.
(719) 389-6157
www.coloradocollege.edu/_athletics/honnen
Honnen is on the Colorado College campus, but it is not restricted to students. There are public skates, figure skating sessions, open hockey times, and learn-to-skate classes. Skate rentals are available. This rink can be a little tricky to find just west of the intersection of Cascade Avenue and Cache La Poudre Street, up a short walkway to the north.

SERTICH ICE CENTER $–$$$$
1705 E. Pikes Peak Ave.
(719) 385-5983
www.springsgov.com

Sertich is in Memorial Park (see the Parks chapter) at the corner of East Pikes Peak Avenue and Union Boulevard. The NHL-size ice also has seating for 2,000, and as such this is a popular place for high school hockey games. There are public skating sessions, a good selection of rental skates, learn-to-skate classes, youth hockey classes, and adult open hockey sessions. Sertich also has a birthday party package, a video game room, skate sharpening, and full-service vending machines, including that all-important hot chocolate.

WORLD ARENA ICE HALL $–$$$$
3185 Venetucci Blvd.
(719) 477-2150
www.worldarena.com/icehall
The World Arena Ice Hall is next to the 8,000-seat World Arena, and it is the big player in ice time in Colorado Springs. The World Arena Ice Hall houses 2 sheets of ice (1 NHL size, 1 Olympic size). The facility hosts world-class athletes at all hours every day as well as public skate sessions, youth and adult hockey leagues, drop-in speedskating, learn-to-skate lessons, private lessons, and is home to the Broadmoor Skating Club (past and present members are US National and Olympic champion figure skaters). Skate rental is available. There is a snack bar, but it is not always open; when it's closed vending machines dole out coffee and hot chocolate. Make sure to check the website or call before heading over as the ice is booked every day from before dawn to almost midnight.

Skating—Inline & Roller

Skating here is not just about the frozen kind. For the inline skater, first read the section on Skateboarding in this chapter—there are a number of skateboard parks that also draw the inline skaters. All skate rinks and courts located in the city parks are free.

There are two regulation-size inline rinks with dasher boards, permanent goals, and lights. Intended exclusively for inline hockey play, they are:

- **Cottonwood Creek Park,** 7040 Rangewood Dr.
- **El Pomar Youth Sports Park,** 2212 Executive Circle

Add to that list the neighborhood parks that have inline hockey courts. Each of these is configured as a multipurpose area that can be used for inline hockey:

- **Buckskin Charlie Park,** 7665 Scarborough Dr.
- **Frank Castello Park,** 7640 Potomac Dr.
- **Explorer Park,** 4260 Bardot Dr.
- **Jared Jensen Park,** 6724 Windom Peak Blvd.
- **Judge Lunt Park,** 4870 Seton Place
- **Kathleen Marriage Park,** 2320 Amberwood Lane
- **Pring Ranch Park,** 5264 Prairie Grass Lane
- **Horace Shelby Park,** 6442 Summit Peak Dr.
- **Springs Ranch Park,** 2990 Pony Tracks Dr.
- **Wilson Ranch Park,** 2335 Allegheny Dr.

For roller skating, there are indoor skate rinks at the two **Skate City** locations (www.skatecitycolorado.com; see the Kidstuff chapter). Skate City charges between $5 to $10 total for admission and skate rental.

In addition, Skate City runs the **CETSports Arena** (3225 Meadow Ridge Dr., 719-597-1235) exclusively for Skate City inline hockey program participants (programs cost at least $55). The state-of-the-art complex hosts both youth and adult recreation leagues (sign up at the CETSports

Arena) and inline club hockey teams (sign up at one of the Skate City locations) and hosts the Thunder, a professional inline hockey team. There are seats for 250 spectators as well as a pro shop, snack bar, grill, and, for the adult spectators, a tavern.

Sledding

There's nothing like rushing down a snowy hill on a sled. **Mueller State Park** (see the Parks chapter) allows sledding and tubing in the Preacher's Hollow, Outlook Ridge, and Elk Meadow areas. For a listing of popular sledding hills closer to town, see the Kidstuff chapter.

Snowshoe/Cross-Country Skiing

The really sweet thing about these activities is, once your equipment is purchased, you can enjoy a quiet, picturesque Colorado winter day absolutely free. Many days after a snowfall local parks and neighborhoods have tracks running through them as people enjoy the untouched snowfall.

Still, there is nothing like heading into serious backcountry on snowshoes or cross-country skis. **Mueller State Park** (see the Parks chapter) in Divide has a number of suggested trails, including some that are up to 7 miles long. Check out the winter activities link on their website for all the details and options (http://parks.state.co.us/Parks/Mueller/ParkActivities/WinterActivities). **Fox Run Park, Palmer Park,** and **Bear Creek Park** (see the Parks chapter for all three) also are prime spots for snowshoeing or cross-country skiing.

One good source for renting or buying Nordic (cross-country) skis and snowshoes is **Mountain Chalet** (www.mtnchalet.com; see the Shopping chapter). **REI** (1376 E.

Woodmen Rd., 719-260-1455, www.rei.com/stores/68) also sells and rents snowshoes but doesn't carry cross-country skis at this location. You can expect to pay about $20 to rent this equipment.

Softball, Baseball & T-Ball

Softball and baseball leagues are a popular pastime in the summer months, primarily through the **City of Colorado Springs Sports Office** (719-385-5981, www.springs gov.com). With more than 50 diamonds throughout the city, in addition to a number of well-maintained sports complexes in every corner of town, finding a team should be easy—now catching that fly ball, that's the hard part! (Also see baseball information in the Kidstuff chapter). There are fees to join any of these teams, starting at about $65.

Swimming

The bad economy almost sank the local pool scene, but a partnership turned out to be the needed lifesaver. There are now four great places to cool off and swim a few laps. Each facility charges about $8 per visit, but they also offer discounted 10-visit punch cards.

The City of Colorado Springs operates the pool at Cottonwood Creek Park (see the Parks chapter).

- **Cottonwood Creek Recreation Center,** (719) 385-6508, 3920 Dublin Blvd. This newish, indoor pool area has the only indoor wave pool in southern Colorado as well as a water slide, current channel and vortex, and zero entry. They also offer lessons and special programs, such as birthday parties. Open 7 days a week.

The other public pools open in the region are operated by Colorado Springs Swim School (719-385-5984, www.csswim school.com), which, as the name implies, also offers swim instruction. At each of the facilities below they offer both a family day pass and a summer family pass to save on the family budget.

- **Colorado Springs Recreation Center,** 280 S. Union Blvd. This big indoor facility at Memorial Park has a zero-entry kids' play area, current river, big water slide, hot tub, and lap lanes. Open 7 days a week.
- **Portal Park Pool,** 3535 N. Hancock Ave. This outdoor swimming pool is not fancy, but it's been a popular spot for locals to cool off for decades. Open 7 days a week in the summer, closed in the winter.
- **Wilson Ranch Pool,** 2335 Allegheny Dr. This outdoor facility is much like the indoor pools, with zero entry, a three-spiral water slide, lap lanes, interactive play feature, current river and vortex, underwater bench, and funbrella. Open 7 days a week in the summer, closed in the winter.

For those seeking a permanent place to swim as part of an exercise regimen, there is a full listing of health clubs, many with big pools, in the Health & Wellness chapter.

Tennis

You might think that, with our snowfall in the winter, Pikes Peak area residents don't go in much for tennis. Nothing is further from the truth.

The City of Colorado Springs maintains more than 45 public tennis courts in citywide parks. Even with this many courts, on a nice summer day it can be hard to find an empty place to play. City tennis courts are free and first come, first served; but if someone is waiting, the general rule is to relinquish the court after an hour of play. The main tennis facility is the **Memorial Park Tennis Center** (719-385-6023, http://memorialparktennis.com). Located just west of Sertich Ice Arena, this facility has 15 courts, 11 of which are lighted. In the summer, there are a number of programs, leagues, camps, and tournaments for youth and adults both at the Memorial courts as well as around town. The most active courts outside of downtown are at **Woodmen Valley Park, Cottonwood Creek Park, Wilson Ranch Park, Monument Valley Park,** and **Sandstone Park.** To see a full listing of the city's tennis courts, go to the city's website, www.springsgov.com.

During the winter the public courts are in a form of hibernation, although they are available for use. It's not unusual to see players on court even in January, if it's a warm, sunny day.

In addition, there are a number of private tennis clubs in town, many with indoor tennis. Most require membership to use the courts. However, if you're a guest at **The Broadmoor** (see the Accommodations chapter) you can use their outside courts, and if you're a tennis player, you should (court fees are about $25 per hour). There are 2 clay courts next to a viewing area, and a number of courts that amble down perfectly manicured grounds. No matter the outcome of the game, you'll enjoy the match for its gorgeous setting and elegant vibe. The Broadmoor also runs a number of destination tennis camps for adults.

Also, if you're a member of the United States Tennis Association (USTA), you're welcome to play at the **Colorado Springs Racquet Club** (719-596-2958, www.cosprings tennis.com) for a small guest fee plus court costs (about $12 per hour for the indoor

courts; the outside courts are free). They have 4 indoor courts and 6 outdoors.

Last, **Life Time Fitness/Lynmar** (see the Health & Wellness chapter) offers a day guest pass plus court fees (about $12 per hour) to tennis players.

Volleyball

The city has a number of sand volleyball courts in parks around the region. If you need something more organized, leagues are available through the **City of Colorado Springs Sports Office** (719-385-5981, www.springsgov.com). Leagues and adult fun also can be found at **The Sand Pits** (719-380-7263, www.thesandpits.com), a sand volleyball complex plus bar and grill on the east side. **Big House Sports** (www.bighousesports.us) runs adult and youth leagues in a huge indoor facility on the east side, which can also be rented out by private parties. With volleyball a very competitive high school sport here, there also are a number of private, club teams for the elite player, but we'll not go into that here—we figure, if you're that kind of player, you already know where to go! The park courts are free but the leagues start at about $65.

SPECTATOR SPORTS

After a day of cycling, hiking, skating, and everything else offered in the Pikes Peak region, sports fans need to chill—preferably at a good game. There's no lack of good spectator sports in the area, with nationally ranked college teams, mainstream major sports, and a few of the left field variety as well. Remember also that if you don't mind a drive, professional sports teams of every league are available just a short hour away in Denver (see the Denver section in the Day Trips & Getaways chapter).

College Sports

COLORADO COLLEGE
www.cctigers.com

One of the biggest sporting draws in southern Colorado is the Colorado College Tigers ice hockey team. Perennially ranked in the top 10 in national polls, the Tigers give rabid fans intense, fast-paced games. When the CC Tigers play the local and national rivals University of Denver Pioneers, it's almost always in front of standing-room only crowds. The CC/DU games come on two weekends a year (in fall and winter), with one game each weekend played at the Tigers' home rink of the Colorado Springs World Arena. Tiger hockey is relatively inexpensive and a big family atmosphere—most of the spectators go a number of times every season, almost all wearing the black and gold Tiger colors. If you go, be prepared to roar. Tickets, schedule, and information can be found on the website. Tickets range from about $9 to $35.

UNITED STATES AIR FORCE ACADEMY (USAFA)
www.goairforcefalcons.com

USAFA teams bring a number of big games to the region. First and foremost, there are the **football** games. Often a contender at bowl games, the Air Force Falcons offer big-time college football with a pre-game show that can't be beat: US Air Force jets always do fly-bys. With military pageantry on the field and seats that look over the plains, this experience can't be beat. When the Falcons play interservice rivals Army or Navy, the stands are packed and the pre-game festivities keep the skies full with everything from F-18s to stealth bombers. It's a spectacle even non-football fans can enjoy.

Other USAFA teams with a strong following and packed spectator seats are the **men's ice hockey** team—especially when they play the local rival CC Tigers. The **men's basketball** team sports a loyal fan base with the hoops crowd. Tickets, schedule, and information can be found on the website. Tickets range from about $5 to $15.

UNIVERSITY OF COLORADO AT COLORADO SPRINGS
www.gomountainlions.com
(719) 255-3601

UCCS plays NCAA Division II, and a number of sports draw a crowd. The men's and women's basketball and women's volleyball teams play in the new 1,200-seat Gallogly Events Center. Tickets and information are available at the website. Tickets are either free or up to $6.

Professional Sports

GOLF

The Broadmoor's famed golf courses host major golf tournaments every few years, including the 2011 US Women's Open. Contact The Broadmoor to find out if an event is happening when you're in town (719-577-5775 or 866-837-9520, www.broadmoor .com). Tickets differ for every event and can be quite pricey.

PIKES PEAK INTERNATIONAL HILL CLIMB

This high altitude road race is a little challenging as a spectator sport since you see the cars zoom by only once, but gearheads love it. The 12.42-mile course begins at 9,390 feet above sea level and ends at 14,110 feet, at the summit of Pikes Peak.

There are 11 classes featuring every type of automobile, from semi trucks to open wheels to motorcycles. Spectators line the road-turned-race track from the bottom to the top, getting a day spent in the mountains as part of the package. Tickets are $45. (Also see the Annual Events & Festivals chapter.)

PIKES PEAK OR BUST RODEO

One of the highest-paying pro rodeo events in the country, the Pikes Peak or Bust Rodeo runs for five days in the height of summer. This perfect family outing features all the excitement of the Old West as well as a carnival and activities like pony rides, gold panning, and mutton busting. In the arena, barrel racers to bull riders take the audience on a thrill ride. Those wacky daredevils, the hard-working rodeo clowns, almost always steal the show. Tickets range from about $5 to $25. (Also see the Annual Events & Festivals chapter.)

SKY SOX BASEBALL
Security Service Field
4385 Tutt Blvd.
(719) 597-1449, (719) 591-SOXX (7699)
www.skysox.com

The Colorado Springs Sky Sox are the Triple-A farm club for the Major League Baseball Colorado Rockies. On any given summer day, you can enjoy a dog and soda while watching big league players sent down to work out some kinks, new whiz kids out to prove themselves, and a field full of big league hopefuls. The intimate, open, 8,500-seat Security Service Field is the highest professional ballpark in the US at 6,531 feet above sea level, and every seat is perfect. The Sky Sox routinely run promotions that allow families to enjoy a day at the park for next to

nothing. All together now, "Take me out to the ball game. . . ." Tickets range from $9 to $12, but there are discounted promotions on a regular basis.

THUNDER INLINE HOCKEY
3225 Meadow Ridge Dr.
http://costhunder.com

Continuing in the "we love to skate here" theme, Colorado Springs is home to the Thunder professional inline hockey team. Games are played at the 250-seat CETSArena (719-597-1235). Find team and schedule information at the Thunder's website. Tickets are $7.

Olympic Sports

DAVE SCHULTZ MEMORIAL INVITATIONAL

This best-of-the-best wrestling tournament has featured world and Olympic champions in years past. The three-day event features Greco-Roman, freestyle, and women's freestyle, from preliminary rounds to the final medal rounds. Tickets range from about $5 to $15. (Also see the Annual Events & Festivals chapter.)

US OLYMPIC TRAINING CENTER

Since one of the nation's elite athletic training facilities is here, it's only natural that regular competition of the highest level takes place on the grounds of the Olympic Training Center. From swimming to shooting to volleyball, world-class athletes—from the US and around the world—can be seen up close and in action at least once a month. Ticket prices vary but are usually quite modest. (Also see the Attractions chapter.)

Other Sports

WOMEN'S FLAT TRACK ROLLER DERBY
Pikes Peak Derby Dames
Colorado Springs City Auditorium
221 E. Kiowa St.
(719) 385-5969
www.pikespeakderbydames.com
You know you're interested. . . . Established in the area in 2005, this women's team has a full schedule throughout the year, played downtown at the City Auditorium. Tickets run $10 to $15 and can be purchased at The Leech Pit (see the Shopping chapter), Play It Again Sports (5338 Montebello Lane, 719-528-5840), or online at www.brownpapertickets.com/producer/10664.

ROCKY MOUNTAIN STATE GAMES
These games are for the people—to both play and watch. There are 34 sports, from rock climbing to racquetball, played all around the area at Memorial Park, the US Air Force Academy, the US Olympic Training Center, and more. All ages and abilities participate, and heartwarming sports moments happen every day. Except for the opening ceremonies, events are free. (Also see the Annual Events & Festivals chapter.)

PIKES PEAK ASCENT AND MARATHON
It's hard for some people to imagine climbing Pikes Peak, let alone running up and then back down the mountain. Held over one weekend in August, the ascent is on Saturday and the marathon is on Sunday. Cheering on the hardy souls is inspirational and priceless—and free. (Also see the Annual Events & Festivals chapter.)

PIKES PEAK INVITATIONAL SOCCER TOURNAMENT
If soccer's your game, this is your event. Elite teams from across the country come to compete over this long weekend in the summer. Some of the best emerging talent is showcased on teams that highlight finesse and skill. One- or three-day passes are a small fee. (Also see the Annual Events & Festivals chapter.)

SHOPPING

From a shopper's perspective, Colorado Springs is a little deceiving. The sheer geographic size of the Pikes Peak region could easily lead one to think there must be one great place to shop—a shopping mecca, as it were, like The Galleria in Dallas or South Coast Plaza in southern California. Um . . . not so much.

But that doesn't mean there isn't good shopping. As long as you're willing to drive, there are a number of eclectic, cool stores where you can spend some dough or get that special gift.

Most of the unique stores are located either downtown or to the north, west, or south. The more east you go, the more likely stores will be names you recognize. For some reason, we seem to have more than our fair share of big box stores; if you drive Powers Boulevard on the eastern edge of the city, you'll see a veritable bonanza of the large national chains. The Pikes Peak region also supports various large indoor and outdoor malls and a plethora of strip malls on every side of town. Each of these has what you'd expect: franchises peppered with a few mom-and-pops.

We are an active population, so sports enthusiasts have a lot of choices in brands, type of store, and quality of merchandise. For instance, there are so many (and really good) cycling shops, we could have written a whole chapter on this shopping niche.

What's interesting is that most of the stores worth mentioning have been around for years—and a lot of them for a number of decades. You've got to have something really exceptional going on for a track record like that.

OVERVIEW

The following list of shopping choices is like the icing on the cake: There are more, and there are bigger. But these represent the best and the most diverse. Because the Pikes Peak region spans so many square miles, we tried to list stores that represent a wide range of inventory and style as well as areas of the region.

This is not a full listing of everything available; that wouldn't fit in this book, even if it were devoted only to shopping. If you need something specific, you would be wise

to use this list as a starting point, with Google as your backup.

But if you're looking for something unique, or you want a day spent cruising the local hot spots, this will point you in the right direction. From there, the treasure hunt is up to you.

A note to consignment store junkies: There are a good number of consignment stores in the area. For this book, those stores are listed under the category of goods they sell rather than under a consignment store category.

ANTIQUES

AMERICAN CLASSICS MARKETPLACE
1815 N. Academy Blvd.
(719) 596-8585
So why is there only one store in this category? Because this is the daddy of 'em all. There are a number of excellent small- and medium-sized antiques stores in the area. You could probably find your heart's desire in any one of them (given your heart's desire at the moment). But American Classics Marketplace is where you can lose yourself for 3 hours and come out with almost anything. The endless choices run from valuable antiques to collectible lunch boxes to embroidered napkins to vintage hats to baby gifts. Call it an antiques store or gift or collectibles store or craft store—you name it, they've probably got it somewhere in the 65,000 square feet of space. Open 7 days a week.

i Antiques junkies can find a number of small, eclectic stores in Old Colorado City, along West Colorado Avenue between 21st and 28th Streets.

BOOKSTORES

BARNES & NOBLE BOOKSELLERS
1565 Briargate Blvd.
(719) 266-9960
www.barnesandnoble.com
The Barnes & Noble chain has two stores in Colorado Springs, both situated near the big indoor malls (the second location is at 795 Citadel Dr. E., 719-637-8282). The Briargate Boulevard location is in the north, across the street from Chapel Hills mall. The Citadel Drive location is across the parking lot from The Citadel mall in the southeast area.

Both stores offer children's story times both Friday and Saturday mornings, and both stores participate in the summer reading program where children in grades 1 through 6 can read eight books and get one free.

The Briargate store hosts a writer's group on Thursday, a book club on the last Monday of every month, and features local artists in the cafe.

The Citadel store hosts a book club on the second Tuesday of the month; various writers' groups; and a "Girls of the World" and "Guys Read" activity, which caters to either girls or boys ages 6 through 12, in which they read a book before the event, then show up for a book discussion, activity, and craft.

Both stores feature a Starbucks Coffee cafe, and both regularly host author signings and special events. Open 7 days a week.

BLACK CAT BOOKS
720 Manitou Ave., Manitou Springs
(719) 685-1589
http://manitoubooks.com
Labeling Black Cat Books, in Manitou Springs, just a bookstore is like labeling George Clooney just an actor. The store does sell books—new and used, from children's to historical fiction. But what this store also does is act as a community force.

First, the books. The inventory on-site can be deceiving when one walks into the tight space inside the front door. But there is a large, cozy room downstairs packed with books that customers are encouraged to browse. Since the owner also runs a wine bar and sells beer, you can do this browsing while enjoying an afternoon aperitif. Author visits, book signings, and readings occur often, sometimes many times in a week.

Black Cat Books even runs some fun author events, such as a Banned Book Reading, where the public is invited to bring and read from their favorite banned book.

The store and owner are also major players in the fall writer's conference held in Manitou each year, Author Fest of the Rockies.

Recurring events at the store run the gamut from a knitting group hosted every Sunday afternoon; poetry open mic nights every first and third Monday; a women's lead group on the second Tuesday of the month; a philosophy discussion group, Socrates Cafe, on the fourth Monday of the month; and a spirituality discussion group on the fourth Thursday of the month. Open 7 days a week.

BORDERS
1710 Briargate Blvd.
(719) 266-1600
www.borders.com
Borders, like Barnes & Noble, has locations on either end of town, although Borders has chosen one mall location and one outside a mall area. The north store on Briargate Boulevard is inside the Chapel Hills mall. The south store on Southgate Road is near the Broadmoor neighborhood.

The north store is two floors with a great "All Things Local" section, a story time on Saturday, an American Girl Club that meets the third Friday of the month, and a chess club that meets on Monday.

The south location (2120 Southgate Rd., 719-632-6611) offers a story time and crafts for kids every Saturday morning and live music on Saturday evenings.

Both stores offer a Seattle's Best Coffee Cafe. Book signings and special events are regularly held at both stores, which are open 7 days a week.

COVERED TREASURES BOOKSTORE
105 2nd St., Monument
(719) 481-2665
The entrance to this store is right off the street and up a few concrete steps. From the quiet wood shingle/sign above the door, it's hard to guess what kind of store this might be, but the surprise for bookies is close to enlightenment. This is a big, smart bookstore in a small bookstore's skin. The new books offered are inspired choices, both bestseller and mid-list, underground goodies. There are also a number of Colorado hiking guides, a fine selection of greeting cards, all categories of new and used books, and a coffee if you choose. Open 7 days a week.

HOOKED ON BOOKS
3918 Maizeland Rd.
(719) 596-1621
www.hookedonbooksonline.com
This almost 30-year-old, independent bookstore is run by people serious about books and the book world. This makes a certain sense, because the store feels like a comfortable, neighborhood library. They offer used and discounted new books and carry more than a quarter million books in the store. They offer special orders for out-of-print books and will order new books, usually at a discount. They carry a big selection of historical nonfiction, art and vintage books, and children's, among others. They also offer audio book rentals. Closed on Sun.

POOR RICHARD'S BOOKSTORE
320 N. Tejon St.
(719) 578-0012
http://poorrichardsdowntown.com
Poor Richard's Bookstore is part of a four-store, Poor Richard's complex in the north downtown area. The entrance to the

bookstore is slight, but the inventory travels so far back, you can feel like you're Alice falling down the rabbit hole. The books are mainly used, but there is a good selection of new books in every category along the front wall. They also carry a serious card selection, fun book and non-book related gifts, and old, rare, out-of-print and collectible books. Free Wi-Fi and adjoining Rico's cafe make this a great place for someone looking to kill time in a bookstore environment. Open 7 days a week.

BOUTIQUES & GIFT SHOPS

ABATINA
1713 S. 8th St.
(719) 471-2290
This lovely little gift shop on the south end of town is just a delight. The quirky items run from African beads to cookbooks for college students. You never know what will be out, and that's what keeps locals going back anytime they need a present or special something. Lotions, baby gifts, jewelry, home decor, garden items, and gift wrapping, too. Closed Sun.

CJ KARD
214 N. Tejon St.
(719) 634-3339
www.cjkard.com
This downtown store is always fun to enter. The more than 20-year-old shop specializes in cards and stationery, but they also carry some gift and home items, books, and knick-knacks. The birthday, anniversary, thank you, and blank cards are the usual Far Side variety up to handmade pieces of art. They also offer custom invitations. Open 7 days a week.

GARDEN OF THE GODS TRADING POST
Garden of the Gods Park, southwest edge
(719) 685-9045, (800) 874-4515
www.gardenofthegodstradingpost.com
Built to resemble a Pueblo Indian home, this iconic store is a bit like walking into the past. A little kitschy, but it feels appropriate.

For souvenir hunters, this is pretty close to a gold mine. The trading post carries almost any item you can think of with the name "Colorado" imprinted on it, T-shirts, wind chimes, aspen leaf jewelry and art, Minnetonka moccasins, and about 38,000 other choices. The post also carries art from Colorado artists, American Indian jewelry, baskets, sand painting, Navajo rugs, and Pueblo pottery.

An outside cafe specializes in buffalo burgers, which are good but pale in comparison to the amazing view of the rocks in the park. Open 7 days a week.

✳RICH DESIGNS
1731 Mt. Washington Ave.
(719) 475-1200, (800) 369-6909
www.richdesignsgallery.com
It's hard to know how to classify Rich Designs, other than to say this longtime Colorado Springs gallery/florist/interior design/home furnishings/gift boutique is one of the town's true gems. The store is more than 6,000 square feet of unusual, beautiful, eclectic goods painstakingly arranged in various home tableaus. This is not the art of shopping, this is shopping as art. The Holiday Spectacular Open House, usually every November, is not to be missed. They also hold an Art of Living event in September, benefitting the local hospice. Open Tues through Sat.

THE SHOPS AT THE BROADMOOR
1 Lake Ave.
(719) 634-7711
www.broadmoor.com

The Broadmoor, a historical, five-star resort, is by definition somewhat separate from the daily lives of most people living and working in Colorado Springs. So it's perhaps not a surprise that locals rarely think about shopping at The Broadmoor. That's a bit of a shame, because The Shops at The Broadmoor have a high-quality selection of goods, and the recently remodeled shopping area is conducive to viewing the wares. There's also the potential for a coffee or cocktail by the lake when one tires of shopping. With a backdrop like that, an afternoon spent shopping is like a little retreat.

There are about 25 stores all together, but a few are stand-outs. **Luma** is an intriguing, unusual collection of fine American crafts, clothing, jewelry, lamps, mirrors, and outdoor art.

The Boutique at the Broadmoor carries designer fashions, jewelry, bags, intimate apparel, and gifts and toys for children.

i A nice break while shopping at The Broadmoor is to pop into the elegant Hotel Bar, next to the lake. Nibbles of exotic nuts accent your very svelte Cosmopolitan—or tea, whatever you please!

The **Cosmetic Shop at the Broadmoor** features skincare and cosmetic lines from Trish McEvoy, Bobbi Brown, Laura Mercier, and Kiehls, among others. Makeovers are also available upon request.

For those who find a shopping excursion incomplete without a shoe store, **Yarid's Shoes** fits like Cinderella's slipper.

Shoe designers from Stuart Weitzman to Tory Burch are available for women, and men's shoes run from Cole Haan to Merrells. All stores open 7 days a week.

SPARROW HAWK
120 N. Tejon St.
(719) 471-3235
www.sparrowhawkcookware.com

This gourmet cookware store, located downtown, is the serious cook's recipe for an excellent kitchen. Picture a big box store like Bed, Bath & Beyond. Condense down only to items of exceptional quality. Pare away to cookware and beautiful kitchen tools. Simmer down to a space about 1/100th the size. Welcome to Sparrow Hawk.

The longtime downtown icon is actually in a slightly more roomy space than in decades previous, when they were around the corner. Before the move, the store was so snug customers held elbows and bags tight against the body to protect against breakage—the goods, not the body.

The new location, though, offers comfortable aisles with the same excellent selection of all things foodie. There are extensive cookware and knives sections, anything you could imagine for setting a table, glassware, spices, high-end food processors and blenders, ice cream makers, bread makers, yogurt makers, and panini grills. You can even find some spoons. They'll also gift wrap. Open 7 days a week.

WHICKERBILL
742 Manitou Ave., Manitou Springs
(719) 685-1540

Whickerbill is a whimsical store for cooks, people who like to decorate their homes, and those in the market for a gift. This is the kind of store where you don't need to have something in mind; by the time you've walked down the length of the store, you've spotted three things you want for yourself and at least two perfect gifts. They carry the svelte line of littala Finish home wares, quirky and fun Patience Brewster items, Japanese bowls, candles of all lengths, wine glasses, and hand-painted (and often oddly shaped—like a chicken) handbags. Open 7 days a week.

Flea Markets

Although others come and go, Colorado Springs has two legitimate flea markets.

Colorado Springs Flea Market
5225 E. Platte Ave., between Academy and Powers
(719) 380-8599
www.csfleamarket.com
This huge, outdoor flea market has been around for more than 30 years. It's the traditional big open area where you can find trash to treasures. There are usually about 500 vendors on the 30-acre, paved site. Open both days every weekend, year-round.

American Indoor Flea Market
2727 Palmer Park Blvd., just west of Circle
(719) 219-1898
For those winter months, the mere fact of indoors has quite an advantage. Not as large as the other flea market, but you don't have to wear mittens. Open every day.

FARMERS' MARKETS

Situated on the lip of the plains, the Pikes Peak region has large and small, longtime farms and ranches within a few hours in all directions. This makes for a bountiful choice in farmers' markets. The last few years have seen an explosion of new locations and days, as well as some fissures in the organization of which farmers attend which markets. Still, the end result for the consumer is a farmers' market in every direction of town, each with at least a decent selection of fresh goods.

Especially good in Colorado Springs are the roasted green chilies, which are usually roasted on-site. When the chilies are roasting, the smell is overwhelming, but in a sweet, earthy, agreeable way. Most vendors have trouble keeping up with the demand. Locals know that these are only available for a short while in the late summer and early fall, so they buy to both eat fresh and to have in the freezer all winter. If you drive to a market where you purchase roasted chilies, the aroma will linger in your car for days.

Also good in the area are tomatoes from the Pueblo farms, melon from Rocky Ford, peaches from the western slope of Colorado, and honey. If you've never tasted fresh honey, it should be on your bucket list.

Especially early in the season, be wary of farm stalls that carry fruits with little stickers that say, "Grown in California." You might as well buy those in the grocery store, because they're not coming from local farms.

Also, two markets are a little different from the rest: They are the markets sponsored by the Colorado Farm and Art Market, and they're at The Margarita at Pine Creek and at America the Beautiful Park. These markets sell as much arts and crafts items as produce. Some people like these markets the best because it's more like a shopping excursion. The produce is just as good as at the other markets, but can be lacking in choice and variety, so it all depends on what you want.

The farmers' markets run from late spring through late fall.

Monday

ACACIA PARK
Bijou and Tejon Streets

MEMORIAL PARK
Pikes Peak and Union Avenues
This is the traditional biggie, held in the same location Mon and Thurs.

Tuesday

FOUNTAIN FARMERS' MARKET
Fountain City Hall, Ohio and Main Streets

Wednesday

AMERICA THE BEAUTIFUL PARK
126 Cimino Dr.
This is one of the Farm and Art Markets.

Thursday

FIRST AND MAIN TOWN CENTER
Powers Boulevard and Constitution Avenue

MEMORIAL PARK
Pikes Peak and Union Avenues
This is the traditional biggie, held in the same location Mon and Thurs.

Friday

MANITOU SPRINGS
Soda Springs Park, 1000 Manitou Ave.

WOODLAND PARK
Center and Henrietta Streets

Saturday

THE MARGARITA AT PINE CREEK
7350 Pine Creek Rd.
This is one of the Farm and Art Markets, in a gorgeous setting outside an eclectic restaurant.

MONUMENT
146 Jefferson St.

OLD COLORADO CITY
24th Street and W. Colorado Avenue

GARDEN SHOPS

GOOD EARTH GARDEN CENTER
1330 N. Walnut St.
(719) 473-3399
www.goodearthgardencenter.com
This business could easily be subtitled Good Mood Garden Center. It's off a smaller street just west and north of downtown, and in the summer the stone walkways are lined by flowering plants and covered by big shade trees. The metal "dinosaur bed," a flower bed with large, metal-dinosaur yard art, gives off good vibes. The grounds are easy to navigate, helped by the clear map posted at the yard's entrance. The retail section offers a nice selection of supplies and goodies. Open 7 days a week.

RICK'S
1827 W. Unitah St.
(719) 632-8491
http://ricksgarden.com
Rick's has been a Colorado Springs staple for about half a century. The store rambles down multiple aisles and into side buildings, filled with necessities like hoses—about 20 varieties—to treasures like Living Geeky yard art. And then there are the acres of outside grounds, down the hill. Rick's is the kind of

garden store where you feel like getting your hands dirty. Closed Sun.

SPENCER'S LAWN AND GARDEN CENTERS
1430 S. Tejon St.
(719) 632-2788
www.spencersgardens.com
Spencer's main store is located on the south end of town, and it's been a tried-and-true Colorado Springs gardening resource for years. The staff is always available to help you determine what will work best in your yard, and they're knowledgeable about this tricky Colorado climate. The store also carries a number of garden tools, supplies, and fun decorations. They are also one of the only places in town where you can get a large Christmas tree. Open 7 days a week. A second Spencer's location is at 4720 Center Valley Dr. in Fountain (719-392-2726).

SUMMERLAND GARDENS
124 E. Cheyenne Rd.
(719) 477-0267
http://summerlandgardens.com
Summerland is a garden shop—and more. The retail store is so unique and packed with such artistic knickknacks, paintings, and other funky little things, it's a strong gift shop in its own right. Summerland is cheerful, bright, funky, and eclectic. Locals and visitors alike get lost in this cool little establishment, set in a house that has been home to many iconic businesses over the years. Open 7 days a week.

KIDS' CLOTHING & TOYS

THE AMERICAN TOY STORE
906 Manitou Ave., Manitou Springs
(719) 434-2133
www.americantoystore.com
This store takes the guesswork out of shopping for American-made toys. If it's sold here, it is made in the USA. The more than 1,000 toys filling the shelves are all high-quality and safe—no Chinese paint jobs on these babies. Toys include everything from games, puzzles, and books to Slinky toys, wooden jumbo marshmallow shooters, wagons, footballs, and K'nex NASCAR and Sesame Street items. Open 7 days a week.

LITTLE RICHARD'S TOY STORE
324 N. Tejon St.
(719) 578-5848
http://poorrichardsdowntown.com
Little Richard's Toy Store is part of a four-store, Poor Richard's complex in north downtown. It's packed full of unique play things for kids of all ages—but mainly for the little guys. The specialty of the store is interactive, imagination-stirring toys that do more than entertain. The smallish space is crammed full of action toys, puzzles, plush puppets, mobiles, games, costumes for an afternoon of dress up, mobiles, and more. It would take a hard heart to walk out without at least something for the little person in your life. Open 7 days a week.

MOUNTAIN MOPPETS
2532 W. Colorado Ave.
(719) 633-3473
www.mountainmoppets.com
This cute, almost 30-year-old store in Old Colorado City is a favorite of grandparents, aunts, family friends . . . anyone looking for a children's gift. Parents like it too, especially the middle-rack, where out-of-season clothing is marked on sale. The quality clothing is stylish and sturdy, the kind that lasts and gets passed on to each sibling and then to others as well. They carry everything from

cloth coats to fancy swimwear for infants on up to elementary grades. They also carry fun accessories like hair bows and headbands, dress-up clothes, and designer footwear. Open 7 days a week.

PLINKETY PLINK MUSIC BOX SHOP & YOYO LOCO
744 Manitou Ave., Manitou Springs
(719) 471-2726
www.yoyoloco.com

This distinctive, alternative toy store carries more yoyos and yoyo supplies than you probably knew existed. The musical toys are just as varied, from snow globes to music boxes to clocks. They also showcase wind-up toys with crazy shapes and crazy names like Mxykikker and Pintacuda. Perhaps not the store for every buying occasion, but when it's right, there's nothing like it. Days open vary by season, but usually open Fri through Mon and can be closed Tues through Thurs.

MALLS & SHOPPING DISTRICTS

CHAPEL HILLS MALL
N. Academy at Briargate Boulevard
www.chapelhillsmall.com

Chapel Hills is an indoor mall, which is almost too bad: It looks over most of the city, with an incredible view of Pikes Peak and the US Air Force Academy. Still, we are a city with snow in the winter, so an indoor shopping mall can be the attraction all to itself.

There are more than 150 stores, a fairly large and adequate food court, a 15-screen movie theatre, a kids' play area, and seasonal entertainment.

Chapel Hills mall has definitely benefited from its north location. Over the past decade, most of the city's growth has occurred north

and east. Because of that, the mall's anchor stores have been solid for a number of years. Dillard's, Macy's, Sears, and JC Penney are longtime tenants, while a newer Dick's Sporting Goods has replaced a private ice rink. Some of the smaller stores run from the national chains (Aeropostale, Gap, and the like) to a few independent stores and kiosks that offer local goods.

THE CITADEL
S. Academy at US 24
www.shopthecitadel.com

The Citadel is Colorado Springs's other indoor mall—and the determining factor in whether one goes to The Citadel or Chapel Hills is all location. Chapel Hills is north, The Citadel is south.

Anchor stores are Dillard's, JC Penney, and Burlington Coat Factory, and there are more than 150 stores in all. Victoria's Secret, Buckle, Express, and Hollister are some of the specialty stores. The food court is pretty decent for a mall, with a number of fast food choices, such as McDonald's, Chick-fil-A, and Panda Express as well as a few different choices, like Gyros Plus and Hibachi San. There is also a Hooters and Ruby Tuesday inside the mall.

Special events are hosted throughout the year near the two-level food court, such as live performances during the Kennedy Center Imagination Celebration, which has its local home in the mall.

DOWNTOWN
Multi-block area surrounding Acacia Park, Tejon Street, and Bijou Street

Downtown Colorado Springs is old, new, funky, conservative. This quiet juxtaposition makes for a definite personality all its own.

SHOPPING

The shopping is along unique storefronts shaded by mature trees and intriguing public art. Most stores are independent and locally owned. Buildings are old brick, new steel and glass, or adobe.

The stores are heavy in the women's clothing arena, with jewelry, music, and gift and book shops in between.

Restaurants are plentiful, and many find a respite from the rigors of power shopping by watching kids splash in the goofy, carefree Uncle Wilbur Fountain (summer only). If the music's not playing, it's worth waiting until the man with the tuba makes his appearance, usually every 30 minutes.

Because it is downtown, there are a number of events during the year that have streets blocked off for pedestrian traffic. There are also a number of parades down Tejon Street, including the Festival of Lights Parade in the holiday season and the Pikes Peak or Bust Rodeo Parade, which opens the rodeo event every July.

OLD COLORADO CITY
West Colorado Avenue area, between 21st and 31st Streets
www.shopoldcoloradocity.com
Old Colorado City is an absolute favorite with tourists. Its brick buildings are reminiscent of the Old West, but the restaurants, frequent festivals, and shops—lots and lots of shops—are contemporary and varied.

These West Side shops cover everything from art to women's clothing. Out-of-towners love all the souvenir shops, and antiques freaks can while away whole days in the myriad antiques stores up and down the blocks. Collectibles of almost every form can be seen, from Pez dispensers to imported lace. There are a number of Indian/Tibetan clothing establishments, at least 10 quirky

and/or vintage women's clothing shops, candles, pottery and glass stores, and fine linens and ceramics.

A number of restaurants dot the area, and ice cream and chocolate stores tempt at major corner intersections. At night, bands and DJs regularly appear in bars and an upstairs club.

The biggest festival is Territory Days, held every Memorial Day weekend. The festival was first held decades ago to commemorate Old Colorado City being the first capital of the Colorado Territory, back in 1861. Unfortunately, that distinction was rescinded almost immediately when the local's rowdy, colorful lifestyle wasn't thought to be conducive to a governing body. The locals are pretty tame by comparison now, but the Territory Days Festival is a rollicking event, with over 180 craft, commercial, and food booths catering to about 100,000 guests.

In the fall, Old Colorado City hosts the Giant Pumpkin Weigh-off, and various other events and festivals come and go through the year.

THE PROMENADE SHOPS AT BRIARGATE
1885 Briargate Pkwy.
www.thepromenadeshopsatbriargate .com
This outdoor shopping mall is the newcomer to the shopping areas. Although quite close in proximity to Chapel Hills, it's really a different kind of animal.

First, most stores are national chains, but there is no one anchor store. And the stores that are here tend to be of the higher-end variety for clothing, housewares, and high technology. Apple, Williams-Sonoma, Pottery Barn, Ann Taylor, and Banana Republic are some of the examples.

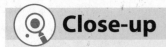

Close-up

Parking Downtown

Parking downtown is really not that hard. It just feels that way sometimes. Knowing what your choices are makes it easier to find a spot quickly. Lunch hours can be especially trying, so have a plan, park, and get on with it.

PARKING METERS

The City has approximately 2,400 parking meter spaces, most downtown. They accept either quarters and dimes (no nickels or pennies) or the Easy Park card.

The Easy Park is a pre-purchased card that allows you to choose the amount put on the meter each session. They can be purchased at:

- The city's Parking Administration office in the City Administration Building Parking Garage, 130 S. Nevada, SE corner of the 2nd floor.

- Online at https://secure.springsgov.com/easypark

Easy Park re-load kiosks, where you can put more money on your card, are located at:

- 218 N. Tejon, next to Jose Muldoon's

- 6 S. Tejon, in front of US Bank

- 127 E. Vermijo, NW corner of Vermijo and Tejon

- 107 N. Nevada, SE side of City Hall

- 2418 W. Colorado, in Old Colorado City in front of Michael Garman

It's wise to mind the meters—they are watched closely and tickets are given in what seems like seconds after the meter expires.

PARKING GARAGES

All of the parking garages are run privately. The garages are at:

- Bijou and Cascade Parking Garage, 215 N. Cascade; 305 spaces

- City Administration Building Parking Garage, 130 S. Nevada; 1,642 spaces

- Kiowa Street Parking Garage, 127 E. Kiowa; 650 available spaces

PARKING LOTS

There are also a few parking lots downtown, all privately run. They are at:

- Pikes Peak just east of Tejon, across from Kimball's Twin Peaks Theater. This one can get a little pricey depending on the day and time, but it is convenient.

- Pikes Peak just west of Tejon, across from Phantom Canyon Brewing Co.

Large restaurants are positioned within the parking area and a number of smaller eateries are next to shops. Biaggi's Ristorante Italiano, P. F. Chang's China Bistro, and Ted's Montana Grill are all popular and tend to get crowded; reservations are wise but not required. For more casual dining, California Pizza Kitchen and Panera Bread are, among others, available.

Artwork lines the well-tended and wide sidewalks, and there are occasional special events.

MENS' CLOTHING

RUTLEDGE'S
102 N. Tejon St.
(719) 632-7654
This classic men's store has been a cornerstone in Colorado Springs for decades—literally. First located on one corner downtown, a few years ago it moved to another prominent corner in the downtown shopping district. This is the kind of store where men (or the women who shop for them) care about the name and/or quality of clothing they buy. It's a great place to shop for a gift or special outfit, or everyday wear for the select shopper. They carry everything from suits to shorts and accessories. Open Mon through Sat.

WILLIAM KURTZ LIMITED
10 E. Pikes Peak Ave.
(719) 635-2126
www.williamkurtzltd.com
This men's specialty store, opened in 1995 by owner Bill Kurtz, is tucked into a quaint space in a historic building downtown. It offers casual to dressy clothing of the Tommy Bahama, Tallia, Thomas Dean variety. The service is understated but helpful, and they run

a trunk show for women looking to buy their men gifts during the holiday season. They also carry a few accessories, including Cole Haan shoes. Open Mon through Sat.

MUSIC STORES

COLORADO GUITAR EMPORIUM
2997 Broadmoor Valley Rd.
(719) 200-9660
www.coguitaremporium.com
This fine music store is tucked into a strip mall on the south end of town, near the intersection of CO 115 and Cheyenne Mountain Boulevard. The owner, Steve Scheller, is known as an accomplished professional rock and jazz musician who has played with some big acts. Probably in large part due to this connection, musicians feel at home here. Aside from their excellent selection of guitars, amps, and basses, they also offer lessons for both children and adults, repair from set-ups to resetting a neck, sheet music, and accessories. Closed Sun.

THE DULCIMER SHOP
740 Manitou Ave., Manitou Springs
(719) 685-9655
http://dulcimer.net
Located in Manitou Springs, The Dulcimer Shop hand crafts dulcimers and guitars on-site. The almost 40-year-old store also carries violins, mandolins, banjos, and other acoustic instruments as well as ethnic pieces such as African drums, shakers, and gourds. The shop sponsors the Manitou Springs Mountain Music Festival, held on the last weekend of August, with three days of local and national talent. Open 7 days a week.

GRANER MUSIC
4460 Barnes Rd.
(719) 574-2001
www.graner-music.com
Graner is a hopping place. With a north location as well as the Barnes Road store, Graner has kids and adults lined up for lessons at almost all hours. They are a big supplier of the band and orchestra market, lately serving even communities north of Colorado Springs. They offer a full-service repair shop, a loaner program for instruments in the repair shop, new instruments of all kinds, and sheet music and books. Closed Sun.

INDEPENDENT RECORDS AND VIDEO
3030 E. Platte Ave.
(719) 473-0882
www.beindependent.com
This big music store has been a Colorado landmark since 1978, when records were still the thing to buy. Locations around town include downtown on Bjiou and on West Colorado Avenue in Old Colorado City. They also have Pueblo, Fountain, and Denver locations. If they don't stock the music or movie you want, they will order it for you. Open 7 days a week.

MEEKER MUSIC
113 E. Bijou St.
(719) 471-8940
http://meekermusic.tripod.com/
Meeker is a family-owned, longtime Colorado Springs music store that, like Graner, is a big supplier in the instrument rental market for bands. The downtown store (there are two others, one north and one in Fountain) has an impressive selection of sheet music. They also sell new instruments and offer a full-service repair shop. Closed Sun.

SPORTS SHOPS

Cycling

COLORADO CYCLIST
3970 E. Bijou St.
(719) 591-4045 or (800) 688-8600
www.coloradocyclist.com
Locally owned and operated, Colorado Cyclist is a bit different from the other bike shops listed here. That's because the operation is run as a large online retailer. If you're looking for a more locally focused shop, these people are probably not your first stop, although they do know the area and cycling like the experts they are. What's interesting for seasoned cyclists is that, if you've ordered bike supplies online, you've probably ordered from them. If you want to see the shop and talk to the people in person, you have that opportunity at their retail store on the east side of town. Open 7 days.

CRITERIUM
6150 Corporate Dr.
(719) 599-0149
http://criterium.com
Criterium's store sits right on the bike path on the north end of town. The newer, airy building sports an extensive retail shop, which is especially deep in clothes. The staff is friendly and helpful, and they are happy to help new riders or visitors find the best bike trails. Criterium also offers bike rentals if you haven't brought your own bike (BYOB). Mechanics are quick to service repairs, and an assortment of new bikes, from the purple-streamered kid's variety to the pro road bike, are on-site. Open 7 days a week.

Manitou Springs

Manitou is close to Colorado Springs, but the two towns have very separate personalities. Manitou is a great place to get your groove on and get in touch with a more natural, independent spirit. There's shopping, an arcade, restaurants, and coffeehouses. Pushed into the base of Pikes Peak, Manitou has a more mountain feel than Colorado Springs. People find Manitou either nirvana or a little too hippie: It's all in your perspective. Visitors tend to enjoy walking its streets for an afternoon.

OLD TOWNE BIKE SHOP
426 S. Tejon St.
(719) 475-8589
www.oldtownbikeshop.com

In business since 1976, Old Towne Bike Shop is a well-known and respected mainstay downtown. It's known for excellent customer service and skilled bike mechanics, and they can knowledgeably serve anyone from a first-time rider to the high-end racer. Old Towne's owner is vocal about the green lifestyle; there are solar panels on the roof and frequent dialogue about bike commuting rather than relying on fossil fuels. A full service and retail area supply both the serious and amateur cyclist. Closed Sun.

PROCYCLING
600 S. 21st St.
(719) 266-4047
http://procyclingwarehouse.com

Located in a historic—and very cool—renovated railroad station roundhouse, Procycling is geared exactly where you'd expect: to the pro cyclist. The mountain bike mechanics are especially well known, but the store also serves the road bike crowd, from beginner to expert. They carry a good retail selection and a number of select bike brands. Open 7 days a week.

TED'S BICYCLES
3016 N. Hancock Ave.
(719) 473-6915
www.tedsbicycles.com

Tucked into an old neighborhood north of the downtown area, Ted's has been here just about as long as people have been riding bikes. The family shop—both run by and for—is known for personal service. There is a retail shop, and although they service and rent all kinds of bikes, they are considered one of the best BMX bike shops in southern Colorado. Closed Sun.

Fishing

ANGLER'S COVEY
295 S. 21st St.
(719) 471-2984
www.anglerscovey.com

Angler's Covey is more like a fishing destination than a store. Located in a new, 6,500-square-feet, West Side building, the longtime fly-fishing shop features ample room and even outside casting ponds. The store carries rods and supplies from a number of reputable manufactures such as Orvis, Patagonia, Ross Reels, and Action Optics. They offer classes and camps, from fly-tying basics to streamside introduction. They arrange Orvis-endorsed guides for customized trips, available on an individual basis or for groups like corporate retreats. The store is also a central location for information and meetings of a number of local fishing groups. Open 7 days a week.

Hiking & Climbing

MOUNTAIN CHALET
226 N. Tejon St.
(719) 633-0732 or (800) 346-7044
www.mtnchalet.com
Since 1968, this mountaineering store has been a feature in the downtown landscape. It caters to serious mountain folks, but even those who are a bit more casual about adventure enjoy walking through the packed store. Mountain Chalet is focused on the supplies, clothing, and information needed for climbing, hiking, camping, and backcountry skiing. They also run a rental program for such things as climbing shoes, backcountry skis, snowshoes, and tents. Their famed T-shirt, "Colorado: Don't Trust Anyone Under 14,000 Feet," which is illustrated with a map of all the Fourteeners in the state, is one of the most authentic and unique souvenirs you can get in the area. Open 7 days a week.

Running

COLORADO RUNNING COMPANY
833 N. Tejon St.
(719) 635-3833
www.corunco.com
This award-winning running company is located downtown, across the street from Colorado College. The customer service is attentive and friendly, and they offer a good selection of shoe brands and running accessories. Gait analysis is free and suggested, and the knowledgeable staff is keen to make sure people buy the right shoe for whatever it is you do in them. The store sponsors

a number of recurring runs, publishes a newsletter, and is generally an all-around community organizer, for both the running community and the public good. Open 7 days a week.

Ski & Snowboard

THE SKI SHOP
1422 S. Tejon St.
(719) 636-3355
www.theskishopinc.com
This extended-family run business has been in their hut-like location on the south end of town since the '50s. Multiple generations of loyal customers keep walking in the door for the same excellent service and quality products. Unlike the big box stores that offer ski and snowboard equipment, the staff at The Ski Shop are deeply in touch with the passion that drives people to spend their weekends (and a few mental health weekdays) on the slopes. They have new and used equipment; offer repair and tune-ups, boot fitting, demo use, and rentals; and sponsor a massive ski, snowboard, and clothing swap every October. Open 7 days a week.

SPECIALTY FOOD STORES

ASIAN PACIFIC MARKET
615 Wooten Rd.
(719) 573-7500
This eastside market is the go-to joint if you're cooking anything Asian. They carry fresh and frozen seafood, large packages of panko, exotic condiments, and sushi supplies, and there is an Asian deli. They also have a good selection of Hawaiian products and a few trendy side items like Ramune, a Japanese soft drink sealed with a marble. Open 7 days a week.

THE OLIVE TAP
906 Manitou Ave., Manitou Springs
(719) 358-9329
http://theolivetap.com/manitou/
Olive oil has its groupies, and this is the place for them. Tastings are encouraged as the staff waxes romantic about artisan, 100 percent pure extra virgin olive oil and its virtues. Features olive oil imported seasonally from Italy (of course), Greece, Argentina, and Tunisia as well as from the US and other countries. Oils are flavored with lemon, blood oranges, and porcini mushrooms, among others. A spice locker offers spices and herbs, and the store carries a good supply of balsamic vinegars, sauces, and gift baskets. Open 7 days a week, but can vary by season.

✳RANCH FOODS DIRECT
2901 N. El Paso
(719) 473-2306 or (866) 866-6328
www.ranchfoodsdirect.com
Ranch Foods Direct is a bit like the poster child for the slow-food, low-mileage, all-natural, humane-treatment philosophy of eating.

Mike Callicrate, a Colorado native with a degree in animal science from Colorado State University, runs a large, independent feed yard in St. Francis, KS. That antibiotic-free, hormone-free meat is sold out of the Colorado Springs fabrication plant and retail store, Ranch Foods Direct. The meat is also sold in a few other independent stores and at many local eateries—who almost always make a big point of the Ranch Foods Direct connection.

For out-of-towners, the Callicrate name might not mean much, but in Colorado, Callicrate is known as the Rolls Royce of beef. Those in the industry credit the "rinse and chill" method used in processing as one additional reason for the meat's superb quality.

The store, hidden down an industrial street and then deep to the side of the meat fabrication plant, used to have a number of open parking spaces out front. Not so much anymore. As the store grows in reputation, parking for the tiny retail space is getting tight.

No matter. People are almost religious in loyalty to Ranch Foods. In addition to Callicrate beef, the store also carries organic pork, chicken, lamb, buffalo, eggs, cheese, and small amounts of produce and baked goods. Everything comes from independent, local farms and ranches. Photographs and biographies of all the suppliers hang at the back of the store.

Christmas prime ribs and Thanksgiving turkeys are especially popular and are best ordered well in advance. Home deliveries are also offered. Closed Sun.

WESTERN APPAREL

THE COWHAND
200 W. Midland Ave., Woodland Park
(719) 687-9688
www.thecowhand.com
In downtown Woodland Park, The Cowhand has been in the same family for 45 years. You'll find authentic Western hats; belts with bold buckles; Western clothing for men, women, and children; quality leather goods; and home accessories; as well as great Southwestern jewelry, both costume and high-end. There's a separate room full of cowboy boots, from ropers to dress boots, plain and fancy. The store is packed wall to wall with great goods that will tempt you to get your cowboy

on. Look here for the cute stick horses for kids—they make great souvenirs or Christmas presents for little buckaroos. Open 7 days a week.

LORIG'S
15 N. Union Blvd.
(719) 633-4695
www.lorigscolorado.com
Lorig's has serious history in Colorado Springs, going back all the way to mining camps in the Gold Rush and American Indian trading posts. They carry all things Western, including apparel for men, ladies, and children; belts; buckles; bolo ties; and, of course, hats and boots. They also stock a significant uniform collection, from safety-toe boots to Carhartt garments to sentry caps. New styles in hats appear every March. Closed Sun.

WOMEN'S CLOTHING

COLORADO CO-OP
315 N. Tejon St.
(719) 389-0696
www.coloradoco-oponline.com
The name here is a little misleading: The merchandise is actually from all over, including Italy and France. The women's boutique carries clothing, jewelry, shoes, and accessories, including some eco-friendly lines. All selections are made by small designers who have a clean, contemporary, fashion-forward aesthetic. The store is not a large space, but it gives a nod to the clothing with its airy, urbane ambiance. With a wide range of price points, this is also a good place to find gift items and select skincare products. Open 7 days a week.

DRAMA BOUTIQUE
107 N. Tejon St.
(719) 329-0500
http://drama-boutique.com
Drama is one of the newer women's clothing stores on the scene, and they've positioned themselves well on one of three golden blocks of retail shopping downtown. Drama has a hip, chic, and mature-but-edgy sensibility to the clothing. This is a good place to go if you want something that'll make you feel stylish and now, even (or especially) if it's only a pair of jeans. Closed Sun.

> **i** There's a 3-block golden zone of women's clothing stores downtown, where just about every other store caters to those who love clothing and accessories: from North Tejon at Boulder Street head south to North Tejon at Pikes Peak Avenue.

EVE'S REVOLUTION
1312 W. Colorado Ave.
(719) 633-1357
www.evesrevolution.com
So you're shopping with your 20-year-old daughter and your 60-year-old mother. Where can you go? Just see Eve. This trendy, forward-thinking new apparel and consignment shop is hip, current, whimsical, and down to business. Now in her second decade in this cute cottage store, Eve has a knack for finding new clothing that is just unusual enough to be interesting while being comfortable enough for real life. Her consignment selections (about 50 percent of the merchandise) are carefully selected for only better brands that have been untouched or very lovingly tended.

Bags, accessories, and shoes line the walls. With frequent special events, you just might walk into something fun, like champagne and cupcakes. Even if you don't buy anything, Eve's is a great shopping excursion. Open 7 days a week.

KIRK & HILL
129 N. Tejon St.
(719) 635-7038

This locally owned women's clothing store is downtown, with a second location at The Promenade Shops at Briargate. It's been around for decades, and is one of the first stops when a nice dress is in order. It also carries more casual items as well as jewelry and accessories. Closed Sun.

THE LEECH PIT
802 N. Nevada Ave.
(719) 634-DORK (3675)
www.theleechpit.com

Driving by The Leech Pit, you will have one of two reactions: either slam on the brakes and find the nearest parking space, or gun it, thinking, *I would never enter that store*. If you're in the latter group, hold on a second. The Leech Pit does exude an element of punkish, screaming fun, but it also offers some of the best clothing, music, and collectibles around. The extensive women's resale clothing and shoes go from '70s happy face to a deep selection of cowboy boots. The men's selections are crammed with pearl-button Western shirts to concert T-shirts. And trying the new duds on requires at least one trip to the anatomically correct dressing rooms. Yes, that's right. You want to go see the place now, don't you? Be sure to notice the Doll-O-Ramas (dolls as funky dioramas),

hobo-style Leech nickels, and a multitude of pop culture items. That's one part of the store. The other is one of the most extensive selections of vinyl this side of Denver. From the birth of cool on, including jazz, soul, funk, hip hop—it's all here. Well, unless it's "square or churchy." That, they don't carry. Open 7 days a week.

REGINA'S
119 N. Tejon St.
(719) 634-6833
http://reginasonline.com

Regina's is another longtime, downtown retail icon. The store is large and open, making it easy to see all the items on hand. The clothes run from sedate sportswear to bling, with a small but excellent choice of shoes as well. A sale rack toward the front usually features quality clothing in popular sizes. Closed Sun.

SWISH
1816 W. Colorado Ave.
(719) 635-8375

We're talking vintage, baby. Like a fine wine, some people just prefer it the older the better. For those folks, Swish is the hands-down favorite among locals. They carry the usual suspects in women's clothing as well as coats, hats, gloves, robes, lingerie, and scarves. They also carry a few new items, all made with the flair of the past. Closed Sun.

✳TERRA VERDE
208 N. Tejon St.
(719) 444-8621
www.terraverdestyle.com

This is the big player in Colorado Springs's women's clothing boutiques. The mostly casual styles are current, wearable, high-quality, and different from anything else available. The prices are reasonable for the quality. The staff is exceptionally helpful or will leave you alone, if wanted. Best-suited for the 20- to 50-something woman, the 6,500-square-foot store is always full of shoppers but rarely feels crowded. This is the go-to store for men who don't know what to buy the woman in their lives. Terra Verde also carries shoes, hats, bags and jewelry, home decor, books, bath and body items, and some baby clothes and toys. The free gift wrapping is a piece of art, and something from Terre Verde is usually the most anticipated gift in the birthday pile or under the Christmas tree. Open 7 days a week.

ANNUAL EVENTS & FESTIVALS

olorado Springs and the Pikes Peak region are *happening*. The area showcases an eclectic mix of events from sports (lots of them) to the arts to food to just plain fun.

With the US Air Force Academy and the US Olympic Training Center here, along with other colleges and sports organizations, there is a sports event every week, if not every day. From college football to Olympic team competitions, a sports fan never has to wait long for something to see.

For foodies and wine-lovers, delicacies abound. Apparently we in the Pikes Peak region love the finer things in life, because there are a host of delectable events throughout the year.

And for the more underground, off-the-radar personalities, the unique is alive and well in Colorado Springs . . . and especially in Manitou Springs. Pick a month and you're sure to see something of interest.

Note that there are two Memorial Parks in the region. In this listing, if it says only "Memorial Park," that's the big one at Pikes Peak Avenue and Union Boulevard in Colorado Springs. If it says, "Memorial Park, Manitou Springs," that's in Manitou on Manitou Avenue.

JANUARY

✳THE GREAT FRUITCAKE TOSS
Manitou Springs High School Track
401 El Monte Pl., Manitou Springs
(800) 642-2567
www.manitousprings.org
It's the ultimate in re-gifting: First, receive the worst present possible from your dotty old aunt and then use that unappetizing gift to entertain a whole community. Just don't tell aunty.

The Great Fruitcake Toss is exactly what is says, and this no-respect, rowdy event is wildly popular. Fruitcakes are tossed, propelled, sling-shot, and hurled by people wearing kilts, parkas, and wedding dresses. Trophies or ribbons and bragging rights

go to the winners in categories for kids, distance, accuracy, and "catch the fruitcake." The latter puts a team across a field where they try to catch the airborne food with any implement found in the garage that morning—fishing nets, baseball gloves, buckets, whatever. There are also fruitcake beauty competitions, with categories for most beautiful, ugly, creative, and the like. Past events have also included games such as spatula relay races.

There are rules about the mechanical and pneumatic devices used to launch the sweet crumbs, and there are weight classes of cake. To ensure that people aren't loading their desserts with heavy inedibles such as marbles and weights, there are Fruitcake Toss Tech Inspectors.

It's all in good fun, and even aunty might approve if she spent a joyous, brisk winter day in the park, cheering the flying fruitcake. Free admission, although contestants must donate either one nonperishable food item or a cash donation to the local food kitchen.

A limited number of fruitcakes are available to rent for $1 if one is fortunate enough not to receive the prized gift. Several local inns also offer cakes for the day.

FEBRUARY

DAVE SCHULTZ MEMORIAL INVITATIONAL
US Olympic Training Center
1750 E. Boulder St.
(719) 598-8181
www.usawrestling.org
This senior-division wrestling competition was started in the '90s to honor a man who was an accomplished wrestler and ambassador to the sport, and it continues in the spirit of friendship, sportsmanship, and goodwill. This elite-level competition hosts more than 300 athletes from around the globe, including India, China, Uzbekistan, and Canada. The tournament is held on the first weekend in Feb.

PRESIDENT'S DAY YOUTH HOCKEY TOURNAMENT
Various Ice Rinks
www.csaha.com
Detroit might be hockey town the rest of the year, but on President's Day weekend, hockey town is Colorado Springs. This ice hockey tournament hosts youth from mites (8 and under) to AAA midgets (under 18

years old with serious skills). Teams come from states across the US and as far away as Slovakia, Sweden, and, of course, Canada. Past events have hosted more than 80 teams along with their coaches and parents. So word to the wise: If you need a hotel room on President's Day weekend, book early.

Games are played at the five rinks in town, and there is a grand opening ceremony featuring a Presentation of Teams held at the 8,000-seat Colorado Springs World Arena. Admission for spectators is by weekend pass or day passes, which can be purchased at the venues.

MUMBO JUMBO GUMBO COOK-OFF & CARNIVALE PARADE
Soda Springs Park (cook-off) and Manitou Ave. (parade), Manitou Springs
(800) 642-2567
www.manitousprings.org
On the Saturday before every Fat Tuesday, Manitou cooks it up hot and spicy. First, both amateur and professional chefs use their secret recipes to bubble up some gumbo like they do in Louisiana. The public can taste the shrimp, rice, and andouille sausage creations for a small fee, and winners not only get bragging rights, they also win cash prizes and trophies.

After the public feast, the town jazzes it up with a Carnivale Parade down Manitou Avenue. Parade goers sashay in a vivid collection of boas, musical instruments, and sequined masks rarely seen this far north. Those wishing to march just show up prior to the start of the event. Since this is a family-friendly day, bring your mojo but leave those To Go cups at home.

CRIPPLE CREEK ICE FESTIVAL
Downtown Cripple Creek
(877) 858-4653
www.visitcripplecreek.com

A lot of people like to head to a warm, sandy beach in February. For those who find sand irritating, or who just can't afford the plane ticket, there's a cool alternative—literally. The Ice Festival features sculptures that range from the mythical to the magical. Spectators can watch as the ice is carved with chain saws and carving tools, and there is an ice maze, ice slide, a dueling chain saws competition, a martini bar (they are better when they're cold, you know), and retail and food vendors on the street and in a heated tent. The festival runs for two weekends, and new sculptures are carved through the last weekend.

MARCH

WINE FESTIVAL OF COLORADO
SPRINGS
Various Locations
(719) 634-5583
www.csfineartscenter.org/Wine
Festival.asp

Now in its third decade, the Wine Festival of Colorado Springs is one of Colorado's premier wine events. Past themes have included "The Wines of South Africa: Old World Meets New," "Women in Wine," and "Pinot Noir from Around the World." Held at The Broadmoor hotel with additional, supporting locations around town, the weekend event is a fine mix of more than 300 wines, elegant food, Grand Tasting & Wine Market Auction seminars, pairings, and the Gourmet Winemaker Dinner & Live Auction. The festival benefits the Colorado Springs Fine Arts Center and is open to the public. Reservations are required

except for the Grand Tasting, where walk-ins are welcome. Special rates for lodging during the festival are offered by The Broadmoor as well as the Garden of the Gods Club.

ST. PATRICK'S DAY PARADE
Tejon Street
www.csstpats.com

A pot o' gold awaits downtown every St. Paddy's day. The rainbow of activity starts with a 5K race, followed by a Leprechaun Fun Run. And then at noon sharp, the parade begins. Marchers, bands, floats, flags, bagpipes, and leprechauns honor this religious and Irish holiday with the best green finery and blarney around. Past parades have been witnessed by more than 30,000 lads and lassies, all with Irish eyes smiling. Grandstand and reviewing stand tickets are available to the public, but the parade is free otherwise. Arrive early for your best seat on the curb. If you're late, you better hope to find a four-leaf clover en route because the crowds can get thick and good viewing spots can be hard to find.

> **i** After the St. Paddy's Day Parade, head to Jack Quinn Irish Alehouse and Pub (21 S. Tejon St.) for some shared blarney and a bit of Irish fare.

APRIL

VICTORIAN EASTER EGG HUNT
Miramont Castle
9 Capitol Hill Ave., Manitou Springs
(888) 685-1011
www.miramontcastle.org

For those looking for a little more than the backyard Easter egg hunt, this is the ticket. The delightful Miramont Castle hosts a Victorian Easter egg hunt and tea for children ages 2 to 10. The little guys won't have any trouble finding eggs with the generous supply hidden on the grounds, and the child who finds the golden egg wins a special Easter basket. Children must be accompanied by an adult, and reservations are required—and fill up early. Tea seatings are scheduled three times during the day.

PIKES PEAK WRITERS CONFERENCE
Colorado Springs Marriott
5580 Tech Center Dr.
www.ppwcon.org

First held in 1993, this highly regarded writers conference has been a force in the Colorado writers market from the start. This is the place writers come to be with their own and make those industry contacts that might—just might—propel them into an actual book. Past faculty have been bestselling authors like Nora Roberts and Robert Crais. Industry professionals like Donald Maass lead workshops that leave the participants enthused, focused, and excited. There are read-and-critique sessions where top agents and editors read participants' material aloud to the room, then give their knowledgeable thoughts on that work. There are specialized workshops and lectures, agent and/or editor pitch sessions where participants get to meet one-on-one with the people in a position to sign them on, meeting time with other writers, and banquets with impressive keynote speakers. There is also the Pikes Peak Writers Fiction Contest. The contest deadline is the previous winter, and the conference registration opens early in the year.

MAY

CAÑON CITY MUSIC & BLOSSOM FESTIVAL
Various Locations, Cañon City and Florence
www.ccblossomfestival.com

This family event is the only community-run band festival in Colorado. The Cañon City Music & Blossom Festival showcases national high school and middle and junior high school bands. Competition is held in concert, jazz, orchestra, and parade performances. The parade features marching bands, floats, and a parade court. Food vendors selling everything from tacos to corn dogs line the parade route.

UNITED STATES AIR FORCE ACADEMY GRADUATION
USAFA Falcon Stadium
(719) 333-2025
www.usafa.af.mil

Families of graduates are usually the only ones interested in a graduation ceremony. Because this school is just a little bit different, so are the norms. The graduation speaker usually is the President of the United States, Secretary of Defense, or other high government official. When they graduate, the approximately 1,000 cadets throw their hats up in the air all at once—it's an inspirational sight. It's hard work to get through this school, and their relief at making it is palpable. Children ages 7 to 10 attending the graduation are allowed on the stadium floor to pick up a hat from the hat toss.

But the best part of the graduation ceremony for the casual observer is the air show. This is, after all, the US Air Force Academy and thus The Thunderbirds perform every year, weather permitting. The aerial show by the team of pilots in F-16 Fighting Falcons usually lasts about 45 minutes and can be seen from most of the city. Tickets to enter the graduation are free but must be acquired beforehand from the US Air Force Academy.

Watching The Thunderbirds

You don't have to go into the stadium for a good view of The Thunderbirds during the US Air Force Academy graduation. CO 83 runs parallel and just east of the USAFA grounds. Especially at the intersection of CO 83 and Interquest Parkway, pull into any parking lot, turn off your car, and look up for a perfect view. It is not safe to pull over and park on I-25, unless you're in the scenic view area accessible from the south-bound lanes of I-25. This fills up well before the planes fly, so if you intend to park there, have a Plan B ready.

TERRITORY DAYS
Old Colorado City
www.shopoldcoloradocity.com
Every Memorial Day weekend Old Colorado City turns into a rollicking, Old West block party. The festival started in 1975 as a salute to Old Colorado City's history as the first capital of the Colorado Territory in 1861. That honor was quickly taken away when lawmakers discovered the inhabitants were a bit on the shady, colorful side. Residents today are a bit more respectable but still love a good party. The event runs for 3 days and hosts more than 180 craft, commercial, and food booths. Depending on the weather (late snow can be a real party pooper), 80,000 and up to 150,000 people enjoy the event every year.

JUNE

MANITOU SPRINGS COLORADO WINE FESTIVAL
Memorial Park, Manitou Springs
(800) 642-2567
www.manitousprings.org
This wine festival, which is always held on the first Saturday in June, showcases Colorado wineries exclusively. The number of wineries is kept to about a couple dozen, so participants are carefully selected. There is live entertainment and several food and gift vendors. There is a cost to taste, but otherwise families and designated drivers are free to stroll the grounds and enjoy the festive atmosphere.

FRONT RANGE INVITATIONAL SOCCER TOURNAMENT
Various Locations
(719) 590-9977
www.rushpikespeak.com
This soccer tournament gets the ball rolling. Usually held the first weekend in June, it serves as the kick-off for the summer season of soccer competition. Now more than two decades old, it lays the field for excellent competition for non-premier teams. The Front Range Invitational Tournament hosts age groups ranging from U11–U18 competitive challenge level of play, and offers competition suitable for all age's groups.

DONKEY DERBY DAYS
Downtown Cripple Creek
(877) 858-4653
www.visitcripplecreek.com

This old mining town is unique in many ways, none of which are as hilarious as the Donkey Derby Days. Now in its eighth decade, the event allows anyone to toss their name into a hat for the chance to pay a small fee and run the derby. Only 8 two-person teams get to race, which consists of trying to lead a donkey for a mile, stopping to bob for apples, navigate a slalom course, and kiss a (cardboard) prostitute. Entry fees go to the feeding and care of the small herd of wild donkeys that still roams the town. Really.

The weekend event also offers much more than a race. There's a parade at noon on Saturday, and the streets are lined with more than 60 vendors, selling everything from art to kettle corn. Typically, there's also homemade ice cream and barbecued beef, among other goodies. There are frivolous competitions, from tobacco-spitting to bubble-gum blowing. There is a beard competition where bearded men are rounded up off the streets and asked to compete; women from the audience are judges. There's also a watermelon-eating and seed-spitting contest and sack races for all ages. One especially popular event is the Mountain Mama competition; would-be Mountain Mamas dress up in a fireman's costume while holding a baby (doll). They have to do all kinds of things while they're in the gear, like diapering a baby and making a cream pie. Any Mountain Mama who drops the baby gets penalized. Seems fair!

There are games for little kids and a treasure hunt for older kids. No pre-registration is required for any event. It's a free-for-all, in every sense of the word. Winners get trophies, ribbons, or cash prizes. Any profits go to the aforementioned wild donkeys.

SPRINGS SPREE
Memorial Park
www.springsspree.org

Springs Spree is a big, 2-day summer party that's been happening for more than 30 years. The event celebrates hot-times-in-the-summertime with a relaxed, kick-back attitude and music, food, vendors, games, and demonstrations. Usually held on Father's Day weekend, past years have included hamster ball rides, karate, and American Indian dance exhibitions, local and national music acts, and a classic car show. The crowds are big and the sun is hot, so wear sunblock and be ready to party.

COLORADO COLLEGE SUMMER FESTIVAL OF THE ARTS
Colorado College
**www.coloradocollege
.edu/summerprograms/
summerfestivalofthearts**

As one of America's premier learning institutions, Colorado College brings an intriguing, enlightening group of summer programs to students and the community all summer long. There are lectures, performances, movies, readings, openings, and more from June through August. Two of the keystones to this festival, though, are held in June. They are the Summer Music Festival and the Dance Festival, each a 3-week long, intensive study program for select students and internationally acclaimed faculty. Some performances and rehearsals are open the public, which allows a rare and spectacular view of some of the world's most inspired, unique artistic talents.

CLAYFEST
Soda Springs Park, Manitou Springs
(800) 642-2567
www.manitousprings.org

You can show up and just look around, but this festival is really all about getting your hands dirty. There are pottery-making competitions for artists and amateurs, demonstrations of wheel-throwing and free-form techniques, finished work to view and purchase, workshops, and more. This 1-day event is for those interested in all things clay.

PIKES PEAK INTERNATIONAL HILL CLIMB

Pikes Peak Highway
(719) 685-4400
www.ppihc.com

First run in 1916, this is known as the "Race to the Clouds." The Pikes Peak International Hill Climb is serious racing mixed with a little bit of insanity. And so, of course, the race is very popular with drivers! The race starts near the bottom of Pikes Peak and runs up 12.4 miles to the top of the 14,115-foot mountain. With 156 (tight) turns and an average 7 percent grade on both paved and gravel roads, this is one grueling, courage-laden race. Here's some perspective: When a tourist drives this road, it takes about an hour, and much of that is white knuckles on the steering wheel as the car goes through hairpin turns with thousand-foot drops off to the side. The race drivers do that road in about 10 minutes. As a spectator, you can only plant yourself at one spot along the race course, but even that is thrilling and staggering to watch. It should be pointed out that the drivers are racing the clock, not each other—the cars are not on the course all at the same time.

The race includes categories for cars, trucks, motorcycles, and quads. A number of technical and public pre-race activities happen in town and on the mountain the week before the race. Tickets are required, and those with tickets must be on the course early in the morning, prior to the first driver going up. The course is then closed to the driving public until all the racers have finished.

i Pack a cooler of food and drink before heading up to the Pikes Peak International Hill Climb. Since the road is closed once the race starts, it's a good but long day on the mountain, with no access to vendors. Just watch the carbonated drinks—depending on how high up the mountain you go, they could explode.

JULY

✳ PIKES PEAK OR BUST RODEO

Norris-Penrose Event Center and Downtown
www.pikespeakorbustrodeo.org

It's pretty obvious when the rodeo comes to town. First, there's a massive, community pancake breakfast, where soldiers from Fort Carson cook up more than 1,000 pounds of pancake batter and more than 1,500 eggs. Hungry citizens get to satisfy their hearty appetites while sitting on bales of hay in the middle of the blocked-off streets downtown. A week later a parade hits the same streets. You can bet there's a lot of horseflesh in this particular parade. At that point, people know to pull on their boots, saddle up, and ride over to Norris-Penrose Event Center—because this is the big one.

i All the seats at the rodeo are close, but the best seats for the popular saddle bronc, bareback, and bull riding are on the west end, by the bucking chutes.

The Pikes Peak or Bust Rodeo is more than 70 years old, and it's one of the premier rodeos sanctioned by the Professional Rodeo Cowboys Association (PRCA). With top-dollar prizes and exposure, both seasoned hands and up-and-coming cowboys show up in their quest for a World Championship title. The big crowd favorite is bull riding, but barrel racing, saddle bronc riding, and all the other events are popular, too. The rodeo always features special events like an Armed Forces Night and Real Cowboys Wear Pink night in support of breast cancer (since 1946, the Pikes Peak or Bust Rodeo Days has donated proceeds to charitable programs and services benefiting local military personnel and their families). Showy, thrilling acts run in between the PRCA events, such as a Western show (one year it was a horse and rider that somehow convinced a full-grown bison to hop on top of a truck), drill team action that'll make your heart stop, and the daring, silly rodeo clowns who keep the cowboys safe.

There's a carnival outside the ring and a general feel that the West has arrived. Just watch your step. The downtown events are free, but you need a ticket to see the rodeo. Try to get seats down by the bucking chutes for the closest views of the bull riding. If you intend to buy tickets the day of, show up early as the line can get long and take some time.

PIKES PEAK INVITATIONAL SOCCER
US Air Force Academy
(719) 590-9977
www.rushpikespeak.com
This highly competitive soccer tournament has been attracting teams from almost every state for close to 40 years. Past events have seen more than 5,000 teams and 100,000 players who have traveled to the Pikes Peak region to participate. Held at the gorgeous US Air Force Academy, the tournament is played on the Academy's 24 perfectly manicured grass fields. If soccer's your game, pack some sunblock and water, bring a folding chair, and sit on one of the three terraces along the fields for great soccer and a breathtaking view of the region.

EL PASO COUNTY FAIR
El Paso County Fairgrounds, Calhan
www.elpasocountyfair.com
First started in 1905, the fair is sweet, hard-working entertainment that welcomes as many as 40,000 fairgoers every year. Held in the rural community of Calhan on the eastern plains, the fair started as a thanksgiving celebration for a bountiful potato harvest. At that time, the fair was simple: a potato bake and bean bake, horse races, and spontaneous games. Well, the fair has grown up. The fair now features a full-range of 4-H competitions, a carnival, ice cream-and watermelon-eating contests, and more. Entertainment in past years has included African acrobats, auto races, concerts, an outdoor movie night, a demolition derby, and a mud drag. The fair lasts for 1 week at the end of summer.

ROCKY MOUNTAIN STATE GAMES
Various Locations
www.coloradospringssports.org
The Olympics always get people psyched up to get off their couch and go for the gold. The Rocky Mountain State Games provide the chance for any Colorado athlete to do just that—from beginner to weekend warrior to Olympic hopeful. This also includes the physically disabled, visually impaired, and Paralympic competitors who

are residents of Colorado. It is the state's largest Olympic-style, multi-sport event, always held in late July.

The games include more than 30 events and regularly host more than 6,000 athletes. All competitors have the chance to walk in an opening ceremony, featuring an Olympic-style parade of the athletes and a lighting of the Rocky Mountain State Games flame. The opening ceremony is held at the 8,000-seat Colorado Springs World Arena. From there the action takes place at more than 25 sports venues across the city, such as the US Air Force Academy, the US Olympic Training Center, and local high schools and recreational facilities.

The Rocky Mountain State Games are among 39 such events staged in various states. Winners qualify to compete at the national State Games of America, which have been held in Colorado Springs three times in the past.

AUGUST

PIKES PEAK ASCENT AND MARATHON
Barr Trail, Pikes Peak
(719) 473-2625
www.pikespeakmarathon.org
The Pikes Peak Ascent and Pikes Peak Marathon are not just running, they're more like survival of the fittest in action. Both are up (and the marathon is back down) the 14,110-foot Pikes Peak, starting from Manitou Springs. The first 10 miles log a gain of almost 6,000 vertical feet, and the brutal, grueling mountain makes runners' legs, lungs, heart, and mind cry for mercy. And then there are the last 3 miles and an additional 2,000 feet of vertical gain—above treeline. At this point of limited oxygen, most runners take 30 minutes or more, some

much more, just to cover a mile. Adding insult to injury, at any point it might start to snow!

For those doing the ascent only, which is run on the third Saturday in August, sweet relief is at the top. For those running the marathon the next day, their tired legs and body need to negotiate everything in reverse, including protruding rocks that easily trip up tired bodies, sending runners crashing to the ground. It's rare to see a racer unscathed at the finish line.

And yet, the event requires a competitive entry registration because it is so popular. Part of the reason entry is so difficult to acquire is that the Forest Service limits runners to a total of 1,800 in the ascent and 800 for the marathon. Entry opens in the early spring and usually fills up the first day—if not in the first hour. Runners must be 16 years old on the day of the run and fulfill other qualifications. For those running the other direction as quickly as possible at the mere thought of this event, it is more than entertaining and inspiring to watch the start and/or finish of either race.

COLORADO STATE FAIR
Colorado State Fairgrounds, Pueblo
(800) 876-4567
www.coloradostatefair.com
Save room for corn dogs and deep-fried Twinkies when visiting this massive, 2-week extravaganza. The fair sports the usual suspects: horse show, 4-H competition, quilt contest, and salsa challenge, as well as about 50 other competitions. There's the Professional Rodeo Cowboys Association–sanctioned rodeo, now in its sixth decade at the Colorado State Fair. There's a carnival with every shooting-duck booth and whirligig ride you could imagine, and there's monster

trucks and demolition derbies. There are more than 300 vendors of crafty and unique goods and more than 50 food concessions. When evening rolls around, big-name music acts take the stage; past fairs have hosted Charley Pride to Garth Brooks. Fiesta Day celebrates the Hispanic culture in Colorado with a parade, mariachi music, special demonstrations, and the presentation of the Fiesta Queen. It's a good old-time fair with some pretty up-to-date entertainment. The fairgrounds are large, so wear boots that are made for walking.

SEPTEMBER

✳COLORADO BALLOON CLASSIC
Memorial Park
(719) 471-4833
www.balloonclassic.com
Colorado Springs becomes a colorful, floating wonderland every Labor Day weekend when the balloon festival comes to town. Now one of the largest hot-air balloon festivals in the US, it's the longest continuously run balloon festival in the Rocky Mountain region. Started in 1977, this event gets even lazybones out of bed at the crack of dawn to see up to as many as 130 vibrant, firebreathing balloons ascend into the deep blue Colorado sky. Just past the field where the balloons take off is Prospect Lake, affording a glorious mirror view of the flying orbs. With shapes from the traditional oval to castles to bunnies, these balloons always delight and surprise the more than 30,000 people who come out to watch each day. The only problem is when the winds roll over the top of the Front Range and keep the balloons grounded. On Saturday and Sunday evenings there is a mesmerizing BalloonGlo. Just as dusk hits, the pilots inflate balloons firmly tethered to the ground, and Memorial Park is alive with the illuminated, bouncing, joyous craft. Admission is free, and food and merchandise vendors are available near the balloon launch area.

i When attending the Colorado Balloon Classic, arrive early. Parking can be tight and you'll have a 10 to 15 minute walk to reach the balloon ascent area.

COMMONWHEEL ARTS & CRAFTS FESTIVAL
Memorial Park, Manitou Springs
(719) 685-1008
www.commonwheel.com
This juried art show and sale features artists of all media, from painting to pottery. Held every Labor Day weekend, this eclectic mix of arts and crafts features some of the best artists of the region and beyond. Food and entertainment make this an event that's a joy to walk through, even if one isn't currently in the market for a new piece for the living room wall.

IAFF FALLEN FIREFIGHTERS OBSERVANCE
Memorial Park
www.iaff.org
The IAFF Fallen Fire Fighter Memorial honors professional firefighters and emergency medical personnel who have given their lives in the line of duty. Each September, the IAFF conducts a respectful, touching ceremony to honor those who have given their lives in the line of duty during the previous year. The uplifting and reverent ceremony is for family, friends, and the public who wish to show their gratitude.

Located in Memorial Park in clear view of Pikes Peak, the Memorial's moving centerpiece is a bronze likeness of a firefighter descending a ladder while cradling an infant in one arm. Towering 20 feet above the park's greenery, the sculpture epitomizes the courage and bravery displayed daily by professional firefighters across the continent. Bordering this sculpture is a Wall of Honor, which lists the names of brothers and sisters killed in the line of duty since 1976, when the US federal government first began tracking line-of-duty deaths in the fire service. As the original wall has filled to near capacity with names of fallen heroes, a second wall was erected just a few steps from the original Wall of Honor. Paving stone, monument lighting, flag standards, and walkways make this a beautiful tribute.

PIKES PEAK LAVENDER FILM FESTIVAL
Colorado College
(719) 633-5600
www.pplff.org
This is a story of turning lemons into lemonade. In the early '90s, Colorado Springs took the national spotlight as the base for anti-gay activities and laws. Early festival producers pulled together resources and talent to try and improve the city's community and reputation by featuring quality lesbian, gay, bisexual, and transgender films. The first Lavender Film Festival was held in 2000. Now a 3-day event, the festival selects and shows the best short films and features screened at the annual San Francisco International LGBT Film Festival the previous summer. The festival has persisted through some rough spots but is now the only consistently run LGBT film festival in Colorado. Past years have seen more than 1,000 film buffs enjoy the weekend, and the films get better every

year. Your best bet is to plan early and buy a weekend pass, but tickets are available at the door.

OCTOBER

BOO AT THE ZOO
Cheyenne Mountain Zoo
4250 Cheyenne Mountain Zoo Rd.
(719) 633-9925
www.cmzoo.org
On late October evenings, the zoo turns from wild habitat to just plain wild. The zoo lets its hair down for roaring good fun for the young Halloween crowd. Your young monsters and ghosts can slink through a spooky haunted house and ghoulish graveyard, enjoy animal encounters, trick-or-treat at spooky treat stations (all treats are orangutan-friendly!), fly through a bat cave, do the Monster Mash down a lighted pumpkin path, ride the Boo Carousel, get knee deep in the Swamp Monster's Slime Factory at the Sky Ride Summit, and see some of those classic zoo favorites—lions, tigers, and bears. Oh my! Special zoo tickets required, sold at the zoo only on each Boo evening. Dig out the flashlight, pull on your costume, and head to the zoo for the wildest fall festival around.

HAUNTED MINES
Western Museum of Mining and Industry
225 N. Gate Blvd.
(719) 488-0880
www.hauntedmines.org.
Creepy, creaky thrills never had such a perfect backdrop. The Western Museum of Mining and Industry runs the Haunted Mines every fall to help support the nonprofit museum, and it's a brilliant mix of supply and demand. The 27-acre grounds of the Mining Museum are turned into an

indoor, outdoor, and underground experience designed to be both physically and psychologically challenging. Teens love this event. Dress for the outdoors as if you were going hiking, complete with sturdy footwear. Be prepared to crawl (and scream) through dark passageways. You might get slightly wet as you pass by the swamp, and know that the bats are real, not props. Terror will be enjoyed through sounds, lights, fog and smoke, wind, water, heat, and other paranormal effects. Monsters dwell here, but they do not touch. Not recommended for children under 12 unless they're very brave and accompanied by an adult. Admission comes with a fee—maybe more from your fear than your pocketbook. Food is available.

EMMA CRAWFORD FESTIVAL & MEMORIAL COFFIN RACE
Manitou Avenue, Manitou Springs
(800) 642-2567
www.manitousorings.org
This ghoulish, all-in-good-fun festival takes some sad heritage and turns it into a street party worthy of the most rollicking Irish wake. Emma Crawford was a local of importance in the 19th century. Upon her demise, her civic standing became a little unstable as her coffin washed down from its supposed final resting place on Red Mountain to the town below. Her fate is celebrated with a coffin race of about 600 feet down Manitou Avenue. Teams are four somber runners who push a coffin-like vehicle with an Emma look-alike in the coffin. This is grave enough competition to require qualifying heats, and helmets for all Emmas. A Parade of Coffins, awards for the best grim Emma and most creative coffin, and other events put the final nail in this daylong event.

NOVEMBER

ROCKY MOUNTAIN WOMEN'S FILM FESTIVAL
Fine Arts Center and Colorado College
(719) 226-0450
www.rmwfilmfest.org
The first weekend in November has long been a time for laughter, tears, exuberance, insight, more tears, and exhaustion. The Rocky Mountain Women's Film Festival is all of life's poignant moments and emotions compressed into one weekend. As much as that can be hard to take in, it's something the community looks forward to and supports year after year. In fact, this is the longest continuously running women's film festival in the world. Since 1988, women and a few brave men have come with tissues in hand to be entertained and enlightened. The festival screens documentaries, features, animation, and, always the crowd pleasers, shorts. The women part is actually a little misleading; a film must be directed or produced by a woman to quality for screening here, but in fact this is a deeply satisfying, expansive view of humanity. Weekend passes and day passes are available prior to the event, and a lavish opening night party and screening are always a big night out.

DECEMBER

FESTIVAL OF LIGHTS PARADE
Tejon Street
(719) 649-9111
www.coloradospringsfestivaloflights.org
Everyone loves an old-fashioned parade, and this is it. The Festival of Lights Parade marks the true beginning of the holiday season in the region. The parade is like a Frank Capra movie, all sweetness and innocent joy. Floats are either on the bed of a truck or

on a trailer pulled by a truck. There are high school bands, horse units, dogs, music, and, of course, Santa on the last float. This is one of those Murphy's Law items: If it can, it will snow. The parade is held in the cold winter evening, so families bundle up on the curb, parkas and mittens pulled out for probably the first time each year. Vendors offer food off of carts, and all the downtown restaurants are open hoping to catch the pre- and post-parade crowd. It's light-hearted fun, but all proceeds go to a serious purpose: to fill the Empty Stocking Fund, a local charity for local health and human service agencies that help people in crisis and assist others in attaining self-sufficiency.

NEW YEAR'S EVE FIREWORKS ON PIKES PEAK
Pikes Peak
www.adaman.org
Anyone out banging pots and pans to ring in the new year is lit from above—with fireworks. Since 1922, the Pikes Peak AdAmAn Club has ushered in the new year with a brilliant fireworks display ignited on the summit of Pikes Peak. And they didn't drive up; they hiked the Barr Trail, often accomplished on icy and snow-swept slopes with wind chills of -50 degrees.

The AdAmAn Club started with five men who had the idea to add only one new member each year. Thus, the name AdAmAn (add a man). Each year, members choose one new member from a list of applicants, which can be quite long, and now includes women. Most successful new members have joined the AdAmAn Club after several previous years as a guest.

The climbing party of members and guests leaves the trailhead of Barr Trail on December 30, with an overnight stay at Barr Camp. On December 31, they flash mirrors from their location at timberline, and by evening they've made it to the top. There are years when storms preclude the event. But when skies are clear, the fireworks are a magnificent sight that can be seen for hundreds of miles along the Front Range of the Colorado Rockies and deep into the eastern plains.

DAY TRIPS & GETAWAYS

Colorado is truly an amazing place. No matter which direction you go from the Pikes Peak region, the scenery is stunning, food tends to be excellent, and there are more activities to choose from than can be done in a day or weekend. From world-class skiing to relaxing in a vapor cave to boutique shopping, Colorado has it all. It is a tourist destination extraordinaire, and almost every corner of the state is set up to pamper and entertain anyone who visits.

New Mexico is a short jaunt away, and many choose to drive south for something with a little more Southwest flair. Both Taos and Santa Fe can be reached in a half day's drive, and each is a unique, refreshing dose of the land of enchantment.

Colorado is probably best known for the ski areas, but travelers can get as much (or more) satisfaction around the state in summer and fall. Spring tends to be unsettled: snow, sun, flowers, more snow . . . But no matter what time of year, Colorado and the surrounding area is the perfect travel choice.

DAY TRIPS

There is so much to do in the Pikes Peak region, it's hard to make other plans. But, for those who want to hop in the car for a short road trip, there's no shortage of things to do and places to go. Some of the areas highlighted are actually in the Pikes Peak region—Cañon City and Woodland Park. But they deserve more than a few passing sentences or spotlights on a business, and so we look at them in total here.

There are also places most definitely not in the Pikes Peak region. Ultra-liberal Boulder is politically as far from conservative Colorado Springs as you can get, but it's really just up the road. And it is amazing how many different adventures can be had within 2 hours of the Springs. Unless you're looking for an ocean, chances are you can find your preferred activity. If a weekend away is in your plans, some of the world's most beautiful towns and resorts are barely half a day's drive.

✳Boulder

Boulder, which is only an hour and a half north via I-25 and CO 36, is first and foremost home to the main campus of the **University of Colorado** (CU; www.colorado.edu). The dramatic, 600-acre campus hosts 30,000 students in 85 majors and boasts 23 NCAA championships and 17 astronaut alumni who have flown in space. A walk through the lovely campus is a good way to spend a few hours, and lends easy proximity to the student hangout, The Hill. Restaurants, bars, and shops fill the short, inclined streets. For breakfast, the hole-in-the-wall **Dot's Diner** (1333 Broadway St., 303-447-9184) is good, especially egg dishes like huevos rancheros, and the affordable bill keeps it popular with the student crowd.

Downtown (and just down the hill) is the **Pearl Street Mall** (www.boulderdown town.com), a multi-block, pedestrian-only shopping, dining, social space. There is always something going on here, and street entertainment is a daily constant. Halloween is a special time for the ebullient residents, and the area seems to split its seams in revelry. Go with a sense of adventure—and a costume.

Any time of year is a good time to shop at the Pearl Street Mall. Browse the well-stocked, independent, three-story **Boulder Book Store** (1107 Pearl St., 303-447-2074, http://boulderbookstore.indiebound.com). **The Peppercorn** (1235 Pearl St., 303-449-5847, www.peppercorn.com) is a fun, funky potpourri of kitchen, bath, and home decor accessories. One of the most popular activities on the mall is dining, especially when the weather's nice enough to sit outside and people watch. Two local favorites are the award-winning **Frasca Food & Wine** (1738 Pearl St., 303-442-6966, www.frasca foodandwine.com) and **Black Cat** (1934 13th St., 303-444-5500, www.blackcatboul der.com), which runs both a bistro and organic farm. **The Laughing Goat** (1709 Pearl St., 303-440-4628, http://thelaughing goat.com), with locations both on the mall and in the library on the CU campus, is a great place to just chill—an art form in Boulder.

For the science oriented, there are two spots to visit. **The National Center for Atmospheric Research (NCAR)** (1850 Table Mesa Dr., http://ncar.ucar.edu) was established in 1960 to study our atmosphere and how weather and climate affect the earth. More than 120 PhD researchers and hundreds of visiting scientists work here. The iconic NCAR building, which can be seen from miles away, hosts visitors, workshops, and school groups. Also in Boulder is the **National Oceanic and Atmospheric Administration's (NOAA) Earth System Research Laboratory** (325 Broadway St., 303-497-3333, www.esrl.noaa .gov/outreach/tours.html). At this facility, scientists study atmospheric and other processes that affect air quality, weather, and climate. When there's a hurricane in the gulf and TV correspondents talk to scientists about where it's going, those scientists are usually speaking from this facility. Tours are once a week.

i In winter, road conditions in Colorado are not a passing interest—they can mean the difference between a safe journey and disaster. Even if it's all blue skies where you are, check the road conditions before heading out. Updates and pictures are at www.cotrip .org/home.htm. You can also call: inside Colorado, dial 511; outside Colorado, dial (303) 639-1111.

Or, indulge your senses in a free, 45-minute tour of **Celestial Seasonings** teas (4600 Sleepytime Dr., 303-530-5300, www .celestialseasonings.com) to see how the teas are blended, packaged, and shipped. Your nose and eyes will tingle in the pungent mint room.

Another interesting jaunt is to **Chautauqua** (900 Baseline Rd., 303-442-3282, www .chautauqua.com), historic grounds and buildings that sit above Boulder. It is the home to films, concerts, and other special events, as well as a place for private events. Chatauqua Park is also the trailhead for the Flagstaff hike, a 5-mile loop up to the top of the mountain and down through Gregory Canyon. Other notable hiking spots are the El Dorado Canyon Trail, an easier hike with bouldering potential. Start at the visitor center, south on CO 170. And the short but spectacular Boulder Falls trail is 9 miles up CO 119 to the trailhead.

If Boulder calls to you more as a getaway than a day trip, make it special by staying at the historic **Boulderado** (2115 13th St., 303-442-4344 or 800-433-4344, www.boul derado.com) or the luxe **St. Julien Hotel & Spa** (900 Walnut St., 877-303-0900, www .stjulien.com).

Cañon City

Cañon City is warmer than Colorado Springs, even though it's only one hour to the south via CO 115. It also offers some of the most dramatic scenery to be found in Colorado, especially at the stunning **Royal Gorge** (4218 CR 3A, 888-333-5597 or 719-275-7507, www.royalgorgebridge.com). A privately owned park flanks the gorge, so the only way to see it is to pay admission. A highlight is to take a stroll across the world's highest suspension bridge, which spans the rim's 1,000-plus-foot drop. Visitors can also check out the very scary Sky Coaster, whereby riders are harnessed up and swung out over the canyon. Park admission includes a free ride to the bottom of the gorge on a vertical tram.

A **Royal Gorge Route train** (401 Water St., 888-724-5748, www.royalgorgeroute .com) takes riders through the gorge, alongside the roaring Arkansas River. You can watch the intrepid whitewater rafters go by,

or you can join them. Signs and advertisements for local outfitters are everywhere (see the Attractions chapter). If you prefer the drier ride of the train, you can take the dinner train and enjoy a leisurely, elegant meal reminiscent of a time long past.

In town, view proof of dinosaurs in the area at the **Dinosaur Depot** (330 Royal Gorge Blvd., 719-269-7150 or 800-987-6379, www.dinosaurdepot.com). Besides a small but fascinating exhibit of paleontological treasures, you sometimes can watch fossils being worked in a lab, and the staff will provide a map so you can explore and locate the place where much of this was found— via a hiking trail just north of town.

The **Museum of Colorado Prisons** (201 N. 1st St., 719-269-3015 or 877-269-3015, www.prisonmuseum.org) lets you see how the criminal half lived in decades past. It's next door to the Colorado State Penitentiary. Nearby Florence is also home to the famed ADX prison—better known as Supermax, which houses the country's most notorious criminals. Just as well, Supermax is not open to visitors.

Several other local museums spotlight the area's history and artists, and the **Holy Cross Abbey Winery** (3011 E. US 50, 719-276-5191 or 877-422-9463, www .abbeywinery.com) offers some award-winning vintages for tasting. The building and grounds at the winery are serene and old-world and worth a look, even if wine is not a favorite.

Since the wide Arkansas River runs up the canyon to the west of town on CO 50, fly fishing is a popular pastime. It's possible that in the next decade portions of the river will be in the national spotlight as the artist Christo has been working with locals and government officials for years to place his

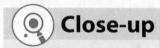

Close-up

Day Trip for Kids

It's a drive, but your kids (and everyone else along for the ride) will remember this day for a long, long time.

First, start at **Bent's Old Fort National Historic Site** (35110 Hwy. 194 E., La Junta, CO, 719-383-5010, www.nps.gov/beol). Bent's Fort is about 2 hours south on I-25 and then east on CO 50 to just outside of La Junta. It rests on what was the boundary with Mexico in the mid-1800s. The reconstructed adobe fur trading post hosts living historians who treat visitors to the sights, sounds, and life experienced by the trappers, traders, and Plains Indians who came together here for peaceful trade in the 1840s. Kids love to explore the rooms on their own, but there are guided tours, too. Planned groups get to learn some skills of the frontiersman, and a book and gift shop is just outside the fort. Kids can earn a Junior Ranger badge by completing a few fun tasks.

Next, head to the **Koshare Indian Museum** (115 W. 18th St., La Junta, CO, 719-384-4411, www.kosharehistory.org) in La Junta. This is not what you think. Yes, there is a traditional museum in the building, and some of the American Indian items here are absolute treasures. But what really sets this place apart is the building and the Indian dances. The Koshare Kiva is a round room used as center stage by the Koshare Indian Dancers, a Boy Scout group (with girls as well) that for decades has studied and brought to life the ancient dances of American Indian tribes. The dancers put on shows a number of nights (check the website for current schedule). The Kiva is a mysterious, cave-like room with a unique log ceiling, valuable pottery used in light fixtures, and rocks that protrude from the walls. Ten large murals by famed American Indian artist Velino Herrera bring a colorful authenticity. When the dancers perform, the dark, circular atmosphere coupled with the song, costumes, and footsteps of the dancers can bring on chills—and not from cold. Depending on the time of year, seasonal dances are featured. Don't worry—the snake dance (with live ones!) is rarely performed.

"Over the River" project. "Over the River" would suspend 5.9 miles of silvery, luminous fabric panels high above the Arkansas River along a 40-mile stretch of the river between Salida and Cañon City.

Good places to eat on your day trip are the surprisingly fine French restaurant **Le Petit Chablis** (512 Royal Gorge Blvd., 719-269-3333), family-owned **Ortega's** (2301 E. Main St., 719-275-9437), and for breakfast, the local favorite **Waffle Wagon** (1310 Royal Gorge Blvd., 719-269-3428).

Denver

Just 1 hour north on I-25, Denver offers big city opportunities. If culture is your thing, visit the intriguing (and that's just the buildings, let alone the art) **Denver Art Museum** (100 W. 14th Ave. Pkwy., 720-865-5000, www.denverartmuseum.org). A recently completed $90 million expansion features a new building by architect Daniel Libeskind, while the first building, which is still in use, features a castle-like exterior with more than a million reflective glass tiles. A deep permanent collection includes more than 18,000 objects of American Indian art, Oceanic art from the South Pacific, and an Institute for Western American Art. Past exhibitions have included the forward, ultra-contemporary "RADAR: Selections from the Collection of Vicki & Kent Logan" as well as "Landscapes from the Age of Impressionism" featuring works by Claude Monet, Eugene Boudin, and John Singer Sargent. There are 2 coffee stands and 1 cafe in the museum if you want lunch or a break. And if you want to make a day/night excursion, **The Brown Palace** (321 17th St., 303-297-3111, www.brownpalace.com) is a historic, ornate hotel within walking distance. Ask for the museum rate.

ℹ️ Everyone loves going to the mountains. In winter, it's the skiers. In summer, it's the hikers. And they all head back to Denver via I-70. The logjam has become so bad that you can count on a virtual parking lot every Sunday afternoon from Georgetown to east of Idaho Springs. Avoid it all and leave another time, or get to the Pikes Peak region via CO 24, over Wilkerson Pass. It's a beautiful drive, and although you'll have some traffic, it won't be anything like the gridlock on I-70.

At **City Park** are two great attractions. **The Denver Museum of Nature & Science** (2001 Colorado Blvd., 303-370-6000, www.dmns.org) includes mummies, dinos, a planetarium, and an IMAX. **The Denver Zoo** (2300 Steele St., 303-376-4800, www.denver zoo.org) is one of the most visited zoos in the country and Colorado's most popular cultural attraction. On 80 acres and home to nearly 4,000 animals, the zoo is recognized internationally as a leader in exhibitry, such as Predator Ridge, a 3-acre exhibit featuring Africa's greatest predators. Years ago the zoo was made famous when twin polar bear cubs, Klondike and Snow, had to be raised by the keepers. Coming spring 2012 is the large Asian Tropics exhibit space, where visitors can watch Asian elephants care for their young, Indian one-horned rhinos cooling off in a shallow stream, and acrobatic gibbons swinging overhead from tree to tree.

Downtown's **Denver Performing Arts Complex** is a 4-block, 12-acre site home to the **Denver Center for the Performing Arts** (1101 13th St., www.denvercenter .org), which showcases popular Broadway touring shows to world-premier plays. This, the largest performing arts complex in the West, is also home to the **Colorado Ballet** (303-837-8888, www.coloradoballet.org), **Opera Colorado** (303-468-2030, www.opera colorado.org), and the **Colorado Symphony** (303-623-7876 or 877-292-7979, www.col oradosymphony.org). If you've got tickets, **The Corner Office** (1401 Curtis St., 303-825-6500, www.thecornerofficedenver.com) is just across the street and a great place for drinks, appetizers, or after-show dinner. If you don't want to drive home late, above the restaurant is one of Denver's most unusual hotels, **The Curtis** (1405 Curtis St., 303-571-0300 or 800-525-6651, www.thecurtis.com), which offers a playful, colorful pop culture atmosphere for your night out. Or stay at the elegant, retro **Hotel Teatro** (1100 14th St., 303-228-1100 or 888-727-1200, www.hotel teatro.com), just a block away.

For sports fans, Denver is a mecca. Downtown is home to **Coors Field** (Colorado Rockies pro baseball), the **Pepsi Center** (Denver Nuggets pro basketball, Colorado Avalanche pro ice hockey, Colorado

Mammoth pro lacrosse), and **INVESCO Field at Mile High** (Denver Broncos pro football and Denver Outlaws pro lacrosse). The **LoDo** (lower downtown) area caters to fans with bars, restaurants, more bars, shops, and hotels. If stadium food is not your thing, try **Jax Fish House** (1539 17th St., 303-292-5767, www.jaxfishhousedenver.com) for oysters, delicate fish, or, surprisingly, great burgers. **Gumbo's** (1530 16th St., 720-956-1490, www.gumbosdenver.net) has great Southern food, and **Jackson's** (1520 20th St., 303-298-7625, http://jacksonsdenver.com) is an always-hopping sports bar and grill with Denver's largest outdoor rooftop patio. It's also right across the street from Coors Field.

Elitch Gardens (2000 Elitch Circle, 303-595-4386, www.elitchgardens.com) will quench your thirst for thrills with the newest ride, Halfpipe. A giant snowboard that fits 16 people in two cars, it spins 360 degrees around a 230-foot long, 100-foot-tall halfpipe. Elitch's also thrills with more rides, a water park, and special events like the Halloween Frightfest. Or, spend a day at the **United States Mint** (320 W. Colfax Ave., 303-405-4757, www.usmint.gov). More than 50 million coins are produced here—daily! Tours are for groups only and those reservations are made online, although individual, stand-by tickets are available. Or, the **Denver Botanic Gardens** (1007 York St., 720-865-3500, www.botanicgardens.org) offers a serene retreat from the city chaos. They also run a mesmerizing corn maze every fall at the Chatfield location.

For those who want to shop, shop, shop, no problem. There are 14 major shopping centers and numerous smaller shopping areas. The **Cherry Creek** area south of downtown has a large, upscale mall and unique, outdoor shopping district as well. It tends to be a bit pricier, but lovely, unique gifts (and occasional bargains) can be found. The **16th Street Mall** is a pedestrian mall running 16 blocks through downtown. The trolley-like shuttle that runs up and down the street aids those with sore feet. **Larimer Square** (www.larimersquare.com) is a historic block with clothing, specialty shops, restaurants, nightclubs, and galleries. It gets festooned for holidays such as Oktoberfest and Christmas.

Fort Collins

Fort Collins is often called Fort Fun by its residents, and they're not being cynical. This university town has grown up from an agricultural area to an energized, cheerful, sophisticated but still casual city. **Colorado State University** (www.colostate.edu), which forms a solid core in the heart of town, brings a college-student, life-is-good feeling. But the year-round residents have made sure the city's lifecycle is more than just semester-based.

Just north of the campus is **Old Town**, a grouping of stores, restaurants, bars, clubs, outdoor amphitheaters, and offices that act as the heart of Fort Collins. **CooperSmith's** (5 Old Towne Sq., 970-498-0483, www.coopersmithspub.com), a microbrew and restaurant, is a popular place to quench your thirst or sit outside on the patio and watch bands play on summer evenings. Diners linger over delicious meals here and at other good Old Town restaurants and watch the ecology-conscious populace pedal by on a fascinating parade of bikes. In August, a local philanthropist sponsors a free, giant music festival, **New West Fest** (www.newwestfest.com), featuring numerous stages, outdoor games, and vendors of all kinds. For 3 days, streets are blocked off, the town puts on party clothes, and Fort Fun is in session.

A half block off Old Town is **The Rio Grande** (143 W. Mountain Ave., 970-224-5428, www.riograndemexican.com), a Mexican restaurant known as much for its margaritas (customers are limited to three) as its fresh, spicy food. Another notable stop is **Jay's Bistro** (135 W. Oak St., 970-482-1876, www.jaysbistro.net). This sleek, inviting restaurant is uptown (live jazz many nights) and delicious.

During the summer, **Horsetooth Reservoir** (www.horsetoothreservoir.com) is a great place to escape the heat (Fort Collins is in what Coloradoans call the banana belt as it's usually about 10 degrees warmer than Colorado Springs). The reservoir is just west of town and is a good place to water-ski, fish, boat (there is a marina), camp, and rock climb. Or take a bike up **Poudre Canyon,** not far from town, for a scenic ride along the Poudre River. Bike rentals are plentiful in town.

The **Fort Collins Museum & Discovery Science Center** (200 Matthews St., 970-221-6738, www.fcmdsc.org) is a little gem, with cabins dating back to 1859, 1864, and 1882, as well as a 1905 schoolhouse. Inside, there are historic displays but also some very cool interactive exhibits in the Discovery Center. Kids adore it.

In winter, students can be seen cross-country skiing across campus, and as in most of Colorado, snowshoeing has taken off as a popular activity. Snowshoes can be rented at most sporting goods stores.

And any time of year, the large **Anheuser-Busch Brewery** (2351 Busch Dr., 970-490-4691, www.budweisertours.com) is worth a visit. The walking tour takes you through the brewery process and on to the stables to see the world-famous Budweiser Clydesdales. Those of legal drinking age can enjoy some samples of innovative or well-known beers, and soft drinks and snacks are also available. Or, visit the nation's first wind-powered brewery, **New Belgium Brewing Company** (500 Linden St., 888-622-4044, www.newbelgium.com). Born out of a European bike trip through beer towns, this home to Fat Tire and other popular microbrews offers tastings and guided tours. Or as they say, you can "control your own destiny" with a self-guided tour.

Pueblo

Once upon a time, we wouldn't have sent anyone to Pueblo. In recent years, that has changed mightily! Once a gray, industrial city, Pueblo has become a greener, cleaner small city with a lot to offer visitors. For starters, it's home to the Colorado State Fair, held at the end of August through Labor Day.

A diverted section of the Arkansas River is now home to the city's own **Riverwalk** project (101 S. Union St., www.pueblohualarp.com), similar to that of San Antonio, but with parks, fountains, sculptures, and landscaped seating areas instead of an encroachment of restaurants and shops. The eateries and stores are slowly coming here, but they're not right on top of the waterway.

The **Nature and Raptor Center** (5200 Nature Center Rd., 719-549-2414, www.natureandraptor.org) outside of town also takes advantage of the Arkansas River and is a place for hiking, biking, bird watching, and fishing. Near the nature center is the Pueblo Raptor Center, a rescue site for injured birds of prey, from tiny owls to giant golden eagles. If you want to see more animals, head to the **Pueblo Zoo** (3455 Nuckolls Ave., www.pueblozoo.org), which is located in scenic, spacious **City Park** and includes a historic wooden carousel.

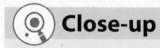

Close-up

Motorcycle Day Trips

With curvy, scenic two-lane highways heading every direction out of the Pikes Peak region, it's no wonder that motorcyclists find this a desirable destination. There are two especially good day trip itineraries for those wearing leather, and choosing which road to follow comes down to the season.

When it's warm (summer and fall), the mountain roads offer views, turns, and changing landscape. Ride west on CO 24, and in Woodland Park turn north on CO 67. The road wanders in and out of the area of the large Hayman Fire of 2002 that burned an estimated 137,000 acres. Spots of dense forest give way to new growth and open meadows. Stop at Deckers for a rest, then head onto CO 126 toward Pine. It'll be an incomparable mountain day.

In winter and spring, choose the low road—lower in elevation, anyway. Ride south out of Colorado Springs on CO 115 toward Cañon City. Continue south on CO 67 toward Florence, and continue on to Westcliffe and the magnificent Wet Mountain Valley. Explore the area up CO 69 toward Texas Creek for remote asphalt, tight turns, and mountain air. Or, from Florence take CO 67, CO 96, and finally CO 165 to the eccentric Bishop castle. Jim Bishop has been single-handedly building the still incomplete, funky structure since 1969. This iron and stone fortress sits in the middle of nowhere, but people come from miles around just to see it once.

Downtown, there's the lovely **Sangre de Cristo Arts Center** (201 N. Santa Fe Ave., 719-295-7200, www.sdc-arts.org), which offers art exhibitions, live performances, and one of the nation's best children's museums. History comes alive at the nearby **El Pueblo History Museum** (301 N. Union Ave., 719-583-0453), where you can see a live dig excavating remnants of early settlements as well as a re-creation of a Pueblo Indian home and *horno* (clay oven). More contemporary history is shown at the lovely **Rosemont Museum** (419 W. 14th St., 719-545-5290, www.rosemount.org), a 37-room Victorian mansion owned by the Thatcher family—some of the city's earliest and most prominent citizens.

The **Steelworks Museum** (215 Canal St., 719-564-9086, www.steelworks.us), located on the old CF&I property, will show the face of labor and steel mills from the 20th century and the **Weisbrod Air Museum** (31001 Magnuson Ave., 719-948-9219, www.pwam .org), with more than 30 aircraft, will show the evolution from biplanes to Vietnam-era helicopters.

If all that activity makes you hungry, Pueblo has some excellent Mexican restaurants (try **Nacho's,** 409 N. Santa Fe Ave., 719-544-0733, or the **Cactus Flower,** 4610 N. Elizabeth St., 719-545-8218) and Italian eateries (such as **Rosario's,** 2930 N. Elizabeth St., 719-583-1822), reflecting well the city's ethnic population. Be sure to try a Pueblo specialty, "the slopper," a burger topped with green chile sauce and cheese (featured in 2010 on Food Network). And don't hesitate to try some of the city's upscale restaurants, too (maybe **DC's on B Street,** 115 W. B St., 719-584-3410, or **Fifteen Twenty-One,**

123 N. Main St., 719-542-9999). There also are some good eats to be found at the city's annual Chile & Frijoles Festival, each autumn.

To make a weekend of it, you can stay at a number of nice downtown hotels or pick a great B&B. And don't forget to watch the walls along the interstate, artfully covered with locally made tiles. For more information on the above attractions, lodging, or how to get a visitors' guide, call (800) 233-3446 or go online to http://destinationpueblo.com.

Woodland Park

Only 20 minutes "up the pass," or west on US 24 Woodland Park was a "resting place for the weary" in the 1880s and '90s for those passing through to the gold fields in Cripple Creek and Victor. It also became a place to carouse, gamble, and drink. Now it's a quiet, family-friendly mountain bedroom community to Colorado Springs, although it definitely has its own, independent personality.

In town, the **Ute Pass History Museum** (222 E. Midland Ave., 719-686-7512, www .utepasshistoricalsociety.org) and its nearby historic village (you'll need to ask if it's not open) is an interesting stop for history buffs. If kids are in your crowd, stop by the **Dinosaur Resource Center** (201 S. Fairview St., 719-686-1820, www.rmdrc.com), a privately funded museum and research facility focusing on dinosaurs and other creatures from the Cretaceous period. Children like the museum because they can handle bones and dino eggs as well as see some pretty amazing rebuilt specimens. Most of their collection comes from Western states, but not much from Colorado. You can't miss it—right on CO 24 in town, there's a giant palm tree outside. When it snows, that's an odd sight.

Woodland Park is a great way to get the full Rocky Mountain experience. Mueller State Park (see the Parks and Sports & Recreation chapters) is a scenic, wildlife-filled space with stunning views and great hiking trails. Or head out to Manitou Lake for a bit of shore-fishing. **Rampart Reservoir** provides a full day's entertainment with fishing, hiking, and mountain bike trails.

Just outside nearby Divide, visit the **Colorado Wolf & Wildlife Center** (4729 Twin Rocks Rd., Florissant, 719-687-9742, www.wolfeducation.org) for an up-close-and-personal look at rescued wolves. Or take a horseback ride at the historic **Triple B Ranch** (27640 CO 67, 877-687-8899, www .triplebranch.com).

Good food before, during, or after your exploring can be found at **The Swiss Chalet** restaurant (19263 E. US 24, 719-687-2001, www.swisschaletofwoodlandpark.com), which is regionally famous for its fine cuisine. **Joanie's Bakery & Delicatessen** (110 E. US 24, 719-686-9091) is a good lunch spot, and **Danny's Corner Bistro** (609 Midland Ave., 719-687-2233), by the movie theaters, serves a mix of simple (burgers) and upscale fare (flash-fried spinach). Also try **Circle H Smokehouse** (locals just say Smokehouse) for some great barbecue (720 W. Browning Ave., 719-687-1828).

GETAWAYS

Colorado as a tourist destination cannot be overstated. Beautiful scenery, thrilling adventures, and world-class skiing, hiking, and hunting are all available. For those more sedentary, resorts and cute B&Bs hop-scotch the state. Other than an ocean, we've got it all. Within a few hours of the Pikes Peak region, visitors can relax, accelerate, schuss, or shop through some of the most amazing, endearing towns and landscapes the US has to offer.

i A lot of Colorado is remote. If an accident happens anywhere in the state, dial *CSP on your cell phone and you will be connected with the closest Colorado State Patrol office. This can also be used to alert authorities to aggressive and/or drunk drivers.

Aspen

No other US town says celebrity and Lifestyles-of-the-Rich-and-Famous quite as well as Aspen. That is not a stereotype—it's true. But there is also much more.

First, about the reputation. Yes, celebrities are around (Jack Nicholson bicycling down a side street, Harry Connick Jr. at a music festival). You might catch glimpses of them, but the rich have private clubs and homes where most of their society is kept. More likely, visitors are treated to people watching the unknown über-wealthy, and they are everywhere (such as a young mother paying for a cheap breakfast out of a jewel-covered, swan-shaped purse).

But it's the homes that are the real stars. Drive south on CO 82 to see some of the most elegant abodes imaginable. **Snowmass Village,** just west on Brush Creek Road off of CO 82, also has a number of (second) homes that amaze and delight.

During the winter, Aspen is, of course, base to four excellent ski and snowboard mountains, **Aspen Mountain, Aspen Highlands, Buttermilk, and Snowmass** (800-525-6200 or 970-925-1220, www.aspensnowmass.com). Lift ticket prices can be astronomical, but when skiing with the stars, what can you expect? Multi-day passes

and lodging packages can soften the blow. In the town of Aspen, the **Hotel Jerome** (330 E. Main St., 877-412-7625 or 970-920-1000, http://hoteljerome.rockresorts.com) offers a historically elegant experience. **The Gant** (610 S. West End, 866-665-0845, www.gantaspen.com) are luxury condos within walking distance to the gondola at Aspen Mountain.

Summertime is short, but shows off the area's exquisite landscape, with delicate flowers, green meadows, and towering peaks. Foremost for visitors is the iconic **Maroon Bells Wilderness Area.** Closed to vehicles most of the day, hikers and gawkers must catch a bus at the Aspen Highlands ski area. The bus drivers narrate the 10-minute trip up a gorgeous valley with interesting area and wildlife information. Once let off the bus by Maroon Lake, hikers can choose a short excursion by the lake and then take the bus back down, or the more intrepid explorers can choose any number of hours- or days-long hikes from here.

Fall shows off the town's namesake, the aspen tree, to its golden best. The trees are usually most spectacular in September when the normally green leaves turn bright golden and seem to "quake" in the breeze.

For those more culturally minded, numerous festivals, conferences, and special events come to town throughout the year. A good place to start researching your special interest in Aspen is the **Aspen Chamber Resort Association** (425 Rio Grande Place, 970-925-1940 or 800-670-0792, www.aspenchamber.org). This association is also a good place to find further lodging, dining, and entertainment choices.

As with any decent hot spot, Aspen has more than its fair share of delicious restaurants. **Krabloonik Restaurant** (4250 Divide Rd., Snowmass Village, CO, 970-923-3953, www.krabloonik.com), just west of Snowmass Village, offers the unusual combination of fine dining and dog sledding. The gourmet menu features game such as boar, elk, and ostrich. **Ajax Tavern** (675 E. Durant Ave., 970-920-6334, www.thelittle nell.com/restaurants/ajax_tavern.aspx) is right next to the gondola at the bottom of Aspen Mountain and thus a great place to sit outside and people watch. The Truffle Fries have a following, and the rest of the menu can be expected to be good to excellent.

i It's easy to get stuck in the snow, and an emergency car kit can literally keep you alive until help arrives. Stock a blanket and hat for warmth (up to 40 percent of body heat escapes through your head); a small LED flashlight (you don't want to use up the car battery); non-perishable food and bottled water; attention grabbers such as flares and hazard signs; a first-aid kit and knife; a cell phone charger; and activities such as books and colors, for kids (or yourself, if you're really there a long time!).

Getting to Aspen from the Pikes Peak region can be an adventure in itself. In the winter you must use I-70 across the Rockies, which takes about 5 hours. But in the summer, **Independence Pass** (www.inde pendencepass.org) is open to cars via CO 82. This route takes about 3 hours. The high, switchback-heavy road offers glorious views of the mountains with 1,000-foot drops off the side. Check to make sure the pass is open before heading that way.

Crested Butte

Crested Butte is 30 miles north of Gunnison, and far from the other pockets of ski towns in both miles and temperament. A 4-hour drive from Colorado Springs, Crested Butte offers the perfect setting for growing wildflowers, which are so bounteous each summer, the town devotes a full week to its annual wildflower festival (www.crested buttewildflowerfestival.com).

Besides wildflowers and surrounding peaks, attractions include ample hiking trails, ranging from easy to difficult, and mountain biking. In fact, Crested Butte calls itself the mountain biking capital of the planet, and is home to the **Mountain Bike Hall of Fame and Museum** (331 Elk Ave., www.mtn bikehalloffame.com). Bicycles are so popular there are public bikes sitting around for anyone to use.

Once a fertile Ute Indian hunting ground, the area later drew miners seeking riches. It now survives as a ski town for **Mount Crested Butte** (800-810-7669, www .skicb.com), which boasts some of the most extreme ski terrain in the nation. The well-preserved town (most of it on the National Register of Historic Places) is a couple of miles down in the valley.

For those who want total proximity to the mountain, good lodging can be found at **WestWall Lodge** (14 Hunter Hill Rd., 888-349-1280, www.westwalllodge.com) for ski-in / ski-out, luxury condos and use of a club, year-round outdoor pool, and full-service concierge. You can even arrange for a massage in your room. **Elevation Hotel & Spa** (12 Snowmass Rd., 800-334-9236, www.ele vationhotelandspa.com) offers a hip, urban atmosphere while keeping a mountain feel. Rooms and suites also come with use of the spa and fitness center. For dining, **Django's**

Restaurant & Wine Bar (620 Gothic Rd., 970-349-7574, www.djangos.us) features European-style small plates and a wine bar. **Uley's Cabin** (12 Snowmass Rd., 970-349-2275 for lunch reservations, 970-349-4554 for sleigh ride dinners and last track dinners) is mid-mountain and open during the ski season only. It's a popular stop for hot chocolate or specialty cocktails on the deck during the day.

Townies, or those not concerned about a short ride to the slopes, could be happy at any number of spots. **The Inn at Crested Butte** (510 Whiterock Ave., 877-343-2111, www.innatcrestedbutte.net) is a comfy boutique hotel and spa, and **The Ruby of Crested Butte** (624 Gothic Ave., 800-390-1338, www.therubyofcrestedbutte.com) is a quaint B&B. **Soupcon Bistro** (127 Elk Ave., 970-349-5448, www.soupconcrestedbutte.com) is a romantic bistro situated in a miner's cabin, **Lil's Sushi Bar & Grill** (321 Elk Ave., 970-349-5457) flies in fresh, hand-picked sushi daily from Hawaii, and **The Secret Stash** (21 Elk Ave., 970-349-6245, www.thesecretstash.com) is great for a pizza or specialty drink.

✳Glenwood Springs

Glenwood, across the Rockies about 3 hours away via I-70, is all about getting away. It's a refresh, reconnect, rejuvenate kind of town. And most of these are done with water.

The **Glenwood Hot Springs** (800-537-7946 or 970-945-6571, www.hotspringspool.com) is a pool, spa, athletic club, and lodge, with the star of the bunch being the pool. The large therapy pool averages 104 degrees and is a boon to aggravated joints and dehydrated skin with all-natural, therapeutic minerals. Just try that after a day of skiing and feel the pain slip away. A few steps from

the therapy pool is a more than 2-block-long big pool, kept between 90 and 93 degrees year-round. There are water slides and a kiddie pool, and all manner of pool toys are allowed.

Adjacent to the pool complex is the **Yampah Spa & Salon** (709 E. Sixth St., 970-945-066, www.yampahspa.com), featuring vapor caves that act as natural underground hot mineral water steam baths. First used by the Ute Indians, modern man enjoys the 125-degree geothermal steam baths while relaxing on slab marble benches in the rocky alcoves.

Other local water features are the **Colorado River,** which runs through town out of the spectacular **Glenwood Canyon.** Rafters and kayakers enjoy the river while bicyclists ride a well-maintained trail next to the rushing water. Bikes can be rented at numerous places in town.

Hiking in the Glenwood Canyon is especially popular to **Hanging Lake,** a tropical wonder almost straight up (or so your legs tell you) a 1-mile trail. The Hanging Lake Trailhead can only be accessed heading east on I-70, but turnarounds and exits are well marked. Plan on a mid-week hike as its popularity keeps the trail especially congested on summer and fall weekends.

Cavers can get their fill at **Glenwood Caverns Adventure Park** (51000 Two Rivers Plaza Rd., 800-530-1635, http://glenwoodcaverns.com). Caves go deep into the mountain, and there are other attractions like an alpine coaster, climbing wall, and kids geology discovery program.

Dining is available at many mom-and-pop restaurants. A standout is **Italian Underground** (715 Grand Ave., 970-945-6422), a small, hidden, dinner-only establishment that tempts diners with heady smells and comfortable ambiance. Or try **Riviera Supper Club** (702 Grand Ave., 970-945-7692), **Daily Bread** (729 Grand Ave., 970-945-6253) for sandwiches on homemade bread served with homemade soup, or **Rosi's Little Bavarian Restaurant** (141 W. 6th St., 970-928-9186) for breakfast.

After yet another round at one of the wet attractions, the historic **Hotel Colorado** (526 Pine St., 800-544-3998 or 970-945-6511, www.hotelcolorado.com) is a good place to check in for the night. Although a little creaky now, the hotel's late 1800s opulence still lends a special feel to a stay. A recent remodel has made it that much better. There are also a number of chain hotels, the lodge affiliated with the pool, and another historic beaut, **Hotel Denver** (402 7th St., 800-826-8820 or 970-945-6565, www.the hoteldenver.com).

Ouray & Telluride

Ouray and Telluride sit in the southwest corner of the state, in the San Juan Mountains. Both are set in valleys with dramatic mountain peaks above the towns, and both are very different from other Colorado mountain areas, probably because they are so distant from the rest of the state's tourism areas. They tend to be more laid back and backcountry—something most visitors there are seeking.

Ouray

At 7,700 feet above sea level, this National Historic District is surrounded on three sides by 13,000-foot peaks. It's no wonder it's often called "The Switzerland of America." As any alternative Swiss city would be, Ouray is an outdoor enthusiast's paradise. Residents and visitors enjoy rock climbing, hiking, four-wheeling, and mountain biking in

the summer and ice climbing, backcountry skiing, cross-country skiing, and snowshoeing in the winter.

Open all the year, the **Box Canyon Waterfall and Park** (www.ouraycolorado .com/boxcanyon) is a dramatic sight, with a 285-foot waterfall plummeting down a narrow, quartzite canyon. The area also has been designated an important bird area by the National Audubon Society. Or, tour the **Bachelor Syracuse Mine** (1222 CR 14, 970-325-0220, http://bachelorsyracusemine .com), which takes you 1,800 feet horizontally into Gold Hill, where you'll see the equipment used in mining, and rich silver veins and other mineral deposits.

One of the best activities is to relax in one of Ouray's several hot springs pools and tubs. The largest is the million-gallon **Ouray Hot Springs Pool** (1220 Main St., www.ouray colorado.com/Hot+Springs+Pool), which is open year-round.

After an active day and a good soak, sate your appetite at the steakhouse **Outlaw Restaurant** (610 Main St., 970-325-4366, www.outlawrestaurant.com), or try two excellent restaurants at the St. Elmo Hotel, which was established in the 1890s: **Bon Ton** (426 Main St., 866-243-1502 or 970-325-4951, www.stelmohotel.com) for Italian or more casual Mexican food at **Buen Tiempo** (515 Main St., 866-243-1502 or 970-325-4951, www.stelmohotel.com). Word to the wise— don't skip the margaritas at Buen Tiempo.

For a good night's rest, the **Beaumont Hotel & Spa** (505 Main St., 888-447-3255 or 970-325-7000, www.beaumonthotel.com) is in a lovely brick building downtown while the **Spangler House** (520 Second St., 970-325-4944 or 800-486-4096, www.spangler house.com) is a B&B with definite charm. The **Wiesbaden Hot Springs Spa & Lodgings**

(625 Fifth St., 970-325-4347 or 888-846-5191, www.wiesbadenhotsprings.com) has a European flair and its own vapor cave soaking pool, outdoor pool, and another small, private, secluded outdoor soaking pool.

i One of the wonderful things about Colorado is the amount of wildlife, and the easy frequency with which we humans enjoy it. The downside is that animals are hit by cars often, usually resulting in significant damage to both cars and animal. Keep your eyes open. Insurance companies do not suggest quick movements to avoid an animal as this can cause your car to rollover. The best solution is to watch for them and give yourself plenty of time to avert a collision.

Telluride

Telluride is known for its high altitude (8,750 feet above sea level), box canyon beauty, skiing, Old West charm, and very contemporary festivals. The entire town has been designated a National Historic Landmark District. Telluride is connected with neighboring **Mountain Village** by a free gondola transportation system—the only one of its kind in North America. At an elevation of 9,500 feet, Mountain Village is a pedestrian-friendly community and home to the **Telluride Ski Resort** (http://tellurideskiresort.com), with a world-class golf course, restaurants, lodging, and shops.

If you come to enjoy the alpine beauty in the summer months, you might also get to enjoy one of the town's signature events: film, jazz, bluegrass, wine, and blues festivals. Summer is also a good time for the usual hiking, biking, fishing, and camping. There's also a disc golf course at Mountain

Village; it's free but you need to bring your own Frisbee. The area's mining history also makes for great off-road adventure for jeeps, ATVs, and motorcycles. Outfitters offer rentals and adventure packages, and on crowded weekends, it's good to book those through your hotel when you make lodging reservations.

Winter is, of course, ski and snowboard season. But that's not all. You can cross-country ski through the **San Juan Hut System,** a ski route connecting Telluride, Ridgway, and Ouray with trails and five interspersed back-country ski huts. Or, get pulled in a sled by huskies on a crisp morning with **Winter Moon Sled Dog Adventures** (970-729-0058), soar above the valley in a glider with **Telluride Soaring** (1500 Last Dillar Rd., 970-209-3497, www.tellurideglidderrides .com), or ice skate in Telluride Town Park or at Capella Hotel in Mountain Village.

When it's time to wind down, head slopeside to the luxurious **Mountain Lodge** (457 Mountain Village Blvd., 970-369-5000, www.mountainlodgetelluride.com) or stay in town at the cute **Aspen Street Inn** (330 W. Pacific Ave., 888-728-1950 or 970-728-5452, www.telluridehotels.com), a quaint B&B.

Telluride has no shortage of good food. **Allred's** (http://tellurideskiresort.com/Tell ski/info/allreds.aspx) is midway between Telluride and Mountain Village on a free gondola ride, and **La Cocina de Luz** (123 E. Colorado Ave., 920-728-9355, www.lacocina telluride.com) is taqueria-style Mexican fare featuring handmade tortillas, a salsa bar, and local, organic ingredients.

✳Santa Fe & Taos

New Mexico is close, and yet a weekend getaway to either Santa Fe or Taos takes your mind to another world. Perhaps it's the mesquite burning in fireplaces (year-round—even summer mornings bring a chill), the close adobe buildings, or the bright silver jewelry worn and sold by everyone, everywhere.

Santa Fe

Santa Fe is a direct route south on I-25 about 5 hours away. Rich in history back to the Tewa Indians and the Conquistadors, Santa Fe is the oldest state capital in the US and among the oldest American cities (along with Jamestown, VA, St. Augustine, FL, and a handful of others.). Its **Palace of the Governors** (120 Washington Ave., www.palace ofthegovernors.org) is believed to be the oldest public building in the US and the oldest state capitol building. The **New Mexico History Museum** (113 Lincoln Ave., 505-476-5200, www.nmhistorymuseum.org) now houses the 400 years of artifacts that had been kept in less-than-ideal conditions at the Palace of the Governors. The 96,000-square-foot museum is adjacent to the Palace of the Governors, and covers everything from prehistoric times to the local contributions to the Manhattan Project, which developed the first atomic bomb.

But this is hardly the only museum worth your time. The **Wheelwright Museum of the American Indian** (704 Camino Lejo, 505-982-4636 or 800-607-4636, www.wheel wright.org) and the **International Folk Art Museum** (706 Camino Lejo, 505-476-1200, www.internationalfolkart.org) also are good choices. The kids find hands-on time at the **Santa Fe Children's Museum** (1050 Old Pecos Trail, 505-989-8359, www.santafe childrensmuseum.org), and **Rancho de los Golondrinas** (334 Los Pinos Rd., 505-471-2261, www.golondrinas.org) is a 200-acre living history site just outside of town.

Art and history are the lifeblood of the town, and art-lovers find themselves in gallery heaven. There are more galleries here per capita than just about anywhere in the US. The old established ones are downtown and along **Canyon Road.** There's also a new art district at the **Railyard** (www .railyardsantafe.com), the **Georgia O'Keeffe Museum** (217 Johnson St., www.okeeffe museum.org), honoring one of the city's most famous artists, and **SITE Santa Fe** (1606 Paseo de Peralta, 505-989-1199, www .sitesantafe.org) for international contemporary art.

The **Santa Fe Plaza,** a block-shaped park in the center of town, is the place for a frequent local Indian Market. It's a chance to buy silver, turquoise, pottery, and other handmade crafts right from the artists. Ask before shooting photos of Native Americans at market or at the nearby pueblos. This is their home and it's only polite.

Almost every visitor stops at the famous **Loretto Chapel** (207 Old Santa Fe Trail, www.lorettochapel.com), which features a mysterious—some say miraculous—circular staircase that baffles engineers and architects who say it should not balance or stand because it has no central support.

Annual events are the **Santa Fe Spanish Market** (www.spanishmarket.org) in July. It taps into the area's rich Spanish heritage, and more than 200 Hispanic artists show their santos, retablos, tinwork, ironwork, pottery, basketry, and needlework. August brings the **Santa Fe Indian Market** (www.swaia .org), a juried show with more than 1,000 Native American artists. It features the paintings, sculptures, jewelry, and other arts and crafts from some of the finest native talent in the Southwest. And the famous **Santa Fe Opera** (301 Opera Dr., 505-986-5900 or

800-280-4654, www.santafeopera.org) season goes through July and August. With world-class opera stars, an outdoor venue with a night sky as the backdrop and the tradition of fancy tailgate parties, this is opera Santa Fe style!

Fall is harvest time—and the scent of roasting green chilies spices the air. Sunny days and cool nights make it the ideal time to visit, weather-wise. There are also smaller crowds because summer is high season, and often packed. Christmas season is magical as celebrations incorporate strong Spanish traditions, such as Las Posadas. Throughout the area, the night is dotted with the warm glow of luminarias or farolitos, candles carefully placed in sand inside a paper bag.

If all this sounds exhausting, try the **Ten Thousand Waves** spa (3451 Hyde Park Rd., 505-982-9304, www.tenthousandwaves .com), just outside of town. The combination Southwest and Japanese ambiance, combined with myriad relaxing treatments, can bring anyone back to life. There are also a few rooms available for lodging.

Other lodging satisfies any whim you have. For deluxe accommodations, the **Inn of the Anasazi** (113 Washington Ave., 505-988-3030, www.innoftheanasazi.com) and **Inn & Spa at Loretto** (211 Old Santa Fe Trail, 866-582-1646, www.innatloretto.com) are two excellent options. Many small, quaint B&Bs are placed throughout the area, such as **El Farolito** (514 Galisteo St., 505-988-1631 or 888-634-8782, www.farolito.com) and its sister property **Four Kachinas** (512 Webber St., 505-982-2550 or 800-397-2564, www.four kachinas.com). There's also a host of national chain hotels.

For foodies, Santa Fe is a feast. You almost can't go wrong. Locals and visitors alike flock to **Cafe Pasqual's** (121 Don Gaspar Ave., 505-983-9340 or 800-722-7672, http://pasquals.com) for any meal of the day. The place is small and tight, so prepare to stand in line and, when you do get a table, the seating is so close you're mostly elbow-to-elbow. **Tia Sophia's** (210 W. San Francisco St., 505-983-9880) is good for breakfast; and for an evening splurge, try two Canyon Road eateries, **Geronimo** (724 Canyon Rd., 505-982-1500, www.geronimorestaurant.com) for eclectic gourmet or **El Farol** (808 Canyon Rd., 505-983-9912, www.elfarolsf.com) for tapas and, some nights, tango. And, of course, you might want to visit the famous **Coyote Cafe** (132 W. Water St., 505-983-1615, www.coyotecafe.com), which is under new ownership but is still amazing.

Taos

Taos is just north of Santa Fe about an hour. From Colorado Springs, it's a 3½-hour drive south on I-25, then west on CO 160 and south on CO 159. Taos is smaller than Santa Fe but no less charming or full of Southwest flair. The **Taos Pueblo** (www.taospueblo .com) is the only living Native American community designated both a World Heritage Site by UNESCO and a National Historic Landmark. The multistoried adobe buildings have been continuously inhabited for more than 1,000 years. Only a few miles from the town's plaza, Taos Pueblo is not a museum—it is the tribe's home, and your journey there will stay in your mind for days.

Also on the not-to-be-missed list is the **San Francisco de Asís Mission Church** (60 Saint Francis Plaza, www.nps.gov/nr/travel/amsw/sw44.htm). You'll know it as soon as you see it because this Spanish Colonial adobe is one of the most photographed buildings in the West. Now managed by the National Park Service, the church features twin bell towers, a large carved altar screen, and a ceiling of *vigas* (beams) that rest on elaborately carved double brackets. Be respectful on your visit as San Francisco de Asis Mission is an active parish.

In the modern town, art is queen. There are a number of museums and almost innumerable galleries tucked into every side alley and street. The **Millicent Rogers Museum** (1504 Millicent Rogers Rd., El Prado, NM, 575-758-2462, http://millicentrogers.org) showcases traditional and contemporary arts and crafts from the many cultures of Northern New Mexico, and the **Taos Art Museum & Fechin House** (227 Paseo del Pueblo Norte, 575-758-2690, www.taosartmuseum.org) showcases the museum's permanent collection of Taos-centered artists. This collection is within the historic hand-built home of Russian-born artist Nicolai Fechin.

Art might own the heart of Taos, but it is not the only game in town. In summer, mountain bikers ride the world-class, 27-mile South Boundary Trail, which for 9 miles follows the rim of the Rio Grande Gorge. Class IV rapids at Taos Box await rafters, or you can float above in a hot air balloon. There are a number of golf courses, and, at **Sipapu** (5224 NM 518, Vadito, NM, 800-587-2240 or 575-587-2240, sipapunm.com), the only 18 basket Mach III alpine disc golf course in the Southwest is both scenic and challenging. Horseback riding, llama trekking, and fishing also are available.

In winter, there are four nearby ski areas, lots of backcountry trails for snowshoe and cross-country ski fans and snowmobiles to rent. And the best part is that at the end of the day, you know you can warm up next to a kiva fireplace while dining on sumptuous meals. Try **El Meze** (1017 Paseo del Pueblo Norte, 575-751-3337, www.elmeze.com) for

excellent and exotic Moorish-Spanish-New Mexican inspired dining, or **Dragonfly Cafe & Bakery** (402 Paseo del Pueblo Norte, 575-737-5859, www.dragonflytaos.com) for eclectic breads, breakfast, and dinner. Near the Rancho de Taos plaza and the famous mission church, **Ranchos Plaza Grill** (8 Ranchos Plaza Rd., 575-758-5788) serves true Mexican fare (watch your timing—when church lets out, the crowd heads to the grill).

Tucked back off the plaza is a quiet jewel of a hotel, **La Posada de Taos** (309 Juanita Lane, 800-645-4803 or 575-758-8164, http://laposadadetaos.com). This quaint B&B is one of the oldest (but now renovated) buildings in Taos, and breakfast on the charming brick patio affords views of the surrounding mountains. Also try **Casa Benavides Bed and Breakfast** (137 Kit Carson Rd., 800-552-1772 or 575-758-1772, www.taos-casabenavides.com), where each room is uniquely decorated with a wild, artistic flair. Return guests always want a different room just to see what it looks like! **The St. Bernard Inn** (112 Sutton Place, Taos Ski Valley, NM, 575-776-2251, http://stbernardtaos.com) puts you right at the lifts at Taos Ski Valley, and they also have condos a short walk farther. **The Taos Inn** (125 Paseo del Pueblo Norte, 575-758-2233, www.taosinn.com) is a local landmark and has been noted by *National Geographic Traveler* as one of America's great inns.

Summit County

Breckenridge, Keystone, Frisco, Copper— they're practically the backyard playground of the Pikes Peak region. From skiing in winter to summer hiking, the road between Summit County and Colorado Springs is well-traveled. It can be done in a day since it's only about 2½ hours away, and many

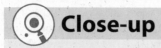

Close-up

✳Rocky Mountain National Park

Rocky Mountain National Park (970-586-1206, www.nps.gov/romo) opens in late May or early June and often closes mid-October when snow blocks the road. And yet it gets about 3 million visitors a year. *National Geographic Adventure* magazine named it one of America's 10 best parks, calling it the "loftiest of all national parks." Bisected by Trail Ridge Road, the park's paved highway makes it for everyone, from visitors in wheelchairs to serious hikers.

Trail Ridge Road threads visitors from park-like valleys that are home to the towns of Estes Park on the east and Grand Lake on the west to the alpine tundra at 12,000 feet. The air is thin, the view is far, and the stupendous wonder of nature is at hand. In 1909, this wonder pushed naturalist Enos Mills to write about the valleys and stunning peaks beyond Estes Park and campaign for the area's preservation. In 1915, it became America's 10th national park.

About a 3-hour drive from the Pikes Peak region, the park headquarters at Beaver Meadows Visitor Center holds exhibits, maps, and a great introductory film that tells visitors about the park's creation. You can also reserve backcountry camping sites here.

At altitudes up to 14,000 feet, the park's peaks impede and create weather. A third of the park is above treeline, which is about 10,000 feet. Here, elk and deer and pronghorns graze; peregrine falcons dart after prey; mountain lions roam the back country, along with bighorn sheep and black bears. Marmots sun themselves on rocks. Beaver build their lodges and create ponds. Gray jays and ground squirrels beg tourists for food (resist!). Foxes and coyotes hunt small mammals and birds, such as the pudgy little pika (a relative of the rabbit) or the shy ptarmigan. If you go up early or come down late, watch for herds of elk grazing not far from the roadways in the foothills. Don't approach them. They look calm but can be dangerous when frightened.

There are two entrances to the park from Estes Park: Beaver Meadows Visitors Center and the Fall River Visitors Center, the latter at the entrance to the old Fall River Road. While Trail Ridge Road is paved, Fall River Road is not. The original road through the park, Fall River Road is open a shorter portion of the year and is less

do pop up for a short time. But after exerting yourself in whatever adventure you choose, it's much more relaxing to plan on a weekend.

Breckenridge is the quintessential description of quaint. Colorful, Victorian buildings mash together along **Main Street** in a way that makes you think it is still a Gold Rush mining town—just cleaner and more festive. The 250-plus downtown buildings on the National Historic Register house shops, restaurants, galleries, and the occasional odd duck, like an oxygen bar. Breck is hip, fun, and picture perfect—bring a camera.

If you'd rather mine for history than a new winter sweater, check out the **Lomax Placer Gulch** tour (301 Ski Hill Rd., Breckenridge, CO) where you can pan for gold, or go the **Washington Mine** (465 Illinois Gulch Rd., Breckenridge, CO) where you traveled than Trail Ridge. But it offers its own attractions, views, and perspective on the park. Savvy travelers go up Fall River Road and come back down Trail Ridge Road, to avoid repeating the entire experience. It doesn't take a 4-wheel-drive or high-clearance vehicle to navigate Fall River Road, but make sure your car is in good condition and take it slow. There are no service stations up here. (Trailers and RVs aren't allowed on this road.)

The top of Fall River Road, at 11,000 feet, intersects with Trail Ridge Road. At this juncture there is another visitor center. There's also a hiking trail carved out of the tundra to a point that is usually cold and windy (speeds of up to 200 mph have been recorded here) but offers spectacular panoramic views of the Gore mountain range. Those who like to climb find a world-class venue here.

It's about 48 miles across the park, from Estes Park to Grand Lake; allow at least 3 to 4 hours to drive it. You'll stop frequently to take pictures and maybe hike. Even from the car you'll most likely see herds of elk grazing, usually either early or late in the day.

Be prepared for any weather. In a single day, you may doff your jacket for a sunny hike and watch a family have a snowball fight in shorts. You can drive up into a thunderstorm, which turns to sleet, then snow, and back down through rain and into sunshine again.

Once out of the park, the town of Estes Park is worth a few hours . . . or days. The quaint town with an incredible backdrop offers hiking, mountain biking, fishing, golfing, four-wheeling, or just sitting on a rock and basking in the high-altitude sun (while wearing sunscreen at all times). You'll want to visit the elegant **Stanley Hotel** (333 Wonderview Ave., 800-976-1377 or 970-586-3371, www.stanleyhotel.com), made famous in the movie *The Shining* when Jack Nicholson's character said, "Here's Johnny!" There are also a number of cozy cabins or romantic bed-and-breakfast inns (**Estes Park Chamber Resort Association**, 800-443-7837, www.estes-park.com). Although summer is high season for tourism, September is a great time to visit as the crowds are down and the quaking aspen trees are turning gold. There's also a **Longs Peak Scottish-Irish Festival** (www.scotfest.com) in September that'll let you know you're in the highlands!

can peer down into a shaft, handle drill steel and core samples, don a hard hat and walk along ore-car tracks, and see the tools and equipment used 100 years ago—from candles to calcium-carbide lights and rock drills to those widow-makers, black powder and dynamite. Both tours can be scheduled with the **Breckenridge Historical Alliance** (800-980-1859).

If you'd rather eat, **Eric's** (111 S. Main St., Breckenridge, CO, 970-453-1401, www .downstairsaterics.com) is an underground (literally—downstairs) hot spot for burgers and an easy time. **The Blue River Bistro** (305 N. Main St., Breckenridge, CO, 970-453-6974, www.blueriverbistro.com) offers far more civilized fare in a chic but comfortable spot on Main Street. **The Hearthstone Inn** (130 S. Ridge St., Breckenridge, CO, 970-453-1148, www.hearthstonerestaurant.biz) might look like something miners would patronize given its cute Victorian setting, but the miners probably wouldn't know what to do with the seared ahi tuna and ginger sea scallops.

Lodging at Breckenridge runs from hotels to condos to private homes for rent. **Beaver Run Resort** (620 Village Rd., Breckenridge, CO, 970-453-6000, www.beaverrun.com) offers hotel rooms and condos slopeside, and both Marriott and Hyatt run vacation club units at the base of the mountain.

Because of course, the mountain is the main attraction. **Breckenridge Ski Resort** (www.breckenridge.com) is one of the most popular mountains in the state—with 30 lifts, terrain parks, and special events almost every week, this is one happening place. Just be careful on the weekends when the crowds can make it close to a demolition derby on the slopes.

Not to be outdone, **Copper Mountain** (www.coppercolorado.com), **Keystone** (www.keystoneresort.com), and **Arapahoe Basin** (www.arapahoebasin.com) also offer that current Colorado gold, snow at its best. Copper is known as a friend to the more experienced ski and snowboard fans, but the 22 lifts range from bunny slope to double diamond (expert). The village is cute and small, set up mainly for those who are there to enjoy the mountain. Numerous hotel, condos, and private homes are available for rent.

Arapahoe Basin, known as A-Basin, is all about the mountain. Lodging must be elsewhere as this old-time ski area does not have accommodations. What it does have is height, incline, and powder. Set at the base of the Continental Divide on Loveland Pass, A-Basin offers steep trails, above timberline bowls, and terrain parks.

Keystone boasts three peaks, the A51 Terrain Park, a mid-mountain extreme tubing experience, and a well-developed main village centered on a lake. Accommodations of all kinds can be made through the resort. The lake is a fun skating spot in winter and paddle-boat spot in summer. A Nordic center caters to cross-country skiers and snowshoers, and instruction is available in both. Keystone also has two challenging, high-altitude golf courses.

Dining in Keystone can be a real adventure at the **Alpenglow Stube** (on Keystone Mountain, 800-354-4386), which requires two gondola rides and a short walk. Once you're there, you're on top of the world. The gourmet cuisine is served in an elegant log lodge, the perfect way to celebrate a fine day of skiing or hiking.

Frisco and **Silverthorne** are the geographical center of Summit County ski resorts, with the ski areas emanating out like a star. The two towns help provide a strong infrastructure to the big ski areas, and lodging, dining, and shopping are everywhere. There's even outlet shopping available. Staying in Frisco or Silverthorne is the best bet for those who want to try various mountains and activities.

For a nice dinner, try the longtime restaurant **Blue Spruce Inn** (20 Main St., Frisco, CO, 970-668-5900, http://thebluespruce.com). Set in a mountain cabin on Frisco's Main Street, the food is sublime and the cozy ambiance a welcome retreat. A good burger can be found at another longstanding joint, **The Moose Jaw** (208 Main St., Frisco, CO, 970-668-3931), also on Frisco's Main Street.

Vail & Beaver Creek

Vail and Beaver Creek are only about a half hour from Summit County, but for some reason it feels farther away. About 3 hours from the Pikes Peak region via I-25, these resort areas tend see a majority of out-of-state visitors who come for week-long stays. The upscale communities cater to a feeling of European opulence and decadence. It doesn't necessarily cost your IRA to go, but it feels like you're splurging when you're there. The hotels are lovely, the unique restaurants are gourmet, and the skiing, hiking, and golf are world-class.

Vail

First, the mountain. **Vail** (www.vail.com) is one of the largest ski areas in the US, with about 5,300 acres of terrain, including 3 terrain parks and 7 bowls. The 31 lifts span a 7-mile-wide area, and Riva, the longest run, is 4 miles long. And then there's Adventure Ridge, a new football stadium–size mountaintop playground meant to keep visitors out well into the night. The family-friendly area has ski bikes, kids snowmobile track, speedy tubing lanes, and more. If you'd rather be just off the mountain, the Solaris area has a CineBistro theater; a bowling alley; and ice skating rink in winter, jet fountain in summer.

Other summer pastimes include hiking, mountain biking, fly fishing, golf, horseback riding, camping, hot air ballooning, and kayaking, with a variety of outfitters and rental shops ready to get you geared up for the day.

Vail Village is like a cultivated European village. The narrow paved roads make for easy walking, especially since cars cannot drive within the village. Shopping and dining tempt down every little alley. **Sweet Basil** (193 Gore Creek Dr., 970-476-0125, www.sweetbasil-vail.com) is a very civilized choice for lunch or dinner, and the wine list compliments anything ordered from the eclectic menu. **The Alpenrose** (100 E. Vail Dr., 970-476-8899) has been around for decades, and it is always a German treat. The omelets are remarkable (they say cooking them very hot is the key), the German fare traditional, and just try to leave without ordering a dessert. For the hip, happening crowd, **Larkspur** (458 Vail Valley Dr., 970-754-8050, www.larkspurvail.com) is the perfect choice. For something completely different, the non-descript **Route 6 Cafe** (41290 US 6, Eagle, CO, 970-949-6393) is a great breakfast (served all day). The funky old gas-station-turned-diner hits you with island music, heavy mugs of coffee, and such local favorites as huevos rancheros with pork green chile, Rocky Mountain trout and eggs, or shredded chicken hash.

Vail has hundreds of large and small hotels, condos, and private rentals, including the boutique hotel **Vail Mountain Lodge** (352 E. Meadow Dr., 888-794-0410 or 970-476-0700, www.vailmountainlodge.com), complete with a club, spa, and fitness center. The luxury **Sonnenalp Resort of Vail** (20 Vail Rd., 866-284-4411, www.sonnenalp.com) offers suites with either a view of Vail Village or the Gore Creek.

Beaver Creek

Beaver Creek (www.beavercreek.com) can be intimidating. Access is only through a guarded gate, and the second (or maybe third) homes you drive by to get to the village is anyone's definition of a mansion. But it is a lovely enclave anyone can share, with a charming, hospitable attitude even with the cloak of exclusivity. It's not big—if you're here, it's because you want to kick back and enjoy the mountain ambiance without interruption.

Again, first to the mountain. For such a compact village, the mountain is quite large. You won't get bored skiing or boarding here—there are 17 lifts, 2 bowls, 4 terrain parks, and a half pipe. Kids can giggle away on the tubing hill. And a Nordic center, which is located through stunning scenery at the top of the Strawberry Park Express chairlift, offers cross-country skiing, snowshoes, and telemark skis. Keep a lookout for porcupines, snowshoe hare, and fox.

The Black Family Ice Rink, outdoors in the center of the village, entertains both day and night, and big outdoor fire pits with huge comfy chairs surround the ice. Shops dazzle and restaurants tempt with specialty cocktails, fine wine, and delectable treats.

In the summer there's a golf course, hiking to Beaver Lake on the mountain, and restful fly fishing. And for those with zen on the mind, the **Allegria Spa** (136 E. Thomas Place, Avon, CO, 970-748-7500, www.allegria spa.com) inside the Hyatt will rub out your cares and aches. The Aqua Sanitas water sanctuary is divine. Ask for seasonal specials.

Beaver Creek dining is exceptional. **Beano's Cabin** (on Beaver Creek Mountain,

970-754-3463) is not just eating dinner, it's a winter wonderland experience. First, there's a 20-minute open-air sleigh ride through the twilight snow. Then as a fire crackles, excellent wine and a culinary masterpiece are served. Summer diners are at a loss as Beano's is open only for the winter season. Another fine choice is the casually elegant **Grouse Mountain Grill** (141 Scott Hill Rd., Avon, CO, 970-949-0600, www.grouse mountaingrill.com), with exceptional food, a knowledgeable yet understated sommelier, and a fantastic view of the valley. If French is your yen, **Mirabelle Restaurant** (55 Village Rd., Avon, CO, 970-949-7728) is *tres magnifique* year after year. When in Beaver Creek in the summer and fall, check if a desired restaurant is open—they often hire out the whole place to wedding parties.

For a restful night, **The Charter** (120 Offerson Rd., 800-525-2139, www.thecharter .com) is the best family-friendly lodging, and **The Osprey** (10 Elk Track Lane, Avon, CO, 866-621-7625 or 970-754-7400, http:// ospreyatbeavercreek.rockresorts.com) has a lift just outside the back door.

SCENIC DRIVES

Colorado has dozens of designated scenic byways and just plain gorgeous drives where everywhere you look there's something beautiful or interesting. Several are close by and can be done in a day; some might entice you into an overnight stay. You can explore a number of nearby attractions and see some stunning scenery, stop for lunch someplace new, and be home that nightfall to sleep in your own bed (or not!). These drives can be as quick or as leisurely as you like. So buckle up—and don't forget the camera. Note that many of these drives take you to places you might want to stop and spend some time (see the Day Trips & Getaways chapter), but we don't address every attraction in every town. Allow plenty of time to dawdle, if that's your inclination. If you aren't a dawdler, then all of these drives can be done in a day—albeit maybe a long one. All of these drives are beautiful in summer and downright gorgeous in the fall when the aspens turn to gold and the scrub oak flashes scarlet. Watch the weather carefully in winter and spring—some of these drives can be treacherous when Mother Nature plays her tricks.

RAMPART RANGE DRIVE

From Colorado Springs, head to the Garden of the Gods Park and the Balanced Rock site. There, catch **Rampart Range Road** and head north and west into the **foothills of the Rockies.** You'll likely see Rocky Mountain bighorn sheep, wild turkeys, and other wildlife along the way as the vegetation changes from scrub oaks to pines. You'll also get some grand scenic overlooks of **Queen's Canyon** and **Williams Canyon.** As you proceed north, you'll pass **Mount Herman, Chimney Peak,** and **Storm Peak,** and finally spot the well-named **Devil's Head** (you can't miss it) up ahead. This road takes you to **CO 67,** and finally into **Sedalia,** which is just west of I-25. You can backtrack and take in the views from the opposite direction or you can head into **Castle Rock** and catch I-25 home.

PHANTOM CANYON & SHELF ROAD

From Colorado Springs, take **US 24** west to Divide, then turn south on **CO 67** to **Cripple Creek.** Spend some time there, if you like, exploring the famous gold camp's history. If nothing else, stop at the visitor center on the way into town for a good overview of the historic district. You'll see lots of evidence of mining (past and present) and ranching. Continue on to **Victor,** where you will find the beginning of **Phantom Canyon Road.** This starts a **65-mile loop** that will leave you mostly out of touch with civilization, so have your cell phone charged in case of car trouble! You'll meander over this unpaved road for many miles, seeing wildlife and easing around blind corners. (Note: Drive slowly and give right-of-way to uphill traffic.) Eventually, you'll come out at **US 50.** Go west to **Cañon City.** There, you can find **Raynolds Avenue** (a state scenic drive sign marks the turn), and head north on the **Shelf Road,** which wends its way back to Cripple Creek. Along the way, you'll come across the **Garden Park Paleontology Area,** lovely **Red Canyon Park,** and a designated rock climbing area. Red Canyon Park is, for sure, worth a detour. The road ultimately ends in Cripple Creek and you can find your way back home from there. Note that this drive is not for the timid and not to be attempted in bad weather.

SCENIC HIGHWAY OF LEGENDS

From Colorado Springs, take **I-25** south to **Walsenburg.** There, catch **US 160** West toward Alamosa, . . . but don't go that far. Turn off at **CO 12** south, toward **La Veta.** This is the last town of any size you'll encounter for many miles on this route, so get gas if you don't have a full tank—and a bite of lunch, if you like. Take a few minutes to explore this artsy little burg before continuing. Heading south, still on CO 12, you'll see the stunning **Spanish Peaks** on your left (to the east), and eventually encounter a massive, natural Dakota sandstone wall that runs parallel to the highway. You'll also see tiny towns settled by early Hispanic farmers and ranchers, coal ovens, and other indications of civilization. If you have time, take a detour to **Cordova Pass** to see the **natural stone arch.** Eventually, **CO 12** comes out at **Trinidad,** the southernmost city on I-25 before you hit **Raton Pass** and **New Mexico.** Return to Colorado Springs via I-25.

FRONTIER PATHWAYS/ WET MOUNTAINS

From Colorado Springs, take **I-5** south to **Pueblo.** Exit on **CO 96** and go west toward **Pueblo Reservoir.** Continue on CO 96 into the **Wet Mountains,** where the land rises from prairie to peak, from cholla cactus to ponderosa pines. You may spot a bison herd, see some antelope, or catch a glimpse of a golden eagle soaring high above, searching for prey. About 30 miles from I-25, you'll intersect with CO 67—but don't take it. Stay on CO 96. As you enter the **montane life zone,** keep an eye out for Rocky Mountain bighorn sheep. Pass through **McKenzie Junction** and the **San Isabel National Forest.** Eventually, you'll get some pretty spectacular views of the **Sangre de Cristo mountains** to the west and enter the towns of **Silver Cliff** and **Westcliffe.** Once you've had a chance to buy a cold drink and stretch your legs, head back toward McKenzie Junction and take **CO 165** south this time. In about 12 or 13 miles, you'll come across a strange sight: **Bishop's Castle.** Reclusive builder Jim Bishop has been constructing this Seuss-like structure for many years and it's worth a stop to take a look. Stay on CO 165 all the way into the town of **Rye** and then **Colorado City,** where you can catch I-25 north for the return trip home.

SOUTH PARK DRIVE

From Colorado Springs, head west on **US 24,** through Woodland Park, through Divide, over Wilkerson Pass, and into **South Park.** Continue on US 24 across the high plains (look for bison and wildflowers), just past the town of **Hartsel** to **CO 9.** Turn north toward **Fairplay.** You'll pass ranches and rolling hills. In Fairplay, be sure to stop at the **South Park City Museum,** a collection of 1800s

Recommended Reading

How do you choose from among the dozens of scenic drives and byways in Colorado? Here are some good resources to help you select the one that suits you. These books often include geological descriptions of each part of each drive, some human history, and even mile-by-mile breakdowns of what to look for.

Colorado Scenic Drives, by Stewart M. Green, lists all the above and more, with detailed point-to-point descriptions, maps, and photos. If that is hard to find, check out his newer book, *Scenic Driving Colorado* published by Globe Pequot Press.

Colorado Byways, by Thomas Huber, offers a detailed look at what you'll see at the various mileage points along some of Colorado's designated scenic byways. He discusses the human history of each area as well as scenic and geologic features.

If you're a member of AAA, the Colorado AAA magazine, *EnCompass,* features a mini tour in every issue (six a year). All members automatically receive the magazine. Or they can go to **www.Colorado.AAA.com** and check out the scenic drives described online.

Or go to the state tourism website, **www.colorado.com,** and search for scenic drives. They have some good tips, too. Also try **www.byways.org/explore/states/CO** for more ideas.

buildings set up like an Old West town. From here, catch **US 285** north and east through several small towns, including **Bailey.** At Bailey, pick up **CO 67** and head back south, toward **Woodland Park,** US 24, and back home to Colorado Springs.

If you want a longer drive with more diversions, from Fairplay you can continue north on CO 9 over Hoosier Pass and into **Breckenridge.** This charming town (see Day Trips & Getaways) has lots to offer and may tempt you to spend the night. Backtrack or head north, catching I-70 east back to Denver, then C-470 to I-25 south and back to Colorado Springs.

SOUTH PLATTE RIVER ROAD

From Colorado Springs, take **US 24** west to **Woodland Park.** Just after you pass

through downtown, look for CO 67 north. You'll pass through woodland areas till you get to **Manitou Lake,** where you can stop and admire the scenery (and toss in your line, if you brought your fishing pole). Wind your way through the **Pike National Forest** till you get to **Deckers,** a small fishing resort town on the **South Platte River.** At Deckers, turn onto **CO 126** toward **Buffalo Creek,** a picturesque little town, then to **Pine,** and finally **Pine Junction.** Not to be missed along this route is a winding road through a gorge with granite walls. From Pine Junction, catch **US 285** to Denver or backtrack to Buffalo Creek and take a scenic, gravel road, **CO 96,** till it intersects with **CO 67** to **Sedalia.** From there, head east to **I-25** and home.

LIVING HERE

In this section we feature specific information for residents or those planning to relocate here. Topics include real estate, education, health care, and much more.

RELOCATION

Colorado Springs is one of the best places to live, work, and play in the US. Backed by the awe-inspiring beauty of Pikes Peak, this community enjoys a lifestyle and richness rare in a city of this size. With our alpine desert climate at 6,000 feet, we enjoy snowfall in the winter and yet bask in an average of more than 300 days of sunshine every year. There are numerous parks, open spaces, and bike and hiking trails. The elementary and secondary schools tend to be excellent, and many are among the best in the state and nationally. The region also hosts two of the most esteemed colleges in the country. Compared to either coast, the cost of living is low with modest utility rates, moderately priced housing, a cost of living below the national average, and one of the lowest tax burdens in Colorado. We are fortunate to have access to two nationally respected health care services, with new and innovative hospitals around town. The corporate and business environment is strong, with 27 *Fortune* 500 companies keeping a presence in the region. Consequently, Colorado Springs also boasts one of the highest educated workforces in the US. The arts and cultural scene is vibrant and active and has depth. There are more than 50 major attractions just within our region. And some of the world's best ski resorts are within a few hours' drive.

We are an amateur sports capital (the US Olympic Committee is just one of many sports organizations based here), a tourist mecca (more than 6 million tourist visits per year), and a favorite place for military personnel to come back to for retirement once they've lived around the world. So if you're one of the lucky new residents of the Pikes Peak region, we say welcome to your new home: You are now one of the luckiest people in America.

OVERVIEW

This chapter lists all those little details that can make moving so hard. No problem! We've found them for you. The first section, **Getting Settled,** helps with that seemingly endless "to do" list in a new location, including how to register your vehicle, find utilities, or get your trash picked up. The second section, **Your Humble Abode,** deals with house-hunting, from neighborhoods to renting to purchasing.

One major note on this chapter: Colorado Springs is but one city, within one county, in the Pikes Peak region. There are actually a number of cities and three counties that make up the Pikes Peak region. For our purposes here, we have listed only services for Colorado Springs, in El Paso County. If you choose to live outside of these boundaries, there might be different sources for you, from utilities to vehicle registration.

Because of this, we've listed here the town halls of surrounding communities, so you can check with them for resources in those areas.

GETTING SETTLED

CHAMBER OF COMMERCE
6 S. Tejon St., Suite 700
(719) 635-1551
www.coloradospringschamber.org
The Greater Colorado Springs Chamber of Commerce was established in 1892, but it's always been forward-looking. Over the last century, the Chamber has influenced major new developments in the region such as Fort Carson (1940s), the United States Air Force Academy (1950s), and high-technology firms (1980s). Currently the Chamber works with all community partners (business, nonprofit, military, and government) to ensure long-term regional prosperity.

Networking is a big part of the Chamber's current activity, from advisory committees, councils, volunteer groups, young professionals' groups, and more. They run active advocacy programs, and the Chamber's collaborative leadership forms a close connection to community leaders, military and elected officials, community-wide resources, organizations, and initiatives.

More than 1,600 members of the Chamber enjoy the opportunity to network at almost 100 events, affordable sponsorships, and advertising opportunities. They also gain from decreased expenses on competitive health benefits, discounted workers' compensation and member savings programs on such items as office supplies.

Outlying City Halls

Fountain
116 S. Main St., Fountain
(719) 322-2000
www.ci.fountain.co.us

Manitou Springs
606 Manitou Ave., Manitou Springs
(719) 685-5481
http://manitousprings-co.gov

Monument
645 Beacon Lite Rd., Monument
(719) 481-2954
www.townofmonument.net

Woodland Park
220 W. South Ave., Woodland Park
(719) 687-9246
www.city-woodlandpark.org

CITY OF COLORADO SPRINGS
30 S. Nevada Ave.
(719) 385-CITY (2489)
www.springsgov.com
The city of Colorado Springs's website is easy to use, and if there's one link on the homepage a newcomer needs, it's the link to "I want to . . . ." On that page you'll find everything from how to apply for a building permit to how to volunteer with the police. There's a community calendar, a city jobs listing, an explanation of the city government, and directions for walking tours through historic districts. There is a link to Summer Heat, an annual weeklong day camp sponsored by the city that introduces young women between the ages of 15 and 19 to career opportunities in the fire service. There are answers to everything from how to recycle to who to call if there's a wild animal in your backyard (Colorado Division of Wildlife, 719-227-5200—welcome to Colorado!). The

easier question is almost, what isn't on this site? Answer: not much!

EXPERIENCE COLORADO SPRINGS
(Convention and Visitors Bureau)
515 S. Cascade Ave.
(800) 888-4748 or (719) 635-7506
www.visitcos.com

Experience Colorado Springs is aimed more at tourists, but it can be a great resource for any newcomer to El Paso, Teller, or Fremont Counties. Their easy-to-use and fun website leads the way to all manner of dining, nightlife, attractions, activities, arts, culture, services, and lodging. A free visitors' guide, maps, and deals and coupons can help anyone start a new life here in Colorado Springs and beyond. The website hosts a community calendar as well as regional history, landmark locations, tips for high altitude, and even helps in planning weddings.

Department of Motor Vehicles

Once you become a Colorado resident (own/operate a Colorado business, be employed in Colorado, and/or reside in Colorado for 90 consecutive days), you have 30 days to qualify for a Colorado driver's license and 90 days to register your vehicle.

Colorado Driver's License or ID Card

You may have either a Colorado driver's license or a Colorado identification card (you can't have both). To get either, you must prove full legal name, identity, age, and lawful presence in the US. Frequently used documents to prove these are passports, driver's licenses from other states, and birth certificates. No matter what type used, documents must be certified originals, certified amended originals, or true copies certified by the issuing agency. US military and their spouses are exempt from obtaining a Colorado driver's license when they have one from another state.

Testing for a driver's license varies widely by situation, but basically if you have a driver's license from another state, you won't have to take the Colorado test. Just show up with the documents to prove who you are and where you live. And then, just like in Casablanca, you wait . . . and wait . . . and wait. . . . It can take hours since only one location issues new licenses, so bring a good book or iPod.

El Paso County Department of Motor Vehicle Locations

(719) 520-6240
www.car.elpasoco.com/motor_vehicle

Centennial Hall
200 S. Cascade Ave.

Powers Branch
5650 Industrial Place

Union Tower Center
8830 N. Union Blvd.

Teens in Colorado have a graduated license process.

- From age 15 years to 15 years, 6 months, a teenager can get a driver education permit. It's good for 3 years and requires that teens have passed the classroom portion of a driver education course.
- From 15 years, 6 months to 16 years, teens can get a driver awareness permit, which is good for 3 years. If a teen goes this route, he or she must hold the permit for 12 months before applying for a full driver's license. At that point, they must prove completion of a 4-hour driver

awareness program or have completed a 30-hour classroom course.

- A minor driver's license is for ages 16 to 20 years old. A teen must have held an instruction permit for 12 months (if under 18 years) and show a completed drive time log (if under 18 years). This license expires 20 days after the 21st birthday.

Colorado Driver's License Locations

It used to be that all Colorado Department of Motor Vehicles locations did almost everything you needed. Now, not so much. Be sure to check if the location you're going to has the service you require. Check at www.colorado.gov/apps/dor/dmv/smartstart/cardCenter.jsf.

2447 N. Union Blvd.
(719) 594-8701
Full-service office, with new Colorado driver's license, traffic records, motorcycle drive tests by appointment (weather permitting), limited reinstatements, and commercial driver's license written tests available.

200 S. Cascade Ave.
(719) 520-6240
Renewals of regular Colorado licenses only.

8830 N. Union Blvd.
(719) 520-6240
Renewals of regular Colorado licenses only.

5650 Industrial Pl., Suite 100
(719) 520-6240
Renewals of regular Colorado licenses only.

Vehicle Title & Registration

A vehicle must be registered in Colorado within 60 days after purchase or within 90 days after you become a Colorado resident. Since counties administer titles and registration, go to the El Paso County Department of Motor Vehicle offices (see box for locations). To register, bring proof of insurance, secure and verifiable identifications (such as driver's license or passport), title, bill of sale showing payment of taxes and fees, and vehicle emissions test for diesel.

To title a car here, go again to the El Paso County Department of Motor Vehicles. Bring all of the items needed to register the vehicle, plus a completed odometer disclosure form. You will be charged for title fees, registration, and any applicable sales tax. The title will be mailed in 4 to 6 weeks.

Libraries

*PIKES PEAK LIBRARY DISTRICT
(719) 531-6333
www.ppld.org
The heartbeat of Colorado Springs and vicinity can be felt at the vital, robust Pikes Peak Library District (PPLD). With 13 libraries, a mobile library service, and virtual resources, PPLD sees an annual circulation of 8.58 million—among the highest circulating systems in the country. Put it this way: If you walk into any PPLD library, you're one of an average 11,800 people per day who do the same. This works out to more than 4,300,000 visits per year. So with that much activity, you know PPLD has something to offer. That something includes a new library in Falcon, an All Pikes Peak Reads program each year (the community reads one book or about one topic and enjoys discussions and presentations on that topic/book), accessibility at all locations that includes large-type

Pikes Peak Library
District Locations

Briargate Library
9475 Briar Village Point, Suite 100
(719) 260-6882

Cheyenne Mountain Library
1785 S. 8th St., Suite 100
(719) 633-6278

East Library
5550 N. Union Blvd.
(719) 531-6333

Fountain Library
230 S. Main St., Fountain
(719) 382-5347

High Prairie Library
7035 Old Meridian Rd., Falcon
(719) 260-3650

Monument Library
1706 Lake Woodmoor Dr., Monument
(719) 488-2370

Old Colorado City Library
2418 W. Pikes Peak Ave.
(719) 634-1698

Palmer Lake Library
66 Lower Glenway, Palmer Lake
(719) 481-2587

Penrose Library
20 N. Cascade Ave.
(719) 531-6333

Rockrimmon Library
832 Village Center Dr.
(719) 593-8000

Ruth Holley Library
685 N. Murray Blvd.
(719) 597-5377

Sand Creek Library
1821 S. Academy Blvd.
(719) 597-7070

Ute Pass Library
8010 Severy, Cascade
(719) 684-9342

keyboards and more, extremely active adult literacy and foreign language programs, free computer use and computer classes, art exhibits, meeting rooms, a wildly successful and vibrant children's program (see the Kidstuff chapter), and more.

i To get a free library card, come to any location and show a picture ID with your current address. You must live within the Pikes Peak Library District, which is most of El Paso County, except for Manitou Springs and Security/Widefield.

Telephone & Internet

There are other choices, but most residents use one of two companies for their telephone (land lines) and Internet service. Cell phones are not covered in our listing because they are the usual suspects from around the US (Verizon, T-Mobile, etc.). Both companies listed here offer significant savings if you "bundle," or let them handle everything, including television.

COMCAST
213 N. Union Blvd.
(800) 266-2278
www.comcast.com

QWEST
(800) 475-7526
www.qwest.com

Television

Television service in the area can be confusing. Both Comcast and Qwest offer significant savings if you bundle services together, including telephone, TV, and Internet. The following companies can also work together; for instance, Qwest offers television service through Direct TV, and they'll even roll a Verizon cellular account into a bundle plan. Starview, the only local company, works with Dish Network. You'll need to do your own research for the plan and provider that best fits your needs, but the following list is a good place to start.

COMCAST
213 N. Union Blvd.
(800) 266-2278
www.comcast.com

DIRECT TV
(888) 777-2454
www.directv.com

DISH NETWORK
(888) 232-8689
www.dishnetwork.com

STARVIEW COMMUNICATIONS LLC
(719) 591-6571
www.starviewcommunications.com

QWEST
(800) 475-7526
www.qwest.com

Trash Pickup

You have choices in trash companies in Colorado Springs since it is a privatized service.

Price can vary but tends to be within a narrow range. Some homeowners associations have service arranged with one company. When this is not the case, perhaps the best way to decide the company for you is to watch the trash cycle in your neighborhood for one week. If one company serves most of the homes, picking that company might help keep your neighborhood less cluttered of empty trash cans on other days. The two biggest players in town are the national firm Waste Management and the locally owned Bestway Disposal. Some of the trash companies are:

BESTWAY DISPOSAL
650 Santa Fe St.
(719) 633-8709
www.bestwaydisposal.com

L & L DISPOSAL SERVICES
1005 S. El Paso St.
(719) 473-4861

ROCKY MOUNTAIN DISPOSAL
P.O. Box 1431
Colorado Springs, CO 80901
(719) 492-2050
www.rockymtndisposal.com

SPRINGS WASTE SYSTEMS
1990 Reliable Circle
(719) 634-7177
www.springswaste.com

WASTE MANAGEMENT
80 E. Chambers St.
(719) 632-8877
www.wm.com

Utilities

In 1924, residents of Colorado Springs voted for a four-service utility, which still serves the region today. Thus, all electricity, natural gas, water, and wastewater services are provided together.

COLORADO SPRINGS UTILITIES
111 S. Cascade Ave.
(719) 448-4800 or (800) 238-5434
www.csu.org

Voter Registration

To register to vote, you must have been a resident of your precinct 30 days prior to election, and you must register 29 days before an election. Registration must occur in the county in which you reside, so for Colorado Springs that means El Paso County.

- **Register Online:** www.govotecolorado .com.
- **US Mail:** print out the form from the website above, fill out completely, and mail to:

  El Paso County Clerk & Recorder
  Election Department
  P.O. Box 2007
  Colorado Springs, CO 80901

- **Fax:** print out the form from the website above, fill out completely, and fax to (719) 520-7327.
- **E-mail:** access the form at the above website, fill out completely, make a PDF format document, and e-mail to carweb@elpasoco.com.

YOUR HUMBLE ABODE

Whether looking for a modest starter apartment or grand dream mansion, there's a lot to choose from in the Pikes Peak region. So much, in fact, we can't begin to list all the available resources here. Consider this a good start, but do your own research to find that apartment complex, home rental by

owner, rental agency, or Realtor firm that will help you feel right at home.

Neighborhoods

One of the first questions asked when meeting new people is, What area of town do you live in? Especially here, that can really tell you about a person. There are more than 100 neighborhoods in Colorado Springs and surrounding regions. (See also the Area Overview chapter.)

The north areas (Monument, Palmer Lake, Black Forest, et al.) are at a higher altitude and thus get more snow. The more mountain feel of pine trees can be found north, west (Rockrimmon, Peregrine, West Side, et al.), and south (Skyway, Broadmoor, Star Ranch, et al.). Gorgeous Victorian homes and cute bungalows can be found downtown (Old North End, Shooks Run, et al.), and south. Newer homes can be found north (Briargate, Pine Creek, et al.) and east (Stetson Hills, Springs Ranch, Woodmen Hills, et al.). Both Peterson Air Force Base and the Army's Fort Carson support many surrounding communities, with living arrangements of every variety.

Many Realtors say that new residents tend to choose a neighborhood close to work. But if that isn't your desire, our best advice is to think hard about what you want. Proximity to hiking trails? New home, or perhaps an established neighborhood? Walking distance to stores? Whatever it is, a respected Realtor or property management consultant can steer you in the right direction.

Renting

There is no one right way to find a rental in Colorado Springs. If you're in the rental market, you need to be a bit resourceful and

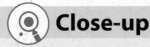

Close-up

Cooking at High Altitude

The usual comment from new residents to the region is, "I love it here. But I can't seem to bake a thing!" Chalk it up to high altitude. With less oxygen and atmospheric pressure in the air, cakes and breads tend to rise fast—and then cave in. And trying to cook pasta for the first time seems like it takes days for the water to boil. Some things you buy, like cake mixes, have high altitude adjustments on the side of the box.

Follow a few simple guidelines and enjoy all the fluffy biscuits you can eat.

- First, don't assume the sea-level recipe will fail. If you do have to modify it, try changing one thing at a time—it might be that one change makes all the difference.

- Sugar: Up to 6,000 feet, reduce by 2 tablespoons per each cup; 7,000 feet and above, reduce by 1 to 3 tablespoons for each cup.

- Liquid: Up to 6,000 feet, increase 2 to 4 tablespoons per each cup; 7,000 feet and above, increase 3 to 4 tablespoons per each cup of liquid.

- Baking powder: Up to 6,000 feet, reduce by ⅛ to ¼ teaspoon per each teaspoon; 7,000 feet and above, reduce by ¼ teaspoon per each teaspoon.

- Allow more time—a lot more time—for water to boil, and baked goods usually need more time at an increased temperature.

For more detailed information, check out the Colorado State University (CSU) Extension information at www.ext.colostate.edu/pubs/foodnut/p41.html.

persistent. That said, there are a few easy places to start.

On Saturday, *The Gazette* newspaper runs the home section, **Springshouses .com.** It is both printed and available online. You can find a decent listing of both apartments and homes for rent. There is also a section called "Apartment Directory" that has a listing of apartments and their area of town, prices, and amenities. It is by no means a complete listing of all apartments in town, but it's a good start.

Also, some Realtor firms in town run a rental locator service. Among others, **ERA Shields** (listed below in Owning section) maintains a relationship with more than 30 apartment complexes in the area. They also represent homes for rent. They have links with two furniture rental companies, one more economical and one more upscale, and can get discounts with moving companies. There is no fee for this service as the vendors pay them. Or, many Realtor firms have property management departments (among others, **Rusinak Real Estate,** 719-594-0100, www.rusinak.com).

There is also Craigslist.com, but the usual cautions and caveats precede this recommendation. The scams and misrepresentations are perhaps as well known with this route as the success stories.

Owning

You can, of course, work without a Realtor. But if you're relocating, the advantages of using a Realtor can't be understated. The city and region varies wildly in types of neighborhoods, housing, weather, schools, and activities, to name just a few aspects. Perhaps the first stop might be at the **Pikes Peak Association of Realtors** (719-633-7718, http://ppar.com). Established in 1902, the PPAR has 3,500 members. The website has everything from tools to find a Realtor, to information on school districts, to calculators, and a glossary for the home buyer.

If you'd rather jump straight to it, listed below are a few of the most respected, most active Realtor organizations in town. As always, do your own research for the company and Realtor agent that is best for you.

ERA SHIELDS REAL ESTATE
5475 Tech Center Dr., Suite 300

130 E. Cheyenne Mountain Blvd.
(719) 593-1000
www.erashields.com

THE PLATINUM GROUP, REALTORS
6760 Corporate Dr., Suite 300
(719) 536-4444
www.platinumhomesales.com

REALLIVING SELECT PROPERTIES
(formerly McGinnis GMAC Real Estate)
5353 N. Union Blvd., Suite 102
(719) 599-9000
www.realliving-selectproperties.com

RE/MAX
2630 Tenderfoot Hill St.
(719) 576-5000

1740 Chapel Hills Dr.
(719) 598-4700

5590 N. Academy Blvd.
(719) 548-8600

216 N. Tejon St.
(719) 576-5000

215 W. Rockrimmon Blvd.
(719) 599-8500

Volunteer

New in town? Don't know a soul? Or maybe you just retired and finally have too much time on your hands. Well, there's a solution. Get out there. Meet people. Do things. Make a difference in the community. Volunteer.

Nearly every church in town—and there are a lot of them—has some sort of outreach program. Like most cities, there is a need for volunteers at the local humane society and other animal rescue places. There are soup kitchens, programs for victims of domestic violence and abuse, services for seniors who are in need (see the Retirement chapter). You can help with a hotline, work for your favorite charity, or support an organization that helps folks suffering from health afflictions ranging from Alzheimer's to heart disease. You name it.

For a list of local agencies that can use volunteers, check out the **Pikes Peak United Way,** www.ppunitedway.org.

Here are some organizations that eagerly welcome volunteers of any age. These are some interesting, fulfilling volunteer jobs that meet needs specific to our region. They could become as full-time as you want (or stay low-key, if you prefer). You'll meet new friends, and you'll be giving something back to the community in which we live. Check them out.

BIG BROTHERS/BIG SISTERS
(719) 633-2443
www.biglittlecolorado.com

Maybe somebody did it for you—mentored you as a kid. Now you can return the favor. Big Brothers/Big Sisters is designed to help kids, one-on-one, by having an adult in their lives who is caring, stable, and attentive. It fosters relationships between responsible adults and kids 7 to 12 who might need just that. This need is especially important in the Pikes Peak region because of the number of youngsters who have a parent deployed overseas on military duty. There's a one-time application fee of $35.

CHEYENNE MOUNTAIN ZOO
(719) 633-9925
www.cmzoo.org/getinvolved/volunteer

There are a lot of ways to help out at the zoo. With hundreds of animals to care for and more than 500,000 annual visitors, there's always something to do. What would you do? Anything from taking care of the animals to adopting an animal, or you can become a zoo docent. Volunteers help keep the zoo running smoothly. Choose from among the animal, horticulture, membership, special events, and education departments, depending on your interests and skills. They do ask for a minimum commitment of 4 hours a month. The Cheyenne Mountain Zoo Auxiliary Docent Program is one of its most successful programs. They give tours and help children to care about wildlife and the natural world. No previous experience is necessary. They'll train you. There are youth volunteer programs, too. To become a volunteer, there is a one-time fee of $46.50 to cover the costs of a background check and other expenses (official shirt, nametag, etc.).

CHILDREN'S LITERACY CENTER
(719) 471-8672
www.peakreader.org

More than 800 local volunteers help kids who are struggling with a basic skill—reading—at the Children's Literacy Center. There are 11 community sites, including one on Fort Carson, where the need is great. Mentors work with children one-on-one. Besides volunteers, there is a need for small prizes for reading achievement, children's books, and games.

FRIENDS OF CHEYENNE CAÑON
(719) 385-6086
www.cheyennecanon.org

Cheyenne Cañon is full of streams, trails, picnic areas, and wildlife. It gets more than 500,000 visitors a year. The local neighborhood started this organization to support the city's efforts to manage the area—an effort especially appreciated during tight budgetary years. Trails maintenance, park hosts, and environmental education programs are supported by volunteers, and there's an ongoing need for public awareness and publicity. If you can handle any of those tasks, they need you. It's a lot of work to maintain a 1,600-acre park!

FRIENDS OF EL PASO COUNTY NATURE CENTERS
(719) 520-6387
www.elpasocountyparks.com

Kids can't get enough of their stimulating nature programs. Adults love them, too. But Bear Creek and Fountain Creek Nature Centers need help. Program leaders are needed for environmental education (especially the many school groups that come through), and anyone with a tree trimmer or shovel is welcome to help maintain the properties. It's a great way to stay in shape and enjoy the great outdoors in the Pikes Peak region. Also, grant writers are sometimes needed. The annual membership fees start at $20.

FRIENDS OF GARDEN OF THE GODS
(719) 219-0108
www.friendsofthegardenofthegods.org
The city's signature park is huge—1,325 acres—and needs lot of work just to keep it beautiful and clean. They have more than 200 members (with a fee of $25 for an individual adult member). Volunteers are always needed to help in the visitor center, act as park guides, perform trail maintenance, and write grants for special projects.

FRIENDS OF THE COLORADO SPRINGS PIONEERS MUSEUM
(719) 385-5990
E-mail: mmayberry@springsgov.com
Founded in 1969, the Friends now number more than 900 members. Their purpose is to provide volunteer assistance and financial support to the Colorado Springs Pioneers Museum for its exhibits and programs, the completion of restoration projects, and ongoing collection acquisition efforts. The group also sponsors fun events to draw the community into the museum. In addition, they publish a teacher's guide to local history, to be distributed in local schools, and help acquire historic documents and photos for the museum's archives. The list is long! The annual adult/individual fee is $25 a year to become a member.

FRIENDS OF THE MANITOU SPRINGS PUBLIC LIBRARY
(719) 685-5206
http://manitousprings.colibraries.org/
friends-of-the-library

Are you good at publicity? Fund-raising? Writing newsletters? Organizing events? And most of all, do you love books and reading? Well, if you live in Manitou Springs, then you should join this dynamic group. Other jobs include database management and serving on the board.

Gardening's Tricky Here

Topsoil? What topsoil? The Pikes Peak region is not known for its rich, dark, loamy soil. It's usually either sand or clay or rock—or all three. If you want to garden here, you have to first amend your soil. Then you have to figure out the growing season (much shorter than wetter, low-altitude areas) and order your seeds and plant accordingly. It's complicated. Wildflowers and tougher blossoms (like sunflowers) do well, but don't expect to grow citrus trees! Certain trees and grasses also do better than others. For some good information to get you started, consult the **Colorado State University Extension Service** (www.ext.colostate.edu) and maybe hook up with one of their local master gardeners for advice. Or stop by the **Xeriscape Demonstration Garden** at the Colorado Springs Utilities site, 2855 Mesa Rd., or call (719) 668-4555. You'll get some ideas on what grows well here, and lots of free brochures.

FRIENDS OF THE PIKES PEAK LIBRARY DISTRICT

(719) 531-6333

www.friendsppld.org

This group was established to support, preserve, and promote our public library system. The support group was established on the 50th anniversary of the Colorado Springs Public Library (March 11, 1955) and incorporated in 1969 as a nonprofit organization. Today, with 900 members, the group sponsors and supports numerous programs and events to further the enjoyment of reading and love for books for everyone. Some of its annual events include seasonal book sales, awards ceremonies (the Frank Waters Award and the Golden Quill Award) honoring local and Colorado authors, the Betty Field Youth Writing Workshop, and other special events. The only skill you need is being able to read, and the only motivation you need is loving books. An individual membership is $20 a year and you can apply online at http://friendsppld.org/MEMBERSHIP-APPLICATION.pdf.

ROCK LEDGE RANCH LIVING HISTORY ASSOCIATION

(719) 578-6777

www.rockledgeranch.com/become-a-member

The Rock Ledge Ranch Historic Site is an educational, nonprofit living history farm and museum illustrating life in the Pikes Peak region in four time periods from 1775 to 1907. It includes the 1860's Galloway Homestead, the 1880's Chambers Home and Ranch, and the 1907 Edwardian Country Estate. The history association members help support the site, owned by the City of Colorado Springs and adjacent to the Garden of the Gods. The group helps preserve and enhance the living history program of the ranch and encourages citizen and volunteer involvement and participation in heritage programs. It also works to preserve the history of Colorado Springs and the Pikes Peak Region. An individual membership is $20 a year.

TRAILS AND OPEN SPACE COALITION

(719) 633-6884

www.trailsandopenspaces.org

If you're really into the outdoors, this is the group for you. You'll get a good workout (no gym for you!) maintaining local trails and open space, befriending orphan parks in need of some TLC, and generally tending to the area's natural beauty. This group also holds some political clout and is responsible for the city acquiring some key properties, such as Red Rock Canyon, for public use.

RETIREMENT

Colorado Springs can have a snowy, cold winter, which means that a good number of retirees go south for the season. Still, there are plenty of year-round senior residents, and a number of services and resources are here to support them. Both Silver Key and the Area Agency on Aging have many programs designed to help seniors stay living independently, in their own homes. There are meals, transportation, and activities that help retirees stay healthy, social, and active. And the housing choices are so deep and varied, we can only give a small glimpse of the options available. Health and hospice care are also here to tend to the ailing and lend dignity and compassion when needed most. So although it might be cold outside, the Pikes Peak region has a warm place in its heart for our seniors.

SERVICES & ORGANIZATIONS

AREA AGENCY ON AGING
15 S. 7th St.
(719) 471-7080
http://ppacg.org/aaa/info
The Pikes Peak Area Council of Government's Area Agency on Aging (AAA) helps older adults in the Pikes Peak region locate the resources they need. Ideally, this helps seniors and those involved in their lives navigate the barriers to independent living, allowing them to stay in their own homes as long as possible. The agency administers programs and services funded through the Federal Older Americans Act and Colorado state funding. AAA also assists with the coordination and development of a comprehensive system of services for seniors in El Paso, Park, and Teller Counties. Their programs run from mastering daily life activities for those with vision impairments to a workshop all about Medicare. There is a

hotline for senior information and assistance and advocates for seniors in nursing and assisted living facilities. Services provided by partners with AAA include audiology, counseling for caregivers, home safety renovation, legal assistance, nutrition education and counseling, respite care, transportation, and more.

> **i** The Area Agency on Aging publishes a Senior Information Directory, or "Yellow Book," with more than 600 services for older adults in El Paso, Park, and Teller Counties. It contains information on adult day care, elder abuse prevention, home-delivered meals, legal services, and more. Copies are available at local libraries and the AAA office or by calling (719) 471-2096.

PIKES PEAK HOSPICE AND PALLIATIVE CARE
(719) 633-3400
www.pikespeakhospice.org

Two community volunteers started this nonprofit organization in the late '70s, and it's grown from serving one patient and family a day to serving more than 240 patients and families daily. The depth of service to the community can be seen in the operating budget for a recent year: $17 million. The agency offers hospice care for those at end of life when the focus is on comfort and caring, as well as palliative care for those with severe, life-limiting disease who may still be seeking treatment aimed at a cure. They operate a pharmacy and offer complimentary therapies to relieve stress, decrease pain, and enhance quality of life. They also offer grief support, including a specialized grief program for children. Hospice and palliative care services are available in a patient's home, in nursing homes and assisted living facilities, and in the agency's own specialized acute care inpatient unit. Since 1998, the Pikes Peak Hospice Foundation has raised funds for the continued support of hospice and palliative care services.

PILLAR
202 E. Cheyenne Mountain Blvd., Suite 101
(719) 633-4991
www.visitpillar.org

Pillar is for those who want a vibrant, interesting life at any age. Pillar brings opportunities for new interests, new friends, and new excursions through classes, tours, trips, and strolls. Past classes have run from the screening and then discussion of a foreign vampire movie to downsizing a home to the impact of German Americans and Irish Americans on Baltimore and Boston to watercolors for the holidays. Classes and excursions are open to any age. The nonprofit organization keeps fees to a minimum so that many can afford the mind and body adventures.

AAA Resources for Seniors

Family Caregiver Support Center
(719) 471-7080, ext. 115
Helps caregivers manage their responsibilities as well as take care of themselves.

Long-Term Care Ombudsmen
(719) 471-7080, ext. 113
Advocate for residents of nursing homes and assisted-living facilities.

Mobility Management
(719) 471-7080, ext. 108
Helps seniors and disabled adults find transportation.

Senior Information & Assistance
(719) 471-2096
Provides information and assistance on all senior issues.

Senior Insurance Assistance Program
(719) 635-4891
Provides counseling in medical insurance and claims assistance.

---

*SILVER KEY SENIOR SERVICES
2250 Bott Ave.
(719) 884-2300
www.silverkey.org

Silver Key has been in the Pikes Peak region since 1971. The local nonprofit keeps seniors engaged, cared for, and valued members of the community by providing services and programs for nutrition, independent living, and transportation. To be eligible, seniors must reside in either Colorado Springs or Manitou Springs and be 60 years or older.

Nutrition services include the national program, Meals on Wheels (719-884-2330). Volunteers deliver hot, freshly prepared meals Monday through Friday and reheatable meals on the weekends. The service can be a permanent arrangement or short term for those who might need extra help, such as after a surgery. The volunteers who deliver the meals also offer some companionship. Meals on Wheels can be arranged on plans for 3, 5, or 7 days a week, and there is a fee.

The independent living services include home care, which assists seniors with non-medical issues such as homemaking and personal care. This service also offers the companionship component, which is sometimes one of the most valuable gifts to seniors. Silver Key also loans health and medical equipment when needed and offers a guardianship program to act as advocates for seniors.

Finally, Silver Key's transportation (719-884-2380) helps those who can't drive, those who aren't comfortable driving, those who need temporary transportation assistance when a car is in the shop, or those who'd rather travel with friends. Rides can be arranged for medical appointments, grocery shopping, or other independent needs. Silver Key also keeps the rides going for social reasons, such as to a free community movie or other event. They post a recreation calendar on the website, which lists all the social trips planned every month.

SENIOR CENTERS

COLORADO SPRINGS SENIOR CENTER
1514 N. Hancock Ave.
(719) 385-5933
Located just northeast of downtown, this active center operates as a rec center for those 55 and older. There are clinical/medical services such as foot and toenail care, blood pressure checks, and massage. Classes—many of them free—include art, computer, and dance. There are lifelong learning classes, legal and business services, support groups, and interest group clubs. A large multipurpose room is available for rental, dances, and more.

FALCON SENIOR SERVICES
www.falconseniorservicesinc.org
A few years ago, a group of friends in Falcon started talking about organizing services specifically for the folks in the eastern-plains area. Out of such humble beginnings, great things are both happening and in the works. Currently under way are plans to fund and build a 6,000-square-foot Falcon Senior Center. In the meantime, a potluck lunch is held every second Wednesday at the Fellowship Hall of Falcon Baptist Church, 11095 Eggar Rd. A main course is provided while members bring sides (a donation toward the main course is requested but not required). The luncheon also features door prizes, a book exchange, announcements, and entertainment or speakers. Also, strength and flexibility exercise classes are offered on Monday and Friday at Grace Community Church, 9475 Grace Church View. Also offered are foot care clinics once a month, and a 10-passenger mini bus with wheelchair lifts is available for those who need transportation. Plans are for the bus to be used for shopping excursions

as well, once volunteers are found to do the additional driving.

FOUNTAIN VALLEY SENIOR CENTER
5745 Southmoor Dr.
(719) 520-6470
Located on the south end of Colorado Springs, this center offers trips and tours, health education and screening, support groups, and legal assistance. They also offer fitness classes as well as arts and crafts from crocheting to porcelain doll making to wood carving. There are also indoor recreation opportunities, such as going to movies or bowling.

TELLER SENIOR COALITION
312 N. Center St., Woodland Park
(719) 687-3330
www.tellerseniorcoalition.org
Located in Woodland Park, this senior center is also the mountain community's agency for senior services. They provide transportation, hold the Golden Circle lunch on-site, provide other nutritional opportunities, help make seniors' homes safer with grants and resources for home improvements, provide respite services for caregivers, run an information and referral line, offer free tax assistance, legal aid, and more. Plus, there are exercise classes and social outings.

HOUSING

The housing for seniors in the Pikes Peak region covers choices for vital, independent retirees to those who need round-the-clock care. Listed here are just a few examples of area options. Further research is needed by anyone in the market, and the best place to start is with AAA's Yellow Book, which lists all facilities by affordable housing organization, assisted living facilities, independent living,

skilled nursing facilities, and retirement and/or multilevel communities.

ACACIA PARK APARTMENTS
104 E. Platte Ave.
(719) 387-6700
These are subsidized apartments, with the rent based on 30 percent of a resident's income. Located downtown across the street from Acacia Park, this handsome brick building—a former hotel—offers 61 units in either an efficiency or one-bedroom configuration. There are elevators and laundry facilities on-site, and the Golden Circle noon meal is served here every day except Sat.

HOUSING AUTHORITY OF COLORADO SPRINGS
831 S. Nevada Ave.
(719) 387-6700
www.csha.us
This affordable housing organization is a resource for apartments for low- to moderate-income seniors. Located in the same facility are the housing authorities for both El Paso County and Manitou Springs. Tenants must meet income guidelines. This organization also oversees the Golden Circle nutrition program.

NAMASTÉ ALZHEIMER CENTER
2 Penrose Blvd.
(719) 776-6300
www.centuraseniors.org/namaste
Operated by Centura Health, Namasté is a 64-bed Alzheimer's facility configured into four pods, depending on a patient's level of functioning. There is also an adult day program specializing in Alzheimer's clients. The lovely campus is tucked behind The Broadmoor and features big pine trees and a small lake that family members can walk

around with the patients. In the highest functioning pod, a large cage of songbirds is in the sitting room, and staff and volunteer groups come in often with craft projects and for companionship. It can be hard to reserve a space as Namasté is quite often at capacity.

REGENCY TOWER APARTMENTS
921 Green Star Dr.
(719) 633-2121
http://regency-apartments.com

These are non-subsidized apartments for adults 55 years and older. The 124 apartments feature either one or two bedrooms and elevators to each floor. Located near The Broadmoor, the building features a common lounge with TV and piano, and a coffee and game room with fully equipped kitchen. Outside is a heated pool and patio with barbecue. Each floor contains a laundry room and extra storage facility. Group social programs are offered.

VILLAGE AT SKYLINE
2365 Patriot Heights
(719) 667-5360
www.brookdaleliving.com/village-at-skyline.aspx

Run by the national firm Brookdale, which has three other facilities in Colorado Springs, Village at Skyline is a multilevel community. The housing choices run the full gamut of continuing care: independent living, assisted living, Alzheimer's and dementia care, and skilled nursing care. Accommodations run from garden homes to apartments to rooms. Set just west of downtown near Bear Creek Park, the large campus is well maintained and convenient to family in south, central, or north Colorado Springs. Services and amenities include meals in a restaurant-style dining room, arts and crafts studio, a golf putting green, a computer center, beauty/barber shop, and fitness center with pool.

SENIOR MEALS

Seniors do not need to go hungry in the Pikes Peak region. Volunteers will deliver food, and there are community meals for those who long for good food and company. There is even help with transportation, if that's needed to attend a community meal.

GOLDEN CIRCLE NUTRITION PROGRAM
104 E. Platte Ave.
(719) 387-6758
www.csha.us/Golden%20Circle%20Information.htm

Golden Circle offers seniors a low-cost, nutritious, delicious hot noon meal. Sponsored by the Housing Authority of the City of Colorado Springs with funding from federal, state, and city grants as well as charitable donations, Golden Circle lunches are served at 24 locations throughout the Pikes Peak region. Intended as a way to help seniors live independently and enjoy time with others, Golden Circle serves about 800 to 1,000 meals every weekday and on Sunday, and a kosher meal is served at a local temple two days a week. The menu changes daily and can feature baked ham, sweet potatoes, and spinach to bratwurst, cabbage, and rye bread. Diners must qualify by being 60 years or older and a few other requirements. There is a minimal suggested cost, but no eligible diner is turned away because of inability to pay. A punch card offering a discount of the suggested cost is available. Reservations are appreciated at most Golden Circle sites, which range from churches to community centers to senior housing developments.

MARION HOUSE SOUP KITCHEN
14 W. Bijou St.
(719) 475-7314
http://ccharitiescs.org
Run by Catholic Charities since 1985, Marion House provides hot, nutritious meals to anyone who needs them. Open 365 days a year, guests include struggling families, seniors on a fixed income, the working poor, veterans, people with disabilities, unsupported teens, and, at only about 30 percent of the guests, the homeless. Most days, more than 600 people are served, although that number rises toward the middle and end of the month. Marion House is operated by a small staff and an army of volunteers.

MEALS ON WHEELS
(719) 884-2330
www.silverkey.org
(See entry under Silver Key in this chapter.)

VOLUNTEERING

There's no need for any senior to feel lonely and useless—a number of local and national agencies specialize in connecting seniors with valuable volunteer experiences. From permanent part-time or by the project, from sitting with other seniors to assisting in the medical field, numerous opportunities are open to seniors in the Pikes Peak area.

SENIOR CORPS
(800) 424-8867 (National Service Hotline)
www.seniorcorps.gov
Senior Corps is a program of the Corporation for National and Community Service, an independent federal agency. The program recognizes that people 55 and over have both the time and experience valuable to a community, and connects willing seniors with myriad needs. Senior Corps has programs for foster grandparents and senior companions. Also available is the RSVP program, which connects seniors with a variety of service opportunities that match their particular skills and availability, from building homes to immunizing children.

SILVER KEY SENIOR SERVICES
2250 Bott Ave.
(719) 884-2300
www.silverkey.org
Silver Key (see entry in this chapter) runs on volunteers. Not only do volunteers assist in the services for seniors, Silver Key actively uses seniors as volunteers. There are plenty of jobs for able-bodied seniors, and even those with mobility and/or other issues. In fact, Silver Key is more willing to work with seniors as volunteers than many other nonprofits in the community. Jobs run from meal delivery to fund-raising to giving companionship, among others. From all aspects of services delivery, Silver Key is very social and prides itself on overall family atmosphere.

VOLUNTEER PIKES PEAK
(719) 955-0762
www.volunteerpikespeak.org
Volunteer Pikes Peak is a web-based database that lists volunteer opportunities from more than 140 local agencies. A collaboration of Pikes Peak United Way and the Center for Nonprofit Excellence, the website is easy to view and navigate, and you can browse all the open jobs as the agencies keep the opportunities current. Volunteer needs run from one day events to long-term commitments.

EDUCATION & CHILD CARE

Diversity in educational institutions does not come more far-ranging than in the Pikes Peak region. From two of the world's most competitive, elite higher education colleges to preschools that focus on those already identified as at-risk, our region encompasses it all.

In higher education, there are a plethora of choices. Colleges and universities cater from interests of general studies to rocket science. There are a number of religious-based curriculums, offering programs for those looking at ministry as a profession. And technical and vocational schools prepare the population for careers as diverse as refrigeration repair and massage therapy.

Elementary through secondary schools are just as diverse. There are traditional public schools, magnet public schools, the option to choice into a different school, and charter schools. That's just public. For private schools there are religious-based, curriculum-based, and boarding schools that allow local day students. If you can't find the right school for your family, you probably just haven't done enough research. And in general, the schools are good. Overall, the students in the Pikes Peak region achieve Colorado Student Assessment Program (CSAP) scores and high school graduation rates 3 to 5 percent higher than the state of Colorado averages.

Preschool and child care are populated by a number of national chains, strong public-funded options and many, many local church, community, or private concerns. It's still a lot of work to explore all the options, but options there are—in abundance.

HIGHER EDUCATION

For a medium-sized city, Colorado Springs is home to some very high-powered learning institutions. Two of the country's best colleges are here, and many good, smaller colleges are here as well. A number of colleges with main campuses elsewhere also run secondary campuses here; most of those are not listed here. Technical and vocational schools are popular in the region, and we seem to have our fair share of religious training available. From aerospace engineer to medical assistant, the Pikes Peak region has access to training for it. In fact, if the amount, quality, and diversity of higher education available are signs of an area's wealth, we in Colorado Springs are rich indeed.

Colleges & Universities

COLORADO COLLEGE
14 E. Cache La Poudre St.
(719) 389-6000
www.coloradocollege.edu

Colorado College, known as CC, is one of America's most prestigious private, liberal arts institutions. The student body is an exceptional group of enthused, intrigued individuals, the great majority of whom graduated in the top 25 percent of their high school class. The college is unique in almost every way—but the first thing to spotlight is the block plan. It divides the academic year into eight 3½-week segments, or blocks. During a block, students take only one course, and the professors teach only one course. The students cover the same amount of material as in a semester system since they take four classes a semester and eight classes in a year. But what this block plan allows is something wholly unlike the traditional semester.

i Colorado College campus overlaps a few blocks of North Cascade Avenue and North Nevada Avenue. Pedestrians have the right-of-way. When driving by and through the campus, slow down and keep a wary eye. Most students and faculty look before entering the street, but a few plunge ahead into traffic. Cross walks, especially on North Cascade Avenue, are marked well with bright yellow paint and flashing lights.

Students in the block plan find complete immersion in that one class. Since it's a given that students do not have responsibilities to another class and/or professor, discussions can go on as long as needed. Schedules can be flexible in terms of time and location, leading to creative research and extended field work opportunities. There is a more hands-on, experiential reference to the learning. In addition, visiting professors and guest lecturers can be engaged since the time frame is condensed. Students do not find themselves cramming for multiple midterms and finals since they have only the one class. And, when it's over, there is an extended break between blocks so both students and professors can rest and rejuvenate before diving into another subject.

This immersion in a subject translates to an acute level of academic rigor and vigor. The school focuses on the traditional liberal arts studies as well as a number of special programs, such as Southwest studies, Russian and Eurasian studies, biochemistry, neuroscience, environmental studies, and a strong across-the-curriculum writing program. The four-year college offers bachelor's degrees in many subjects and a Master of Arts in teaching.

The approximately 2,000 students enjoy a green, sprawling campus just north of downtown. The grounds were reserved by Gen. William Jackson Palmer when he laid out the town of Colorado Springs in 1871. The college opened on May 6, 1874, which was two years before Colorado became a state.

Thus, a few of the buildings are original, constructed with huge blocks of stone and ornate roofs, and are on the National Register of Historic Places. But since the '50s, many of the buildings are new, including the exquisite Cornerstone Arts Center, opened in 2008. Lush lawns separate the buildings, and works of art are placed throughout the campus.

The community of Colorado Springs enjoys the numerous events sponsored by CC, and the college's Division I ice hockey team, regularly ranked in the top 10 in the country, has a loyal, almost rabid following within the area. The CC Tigers, as they're known, cause the fans to dress in stripes, tails, ears, and enough bright yellow to pave another yellow brick road. They play at the 8,000-seat Colorado Springs World Arena, and many of the games are sold out or close to it. (See also The Arts chapter.)

PIKES PEAK COMMUNITY COLLEGE
5675 S. Academy Blvd.
(719) 502-2000
www.ppcc.edu

Founded in 1968, Pikes Peak Community College (PPCC) has seven locations in the Pikes Peak region. PPCC offers more than 150 two-year programs in liberal arts and sciences, career and technical education, and the popular transfer programs, which are used by nearly half the student body. For those not looking to transfer, some of the signature programs include outdoor leadership and recreation technology, which has received national recognition, and zookeeping technology, which is one of only two in the country affiliated with a mountain zoo. Recently, PPCC added a water and wastewater technology program. PPCC's allied health programs, which encompass nursing, emergency medical services, dental assisting, radiology, and other health-related disciplines, account for 25 percent of the school's total enrollment of about 13,000 students. A nationally recognized simulation lab allows hands-on training for nursing and emergency medical students. PPCC's criminal justice and fire science technology programs provide training for the majority of first responder personnel in southeastern Colorado. Being in close proximity to four major military installations and the Air Force Academy, PPCC has a variety of military and veterans' programs that focus specifically on their needs.

REGIS UNIVERSITY
7450 Campus Dr.
(303) 458-4126 or (800) 568-8932
www.regis.edu

Colorado Springs is a satellite campus to Regis University's main, 81-acre campus in Denver, which has earned a top-tier ranking for best colleges and universities by *U.S. News & World Report*. The Jesuit school in the Pikes Peak region has a student population of about 1,000 students and has graduated nearly 30,000 students over the past 30 years. Students tend to be professionals earning degrees while continuing full-time employment. At the Colorado Springs campus, about 10 undergraduate degrees are available, as well as master's degrees in business administration, management, and computer information systems. The campus has recently launched a post-graduate certificate in counseling military families. This degree is offered to master's level counselors who desire specialized training in counseling the military population in clinical mental health counseling or marriage and family therapy.

UNITED STATES AIR FORCE ACADEMY
www.usafa.af.mil

The United States Air Force Academy (USAFA) is one of the nation's premier service academies as well as a military installation. While there, the more than 4,000 cadets live and study on rolling, green grounds that are some of the most beautiful in the region. In the center of the main academic buildings and dorms, the spires of the iconic Air Force Academy Cadet Chapel can be seen from across the Pikes Peak region.

The grueling, four-year program encompasses intellectual, physical, and psychological challenges. Each cadet graduates with a

Bachelor of Science and a commission as a second lieutenant in the Air Force.

While there, cadets undertake a core curriculum of science, engineering, social sciences, and humanities, additional electives required for one of 25 major areas of study. About 60 percent of the cadets complete majors in science and engineering; the other 40 percent graduate in the social sciences and humanities. Some of the most popular majors include management, astronautical engineering, international affairs and political science, history, behavioral science, civil engineering, aeronautical engineering, electrical engineering, and engineering mechanics.

The majority of the academy's nearly 600 faculty members are Air Force officers. They are selected primarily from career-officer volunteers who have established outstanding records and have at least a master's degree; more than 35 percent have doctorates. The academy also has several distinguished civilian professors and associate professors who serve one or more years. Officers from other services are members of the faculty as well, and a small number of officers from allied countries teach in the foreign language, history, and political science departments. Distinguished civilian and military lecturers also share their expertise with the cadets during the academic year.

The academy offers some of the most extensive physical education, intramural sports, and intercollegiate athletic programs in the nation. Cadets take at least three different physical education courses each year. The Colorado Springs community enjoys the proximity to these elite athletes, teams, and facilities. The football games in particular, which usually feature fly-bys prior to games, are community favorites.

The academy offers courses in flying, navigation, soaring, and parachuting, building from basic skills to instructor duties. Cadets may fly light aircraft with the Cadet Flying Team. Those not qualified for flight training must enroll in a basic aviation course. Astronomy and advanced navigation courses also are available. Students bound for pilot training enroll in the flight screening program at the academy and fly the DA-20 Katana aircraft.

Unlike traditional colleges, summers are not time off for the cadets. Over the four years, they are required to complete various training, including 6 weeks of basic cadet training in their first summer, combat survival training during cadets' second summer, and training options such as airborne parachute training and leadership training.

Admission to the academy is extremely competitive and requires a nomination by a member of Congress.

In addition to the college, the USAFA is home to the 10th Air Base Wing, which comprises more than 3,000 military, civilian, and contract personnel. These staff conduct all base-level support activities for a military community of about 25,000 people, including law enforcement and force protection, civil engineering, communications, logistics, military and civilian personnel, financial management, services, and the clinic.

UNIVERSITY OF COLORADO AT COLORADO SPRINGS
1420 Austin Bluffs Pkwy.
(719) 255-8227 or (800) 990-8227
www.uccs.edu
Sitting against a bluff above downtown, the University of Colorado at Colorado Springs (UCCS) campus used to be the little brother in the CU system. Not so anymore. Founded

in 1965, it is the fastest growing campus in Colorado and one of the fastest growing campuses in the nation. There are currently 36 bachelor's, 19 master's, and 5 doctoral degree programs with 6 academic colleges on campus: business, education, engineering and applied science, public affairs, letters, arts and sciences, and nursing and health sciences. In addition, UCCS offers many unique programs such as the bachelor's degree in innovation, geropsychology, and professional golf management. *U.S. News & World Report* has named UCCS a top Western public university and the undergraduate engineering program one of the nation's best.

The 532-acre, sloped campus supports a student population of about 9,000. The average undergrad is slightly older at 24 years, and the military make up a significant percentage of the student body. There are also about 30 US Olympic athletes pursuing degrees at UCCS.

The campus has gone from old, original buildings to innovative, impressive structures as the predominant look. Centennial Hall recently underwent a $17 million renovation, making it now the fourth LEED-certified building on campus. It joins the imposing, contemporary, and environmentally friendly Science and Engineering building, a $56.1 million, 159,000-square-foot home to the departments of biology, mechanical and aerospace engineering, and physics as well as the CU Institute for Bioenergetics and the National Institute for Science, Space, and Security Centers. Also LEED certified are the newer Gallogly Events Center and the Recreation Center, a 54,000-square-foot facility with an elevated, two-lane track, pools, dance studio, a large fitness area, and a bike repair and ski/snowboard tuning shop.

Technical & Vocational Schools

COLORADO INSTITUTE OF MASSAGE THERAPY
1490 W. Fillmore St.
(719) 634-7347
www.coimt.com
The Colorado Institute of Massage Therapy (CIMT) has been in the area since 1985. The school operates out of an office complex in the northwest part of town, and was one of the original three schools in the US to include the International Academy of Neuromuscular Therapy (IANMT) certification into its curriculum. CIMT prepares its 75 students for a professional massage therapy practice through two programs: the year-long, comprehensive neuromuscular/trigger point program or the eight-month integrative techniques certification program. The school gives students access to a variety of faculty, including certified neuromuscular therapists, a chiropractor, physical therapists, massage therapists, a certified fitness therapist, and an exercise physiologist. Students also have the opportunity to provide on-site massage therapy at the hospitals of Penrose-St. Francis Health Services. CIMT has a nearly 95 percent first-time pass rate for those sitting for the National Certification exam (NCBTMB).

COLORADO TECHNICAL UNIVERSITY
4435 N. Chestnut St.
(719) 598-0200
www.coloradotech.edu
Started here in 1965, Colorado Technical University (CTU) offers higher education for working students. Although this was the first campus, there are now five others throughout Colorado and bordering states, and an online capability as well. The more than 2,000 students at the Colorado Springs CTU

campus earn degrees in business and management, criminal justice and legal studies, and engineering and computer science.

FULLER THEOLOGICAL SEMINARY
540 N. Cascade Ave.
(719) 385-0085
www.fuller.edu/colorado
Fuller has been part of the community since 1977, first as a partner with Young Life, and then as a regional campus since 1995. The main campus is in California. About 300 students attend the Colorado Springs seminary, 75 as local students and the remainder who come in for intensive classes a couple of times each year. Located downtown, Fuller is an evangelical, multidenominational, international, multiethnic community that offers a Master of Divinity degree as well as Masters of Arts in Christian leadership, theology, and theology and ministry. Certificate programs are also offered in youth ministry and Christian studies.

INTELLITEC COLLEGES
2315 E. Pikes Peak Ave.
(719) 632-7626
www.intelliteccollege.com
IntelliTec has been in Colorado Springs since 1965. There are two other campuses in the state, including Pueblo, but the Colorado Springs campus is the main one. The college offers career-focused training in allied health care, business, and technology. Programs lead to professional certificates or an associate degree. The Colorado Springs campus population is about 650 students. Specific programs include automotive technician, HVAC–refrigeration technician, computer and networks systems technician, architectural drafting and design/CAD, mechanical drafting/CAD mechanical, medical

administration, and medical assistant. The Pueblo campus has recently started training in cosmetology.

NAZARENE BIBLE COLLEGE
1111 Academy Park Loop
(719) 884-5000 or (800) 873-3873
www.nbc.edu
The Pikes Peak region is home to more than 100 Christian organizations, so the 43-acre Nazarene Bible College campus is a natural fit in the community. The college was opened in 1967 to prepare ministers, rather than the broader assignment of providing liberal arts education for both laity and clergy. Nazarene Bible College is one of the 10 Nazarene institutions in the US given the responsibility and funding to deliver multicultural contextual education. Graduates of the four-year Bachelor of Arts in ministry degree, with a major in pastoral ministries, meet denominational requirements for ordination to the ministry. The approximately 1,500 students have an average age of 38 years and come from across the country and the world.

REMINGTON COLLEGE
6050 Erin Park Dr., Suite 250
(719) 532-1234
www.remingtoncollege.edu
Remington gives students hands-on training so they're ready to enter the workforce. The school works with Colorado Springs employers to make sure the curriculum and training is relevant and in demand. The college has been serving the area for more than 10 years and regularly sees an enrollment of 200 and up. The program covers bachelor's and associate's degrees in criminal justice and diplomas in medical assisting, medical billing and coding, and pharmacy technician. The

school also encourages students to volunteer locally at area schools, on civic committees, and in civic organizations.

PUBLIC SCHOOLS

The Pikes Peak region is not one big public school district. There are many, and they are varied: from huge districts to some so tiny they serve about 300 students in total. In fact, there are twice as many school districts within the region as are listed here. Those not listed tend to be ranching or mountain community schools that serve a very limited population. We figure you know what you're getting into in regards to those school districts.

In the larger districts, differences can be stunning and a family's choice of schools close to overwhelming. There are traditional public schools, charter schools, and the option to "choice" into a public school outside of your neighborhood area. Many citizens do choose to send their kids to the local public school; but for those who want something specific in their child's education, chances are it is offered somewhere in the Pikes Peak region.

i Go to the Colorado Springs/ Pueblo Emergency Reports for a quick check on snow days and school closings: www.flashalertcs.net.

In addition to the programs and services listed here, most public school districts also offer support services for home school, which is very popular in the region. And almost every bigger district has at least one charter school under its umbrella, although the charter schools tend to operate separately while still offering those students some of the benefits of the district, such as the opportunity to play on a large sports team.

ACADEMY SCHOOL DISTRICT 20
1110 Chapel Hills Dr.
(719) 234-1200
www.asd20.org
Academy School District 20, or D20 as it's commonly called, is one of the most well respected school districts in the Pikes Peak region. Standardized test scores remain consistently high across grade levels, schools, and the district in general. A great percentage of high school students graduate, many with national awards, scholarships, and admission to colleges and universities across the country.

The district formed with the construction of the US Air Force Academy in 1957, when nearby schools and the new academy schools consolidated into one district. The past two decades have seen so much growth within D20 boundaries that new schools crop up at a fast pace. And that is one of the keys to the district: a sound tax base, and constituents who tend to vote generously on school issues.

D20 currently consists of about 23,000 students at five traditional high schools, five traditional middle schools, and 18 elementary schools utilizing the K–5, 6–8, and 9–12 grade level configuration. There is also one charter school, an alternative high school, an online high school, an alternative middle school, and a home school academy for K–9. Each school concentrates on core academic subjects, but the way they teach that information can vary widely. Depending on the school, students can participate in the International Baccalaureate (IB) program from elementary through high school, as well as magnet schools with a focus in science, the arts, or math. The district's School in the Woods teaches fourth grade based on the natural sciences in a natural setting within the Black Forest, and The Classical Academy is the largest K–12 charter school in the state.

Academic programs range from Odyssey of the Mind, National Honor Society, DECA, and Future Business Leaders. Every school houses a library/media and computer center.

Co-curricular activities are comprehensive. Music and physical education teachers are in every elementary school, and every high school offers a wide range of performing arts classes and opportunities. Students at all levels are encouraged in sports activities, and intramural and interscholastic athletic activities are strong. D20 schools often compete in various Colorado High School Athletic Association championships.

The district partners with Pikes Peak Community College to offer advanced and vocational classes, and D20 and Colorado Technical University have a program allowing online students to earn college credits. The district also promotes several cooperative corporate ventures, such as the Kennedy Center Imagination Celebration and an innovative elementary hands-on science program funded by Hewlett-Packard.

CHEYENNE MOUNTAIN SCHOOL DISTRICT 12
1775 LaClede St.
(719) 475-6100
www.cmsd.k12.co.us
Located in the southwest corner of Colorado Springs, Cheyenne Mountain School District is another of the excellent school districts in the region. Commonly referred to as D12 or Cheyenne, this district has a total enrollment of approximately 4,600 students in preschool through grade 12. There are five elementary schools offering grades K–6, and one preschool. The district has one junior high school for grades 7–8, a high school for grades 9–12, and a charter school serving grades K–6.

District 12's students are annually near the top of all schools in Colorado in academic achievement. Approximately 90 percent of the high school graduates go

---

Choice in Public Schools

Maybe it's the influence of the independent West—the "don't fence me in" attitude. Whatever the reason, families in the Pikes Peak region get "choice" in their schools. Choice means any student in any Colorado school district can choice into any other school in any school district. The rules include registering within deadlines set by each district (they differ), and when there are space issues, enrollment might be denied.

Families opt to choice into a school outside of their neighborhood schools for almost as many reasons as there are schools: schedule, curriculum, friends, and location. Choicing into schools for sports is frowned upon, and there are a number of barriers to prevent this from happening. But whatever the reason, families are utilizing the choice option in record numbers. Some districts even provide transportation for choice students, but that varies by district and geography.

on to college, many to some of the most prestigious colleges and universities in the nation.

Programs offered district-wide include instructional technology, special education, instrumental music, vocal music, art, drama, world language, and physical education. In addition, there is an early intervention preschool and honors classes at the junior high and high school level.

A newer program at the high school is CU Succeed Gold, which allows students to earn dual credit from the University of Colorado for courses such as AP Economics, AP Psychology, and AP US History. Also new is an EnVision Math curriculum for all students in grades K–6.

The district fronts a full range of co-curricular programs, and its high school sports teams are consistently vying for state championships, especially in men's and women's varsity tennis, women's varsity volleyball, and varsity ice hockey.

Cheyenne is the rare exception to the area in that it does not provide daily transportation.

COLORADO SPRINGS SCHOOL DISTRICT 11
1115 N. El Paso St.
(719) 520-2000
www.d11.org

Colorado Springs School District 11, or D-11 as it's commonly called, is the oldest and largest school district in the Pikes Peak region. The boundaries run as far west as Garden of the Gods, east out to Peterson Air Force Base (it would take a half hour to drive this distance), and as far north as Woodmen Road and south to below downtown. The district has 60 schools and serves about 30,000 students. Over the past

many years, the district has seen the highest gains in CSAP scores of any large district in Colorado.

The schools provide education in almost any form imaginable. First, there are many traditional public schools in the elementary, middle, and high school choices. High school students can enrich their classes with business and marketing, industrial technology, and family and consumer sciences. Full-day kindergartens are in every elementary school. The Galileo School of Math and Science teaches middle school in an interdisciplinary environment. There are English as a Second Language, gifted and talented services, Navy Junior Reserve Officer Training Corp units, and the International Baccalaureate program for K–12. Preschools are available at many elementary schools, and before and after school care is present at most elementary schools. Performing arts magnet schools are available for all grades. Coronado High School offers the CU Succeed Gold program, which allows dual credits at the high school and the University of Colorado-Boulder.

There are alternative schools, such as ACHIEVEk12, an online school for students in K–8 with a tuition-free college preparatory academic program. The Bijou School, Doherty Night School "Success First," and Palmer Night School reach out to the high school age. The Tesla Educational Opportunity Program reaches out to middle and high school students who have experienced difficulties in a traditional school setting.

The programs and services offered reach out to all members of the community with adult and family education classes as well as community education classes.

FALCON SCHOOL DISTRICT 49
10850 E. Woodmen Rd., Falcon
(719) 495-1100
www.d49.org

Falcon is located to the east of Colorado Springs, and "booming" is almost too tentative a description of this area and its school district. There are about 15,000 students, 20 schools, and a recent annual growth rate of close to 6 percent.

The district has adjusted to this quick growth by offering almost every type of education available. Some elementary schools are K–5, some go through middle school and offer K–8. Some middle schools offer grades 6–8, some go further into high school, offering grades 6–10.

The schools offer a host of educational choices; some of these are available district-wide, while some are at specific schools only. There is an International Baccalaureate program as well as a math, science, and space integration program. A school of technology integrates high-tech tools into project-based assignments. Engineering is Elementary curriculum teaches elementary students about engineering and technology concepts, and core knowledge is enhanced with foreign language, art, music, and physical education. Mosaica offers students the competition and private sector efficiency within the public school system. Expeditionary learning provides hands-on, in-depth education. Student Opportunities for Academic Richness (SOAR) provides the challenges needed by gifted and talented students. Summer school opportunities are available. Career academics is a high school curriculum that aims to prepare students for the world past secondary education, including focus in the medical profession, information technology field, broadcasting, and civil air patrol, among others. There is night school for those needing alternative education, and a program called SWAP (School to Work Alliance Program) provides successful employment and increased community connection for those in all categories of disability.

FOUNTAIN-FORT CARSON SCHOOL DISTRICT 8
10665 Jimmy Camp Rd., Fountain
(719) 382-1300
www.ffc8.org

This is one of the most diverse school populations in the district, and one of the most liquid in a long-term sense: about 70 percent of the student population is composed of military families. With the Army planning an increase in the troops stationed at Fort Carson over the next several years, the school district anticipates a significant number of new students. This growth from the current enrollment of 6,500 students should not be a burden as the district has the lowest school mill levy in El Paso County and has no bond indebtedness. Fountain-Fort Carson also has recently received several federal grants totaling over $3 million. These additional funds are planned for new opportunities and to extend existing programs, such as integrating new students in a more comprehensive way, offering extensive after-school options, and creating schools as community centers for both students and families.

The district has eight elementary schools, two middle schools, a high school, and an alternative school. They were the first school district in Colorado to offer laptops to all high school students at registration. Gifted education is available, and each elementary school has both full- and half-day kindergartens. Extended learning provides before- and after-school group tutoring and enrichment programs. Teachers are trained in the latest researched-based practices such as how to differentiate or individualize instruction for all students. Competitive interscholastic and intramural athletics are offered at the middle and high schools, and instrumental music and vocal music programs are available for grades 4–12. Child focus teams design specialized educational programming for students, and there are school-wide character development programs. There are advanced courses available at the middle and high schools, and the district offers strong vocational training programs and partnerships with Pikes Peak Community College, CSU Pueblo, and the University of Colorado at Denver. There are summer learning opportunities for all grades, art and drama classes, world language classes for grades 9–12, and physical education at all elementary, middle, and high schools. In the most recent years, the school district scored above state levels on CSAPs in 20 out of 27 areas.

HARRISON SCHOOL DISTRICT 2
1060 Harrison Rd.
(719) 579-2000
www.harrison.k12.co.us
Harrison School District 2, commonly referred to as either Harrison or D2, educates more than 10,000 students in 14 elementary schools, one K–8 school, three middle schools, two high schools, one alternative school, and three charter schools. The district in the south of Colorado Springs has a strong sense of community and frequently works to meet needs, such as partnering with the Urban League of the Pikes Peak Region to feed more than 200 families a Thanksgiving dinner. This strong sense of community and purpose has led D2

staff and families to create action plans to address needs. Success can be seen in increased high school graduation rates, and 2009 CSAP scores, the most recent available at press time, marked the largest increase in proficiency for Harrison students in the history of the state tests. No other district in the Pikes Peak region and no other large at-risk district in the state improved proficiency as much as the Harrison district that year. Continuing data shows that achievement continues to improve.

LEWIS-PALMER SCHOOL DISTRICT 38
146 Jefferson St., Monument
(719) 488-4700
http://lewispalmer.org
The Lewis-Palmer School District has roots in one-room school houses of the late 1800s. Now the district, which sits in northern El Paso County, has some of the newest, most modern, and advanced schools in the region.

The approximately 5,800 students consistently rank high in the state in both state and national standardized testing. The high school graduation rate is over 95 percent and approximately 85 percent of those graduates continue on to college. The district provides bus transportation and a hot lunch program to its five elementary schools, one middle school, and one high school. There is also one charter school, which serves students preschool through grade 9. Elementary schools cover K–6, and grades 7–8 are at the one middle school.

Athletic programs are available in the middle and high school, and there are special education, gifted and talented services, and English as a Second Language. Additional co-curricular programs are also offered.

MANITOU SPRINGS SCHOOL DISTRICT 14

405 El Monte Place, Manitou Springs
(719) 685-2024
http://sd14web.mssd14.k12.co.us

The approximately 1,500 students attending Manitou schools come from Manitou Springs, Cascade, Green Mountain Falls, Chipita Park, and Cedar Heights—all close-in mountain and foothills communities. The two elementary schools, one middle school, and one high school are well-respected and offer excellent academics. They consistently receive a "High" rating on the Colorado State Accountability Report. But the reason parents send their kids to Manitou schools has more to do with the small-town feel. A child will most likely not get lost in this district. There is art, physical education, music, computer technology, special education, and gifted and talented instruction. Students may choose from many after school programs, particularly at the middle and high school. Class sizes in the elementary schools typically range from 18 to 25 students, and average middle school class size is 24 students. High school class size averages at 22 students.

WIDEFIELD SCHOOL DISTRICT 3

1820 Main St.
(719) 391-3000
www.wsd3.org

Widefield School District 3, informally called Widefield, also serves the residents of Security, portions of Fountain, Colorado Springs, and surrounding rural areas. The district encompasses 59 square miles and, because the Security/Widefield area is the largest unincorporated area in Colorado, the district takes on many of the functions normally provided by municipal governments.

The district manages Widefield Community Education and Recreation Services, better known as the Community Center. In recent years, the Community Center provided a variety of community education and recreation activities for more than 56,000 people. The district also oversees the Security Public Library and has built trails and parks in the area.

The district serves many military families as it lies close to Fort Carson. There are nine K–5 elementary schools, a K–5 charter school, three 6–8 junior high schools, two 9–12 high schools, and an alternative high school. There is also an online K–12 school and a preschool. District enrollment totals about 8,900 students. The district is a strong supporter of neighborhood schools while also offering the choice option.

District-wide programs include full-day kindergarten at every elementary school, child care services for before and after care at all elementary schools, and gifted and talented programs. Widefield annually ranks first or second in Colorado in graduation rates for African-American students and in the upper third in Colorado in graduation rates for Hispanic students.

WOODLAND PARK SCHOOL DISTRICT RE-2

211 N. Baldwin St., Woodland Park
(719) 686-2000
www.wpsdk12.org

Woodland Park School District Re-2 encompasses the northern half of Teller County, which lies up Ute Pass west of Colorado Springs. The district serves about 3,000 students. Three K–5 elementary schools have preschools, the middle school is grades 6–8, and the high school is grades 9–12. There is also an online school.

The district has focused on a balance between traditional instruction in basic skills and innovative instruction. There is also a full range of co-curricular activities including art, band, drama, forensics, and vocal music. There are programs for gifted and talented students, extended learning opportunities, and support services for students who are struggling. Woodland Park students consistently hold the fourth-highest score position of all districts in the Pikes Peak region on CSAPs. The high school offers a number of honors and AP classes, and the district is currently in the middle of an ambitious five-year program to update texts and teaching materials for all K–12 core academics as well as in many elective and exploratory areas.

PRIVATE SCHOOLS

Just as there are many choices in public schools within the Pikes Peak region, there is a variety of private schools as well. Many are religious, but not all. They run from schools serving a church or neighborhood to an elite, college-prep school that attracts boarding students from across the globe.

COLORADO SPRINGS SCHOOL
21 Broadmoor Ave.
(719) 475-9747
www.css.org
The beautiful, historic grounds of the Colorado Springs School (CSS) serve about 450 students from pre-K to grade 12. Founded in 1961, the school offers small class size (about 16) and small student-to-teacher ratio (about seven students to a teaching faculty). With recent SAT scores at 1873/2400 and 1269/1600, recent graduates attend almost all the state schools as well as MIT,

Wake Forest University, and Williams College, among others.

COLORADO SPRINGS CHRISTIAN SCHOOL
4875 Mallow Rd.
(719) 268-2188
www.cscslions.org
CSCS, as it's known in the region, opened in 1971 and has continued to grow since: It seems every time you drive by the campus off of Austin Bluffs Parkway, there seems to be a new building or structure. Recognized as a 2010 National Blue Ribbon School award winner, CSCS strives to provide excellent education from a Christ-centered biblical perspective. Classes average about 21 students. The total population of 900 students from pre-K through grade 12 has daily Bible courses, weekly chapel services, and opportunities for volunteer service as well as strong academics, arts, and sports. Many of the sports teams, especially the varsity volleyball team, often vie for state championships. There is also an online program for high school students. A K–8 Woodland Park campus opened in 2005.

EVANGELICAL CHRISTIAN ACADEMY
2511 N. Logan (Elementary) and 4052 Nonchalant Circle S. (Secondary)
(719) 574-0920
www.ecaeagles.org
Evangelical Christian Academy (ECA) was established in 1971 and now provides a Christian-based education to about 400 students from more than 50 churches in the region. The elementary campus includes grades pre-K–6 and a secondary campus serves grades 7–12. Christian teachers reinforce a relationship between home, church, and school. ECA students' standardized test

scores are consistently above the national average. Low student-teacher ratios are supported with an emphasis on solid study habits and personal discipline.

FOUNTAIN VALLEY SCHOOL
6155 Fountain Valley School Rd.
(719) 390-7035
www.fvs.edu

This sprawling campus for both boarding and day high school students is one of the country's top college preparatory institutions. The rigorous, in-depth academics and full co-curricular program includes 18 Advanced Placement courses, physical education as a mandatory part of after-class life, and a comprehensive arts program with courses in visual arts, theater, music, dance, and film. Boarding students are the majority of the approximately 250 students, and they come from all over the country. International students also make up about 20 percent of the student population.

Founded in 1930, the campus covers 1,100 acres of chaparral landscape and expansive lawns. Adobe buildings lend an iconic feel of the Southwest. There are classrooms, homes for faculty, dorms for students, arts buildings, and barns for the horses the students may ride. There is also a mountain campus near Buena Vista, CO, which is used for retreats and experiential studies. The average class size is 12 with a student to teacher ratio of 6 to 1. Graduates are routinely admitted to the country's elite colleges and universities.

ST. MARY'S HIGH SCHOOL
2501 E. Yampa St.
(719) 635-7540
www.smhscs.org

St. Mary's is a Catholic high school established in 1885. The 360 students study in a college prep program focused on core courses supplemented by electives. AP and honors classes are offered. Average student-to-teacher ratio is 18 to 1, and the school lists numerous academic awards every year, including students who have scored a perfect 800 on the SAT. The campus, which is just east of downtown, has a chapel, classrooms, the Pirate Cove (the mascot is a pirate), stage, gymnasium, art and photography labs, and fitness center. In 2006, the school opened a 25-acre athletic complex a few miles north of the campus. St. Mary's has won numerous state championships in various sports. In recent years, the student body has also posted more than 19,000 hours volunteering with Christian outreach projects.

UNITED CATHOLIC SCHOOLS OF THE PIKES PEAK REGION
www.ucsppr.org

Parochial schools are popular choices in the Pikes Peak region. Organized by the archdiocese, the Catholic schools share standards, a reputation of academic excellence, and accreditation. They are generally from preschool through grade 8. The Catholic high school, St. Mary's, is not governed by this umbrella of schools. Each school in this group can vary in size and activities, but geography is usually the determining factor in choice.

The Catholic schools are **St. Peter Catholic School** (Pre-K–5) in Monument, which is to the north. To the south is **Pauline Memorial Catholic School** (Pre-K–8), which sits directly behind The Broadmoor. Downtown is **Corpus Christi Catholic School** (Pre-K–8), just across the street from Penrose Main hospital, and just east of downtown is **Divine Redeemer Catholic School** (Pre-K–8).

PRESCHOOLS & CHILD CARE

This can be one of the toughest decisions a parent can make: Who takes care of your child, and who is the first to start your child's education process? In the Pikes Peak region, there's no shortage of choices for either one.

For child care, there are a number of the national chains with multiple locations: Creative Play Centers, KinderCare, and Junior Academy Children's Centers are some. Those aren't listed here as you probably know what to expect with them. There are a number of small neighborhood, church-run, and private child care centers—in fact about 800 in the region. We've selected just a few to highlight the different choices. We've also listed a central agency that can provide a list of all licensed day care providers.

For preschool, there are again a host of choices. Most of the big school districts provide some preschool options within elementary schools. There are also church and neighborhood preschools that might be just the perfect fit for your family. So again, we list a few to highlight choices, but the final research will have to depend on the area and/or program for each family.

BUILDING BLOCKS CHILD CARE
3819 N. Academy Blvd.
(719) 591-6114
www.freewebs.com/
buildingblockschildcare
Opened in 1985, this northeast-side child care center takes children from infants to 12 years old. They are licensed for 132 kids at once. They offer transportation to and from school, summer classes, parent meetings,

and child evaluations to track progress and development.

CHILD CARE CONNECTIONS
125 N. Parkside Dr., Suite 202
(719) 638-2070
www.childcareconnections.net
This agency is a parent's dream—a place to find answers without wading through the yellow pages or Google. The site offers provider resources and upcoming events and training for providers and parents. Parent referrals are available on everything from locating child care to tax credits for families. Employers have tools to help their employees find child care and save on lost work hours. For a parent, the journey won't end here, but it will be easier if it's started here.

COMMUNITY PARTNERSHIP FOR CHILD DEVELOPMENT
2330 Robinson St.
(719) 635-1536
www.cpcdheadstart.org
Founded in 1987, Community Partnership for Child Development (CPCD) provides early childhood education and support services for more than 1,900 children living in poverty or challenged by special circumstances. It is a safety net and positive force in the region.

The programs include Head Start (educational, physical and mental health, and nutritional services to children 3 to 5 years of age), Early Head Start (promotes healthy families and school readiness by serving pregnant women and children birth to age 3), and the Colorado Preschool Program (many of the Head Start services for children 3 to 5 years of age). They also offer health, dental, and family support services. CPCD operates more than 65 classrooms in the region, including at all the big school districts, at Early Connections Learning Centers, and the Urban League of the Pikes Peak Region, among others. CPCD's innovative, ground-breaking first-ever therapeutic preschool in the Pikes Peak region serves 3- to 5-year-olds who are struggling with significant behavioral challenges. Family literacy programs are offered in partnership with school districts to serve adults and children who are learning English. Early childhood services support families who are homeless, and CPCD offers specific programs to military families.

Montessori Schools

The Pikes Peak region is a believer in the Montessori method. There are almost 10 independent Montessori schools here as well as a few within the public school preschool choices. The hands-on, multi-age, step-based programs remain somewhat similar at the various schools, but size and costs can be significantly different. Choice might come down to location, and there are Montessori schools close to almost every area, from Monument to The Broadmoor area.

COUNTERPOINT SCHOOL
611 N. Royer St.
(719) 633-9880
http://counterpointschool.com
Counterpoint is a longtime preschool tucked into a downtown neighborhood. It is not big (just a few classrooms), but it has generations of loyal families. The classrooms are organized into learning centers with freedom of movement and easy access to materials. Kids learn through music, art, dance, natural sciences, language arts, and movement. There is a large outside space. They have two preschool classes, two pre-K classes and a sprouts class for 2½- to 3-year-olds. There is early care, after care, and summer programs. Full and half-day classes are offered.

EARLY CONNECTIONS LEARNING CENTERS
104 E. Rio Grande St.
(719) 632-1754
www.earlyconnections.org
Previously known as Child Nursery Centers, the main building (there are numerous locations) is a stunning, historic brick mansion. In the child care and early childhood education business since 1897, this is a big player in the region, and not only because of size. The quality program, family support services, and outreach to needier families makes Early Connections a true asset to the community. And even with its long history, Early Connections is on the forefront: In late 2010, the National Association for the Education of Young Children accredited four Early Connection Learning Centers. Only 8 percent of such centers in the US have received this honor, gained through a rigorous, two-year review process.

The preschool curriculum is literacy-focused with in-depth exploration of books and stories, including use of puppets, dramatic play props, and discussions. Through this storybook approach, they integrate language, literacy, math, science, social studies, music, movement, and physical development into everyday life. Children are encouraged to explore, experiment, and problem solve in activities.

The family services offered include partnerships and referral to agencies for housing, food, transportation, employment, clothing, medical and dental care, language translation, legal services, vehicle repair, and more. A sick room is available so parents don't have to miss work when a child is mildly ill. Some locations offer evening, weekend, and overnight care. Nutritious meals and snacks are provided and health support is available.

GREENSHADE SCHOOL
1019 W. Cheyenne Rd.
(719) 632-2232
First opened in 1978, this nonprofit child care, preschool, and school is set in the wooded Cheyenne Cañon area. With three buildings (one was the first Cheyenne School District building from around 1900), Greenshade accommodates up to 91 children ages 1 to 12. Children use one of the three buildings as determined by age. They offer school pick up for the elementary kids in the Cheyenne Mountain District 12 schools, and feature five playgrounds, each designed for a specific age group. Greenshade offers day camps in the summer. They receive state funding and offer two fee structures so that parents who make under $30,000 per year are better able to afford the services.

RUTH WASHBURN COOPERATIVE NURSERY SCHOOL
914 N. 19th St.
(719) 636-3084
http://rwcns.org
Ruth Washburn isn't for every family, but for those who choose it, it's just the right fit. The preschool for kids ages 2½ to 6 focuses on a child's emotional, physical, social, and cognitive needs. A positive self-image and the ability to engage in caring interactions with others are stressed. Within small classes, children are invited to creatively explore the world and discover how to uniquely express themselves. The outside playground is bigger than the building and the play equipment is unique, inviting, and creative. But what really makes Ruth Washburn distinctive is its structure as a co-op. Parents assist in the classroom and take responsibility for the maintenance, governance, and financial well-being of the school. When a child is at Ruth Washburn, the whole family is involved.

HEALTH & WELLNESS

I n general, people of the Pikes Peak region like to be healthy, and they take care of themselves to stay that way. Colorado is often in the news as one of healthiest or fittest states. Our overweight and obesity rates are lower than the national average, our rate of cardiovascular disease is only about 25 percent of the rate for the US as a whole, and the majority of people in the Pikes Peak region are considered physically active.

This is not to say there aren't issues. The Pikes Peak region's infant mortality rate, which is a good measure of a community's overall social and economic well-being, is about 6.5 deaths per 1,000 live births, well above the goal of 4.5. Methamphetamine use and suicides are also higher than the national average. Luckily there are a number of concerned and active groups addressing these issues from both the public and private sector.

The Pikes Peak region has strong, award-winning medical systems, qualified medical professionals, and state-of-the-art facilities. A number of fitness clubs and venues cover the area, and there are teaching professionals available for every sport and pastime. The populace works to stay healthy and well through nutrition, activities, and lifestyle, which makes this a good place to live, even with future challenges.

HEALTH CARE

The main story in health care is the two large health systems that, combined, provide most of the health care services in the Pikes Peak region. Memorial Health System and Penrose-St. Francis Health Services each run multiple hospitals, urgent care facilities, cancer centers, birth centers, heart and vascular departments, and more. Each has won prestigious industry awards, has a number of physician groups affiliated with their system, and is well-respected in the community.

Hospital Systems

Memorial Health System
MEMORIAL HOSPITAL CENTRAL
  MEMORIAL HOSPITAL FOR
  CHILDREN
1400 E. Boulder St.
(719) 365-5000

MEMORIAL HOSPITAL NORTH
4050 Briargate Pkwy.
(719) 364-5000
www.memorialhealthsystem.com
This city-owned hospital system has a campus downtown and another in Briargate (north). It has a total of about 670 beds and offers a Level-II trauma center and 2 urgent

care centers. There is a children's hospital with a pediatric intensive care unit and the only Level IIIB neonatal intensive care unit in southern Colorado. A recent year saw more than 130,000 visits to the emergency departments. Memorial also has 7 physical therapy and rehabilitation clinics in the Pikes Peak region as well as a sleep disorders clinic. The Printers Park Medical Plaza, part of the Memorial system, offers such diverse services as centers for breast care, disease and wellness, and wound care, as well as rehabilitation for pediatric, pulmonary, and cardiac issues, and a surgery center with 6 operating rooms, 2 gastrointestinal suites, and 1 pain management suite.

i Colorado Springs's high altitude of 6,035 feet can be hard for a body to take. Drink lots of water. Limit alcohol intake. And if you have a heart condition, take it easier than you would at a lower altitude.

First opened in downtown Colorado Springs in 1904 as a 30-bed hospital, Memorial treats everyone regardless of ability to pay; and yet, it uses no tax dollars in its operations. A recent year saw the system provide $73.1 million for the community benefit, including $12 million donated in charity care. The Memorial Health System Foundation was created in 2001 to meet the demands for community-based health care. Areas where the foundation has had a profound impact include the building of Memorial Hospital for Children and Memorial Hospital North as well as in medical services for heart and vascular care, cancer care (including integrative therapies), emergency and trauma care, women's/maternal care, infant care, pediatric care and rehabilitation,

chronic disease management, and wellness and community outreach.

Currently, a commission has recommended the ownership structure should change from city owned to nonprofit. Any changes will have to be approved by the voters.

Penrose-St. Francis Health Services
PENROSE HOSPITAL (CALLED PENROSE MAIN BY LOCALS)
2222 N. Nevada Ave.

ST. FRANCIS MEDICAL CENTER
6001 E. Woodmen Rd.
(719) 776-5000
www.penrosestfrancis.org

A nonprofit, faith-based health care system, Penrose-St. Francis operates two hospitals, one north of downtown and the other northeast off of Powers Boulevard. There are about 525 beds between them. Founded in 1890, Penrose-St. Francis also has several other operations, including 2 urgent care centers, a cancer center, a heart institute, and a healthy learning center, which is dedicated to healthy aging through management of chronic diseases. A recent year saw more than 71,000 visits to its emergency departments. The St. Francis Medical Center (the northern hospital) specializes in maternal-child health with a birthing center, Level IIIA neonatal intensive care unit, and a pediatric unit.

Penrose-St. Francis is the only Colorado system to make the list of America's top 50 hospitals for 2010, as determined by Health-Grades, an independent health care ratings organization. It has also been recognized by HealthGrades for other areas, including pulmonary, critical, and gastrointestinal care.

Penrose-St. Francis is part of Centura Health, jointly sponsored by Catholic Health

Initiatives and Adventist Health System. A recent year saw the Penrose system count $83.9 million in uncompensated and charity care to the community.

Nurses On Call

Got a health question or worry? Both Memorial Health System and Penrose-St. Francis Health Services run a free health advice line staffed by nurses. Physician referrals, classes, and more are also available.

Memorial's HealthLink
5360 N. Academy, Suite 220
(719) 444-CARE (2273)

Penrose's ASK-A-NURSE®
(719) 776-5555

Urgent Care & Walk-In Clinics

EMERGICARE MEDICAL CLINICS
402 W. Garden of the Gods Rd.
(719) 590-1701

4083 Austin Bluffs Pkwy.
(719) 594-0046

402 W. Bijou St.
(719) 302-6942

3002 S. Academy Blvd.
(719) 390-7017
www.emergicare.org
EmergiCare is an independent business run by a local doctor for more than 30 years. There are 4 clinics in Colorado Springs (listed here) and one in Pueblo. Patients do not need an appointment and see a board-certified physician in 30 minutes or less. Each clinic has a triage area, 5 to 6 exam rooms, EKG, pharmacy, lab, X-ray, trauma beds, a minor surgical suite, and a physical therapy room. The clinics also provide non-emergency needs including flu shots, physicals, annual checkups, immunizations, and drug and alcohol testing. EmergiCare also offers occupational medicine and handles work injury treatment, rehabilitation, physical therapy, and chiropractic care. Hours and days vary by location.

EXPRESSCARE PLUS
2141 N. Academy Circle
(719) 597-4200
www.expresscareplus.net
ExpressCare Plus is a privately owned facility that has been serving Colorado Springs for more than 25 years. Walk-ins are welcome, and appointments can be scheduled for regular treatment. Services include family practice, urgent care (minor emergencies), lab and X-ray services, clinical research, and specialist appointments such as ophthalmology, orthopedics, podiatry, and physical therapy. A pharmacy is in the same building. Hours vary by day, and closed on Christmas day.

i Our more than 300 days of sun at high altitude can leave you red in the face—and arms and legs. Use sunblock generously every day as you can burn faster at this altitude.

MEMORIAL HEALTH SYSTEM
Briargate Medical Campus
8890 N. Union Blvd.
(719) 365-2888

Springs Medical Center
2220 E. Pikes Peak Ave.
(719) 365-2888
www.memorialhealthsystem.com

Memorial's urgent and after-hours care centers also offer occupational medicine, and the Briargate facility has a lab, occupational health center, radiology and imaging, and a blood donation center. Hours and days open vary by location.

i The El Paso County Medical Society has a "Find a Physician" link on its website: www.epcms.org. Both Memorial and Penrose also have physician links on their websites as well.

PENROSE-ST. FRANCIS HEALTH SERVICES

Penrose Community Urgent Care
3205 N. Academy Blvd.
(719) 776-3216

Penrose Mountain Urgent Care
41 CO 67, Woodland Park
(719) 686-0551
www.penrosestfrancis.org

Penrose's urgent care is at two facilities, one in Woodland Park. Both offer urgent and acute care for minor illnesses and injuries, limited outpatient lab and X-ray services, and the mountain center offers rehabilitation services. No appointments necessary. Open 7 days a week, but hours vary by location.

Health Care Agencies

ASPENPOINTE
(719) 572-6100 or (800) 285-1204 (Call Center)
(719) 635-7000 (Crisis Hotline)
www.aspenpointe.org

This umbrella organization for 12 agencies provides an integrated approach to mental health needs. It provides individual and family services in mental health, substance abuse, employment and career development, suicide, women's health, education, housing, jail diversion and reintegration, telephonic wellness, and provider network services. There are 21 facilities offering various services and programs across the Pikes Peak region.

EL PASO COUNTY DEPARTMENT OF HEALTH AND ENVIRONMENT
301 S. Union Blvd.
(719) 578-3199
www.elpasocountyhealth.org

The umbrella of duties and services provided by this public health department ranges from issues under the auspices of the Centers for Disease Control (CDC) to meth lab clean-ups per Colorado regulations. At the clinic (appointments are needed, call the number above to start the process), the agency can provide reproductive health care services for men and women, STD screening, diagnosis and treatment, and pregnancy testing and referral to health care providers/agencies. Fees are charged on a sliding scale based on income. Immunizations are also available. The agency also runs the Health Care Program for Children with Special Needs (HCP) that can coordinate medical and social support services as well as services offered through the Colorado Traumatic Brain Injury Trust Fund, support group training and information, and referrals for medical and developmental services and information.

PEAK VISTA COMMUNITY HEALTH CENTERS
(719) 632-5700
www.peakvista.org

This private nonprofit started as a free clinic in the 1970s and has now grown into a federally qualified health center. Peak Vista provides medical, dental, and behavioral health care and health education services to those in need at 16 outpatient health centers. In a recent year, Peak Vista provided over $14 million in charity care to those in the Pikes Peak region. Peak Vista provides low-income, uninsured, and underinsured working families access to primary health care services, dental care, and pharmacy and laboratory services. An agency that exudes integrity, Peak Vista aims for premier medical care and treatment as it services women, children, working families, seniors, and the homeless (a small but advanced, handsome center is physically connected to the local homeless shelter). Regularly scheduled events include senior health education sessions (such as "Boning up on Osteoporosis"), a free men's prostate cancer screening, and a Back in School fair in August for school-age children.

i **Pikes Peak United Way maintains a hotline to help people find non-emergency health and social services resources, such as senior services, family support, community health, and human services. The hotline can also help find assistance in paying rent/mortgage, utilities, or medical/prescription costs, and in finding food, clothing, and housing/shelter. Dial 2-1-1 or (719) 955-0742.**

SET FAMILY MEDICAL CLINICS
825 E. Pikes Peak Ave.
(719) 776-8850
www.setofcs.org
Serve, Empower, Transform (SET) Family Medical Clinics is a nonprofit that serves the uninsured and underinsured in the Pikes Peak region at low or no cost. Now more

than 20 years in the community, SET acts as a safety net for children, families, and seniors in need of basic medical care and holistic wellness services. SET is sponsored by Centura Health, of which the Penrose-St. Francis Health Services is a part, and this sponsorship has allowed the clinic to double patient capacity with expanded clinic hours to 40 hours per week. SET recently received a grant to help ex-offenders stay healthy while re-integrating into society.

A community health partnership committee meets monthly to reduce duplication and share and expand services between Peak Vista, SET, and two other agencies that serve those in need in the Pikes Peak region.

Additional Health Care Sources

Chinese Medicine
Chinese medicine, most notably acupuncture, is popular with the people of the Pikes Peak region. There are more than 50 providers, and most are one-doctor shops tucked into neighborhoods. Proponents use the historical treatments for everything from pain management to weight loss to hormone imbalance. As with any health care provider, an acupuncturist is a very personal choice. These are just a few providers who have served the region for a number of years.

The Acupuncture Clinic (2020 W. Colorado Ave., B-204; 719-634-1669; www.nasacupuncture.com) is on the west side and is run by Na Zhai, who graduated from university in China and has done work in Western medicine in Vienna. Her clinic offers acupuncture, acupressure, Chinese herbology, cupping, and Tai Chi. Some local athletes have used her services for weekend warrior issues such as tennis elbow.

Norman E. Smith L. Ac. (1430 S. 21st St., Suite 201; 719-630-8522; www.caringhealer

.net) is also on the west side and has been practicing a holistic approach to health care for 27 years. His practice includes traditional needle acupuncture, laser beam on acupoints, Korean hand therapy, Chinese herbs, hado medicine, moxabustion, electrical stimulation, infrasonic therapy, and gwa sha, among others. The conditions he treats is a long list, including fibromyalgia, insomnia, and disc pathology.

A respected practitioner on the north side of town is **Chien's Acupuncture & Oriental Medicine** (5125 N. Union Boulevard; 719-533-0008), which treats everything from anxiety stress to infertility to allergies.

Chiropractics

This health care treatment, which focuses on disorders of the musculoskeletal system and nervous system, is another very popular health care method in the Pikes Peak region. There are more than 200 providers in the region, the great majority of who operate in an office as the only doctor. There are also some chiropractic services available at urgent care facilities. As with acupuncturists, a few of the many chiropractors are listed here just to get you started, but choosing a chiropractor is a very personal decision.

Champion Health (9240 Explorer Dr., Suite 215; 719-473-7000; www.champion-health.com) is the birthplace of Active Release Techniques (ART), a soft tissue system/movement based massage technique that treats problems with muscles, tendons, ligaments, fascia, and nerves. People outside of our region come here to work with the doctors at this facility.

Colorado Health and Wellness (1231 Lake Plaza Dr.; 719-576-2225; www.colorado healthandwellness.com) is run by the husband and wife doctor team of John and Gail

Warner. It has been in Colorado Springs since 1993. Their practice also includes nutritional counseling, acupressure, and other educational sources and treatments.

Healing Touch Chiropractic (1422 N. Hancock Ave.; 719-578-0504) offers traditional chiropractic services as well as some Oriental treatments such as acupuncture, and Dr. John Garrison at **The Crossing Healing Arts Center** (627 N. Weber St.; 719-471-7333) has a well-respected practice downtown.

WELLNESS

The Pikes Peak region is active and health-conscious. We tend to work out, play hard, take care of ourselves, and embrace healthy indulgences. It is rare to find a resident of the Pikes Peak region who doesn't have some kind of fitness regimen. Thus, health clubs are numerous and often crowded. On off days, massage is a common way to unwind and get those kinks out. There are plenty of individual massage therapists who work out of homes, independently out of store-fronts, or out of a medical professional's office. Those aren't listed here.

Health Clubs & Spas

ACCOLADE FITNESS
4390 Arrowswest Dr.
(719) 592-1111
www.accoladefitness.com
After incarnations as several different national chains and moving from one location to another, Accolade Fitness (now locally owned) has finally found its place in the Colorado Springs gym scene. It draws young (teenagers with Mohawks and piercings) and old (the white-haired senior crowd) alike. And everyone in between.

That's because of the friendly owners, who greet many guests by name and are always around to fix a machine or answer questions on how to use one. No matter what you like—treadmills, step machines, weight machines, and much more—they are likely to have it in their spacious 17,000-square-foot facility. There are individual TVs in front of most machines, and there's a room strictly devoted to weight training. They are likely the least expensive gym in town, and belong to the Silver Sneakers program (where your health insurance pays your monthly fee, if you qualify). Notably clean, it has showers, locker rooms, dry saunas, and tanning beds, if you're so inclined. Yoga, Zumba, and pilates classes also are offered for an extra fee.

BALLY TOTAL FITNESS
(866) 402-2559
www.ballyfitness.com
There are two Bally's in town, both on Academy Boulevard—one north and one south. The popular workout facilities have Spanish-speaking staff; personal trainers; and classes in step, boot camp, strength training, and more. There is a pool; cardio equipment from cross-trainers to stair-climbers; a children's play center; and a sauna, steam room, and whirlpool. The strength training equipment runs from free weights to machines.

COLORADO INSTITUTE OF MASSAGE THERAPY
1490 W. Fillmore St.
(719) 634-7347
www.coimt.com
This massage therapy school (see entry in Education) offers massage therapy by professionals and students (discounted rates from student therapists). They offer a student sports massage clinic every other

Monday evening for competitive athletes (high school team members love this), and memberships that allow discounted and free massages over a year's period.

CURVES
(800) 848-1096
www.curves.com
There are 14 Curves studios in the Pikes Peak region, from Woodland Park to Cañon City. Membership is good at any location worldwide so members can use other studios when they travel. At home in southern Colorado, there's a Curves near almost every neighborhood. The for-women health clubs offer complete fitness and nutrition solutions, and many members appreciate the Curves 30-minute workout so they can exercise every major muscle group and get on with their day.

LIFE TIME FITNESS/LYNMAR
2660 Vickers Dr. (Lynmar)
Briargate Parkway and Powers Boulevard (Life Time)
(719) 598-7075
www.lifetimefitness.com
Lynmar Racquet & Health Club is a longtime Colorado Springs tennis and workout facility. In 2008 it was purchased by Life Time Fitness, which runs more than 80 fitness centers in the West and East. In May 2011 the facilities moved from the Lynmar building to a new, 180,000-square-foot Life Time Fitness building with 8 indoor tennis courts and a state-of-the-art fitness center with elliptical cross-trainers, rower, weights, and more. The Life Time model caters to a healthy lifestyle and provides members with personal training consultants, spas and cafes, nutrition assessment and education, family activities including a number of indoor and outdoor

pools, rock climbing walls, group fitness classes, and chiropractic clinics.

MATEOS SALON AND DAY SPA
5919 Delmonico Dr.
(719) 266-9295
www.mateosdayspa.com
Mateos has been a longtime community standout. The massage therapists tend to stay for years, and the massages offered run from basic Swedish to a salt glow to a Tuscan Wine Antioxidant Massage. They also have more than 10 hair stylists; offer facials, manicures, and pedicures; and run the Skin Savvy Laser Clinic for corrective and restorative skin care.

24 HOUR FITNESS
(800) 223-0240
www.24hourfitness.com
The three 24 Hour Fitness clubs in Colorado Springs are popular—the one on North Academy Boulevard even draws quite a crowd of the under-30 set late at night. All three clubs are the "Sport" type of 24 Hour Fitness facility, which means they offer a wide variety of equipment and classes. They each have basketball courts, swimming pools, sauna, steam room, whirlpool, free weights, a kids' club, personal trainers, a huge selection of cardio equipment, and classes from spinning to yoga.

VEDA
(719) 578-8332 (south)
(719) 265-5660 (central)
(719) 314-1480 (north)
www.coloradoaveda.com
There are three Vedas in Colorado Springs, all pampering guests with treatments from traditional massage to wraps. They also offer facials, hair care, waxing, manicures and

pedicures, and skin care products. Veda is an upscale spa, and it can be a bit more expensive to go there—but those who do usually walk out happy.

VILLASPORT ATHLETIC CLUB AND SPA
5904 Prairie Schooner Dr.
(719) 522-1221
www.villasport.com
On the northeast side of town, Villasport has made quite a splash—and not just in its 5 pools. The 175,000-square-foot campus has all the new bells and whistles in workout equipment and hosts more than 150 group fitness classes each week, from yoga to spinning. The locker rooms feature a TV lounge, steam room, and whirlpool. There's an NBA-size court. A 12,000-square-foot kids club has area for exercise, art, computer, and dance. Seasonal parties and summer camps are held for the kids, and there are occasional Parent's Night Out events. A full-service spa offers massages, facials, and other body treatments, and there's even a massage suite for two. The indoor and outdoor pools separate areas for lap swim, aquatic classes, waterslides, whirlpool, and water jets.

YMCA OF THE PIKES PEAK REGION
316 N. Tejon St.
(719) 471-9790
http://ppymca.org
With eight locations across the Pikes Peak region and one mountain summer camp for kids, the Y is a big part of the community's healthy lifestyle. In fact, their programs and services reach a quarter of a million people each year. The Y's classic "build strong kids, strong families, and strong communities" motto is seen in youth sports programs, swim lessons, summer camps, group fitness classes, rehab and massage, health

education, personal training, and more. Especially welcome here, the Y serves local military personnel and their spouses and children with outreach programs such as respite child care. The Y provides at least $1.3 million a year in financial assistance and program subsidy so that lower-income youth, teens, and families can participate in healthy programs and services. The Y runs Adventure Guides to foster parent-child bonding, has large and small pools at many locations, and sponsors seasonal activities, such as a Turkey Trot family run on Thanksgiving morning.

Yoga Studios

The Pikes Peak region likes to salute the sun and do the downward dog. Yoga classes are a component at every health club, and there are a number of private yoga studios as well. Located downtown for many years, **Yoga Journeys** (709 N. Nevada Ave., Suite 201; 719-471-7424; www.yoga-journeys.net) is led by Teryl Lundquist, who has been nurturing both the new and experienced student for years. **CorePower** (www.corepoweryoga .com) has a downtown and north location, offers classes at all times of the day, and also runs a yoga teacher training and certification program. For those who like it hot, CorePower also runs bikram yoga classes in rooms 100 to 103 degrees.

MEDIA

The Pikes Peak region is like a lot of the US: Newspapers are struggling; news comes from national and online sources; and local radio competes with satellite, the Internet, and personal devices like iPods. Living locally doesn't mean hearing or seeing locally anymore!

The one daily paper, *The Gazette,* gets some competition from bigger papers out of the region—notably *The Denver Post* and the *Wall Street Journal.* For TV, it's not about what stations, the question is what cable provider. There's Comcast, DirectTV, and Dish network. Each location—even by subdivision—might mean something else. Confusing? You said it!

For radio, we have a lot of country and Christian stations. But more than what kind of station, we have a very revolving environment. One day a station might be rock, and then the next week it's country. You can never be sure, but people have adapted. Put it this way—our media scene is a lot like family. We might not always like it, but we live with it.

DAILIES

THE GAZETTE
30 S. Prospect St.
(719) 632-5511
www.gazette.com

There have been other daily papers in our region, but for many years the only one is *The Gazette.* Now owned by Freedom Communications, *The Gazette* started in 1872 as *Out West* and was published every Saturday for a subscription rate of $3 a year. In 1946, *The Colorado Springs Gazette* merged with the *Evening Telegraph* to become the *Gazette Telegraph,* which it was called for many years. In 1997, it became simply *The Gazette.* The daily newspaper also publishes a number of special publications and editions, such as the monthly *Pikes Peak Parent* magazine. The paper covers national and local news, sports, entertainment, weather, business, and local lifestyle features. There is an online edition, and a number of staff over the years has won prestigious awards, including a Pulitzer Prize in 1990.

WEEKLIES

CHEYENNE EDITION (SOUTH)
WOODMEN EDITION (NORTH)
(719) 578-5112
www.waltpub.com

These free, weekly neighborhood papers cover neighborhood news and regional news important to the area. The *Cheyenne Edition* was first published in 1982 and has a circulation of about 8,200. It's distributed to homes in the Broadmoor, Skyway, Gates

Ranch, and Broadmoor Valley areas. The *Woodmen Edition* has a circulation of more than 16,000 and is delivered to homes in the Peregrine, Pine Cliff, Rockrimmon, and Briargate areas. It was first published in 1992.

i Many locals get *The Denver Post* delivered on Sunday, or even all week. The Colorado Springs news is slim, but the national, state, sports, and arts coverage is a step above the local offerings. Go to www.denverpost.com.

COLORADO SPRINGS BUSINESS JOURNAL
31 E. Platte Ave., Suite 300
(719) 634-5905
www.csbj.com
The *Business Journal,* as it's called locally, is a business-to-business publication that focuses on the biggest sectors of the local economy, from tourism to defense contractors to health care. The weekly print publication has been around for more than 20 years, and an online edition is updated daily with breaking news. Subscribers also receive a daily e-mail on important stories. The audience is mainly CEOs, business owners, and professionals in both the for-profit and nonprofit industries. Through its entire media, the *Business Journal* reaches about 50,000 people per week.

COLORADO SPRINGS INDEPENDENT
235 S. Nevada Ave.
(719) 577-4545
www.csindy.com
The *Independent* is an alternative weekly paper that covers news, culture, and entertainment, many times through insightful, in-depth features. The 36,000-circulation paper can be picked up for free at hundreds

of locations around town, such as restaurants, health clubs, and libraries. Opinionated, whimsical, and forward-thinking, the paper has been published in the region since 1993. Its biggest issues of the year cover the popular Best of Colorado Springs contests for everything from restaurants to nail salons. One recent year saw more than 8,500 people vote.

MONTHLIES & MAGAZINES

COLORADO SPRINGS STYLE
118 N. Tejon St., Suite 405
(719) 632-0422
www.coloradospringsstyle.com
This upscale, glossy magazine focuses on the lifestyle, culture, interests, and homes in the Pikes Peak region. Printed six times a year, its circulation of about 20,000 includes paid subscriptions ($19 year) and newsstand sales in bookstores and supermarkets. It's also put into more than 8,200 hotel rooms and in hospitals, doctor's offices, auto dealerships, and retail stores. Features include travel and dining, spotlights on interesting personalities, and hot topics. Past issues have focused on weddings, a fall fashion guide, and top doctors and dentists.

RADIO

AM Stations

KVOR 740
(719) 593-2700
www.kvor.com
News/Talk

KCBR 1040
(719) 570-1530
www.1040kcbr.com
Christian

KRDO 1240
(719) 575-6245
www.krdo.com
News/Talk

KKML 1300
(719) 593-2700
www.sportsanimal1300.com
Sports

KZNT 1460
(719) 531-5438
www.newstalk1460.com
News/Talk

KXRE 1490
(303) 733-5266
www.radioquebueno.com
Spanish

KCMN 1530
(719) 570-1530
www.1530kcmn.com
Oldies

FM Stations

KTPL 88.3
(719) 593-0600
www.ktpl.org
Christian

KCME 88.7
(719) 578-5263
www.kcme.org
Classical

KEPC 89.7
(719) 520-3131
Pikes Peak Community College

KTLF 90.5
(719) 593-0600
www.ktlf.org
Christian

KRCC 91.5
(719) 473-4801
www.krcc.org
Public radio

KKPK 92.9
(719) 593-2700
www.929peakfm.com
Oldies

KILO 94.3
(719) 634-4896
www.kilo943.com
Rock

KATC 95.1
(719) 593-2700
www.catcountry951.com
Country

KIBT 96.1
(719) 540-9200
www.beatcolorado.com
Hip Hop

KCCY 96.9
(719) 540-9200
www.y969.com
Country

KKFM 98.1
(719) 593-2700
www.kkfm.com
Classic rock

KKMG 98.9
(719) 593-2700
www.989magicfm.com
Top 40

KVUU 99.9
(719) 540-9200
www.kvuu.com
Rock

KGFT 100.7
(719) 531-5438
www.kgftradio.com
Christian talk

KBIQ 102.7
(719) 531-5438
www.kbiqradio.com
Christian

KYZX 103.9
(719) 634-4896
www.1039rxp.com
Alternative rock

KRDO 105.5
(719) 575-6285
www.krdo.com
News/Talk

KDZA 107.9
(719) 540-9200
www.1079kdza.com
Rock

TELEVISION

Southern Colorado has its own television market, distinct from the rest of Colorado, which gets the Denver TV stations. All but one are based in Colorado Springs, and the other is in nearby Pueblo. This means residents in this area get specific weather and event information, which can be timely when storms move in fast. It also means, as a medium-size market, the anchors are either young up-and-coming stars who stay for only a year or so, or are journeymen professionals who love the area and choose to stay here for their career, sometimes anchoring the same station for decades.

KKTV CBS CH. 11
3100 N. Nevada Ave.
(719) 634-2844
www.kktv.com

KOAA NBC CH. 5
530 Communications Circle
(719) 632-5030
www.koaa.com

KRDO ABC CH. 13
399 S. 8th St.
(719) 575-6285
www.krdo.com

KXRM FOX CH. 21
560 Wooten Rd.
(719) 596-2100
www.kxrm.com

KTSC PBS CH. 8
2200 Bonforte Blvd., Pueblo
(719) 630-8800
www.rmpbs.org

INDEX